INSIGHT GUIDE

Japan

APA PUBLICATIONS

Part of the Langenscheidt Publishing Group

ABOUT THIS BOOK

Editorial

Managing Editor
Scott Rutherford
Editorial Director
Brian Bell

Distribution

UK & Ireland
GeoCenter International Ltd
The Viables Centre
Harrow Way
Basingstoke
Hants RG22 4BJ
Fax: (44) 1256-817988

United States
Langenscheidt Publishers, Inc.
46–35 54th Road
Maspeth, NY 11378
Fax: (718) 784-0640

Worldwide
APA Publications GmbH & Co.
Verlag KG (Singapore branch)
38 Joo Koon Road
Singapore 628990
Tel: (65) 865-1600
Fax: (65) 861-6438

Printing

Insight Print Services (Pte) Ltd
38 Joo Koon Road
Singapore 628990
Tel: (65) 865-1600
Fax: (65) 861-6438

© 1999 APA Publications GmbH & Co.
Verlag KG (Singapore branch)
All Rights Reserved
First Edition 1992
Third Edition 1999

CONTACTING THE EDITORS
Although every effort is made to
provide accurate information in
this publication, we live in a
fast-changing world and would
appreciate it if readers would
call our attention to any errors or
outdated information that may
occur by writing to us at:
**Insight Guides, P.O. Box 7910,
London SE1 8ZB, England.
Fax: (44 171) 620-1074.
e-mail:
insight@apaguide.demon.co.uk**

This guidebook combines the interests and enthusiasms of two of the world's best known information providers: Insight Guides, whose titles have set the standard for visual travel guides since 1970, and Discovery Channel, the world's premier source of non-fiction television programming. The editors of Insight Guides provide both practical advice and general understanding about a destination's history, culture, institutions and people. Discovery Channel and its Web site, www.discovery.com, help millions of viewers explore their world from the comfort of their own home and also encourage them to explore it firsthand.

In this, the third edition of *Insight Guide: Japan*, we journey to one of the most captivating and confounding nations. An archipelago of ancient enigmas and exquisite art, Japan offers a traveller the most immense of cities, delicate of cuisines, diverse of environments, and the most confusing of cultures. Our writers and photographers will help reveal it all.

EXPLORE YOUR WORLD
Discovery CHANNEL

How to use this book

The book is carefully structured to convey an understanding of Japan and its culture and to guide readers through its sights and attractions:

◆ The Features section, with a yellow colour bar, covers the country's history and culture in lively authoritative essays written by specialists.

◆ The Places section, with a blue bar, provides full details of all the sights and areas worth seeing. The chief places of interest are coordinated by number with specially drawn maps.

◆ The Travel Tips listings sec-tion, with an orange bar and at the back of the book, offers a convenient point of reference for information on travel, accom-modation, restaurants and other practical aspects of the country. Information is located quickly using the index printed on the back cover flap, which also serves as a handy bookmark.

The contributors

This new edition was edited by **Scott Rutherford**, who lived in Japan for a number of years, first arriving on a photo assign-ment for *National Geographic*. He also wrote most of the Tokyo coverage. This latest edition was based upon the first edition managed by **Malcom Davis**, an editor in Tokyo for many years. Updating the Kanto region, which includes Tokyo, Yokohama and Kamakura, was Tokyo-based **Hugh Paxton**. Tending to the information in the chapters on Kyoto, Osaka, and Shikoku was **Mason Florence**, who has long called Kyoto home. Ranging through the southern extents of Japan – including Chugoku and Kyushu – Hong Kong-based **Ed Peters** couldn't get enough of the country. Important contribu-tors to the previous editions of the guide included **Bill Williams, Matsutani Yuko, Kim Schueff-tan, Steve Usdin, John Carroll, Alex Kerr, Davis Barrager, Mark Schreiber, David Benjamin, Anthony J. Bryant, Bruce Leigh, Rich Blumm, Peter Ujlaki, Peter Hadfield, Arturo Silva, Gail Feld-man, Evelyn Corbett, Wayne Graczyk, Robert McLeod**, and **Otani Eiho**.

Map Legend

— ·· — International Boundary

— ◦ — National Park/Reserve

— — — Ferry Route

✈ ✈ Airport: International/ Regional

🚌 Bus Station

🅿 Parking

ⓘ Tourist Information

✉ Post Office

✝ ✝ ✝ Church/Ruins

✝ Monastery

☾ Mosque

✡ Synagogue

🏰 🏚 Casdtle/Ruins

∴ Archaeological Site

∩ Cave

⚑ Statue/Monument

★ Place of Interest

The main places of interest in the Places section are coordinated by number with a full-colour map (e.g. ❶), and a symbol at the top of every right-hand page tells you where to find the map.

Photo: collecting alms on a pilgrimage in front of a department store.

CONTENTS

Maps

Introduction

History

Features

Tokyo, from
Tokyo Bay.

Insight on ...

Information panels

Places

Travel Tips

A UNIQUE PLACE

Some see the Japanese turning into Westerners. Others see a
Zen-like serenity. The reality is more complicated

A traveller roaming amongst the islands of Japan is usually seeking the exotic, or the wondrous, or the unconventional. And indeed, Japan is often so, in both the cities and along the back roads. Sometimes what's encountered seems illogical or of dubious purpose, but that is a bias of culture and outlook. The traveller will inevitably compare Japan with the West when confronted with the obvious examples of suits and ties on Japan's *sarariman* – the "salary man" or white-collar worker – and the proliferation of fast-food franchises nearly everywhere. The near-cult status of Western pop icons can lull the outsider into believing that East has met West. (Even the Japanese language, as different as it is, uses English loan words, an estimated 10 percent of all words used in daily conversation.) The traveller thinks, *Japan has become like the West.*

Big mistake. In its history, Japan has adopted many things, taking what it wants or needs, adapting, and then discarding that which is of no use. Over the centuries, the Japanese have adopted Chinese writing and philosophy, Korean art and ceramics, and most recently, Western technology, clothes and fast-food. Indeed, since it yielded to Perry's Black Ships in 1853, Japan has adopted things foreign with gusto. Yet that which it adopts from the West or elsewhere becomes distinctly Japanese somehow. A foreign word is chopped in half, recombined with the second half of another bisected foreign or even Japanese word, and – *voilà*, a new word in the Japanese language.

Although Japan derives most of its culture from its Asian neighbours and most of its modernity from the West, the Japanese continue to cultivate a self-image of an almost divine uniqueness. The Japanese repeatedly refer to Japanese things – including themselves – as "special" or "unique" and thus beyond an outsider's understanding. The special Japanese snow once kept out French skis, as did the special Japanese digestive system keep out American beef.

Japan is special, of course. It has become the world's second-strongest economy while evenly – and in comparison with most of the world, uniquely – distributing a growing wealth while generating no significant lower class. Yet, having done so, it has made itself into a uniquely expensive place. While Japan radiates an international image of sophistication and efficiency, the home country is oddly behind the times. Just two-thirds of Japanese dwellings are connected to a modern sewage system, for example. Bureaucrats in the Kasumigaseki government district of Tokyo issue vague, verbal suggestions for corporate guidance that somehow become the equivalent of regulatory edicts. Japanese companies understand the system

PRECEDING PAGES: detail of door, Nijo Castle, Kyoto; harvesting rice in eastern Honshu; bamboo grove in Kamakura; typical urban architecture, Naha, Okinawa.
LEFT: helping a grandson for *shichi-go-san*, when children are blessed at shrines.

and its nuances, but foreign companies trying to start business in the country are like turtles out of water.

There is the nagging legacy of World War II, not to mention the uniquely Japanese forgetfulness regarding it. Other than of the atomic bombings of Nagasaki and Hiroshima, the Japanese don't talk about that war much. Yet, increasingly, neighbouring countries do, and Japan's relations with Korea and China are often rich with the undercurrents of the past. Most recently, national self-confidence weakened after a collapsing, superheated economy lingered as a decade-long recession. Then there was the 1995 Kobe earthquake that killed over 5,000 people and destroyed a supposedly earthquake-proof infrastructure, and a poison gas attack on Tokyo's subways, right in the heart of the government district in Tokyo.

Nonetheless, the Japanese are rightly proud of their country – current self-doubts aside – and of the sophistication and depth of its heritage. Much of its progress and advances have been the result of an inward-looking dedication and spirit. As an island nation, Japan is often focused inwardly in its approach to the world, as when the evening television news leads off with a cherry-blossom story and the remainder of the world is shoved to the end. Yet the Japanese are perhaps more appreciative of the subtleties of the changing seasons than any other people. Rural people will know if the dragonflies that appear in late spring are three days early this year, or if the *tsuyu*, the rainy season, is dragging on a bit longer than normal, say by two days. There is a delicate charm and serenity in such observations. It is a quality that says the people know their sense of place.

There are those, Japanese and foreigners alike, who retain an image of a Japan of Zen-like serenity. It is a wistful image, a nostalgic retreat. The novelist and nationalist Mishima Yukio, who revered the old Japan and chose to rebel and then kill himself for those old-guard principles, wrote that "Japan will disappear, it will become inorganic, empty, neutral-tinted; it will be wealthy and astute." Who knows? Cultures change, shift, disappear. On its surface, Japan appears to be changing. Underneath, one wonders if it is capable of doing so, or if it wants to change. Even Japanese don't know. But for the traveller, Japan as it is today is a supremely embracing and fabulous – and, yes, special – experience.

A note on style

Wherever possible, we use Japanese terms for geographical names, appearing as suffixes to the proper name. For example, Mt Fuji is referred to as Fuji-san. Mountains may also appear with -*zan*, -*yama*, and for some active volcanoes, -*dake*. Islands are either -*shima* or -*jima*, lakes are -*ko*, and rivers are -*gawa* or -*kawa*. Shinto shrines end in -*jinja*, -*jingu*, or -*gu*. Temples are Buddhist, with names ending in -*tera*, -*dera*, or -*ji*. When referring to individuals, we follow the Japanese style: family name first, given name second. ❏

RIGHT: purification before praying at a Kyoto temple.

Decisive Dates

Rise of civilised Japan

10,000 BC: Jomon culture produces Japan's earliest known examples of pottery.

3500–2000 BC: population begins migrating inland from coastal areas.

300 BC: Yayoi Period begins with the migration of people from Korea, who introduce rice cultivation.

AD 300: start of Kofun Period as political and social institutions rapidly develop. The imperial line, or Yamato dynasty, begins.

500–600: Buddhism arrives in Japan from Korea.

Time of the warlords

710: a new capital is established in Nara.

794: the capital is relocated to Kyoto. While the court expands, rural areas are neglected.

1180s: estate holders respond to the imperial court's disinterest in the rural areas by developing military power. Conflict amongst warlords ends Heian Period.

1185: Minamoto Yoritomo is victor of the estate-lord struggles and is granted the title of shogun. He establishes his base in Kamakura. The weakened imperial court, however, stays in Kyoto.

1274: Mongols from China unsuccessfully attempt an invasion, landing on Kyushu.

1281: Mongols again attempt an invasion but are turned back by typhoons.

1333: Muromachi Period begins as shogun Ashikaga Takauji returns capital to Kyoto, confronting the imperial court and further eclipsing its influence.

1467: relations between shogun and provincial military governors break down, leading to the chaotic Age of Warring States. Power of feudal lords (daimyo) increases.

1573: warlord Oda Nobunaga overruns Kyoto and conquers the provinces, thus beginning the process of unifying the islands.

1582: Nobunaga is assassinated and replaced by Toyotomi Hideyoshi, who continues Nobunaga's unification efforts.

1590: all of Japan is under Hideyoshi's control.

1592: Hideyoshi attempts invasion of Korea.

1597: Hideyoshi again attempts an invasion of Korea, but dies a year later.

1600: Edo Period begins as Tokugawa Ieyasu takes control after defeating opposition warlords in the Battle of Sekigahara.

1603: Tokugawa moves capital to Edo (present-day Tokyo), begins 250 years of isolation from the world. Edo becomes the largest city in the world.

1853: Perry arrives with U.S. naval ships and forces Japan to accept trade and diplomatic contact. The shogunate weakens as a result.

Return of imperial rule

1868: Meiji Restoration returns the emperor to power. The last shogun, Yoshinobu, retires without a fight. The name of the capital is changed from Edo to Tokyo (Eastern Capital).

1872: samurai class is abolished by imperial decree.

1889: new constitution promulgated.

1895: Japan wins the Sino-Japanese War.

1904–06: Japan wins Russo-Japanese War, the first time that an Asian nation defeats a European power.

1910: Japan annexes Korea.

1912: Meiji emperor dies. Taisho emperor ascends to the throne.

1918: Japan hit hard by economic chaos, rice riots.

1923: Great Kanto Earthquake hits Tokyo area, killing tens of thousands and nearly destroying the city.

1926: Taisho emperor dies. Hirohito ascends the throne to begin the Showa Period.

1931: the Japanese occupy Manchuria and install China's last emperor, Pu-yi, as leader of the new Manchuguo. Japan leaves the League of Nations.

1936: a bloody military uprising, one of many during the 1930s, almost succeeds as a coup d'etat.

1937: Japan begins a brutal military advance on China. In Nanjing, the army runs riot, killing from 150,000 to 300,000 civilians in six weeks.

1941: Japan attacks Pacific and Asian targets. Within a year, Japan occupies most of East Asia and the western Pacific.

1945: American bombing raids destroy many of Japan's major cities and industrial centres. In August, two atomic bombs are dropped on Hiroshima and Nagasaki. A week later, Japan surrenders.

1946: a new constitution is issued under Allied occupation forces, placing sovereignty with the people rather than the emperor.

1952: San Francisco Peace Treaty settles all war-related issues and Japan is returned to sovereignty, except for some Pacific islands, including Okinawa. Japan regains its prewar industrial output.

End of the dream

1990: the so-called "economic bubble" of overinflated land values and overextended banks begins to deflate.

1991: completely dependent on imported oil, Japan receives international criticism for not contributing its share to the Gulf War against Iraq.

1992: Japan's worst postwar recession begins, which will last to the end of the decade.

1993: a series of publicised scandals, including institutionalised bribes and collusion, creates a backlash of voters, who replace Liberal Democratic Party members with independents. A coalition government is formed and lasts seven months, replaced by another coalition led by the socialist party.

1955: socialist factions merge to form Japan Socialist Party; in response, the Liberals and Democrats join to create the Liberal Democratic Party (LDP)

1964: the Summer Olympics are held in Tokyo. The bullet train (*shinkansen*) begins service.

1972: U.S. returns Okinawa to Japan.

1980s: Japan's economy blossoms into the world's second-most powerful. Banks extend easy loans to corporations and small companies based on the inflated land values.

1989: Hirohito dies, replaced by his son Akihito to begin the Heisei Period.

LEFT: Prince Shotoku Taishi with two princely escorts.
ABOVE: 1964 Summer Olympics in Tokyo.

1995: an earthquake hits the Kobe area, near Osaka and Kyoto, and kills more than 6,000 people and leaves 300,000 homeless. Two months later, a religious cult releases nerve gas in the Tokyo subway system, killing 12 and destabilising Japanese confidence in the safety of their society.

1996: the LDP returns to power.

1998: the Winter Olympics are held in Nagano. The international community prods Japan to resuscitate its economy, essential to bring the rest of Asia out of economic recession. Several banks close and bankruptcy rates continue to rise. The Chinese president berates Japan during a state visit for not sufficiently apologising for World War II.

1999: efforts to revive the economy continue. ❑

JAPAN'S EARLY CENTURIES

Migrations of people from the mainland across now-submerged land bridges

evolved into a feudal system of warlords and an aesthetic of profound elegance

The lands that are now the Japanese archipelago have been inhabited by human beings for at least 30,000 years, and maybe for as long as 100,000 to 200,000 years. The shallow seas separating Japan from the Asian mainland were incomplete when these people first settled on the terrain. After people arrived, however, sea levels rose and eventually covered the land bridges.

Whether or not these settlers are the ancestors of the present Japanese remains a controversy. Extensive archaeological excavations of prehistoric sites in Japan only began during the 1960s, and so a clear and comprehensive understanding of the earliest human habitation in the archipelago has yet to emerge.

It is generally agreed that Japan was settled by waves of people coming from South Asia and the northern regions of the Asian continent, and that this migration very likely occurred over a long period.

Jomon Period (ca 10,000–300 BC)

The earliest millennia of Neolithic culture saw a warming in worldwide climate, reaching peak temperature levels between 8000 and 4000 BC. In Japan, this phenomenon led to rising sea levels, which cut any remaining land bridges to the Asian mainland.

At the same time, the local waters produced more abundant species of fish and shellfish. New types of forest took root, sprang up, and thrived. These natural developments in the environment set the stage for the Early Jomon Period. Japan's earliest pottery – belonging to the Jomon culture – has been dated at about 10,000 BC, possibly the oldest known in the world, say some experts.

The Early Jomon people were mostly coastal-living, food-gathering nomads. Dietary reliance on fish, shellfish, and sea mammals gave rise to the community refuse heaps known

as shell-mounds, the archaeologist's primary source of information about these people. The Early Jomon people also hunted deer and wild pig. Artifacts include stone blade tools and the earliest known cord-marked pottery (*jomon*, in fact, means cord-marked).

In the Middle Jomon Period (from about

3500 to 2000 BC), the locus of life shifted away from coastal settlements toward inland areas. By this time, fish and shellfish may have been depleted by lower sea levels, or perhaps more reliance may have been placed on plants as the dietary staple. Grinding stones, capped storage jars, and other Middle Jomon artifacts indicate a much more intense involvement with plant cultivation. Middle Jomon came to an end when tree crops in inland hilly areas failed to provide sufficient sustenance.

The Late Jomon Period, dating from around 2000 BC, is marked by a resurgence amongst villages of coastal fishing along the Pacific coasts of the main islands.

PRECEDING PAGES: old illustration from the classic *Tale of Genji.* **LEFT:** a clay figure, or *haniwa*, from the Jomon Period. **RIGHT:** earthenware, Jomon Period.

Yayoi Period (ca 300 BC–AD 300)

Named after an archeological site near Tokyo University, the Yayoi Period was a time of significant cultural transition and ushered in by peoples who migrated from rice-growing areas of the Asian mainland, starting around 300 BC, into northern Kyushu via Korea and, most likely, Okinawa. (Northern Japan, in fact, lingered behind the rest of the archipelago, with the Jomon culture persisting well into northern Japan's early historic periods.)

In a brief 600 years, Japan was transformed from a land of nomadic hunting-and-gathering communities into one of stationary farming villages. The growth of tightly-knit, autonomous rice-farming settlements was so rapid in Kyushu and western Honshu that by AD 100 such settlements were found in most parts of the country, except for the northern regions of Honshu and Hokkaido.

Kofun Period (ca 300–710)

The break with Yayoi culture is represented by the construction of huge tombs of earth and stone in coastal areas of Kyushu and along the shores of the Inland Sea. *Haniwa*, hollow clay human and animal figures (*see photograph on page 24*), and models of houses decorated the perimeters of these tombs. These were made, some experts have speculated, as substitutes for the living retainers and possessions of the departed noble or leader.

Political and social institutions developed rapidly. Each of the community clusters that defined itself as a "country" or "kingdom" had a hierarchical social structure, subjected to increasing influence by a burgeoning central power based in the Yamato Plain, in what is now the area of Osaka and Nara. The imperial line, or the Yamato dynasty, was most likely formed out of a number of powerful *uji* (family-clan communities) that had developed in the Late Yayoi Period.

Buddhism came to Japan in the 6th century from Korea. Although it is said that writing accompanied the religion, it may be that Chinese writing techniques preceded the religion by as much as 100 to 150 years. In any case, it was literacy that made the imported religion accessible to the nobility, also exposing them to the Chinese classics and to the writings of sages such as Confucius. Social and political change naturally followed an increase in literacy.

DESCENDANTS OF THE SUN GODDESS

Shinto mythology has the Japanese emperor, via the Yamato dynasty, claiming direct descent from Amaterasu Omikami, the Sun Goddess and the supreme deity. As late as the early 1940s, it was officially ordained that the emperor was traced back to Jimmu, descendant of the Sun Goddess. Archaeologists could dig but not counter the myth. Today, the claim of the emperor's descent from the Sun Goddess is made by only a few Japanese, notably right-wing nationalists. It has been officially denied both by the government and by the Imperial Household Agency, which administers the affairs of the imperial family.

The power of the Soga clan was enhanced by exclusive control of the imperial treasury and granaries and by the clan's monopolistic role as sponsor for new learning brought in from the Asian mainland. Their consolidation of political power culminated with Soga daughters chosen exclusively as the consorts of emperors, with Soga clansmen filling important court positions. Reforms were aimed primarily at strengthening the central government and reducing the power of other clans at the imperial court. The reforms were far-reaching, including changes in social structure, economic and legal systems, provincial boundaries, bureaucracy, and taxes.

Nara Period (710–794)

An empress in the early 8th century again constructed a new capital, this one in the northwest of the Yamato Plain and named Heijo-kyo, on the site of present Nara. The century that followed – the Nara Period – saw the full enforcement of the system of centralised imperial rule based on Chinese concepts (the *ritsuryo* system), as well as flourishing arts and culture.

With the enforcement of the ritsuryo system, the imperial government achieved tight control, placing administrative control in a powerful grand council. All land used for rice cultivation was claimed to be under imperial ownership, which later led to heavy taxation of farmers.

Heian Period (794–1185)

In the last decade of the 8th century, the capital was relocated yet again. As usual, the city was built on the Chinese model and was named Heian-kyo. It was the core around which the city of Kyoto developed. Its completion in 795 marked the beginning of the glorious 400-year Heian Period; Kyoto remained the imperial capital until 1868, when the imperial court moved to Edo, soon to be renamed Tokyo.

The strength of the central government continued for several decades, but later in the 9th century the ritsuryo system gradually began to crumble. The central government was interested in expanding the area of its influence farther and farther from the capital, but provincial government became harder to manage under the bureaucratic system.

This was modified so that aristocrats and powerful temple guardians could own large estates (*shoen*). Farmers, working imperial lands but faced with oppressive taxation, fled to these estates in large numbers. Thus the estate holders began to gain political – and military – power in the provinces.

Provincial areas were neglected by the imperial court. Banditry became widespread and local administrators were more interested in personal gain than in enforcing law and order. The result was that the lords of great estates continued to develop their own military power, eventually engaging in struggles amongst themselves. The fighting ended the Heian Period dramatically and decisively.

LEFT: bronze vessel from the Yayoi Period.
RIGHT: Minamoto Yoritomo of Kamakura Period.

Kamakura Period (1185–1333)

The victor of the struggles, Minamoto Yoritomo, was granted the title of *shogun*. He established his base at Kamakura, far from Kyoto and south of where Edo Tokyo would arise. There he established an administrative structure as well as military headquarters, creating ministries to take care of samurai under his control. He had, in effect, come to dominate the country by assuming control of justice, imperial succession, and defence of the country. He remained in Kamakura, refusing to go to the imperial capital for any reason.

Nevertheless, he convinced the emperor to

sanction officials called *shugo* (military governors) and *jito* (stewards) in each province. The former were responsible for military control of the provinces and the latter for supervising the land, plus collecting taxes. Both posts were answerable directly to the shogun himself, thus government by the warrior class, located at a distance from the imperial capital, was created. This governing system was based on obligation and dependency, not unlike that of medieval Europe, and so it can be called a true feudal system known as *bakufu*, or shogunate. The imperial court was, in effect, shoved into a corner and ignored. The court remained alive, however, though subsequent centuries saw its impoverishment. Still, it kept an important function in ritual and as symbol until 1868, when the emperor again became the acting head of state.

Although the Kamakura Period was relatively brief, there were events and developments that profoundly affected the country. A revolutionary advance of agricultural techniques occurred that allowed greater production of food.

Consequently, there was an increase in population and economic growth, with more intense settlement of the land, better commerce and trade, the growth of local markets, and the

beginnings of a currency system. Contact with China resumed on a private basis.

Strong Buddhist leaders arose who preached doctrines that appealed to both the samurai and the common people, and Buddhism became a popular religion, whereas in the past it had been the monopoly of the aristocracy.

The complexities of civil rule became top-heavy; the system of military governors and stewards started to crumble. More strain was added by the defence of the country against the two Mongol invasions in 1274 and 1281, both of which were unsuccessful due in great measure to the fortuitous occurrence of typhoons that destroyed the invading Mongol fleet.

Muromachi Period (1333–1568)

A subsequent shogun, Ashikaga Takauji, returned the capital to Kyoto, bringing the shogunate nose to nose with the imperial court and effectively eclipsing any power, political or economic, that the court may have retained. At the same time, the Ashikaga shogun and vassals, in the age-old pattern of conquering warriors anywhere, caught aristocratitis and actively delved into such effete pursuits as connoisseurship and cultural patronage after the manner of the old aristocracy.

The name of the period, Muromachi, comes from the area of Kyoto in which a later Ashikaga shogun, Yoshimitsu, built his residence. His life represents perhaps the high point of the Ashikaga shogunate. Yoshimitsu took an active role in court politics as well as excelling in his military duties as shogun.

Overall, the Muromachi Period introduced the basic changes that would assure the economic growth and stability of the coming Edo Period. Agricultural techniques were improved, new crops were introduced, and irrigation and commercial farming expanded. Guilds of specialised craftsmen appeared, a money economy spread, and trade increased markedly. Most importantly, towns and cities arose and grew; such development was accompanied by the appearance of merchant and service classes.

A later Ashikaga shogun was assassinated in 1441, which started the decline of the shogunate; the relationship between the shogun and the military governors of the provinces broke down. A decade of war and unrest marked the total erosion of centralised authority and a general dissolution of society. It ushered in the Age of Warring States, a century of battle that lasted from 1467 until 1568.

The almost total decentralisation of government that occurred in the Age of Warring States saw the development of what might be called a true type of feudal lord, the *daimyo*. The need to defend territory by military might meant that the political unit became contiguous with its military potential. The daimyo became what he was by right of conquest and might, backed up by vast armies.

During this century of warfare, with its ethic of ambition and expansion by force of arms, it is not surprising that the idea of unifying – or subduing – the entire country occurred to a few of the warriors, leaders of vision and ability.

Momoyama Period (1568–1600)

This short Momoyama Period is somewhat of a historian's artifact, more the climaxing of the Muromachi Period. But it has been accorded a name, perhaps because the Ashikaga shogunate ended in 1573 (the Muromachi Period is when the Ashikaga shogun ruled), notably when Oda Nobunaga (1534–82), the first of three leaders to go about the business of unifying the country, overran Kyoto. The other leaders were Toyotomi Hideyoshi (1536–98) and Tokugawa Ieyasu (1542–1616).

Nobunaga conquered the home provinces in a rigorous manner. He eliminated rivals in the

SADO: THE TEA CEREMONY

Sado – the way of tea – attained its fundamental character under Toyotomi Hideyoshi's tea master, Sen no Rikyu. Making the tea is not the challenge; it is making it in the right spirit that consumes a lifetime of effort. Implements and procedures have value only towards a higher objective – the ability to show sublime hospitality. The years of training are to make the motions appear casual and effortless.

Although tea drinking appeared earlier, it was not until the 12th century that the special strain of tea bush and the technique for making powdered green tea (*matcha*) were brought from China. First planted in Uji, near Kyoto, matcha – loaded with caffeine and vitamin C – helped meditating Zen monks keep their concentration.

While matcha had became a stimulant of the rich merchant class by the 15th century, it retained its Zen connection through Rikyu, who noted that "all people are equal in the tea room". The room's door, for example, is so low that all guests must bow equally to enter.

---

usual military fashion and is known particularly for razing the temples of militant Buddhist sects around Kyoto that opposed him. Temple burning aside, he had a flair for culture.

Although he brought only about one-third of the country under his control, Nobunaga laid the foundation for the unification that would later follow. He was assassinated by a treacherous general in 1582.

Hideyoshi, Nobunaga's chief general, did away with Nobunaga's murderer and set himself up as Nobunaga's successor. With military brilliance, statesmanship, and a certain amount of brass, he proceeded vigorously with the job of unifying Japan. By 1590, all territories of the country, directly or by proxy, were essentially under his control. But the government was still decentralised in a complex network of feudal relationships. Hideyoshi's hold on the country, based on oaths of fealty, was slippery at best. Still, he effected sweeping domestic reforms. The action that perhaps had the longest-lasting social impact on Japanese history was his "sword hunt", in which all non-samurai were forced to give up their weapons. (To this day, there are strict regulations on weapons of any sort in Japan, whether knives or guns.) A class system was also introduced. In some areas, rich landlords had to make a difficult choice: declare themselves to be samurai and susceptible to the demands of the warrior's life, or else remain as commoners and thus subservient to the samurai class.

Hideyoshi made two attempts to conquer Korea in 1592 and 1597 with the aim of taking over China. His death in 1598 brought this megalomanic effort to a swift end.

The cultural achievements of these three decades were astonishing. The country was in political ferment, yet glorious textiles, ceramics, and paintings were produced. ❑

LEFT: *sumi-e* (ink painting) from Muromachi Period.
RIGHT: shogun Toyotomi Hideyoshi.

THE EDO PERIOD

The rise of the great shogunates and their samurai warlords instilled in the Japanese culture ways of thinking and behaviour that persist even today

The political, economic, social, religious, and intellectual facets of the Edo Period (1600–1868) are exceedingly complex. One often-cited general characteristic of this time is an increasingly prosperous merchant class occurring simultaneously with urban development. Edo (now modern-day Tokyo) became one of the world's great cities and is thought to have had a population in excess of one million at the beginning of the 18th century, greater than London or Paris at the time.

The Tokugawa shogun

For many years, the shogun Hideyoshi had bemoaned his lack of a male heir. When in the twilight of Hideyoshi's years an infant son, Hideyori, was born, Hideyoshi was ecstatic and became obsessed with founding a dynasty of warrior rulers. So he established a regency council of leading vassals and allies, foremost of whom was Tokugawa Ieyasu (1542–1616), who controlled the most territory in the realm after Hideyoshi. Members of the council swore loyalty to the infant; the boy was five at the time of Hideyoshi's death.

The death of Hideyoshi was naturally an opportunity for the ambitions of restless warlords to surface. Tokugawa Ieyasu had about half of the lords who were allied with Hideyoshi's son sign pledges to him within a year of Hideyoshi's death. In 1600, however, he was challenged by a military coalition of lords from western Japan. He won the encounter in the Battle of Sekigahara (near Kyoto) and became the islands' *de facto* ruler.

In 1603, Tokugawa Ieyasu was given the title of shogun by the still subservient but symbolically important emperor. He established his capital in Edo (now Tokyo), handed his son the shogun title in 1605, and then retired to a life of intrigue and scheming aimed at consolidating the position of his family. (Ieyasu himself would die in 1616.)

The primary problem facing Ieyasu was how to make a viable system out of the rather strange mix of a strong, central military power

and a totally decentralised administrative structure. Eventually he devised a complex system that combined feudal authority and bureaucratic administration with the Tokugawa shoguns as supreme authority from whom the various lords, or *daimyo*, received their domains and to whom they allied themselves by oath.

While the military emphasis of the domain was curtailed, each daimyo had considerable autonomy in the administration of his domain. The system sufficed to maintain peace and a growing prosperity for more than two centuries. Its flaws were in its inability to adapt well to social and political change, as would later be seen. Whether this fragile conservatism was inherent in the system or in the people who ran the system can be argued endlessly.

Ieyasu was Napoleonic in his passion for administration, and he thought of every device possible to assure that his descendants would retain power. Wanting to keep an eye on the daimyo, in 1635 he established the *sankin kotai* system, which required staggered attendance in Edo for the 300 independent feudal lords. The shogunate set up a rigid class hierarchy – warriors, farmers, artisans, merchants – and adopted a school of neo-Confucianism as the theoretical basis for social and political policy.

Whether in Edo or the countryside, every individual knew exactly what his or her position in society was and of how they were to behave. Sometimes encouraged with the sword, the emphasis on Confucian obedience and proper relations between superior and inferior filtered down to the lowest strata of society. People in a daimyo's domain had little recourse

increased, but at times the shogunate quelled conspicuous consumption of merchants.

Growth of Edo

When Ieyasu first settled down in what eventually would become modern Tokyo, the area was little more than a collection of scattered farming and fishing villages. The little town of Edojuku, at the mouth of the Hirakawa River, contained only about 100 thatched huts in the shadow of a dilapidated castle, built in 1457 by the minor warlord Ota Dokan. A sophisticated poet and scholar, in 1485 he was betrayed and butchered at the behest of his own lord.

if their lord was autocratic, unprincipled, or arbitrary. As with today's Japan, there seems to have been a predisposition towards xenophobia, yet it was somehow coupled with an attraction toward things foreign. The xenophobia won, however, and the result was brutal and bloody for those tainted by the outside world. Indeed, for most of the Tokugawa decades, Japan's doors were closed to the outside.

Long years of isolated peace slowly replaced the warrior's importance with that of the merchant. Standards of living for all classes

LEFT: Tokugawa Ieyasu, the first Tokugawa shogun.
ABOVE: Nihom-bashi in Edo (Tokyo) and Fuji-san.

A SAMURAI'S WAY OF LIFE

The way of the samurai – *bushido* – was a serious path to follow, "a way of dying" to defend the honour of one's lord or one's own name. Often that meant *seppuku*, or ritual disembowelment. An unwritten code of behaviour and ethics, bushido came to the foreground during the Kamakura period. In the Edo period, bushido helped strengthen *bakufu*, or the shogunate government, by perfecting the feudal class system of samurai, farmer, artisan, and merchant. The ruling samurai class was by far the most powerful. Only when the economy shifted from rice-based to monetary did the merchants take control of Edo, the samurai increasingly in debt.

Ieyasu brought with him to Edo a ready-made population of considerable size. Huge numbers of peasants, merchants, and *ronin* (masterless samurai) poured into the new capital of the shogun to labour in the construction of the castle, mansions, warehouses, and other infrastructure required to run the giant bureaucracy. The courses of rivers were changed, canals were dug, and Hibiya Inlet, which brought Tokyo Bay lapping at the base of the castle hill, was filled in.

When the major daimyo and their entourage were in town, the samurai portion of the city's population probably topped 500,000, maybe even outnumbering the commoners. The samurai allotted themselves more than 60 percent of the city's land. Another 20 percent went to hundreds of shrines and temples, which formed a spiritually protective ring around the outer edges of the city.

By the early 1700s, an estimated 1 to 1.4 million people lived in Edo, making it by far the largest city in the world at the time. During the same period, Kyoto had a population of 400,000, and Osaka, 300,000. In 1801, when Britain's navy dominated the seas, Europe's largest city, London, had fewer than a million inhabitants. Japan's population hovered around

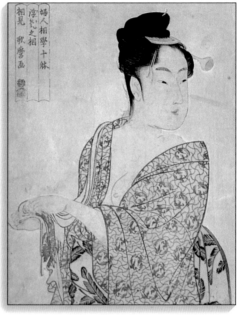

THE 47 MASTERLESS SAMURAI

In 1701, a warlord named Asano from near Hiroshima became angered at the taunting of a *hatamoto* named Kira, who had been assigned to teach him proper etiquette for receiving an imperial envoy. Asano drew his sword and wounded Kira. Asano was ordered to commit ritual disembowelment, or *seppuku*. He did so. His lands were confiscated and his samurai left as *ronin*, or masterless warriors. A year later, the ronin took revenge by attacking Kira's Edo mansion. Chopping off Kira's head, they took it to Asano's grave so that his spirit could finally rest. In turn, the 47 ronin were ordered by the shogun to commit seppuku, which they did as a group.

30 million for most of the Edo era; less than two million belonged to the samurai families.

In general, the samurai gravitated to the hilly parts of the city, or Yamanote, while the townspeople congregated – or were forced to do so – in the downtown lowlands, or Shitamachi, especially along the Sumida River. More than half of Edo's residents were crammed into the 15 percent of the city comprising Shitamachi, with a population density of about 70,000 people per square kilometre. Almost from the start, both Yamanote and Shitamachi began to encroach through land-fill onto Tokyo Bay. (Even today in the modern city of Tokyo, these two districts retain distinctive characteristics.)

The Edo castle

The grounds of Ieyasu's huge castle, including the defensive moat system, were extensive. The complex was not actually completed until 1640 but was razed by fire seven years later.

Like everything else in Edo Tokyo, the castle underwent many resurrections following fires and earthquakes. Little of the Tokugawa castle remains today; in fact, there are no visual representations in art or print of the castle itself to tease our curiosity.

> ### SHIFTING VICES
>
> The shogunate unsuccessfully tried banning both *kabuki* and prostitution. Eventually, the shogunate simply moved them to less desirable locations.

from Kyoto converging on the city were not also important. They were, especially the famous Tokaido, or East Sea Road, along which most of the feudal lords from Osaka and Kyoto travelled to Tokyo for their periodic and mandated stays in Edo. Tokaido also formed the central artery of the city itself between Shinagawa and Nihombashi.

The dichotomy between the refined – albeit somewhat constipated – culture of upper-class Yamanote and the robust, plebeian art and drama of lower-class Shitamachi

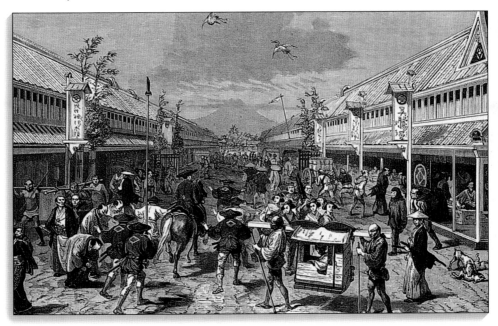

But the shogun's capital must have been a truly impressive city, backed by Mt Fuji and laced with canals. It is often forgotten nowadays that most of Edo's supplies came by sea, especially from Osaka. In fact, one of the reasons Ieyasu had chosen the area for his capital was its easy access to the sea. But the swampy shore of Tokyo Bay itself was unsuitable for building docks and wharfs; instead, canals and rivers threading inland from the bay served as ports. This is not to suggest that the five great highways from the provinces and especially

(which Edward Seidensticker aptly dubbed respectively as the "high city" and "low city") has been a consistent feature of life in Edo. The Edokko (Children of Edo) took delight in delight, and this appreciation of pleasure is grandly reflected in the popular culture of the time – the colour and splash of *kabuki;* the *bunraku* puppet drama; *ukiyo-e* woodblock prints depicting the world of actors, sumo stars, courtesans, and geisha; the pleasure quarters, licensed and unlicensed; and the vigorous publishing world of both scholarship and trashy stories. All of these reflected the Edo pleasure in the material world and in a kind of high consumerism. The fact that men outnumbered

LEFT: Edo woman in kimono, and print by Utamaro.
ABOVE: street life in Edo, or present-day Tokyo.

women – two to one as late as 1721 – probably contributed to making the male population more than a bit rowdy and cantankerous. It would certainly explain the emphasis on catering to the sensual pleasures of men and in the rise of woodblock prints of a rather graphic if not exaggerated sexual nature.

Rise of the merchants

The establishment of the shogunate caused many economic changes. After the shogunate eliminated international trade, merchants and the increasingly powerful commercial conglomerates (*zaibatsu*) turned their attention to

domestic distribution and marketing systems. The highways built by the Tokugawas, along with their standardisation of weights, measures and coinage, helped with the rise of the zaibatsu. (These zaibatsu lasted until World War II; they were then broken up by the Occupation forces.) Just north of Nihom-bashi, the bridge from which all distances in Japan were measured, stood the major dry-goods stores, including Echigoya (now Mitsukoshi), established in 1673 during the Edo Period, along with Sumitomo and other present-day zaibatsu.

The samurai received their stipends in rice, but the economy was increasingly dependent upon money – not to the shogunate's liking, as the shogunate's economic foundation was based upon taxes paid in rice. The result: the samurai borrowed from the merchants and increasingly went into debt.

Yet it was still controlled with rigid social and governmental systems. Internal pressures demanded change. Moreover, the world itself was not about to allow Japan to keep its doors closed. The industrial revolution was gaining momentum in Europe. The Western powers were casting about for more countries into which to expand economic influence.

While others had tried rattling Japan's doors, it was the United States that yanked them open in 1853 with Commodore Matthew Perry and America's East India Squadron – the famous "Black Ships". He reappeared the following year with additional ships to back up the action and was successful. Many in Edo were not especially giddy with delight in the shift of tides. When the first American consul, Townsend Harris, was allowed to enter Edo in 1857, he was greeted by a crowd of thousands – and absolute silence. Nevertheless, in 1858 a treaty of friendship and trade was signed with the United States, followed shortly by treaties with other Western powers.

The turmoil and tumult of the 15 years from 1853 to 1868 have been well documented in many books. The sense of Japan afloat in a sea of hostile powers who possessed more technology and had voracious ambitions may have acted to direct domestic energies away from internal wrangling. The shogun was in a tight squeeze with the arrival of Perry. His domestic response – a consensus with the daimyo regarding how to respond to the Black Ships, then encouraging them to strengthen defenses in their own domains – eventually diluted his control over the daimyo. At the same time, an anti-Tokugawa movement amongst lower-level daimyo was stewing near Osaka and Kyoto. Rebel daimyo captured the then-powerless emperor and declared the restoration of imperial rule. Shogunate forces sought to reverse the situation in Kyoto but were defeated. The shogun yielded to the imperial court in 1868 – the Meiji Restoration. The emperor ascended again to head of state. The reign of the Meiji emperor would last from 1868 until 1912. ❏

LEFT: Perry's American fleet at Uragawa.
RIGHT: Edo-Period leisure depicted in *ukiyo-e*.

THE MODERN ERA

*Once militarism was replaced by consumerism, Japan rapidly became
one of the world's richest, safest, and most advanced countries*

The Meiji Restoration of 1868, in which the ascension of the Meiji emperor as the nation's leader returned Japan to imperial rule, was a revolution of considerable proportions. Yet it was accomplished with surprisingly little bloodshed. The last shogun, Yoshinobu, in statesman-like fashion retired and gave up the Edo castle rather than precipitate a full-scale civil war. Power was officially returned to the emperor in the fall of 1867. (The samurai class would be abolished by imperial decree in 1872, leaving breathing space for the merchant class.)

But shogunate residue remained in Edo and not all the samurai gave up easily. At the Tokugawa family temple of Kan'ei-ji, most of which is now Tokyo's Ueno Park, 2,000 die-hard Tokugawa loyalists – the Shogitai – chose to make a last stand in a bloody, one-day battle. During this Battle of Ueno, the Shogitai burned most of the Kan'ei-ji complex to the ground. Hundreds of the Shogitai were killed, their bodies left to rot by the victors. (Days later, however, with the new emperor's permission, monks released the souls of the Shogitai with a funeral pyre.) Today, Kan'ei-ji, a huge Buddhist temple complex with nearly 100 buildings, is and has long been a mausoleum temple for all three generations of the Tokugawa family. Only Ieyasu and his grandson Iemitsu are entombed elsewhere, in Nikko, to the north.

Meiji Period (1868–1912)

In 1868, an imperial edict changed the name of Edo to Tokyo, or Eastern Capital, and Emperor Meiji moved his court from the imperial capital of Kyoto to Tokyo. But before leaving Kyoto, the emperor issued an extremely important document proclaiming that "knowledge shall be sought throughout the world so as to strengthen the foundations of imperial rule... Evil customs of the past shall be broken and everything based upon the just laws of Nature".

PRECEDING PAGES: celebrating the emperor's birthday outside the palace. **LEFT:** Mutsuhito, the Meiji emperor. **RIGHT:** exposition in Ueno Park, Meiji Period.

Because at the end of the Edo Period the office of emperor had no longer been tied to a political system, the emperor's "restoration" was used as a symbol and vehicle for choosing from a wide range of governmental structures. The quality of the nation's new leadership, and the political, economic, and cultural choices

they made, can be seen as nothing less than spectacular. The tremendous support the government gave to the corporate *zaibatsu* and other favoured companies would appear to indicate the installed system was state capitalism, but such an assessment can be deceiving. There was, in fact, a dual economic structure: the huge industrial-and-trade zaibatsu conglomerates and the small cottage industries. (To a certain extent, this dual structure of manufacturing continues to this day.)

In a few decades, Japan effectively restructured itself as a political entity. In retrospect, this seems astonishingly radical. Yet it did not happen overnight, but rather by a series of incremental modifications to the political system. The first new governmental structure was a compromise between old and new. It cleverly borrowed names from archaic imperial institutions to give an aura of tradition to what was hardly traditional.

Meeting the Western powers as an equal was one of the guiding concerns of the Meiji years. This meant adopting anything and everything Western, from railroads to ballroom dancing. The pendulum first swung to extremes, from a total rejection of all native things (including an urge to abandon the Japanese language) to an emotional nationalism after the excesses of ini-

tial enthusiasm for foreign imports. Japan took to Western industrialisation with enthusiasm. But the employment of numerous foreign advisors (upwards of 3,000) ended as soon as the Japanese sensed that they could continue perfectly well on their own.

An urgent need of the Meiji leaders was modification of the unequal treaties with the West, which previously had been negotiated by the shogunate. This issue alone was not resolved until the 1890s and saw the fall of several highly competent leaders.

After a number of unsuccessful drafts over the years, a new constitution for the country was promulgated in 1889. This Meiji Constitution helped Japan become recognised as an advanced nation by the West. Another factor was Japan's success in the Sino-Japanese War of 1894–95, which proved the country's ability to wage modern warfare.

But the clincher in making Japan a true world power was winning the Russo-Japanese War of 1904–06, the first time that an Asian nation had defeated a European power. It didn't stop there, however. In 1910, Japan annexed Korea, ostensibly by treaty but actually under military threat. It would occupy Korea until the end of World War II in 1945.

Emperor Meiji died in 1912. By then, Japan had consolidated its economy, defined a political system, changed its social structure, and become an advanced nation in many ways.

Taisho Period (1912–26)

The short reign of Emperor Taisho saw the 20th century catch Japan in its grasp and carry it off on a strange and sometimes unpleasant odyssey.

World War I proved an enormous economic boom, and Japan seized the chance to enter Asian markets vacated by the European powers. But the inevitable deflation hit hard and there were major rice riots in Tokyo in 1918.

The following year, most politics became extremely polarised as the labour movement and leftists gained momentum. A new right, which believed in the politics of assassination rather than the ballot box, emerged from the political shadows.

A series of political murders, including of prime ministers and former prime ministers, followed over the next 15 years, helping to create the climate of violence that eventually would let the military intervene in politics.

OF EMPERORS AND CALENDARS

Japan has a British-style constitutional monarchy and parliament. Since the 1868 Meiji Restoration, there have been four emperors, since World War II a figurehead:

- **Meiji** (Meiji Period)   1867 (1868)–1912
- **Taisho** (Taisho Period)   1912 (1915)–1926
- **Hirohito** (Showa Period) 1926 (1928)–1989
- **Akihito** (Heisei Period) 1989 (1990)–Present

(Coronation dates in parenthesis.)

Japan uses two methods for indicating the year: the Western system (i.e., 1999) and a system based on how long the current emperor has reigned (i.e., Heisei 11). The latter appears frequently on official documents.

The big event of the 1920s was the Great Kanto Earthquake. It struck around noon on 1 September 1923, when a good percentage of the city's charcoal and gas stoves were lit. Fire, not the quake itself, caused the most damage. Ninety percent of Yokohama was destroyed.

During the Taisho Period, Japan began to bubble intellectually. The growing prosperity (and the accompanying problems), the shrinking size of the world, and the relative youth of Japan as a world power contributed to the "Taisho Democracy", which was actually little more than a time of good, healthy, intellectual ferment. Still, this bright spot was important as

sliding into world war. Historians' analyses of why and how militarism developed in the 1930s has produced a rash of theories, some of which argue a conspiracy going back to Meiji days. Whatever the political, economic and social forces that produced the military government and the aggressive war effort, some observations can be made. The distribution of wealth was still uneven. The establishment factions included big business (the zaibatsu), the upper crust of government, and the military interests.

Political power within the country favoured establishment interests; suffrage was not universal. Non-establishment interests were weak

a precursor to Japan's plunge into the dark period of militarism and war and as a foundation for the country's emergence afterwards.

Showa Period (1926–89)

With the death of the Taisho emperor in 1926, Hirohito succeeded to the throne to begin the Showa Period. Japan's isolation from World War I had kept the nation free of Europe's war-weary cynicism, and, too, of the horrors of such war. But within a decade, Japan itself would be

LEFT: *ukiyo-e* print depicting the emperor promulgating the Meiji constitution. ABOVE: busy street in Tokyo's Shibuya district in the early 20th century.

because they had little recourse for expression, other than through imported political concepts – socialism and communism – that were distrusted and feared. In fact, non-establishment interests never received adequate representation in government until after World War II.

Japan, still sensitive to Western righteousness regarding Asia even half a century after opening up to the West, felt insecure. This and domestic economic and demographic pressures made military hegemony seem a viable alternative, at least to the military. Indeed, the military and its supporters were increasingly frustrated by what they saw as ineffectual and compromising civilian policies.

Militarism's rise and fall

The pivotal point was the Manchurian Incident of 1931, in which Japanese military forces occupied Manchuria and set up the state of Manchuguo. Protest over this action by the League of Nations resulted in Japan leaving the League and following a policy of isolation. Within the military itself, extremist factionalism grew, and during the 1930s several plots of one kind or another sought to take over power. The most famous is the 26 February Incident of 1936, a bloody military uprising that might have been a coup d'etat had it not been based on vague, romantic ideas that did not include a practical plan of how to use power. This bolstered the civilian resistance to military involvement in politics. But in the summer of 1937 war erupted in China and Japanese troops began a brutal campaign against the Chinese, notably in the occupation of Nanjing and the slaughter of from 150,000 to 300,000 civilians.

Seeking to discourage Western intervention in Japan's Asian expansion, the Japanese military launched pre-emptive attacks not only on Pearl Harbour in December of 1941 but against European colonial holdings throughout Asia.

In less than a year, Japan possessed most of

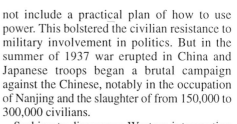

SURRENDER PREVAILED

Evidence suggests that the Japanese military ignored civilian officials' pleas to end the war. Three days after the atomic bomb on Hiroshima, the imperial army's chief of staff assured the civilian government that a foreign invasion of Japan would be turned back. Informed of the second atomic bomb on Nagasaki, he repeated his claim. Still, on 14 August Hirohito prepared a surrender announcement. That night, 1,000 members of the army attempted a coup by surrounding the Imperial Palace, executing the emperor's guard commander, and searching for the emperor's surrender edict. The coup was thwarted, and Japan surrendered.

East Asia and the western Pacific. Japanese occupation was often savage and inhumane. But by early 1945, Japan was on the defensive, its major cities (except Kyoto and Nara, because of their historical heritage) levelled by American bombing raids.

Despite Germany's defeat in May of 1945, Japanese military leaders would not yield. The Allies and most Asians say it was necessary, the Japanese say not, but in mid-August of the same year, atomic bombs were dropped on Hiroshima and Nagasaki. A week later, the war was over. (Later, it would turn out that the Japanese had been developing their own atomic bomb with German help.)

On 15 August 1945, Emperor Hirohito spoke on the radio – the first time commoners had heard his voice – and declared an unconditional surrender. Japan lost its empire, its right to independent foreign policy, the emperor's claim to divinity, and the army. More than 6 million soldiers and civilians returned home to Japan. War-crime trials convicted several thousand Japanese; 920 of them were executed.

A new 1946 constitution issued under the mandate of Gen. Douglas MacArthur's occupation government guaranteed Western-style liberties, established a British-style parliamentary system, dismantled the prewar industrial

democracy by politicians; and modern Japan's collective inability to recall much of Asia's history involving Japan between 1910 and 1945.

The decades following the war were of well-coordinated corporate and bureaucratic efforts to revive both business and the country. Protected by the American military umbrella to the end of the 20th century, Japan was able to funnel full economic resources into its economy.

Meanwhile, the provincial millions who continued to flow into Tokyo – its population more than doubled after 1950 – often found homes along the rail lines leading out from the main terminals of Shibuya, Shinjuku and Ikebukuro.

zaibatsu, and renounced war as national policy. With the signing of the 1952 San Francisco Peace Treaty, American occupation of the country ended and Japan was sovereign.

The sun rises again

Three significant characteristics help define postwar Japan up to the present day: government-coordinated industrialisation and spectacular economic growth; the mocking of

LEFT: beheading a Chinese civilian; a Japanese newspaper recounts a contest between two Japanese army officers to see who could behead 100 Chinese the fastest. ABOVE: blessings for the warriors, 1945.

INSTITUTIONALISED FORGETFULNESS

Collectively Japanese seem unable to recall 50 years of Japanese aggression capped by a Pacific war killing 20 million people. But Japan's neighbours – Korea, the Philippines, and China – do. Recently, the Imperial Army's own documents confirming the brutality have been surfacing, and aging veterans have publicly purged their nightmares. But schools still minimise Japan's aggressive past, if mentioned at all, and conservative politicians still rewrite history. In 1994, the Minister of Justice declared that the 1937 Rape of Nanjing – 150,000 to 300,000 Chinese were slaughtered by an out-of-control Japanese army – was an unsubstantiated myth.

These rail lines were usually constructed by department store firms, which had major stores near the station and branches at most stations along their private lines. Real estate firms grabbed up land along the tracks and sold pre-fabricated "rabbit hutches" to the *sarariman* ("salaryman") – male white-collar workers – who had not yet abandoned the dream of owning their own home. In the process, a nightmare of urbanisation at its worst was created, and few can deny that urban Japan today is an aesthetic catastrophe.

With the urban population's explosive rise, farming's importance dropped to a fraction of the nation's gross national product, although the farmers' political power actually increased. Unusual for a developing or developed country, Japan's new national wealth was evenly distributed amongst the people, leaving almost no one in an economic lower-class. Unemployment remained low. Industrial labour disputes and strikes were minimal.

During postwar reconstruction, government regulation had served Japan's interests well. But as Japan joined the advanced economies in the 1960s and especially the 1970s, the one-way nature of Japan's markets strained relations with others, especially with the U.S., its largest market, and Europe. Over-regulation and chummy business-government relationships saddled consumers with ridiculously high prices (US$700 hook-up fees for a single phone line and domestically sold televisions costing twice their export price) for nearly everything except umbrellas, cheap in this rainy land.

High rates of household savings created excess capital, used by business and the government for funding massive infrastructure projects. The economy accelerated with uncanny momentum, surpassing every other country except the United States. Japan became the new global paradigm for success and potency. The stock market was on a trajectory that, in the late 1980s, momentarily exceeded the New York Stock Exchange in volume and vigour. Real estate in Japan became the planet's most valuable, and banks dished money out, securing the loans with highly overvalued land. (These loans came back to haunt the banks in the 1990s when several banks collapsed, while others had to be propped up by government support.) Japan's rising sun seemed, for the moment, to outshine most of the world.

Heisei Period (1989–)

Emperor Hirohito died in 1989, the longest reigning emperor (62 years) in Japan's recorded history. His son, Akihito, took the throne and adopted the period name of *Heisei,* which means "attainment of peace". He and his family have made sustained efforts to humanise the imperial family and to tangentially deal with Japan's brutal past. But as a politically neutered

---

A WOMAN'S DESTINY?

Crown Prince Naruhito remained single until his early thirties. When he married, talk soon turned to an heir. His wife, Owada Masako, had a blossoming career in the diplomatic corps. Younger Japanese women saw in her a modern woman – educated abroad, stylish, independent. Japanese agree, however, that marriage and the Imperial Household Agency have quenched Masako's independent ways. (Michiko, the current empress and a commoner like Masako, was long poorly treated by palace staff.) Many years after the marriage, the princely couple has had no children; the press is now obsessed as to why Masako has "failed" to produce an heir to the throne.

LEFT: Akihito and Michiko, the future emperor and empress in 1959. **RIGHT:** Seto Ohashi, between Shikoku and Honshu, during construction.

figurehead, the emperor is not permitted to address politics, history, or his father's place in history. Every public utterance of the imperial family is controlled by either the Imperial Household Agency, which administers the affairs and behaviour of the imperial family, or the bureaucrats of government.

Atop the cauldron of hyper-inflated land values, Japan's "bubble economy" superheated in the late 1980s, only to begin collapsing in 1990. The stock market lost half its value in a short time, banks lost still-unspeakable amounts on loans secured by now-deflated land values, and a blossoming Japanese self-righteousness as

economic superpower took a cold shower. The country went into a deep recession lasting through the end of the 1990s, a stagnation long recognised by all except the bureaucrats at the Ministry of Finance and officials at the Bank of Japan, at least until it was too late.

But in politics, life at the very top remained very good. For nearly four decades, one political party has dominated Japan – the dubiously named Liberal Democratic Party, or LDP. Conservative, unprogressive, and decidedly undemocratic by Western standards, the LDP seemingly serves only to make its leaders wealthy; national leadership and representation

JUST BUILD AND NO ONE WILL COME

One of the major engines of growth in postwar Japan has been the construction industry. Following the war, most of Japan's infrastructure had to be rebuilt. Thirty years later, this development became institutionalised to the point that it is a major political tool. Today, no other nation comes close to the nearly 10 percent of GDP that Japan spends on public works. Much of this money comes from Japan's postal savings and pension funds. Public opinion has lately embraced the belief that many of these projects are useless efforts solely for politicians' gain and glory.

Bullet-train lines have been built to backwater towns. Two huge and quite expensive bridges between Shikoku

and Honshu carry less than half the traffic that planners claimed, and tolls are more than US$50 one-way. The world's longest (9.5 km) underwater tunnel, the Aqualine Expressway under Tokyo Bay that opened in 1998, is rarely used, perhaps because of a US$40 toll and because it goes nowhere important. In the 1980s, Tokyo's former governor initiated an immense "sub-city" in Tokyo Bay at an estimated cost of US$100 billion. The city intended to sell or lease reclaimed land for huge profits. The economy's collapse instead put Tokyo deep in debt.

For a nation with a population growth of 0.2 percent, construction projects keep coming, useful or not.

of the people's wishes are inconsequential and inconvenient sidelines. Agriculture accounts for just 15 percent of Japan's GNP, but the LDP has subsidised and coddled the farmers at the expense of the urban majority. Through arcane electoral laws, rural voters have twice the voting weight of city dwellers. Nobody complains, not entirely unexpected. (Indeed, in the times of sword-swinging samurai, the wayward opinion or complaint was lopped off along with the speaker's head. It was best to remain obscure.)

> ### GOVERNMENT DETAILS
>
> Japan's government is called a parliamentary democracy. The prime minister, of the majority party, comes from the Diet. The emperor is head of state.

unknown illnesses, a traditional exile in Japan.

The LDP fell from grace in 1993 in an unusual backlash by voters, to be replaced by a coalition government led by Hosokawa Morihiro, descended from a powerful Kyushu family whose independence and opposition to central government goes back several centuries. With a head of thick young hair, Hosokawa invigorated the nation with calls for substantial reform. Seven months later, he resigned because of scandal. Succeeding him was a coalition led by the socialist party

Institutionalised and immune to legal redress, *seiji fuhai,* or political corruption, festered unimpeded at the highest corporate and governmental levels. By the 1980s, *The Economist* opined, the ruling LDP government was "choking on its own corruption".

In 1992, the last of the LDP's omnipotent kingpins and powerbrokers, Shin Kanemaru, was caught not only in one of the predictable scandals that sprouted regularly like the new rice crop, but prosecutors searching his house uncovered a stash of gold bullion worth millions. Like most politicians and corporate leaders seeking refuge from public scrutiny, he retreated to a hospital to rest and recover from

and a well-meaning but weak prime minister. In the meantime, the LDP resuscitated itself by returning to control in 1996.

The collapse of the economic bubble was a shocking flame-out for the Japanese, who had thought themselves atop the fastest, safest rocket around. Perhaps even worse than the economy's rapid flattening was the subsequent stagnation and recession that lasted until the end of the 20th century. Nothing, it seemed, not even a series of economic jolts by the government, could get the economy accelerating. Banks started sinking beneath massive amounts of bad loans left over from the bubble economy, though dubious accounting practices discounted elsewhere in the developed world kept most debts hidden. An increasingly strong yen – severely over-valued – quenched corporate profits as exports plummeted. And at home, where manufacturers had for decades over-priced consumer goods so as to subsidise low export prices and thus gain market share (considered more important than immediate profits), new discounters started bypassing Japan's notoriously inefficient distribution system and buying direct from American and European manufacturers. Japan became the only country in world history to undergo a substantive deflation of consumer prices.

1923. For decades, and most recently after the California earthquakes of the early 1990s (which received extensive coverage and analysis by the Japanese press), the Japanese people were explicitly reassured by government, corporate, and academic experts that Japan's architectural design and construction techniques were unsurpassed in the world, and that collapses of expressways and high-rises in an earthquake could not happen in Japan. In fact, they simply *would* not happen.

In January of 1995, an earthquake hit Kobe, an important coastal port near Osaka. Kobe had been declared a low-risk area for earthquakes.

Shaky foundations

Two events within two months in the mid-1990s further evaporated Japanese self-confidence and world opinion. One was beyond anyone's control and the other was thought impossible within the social safety of Japan.

Ten percent of the world's earthquakes occur in Japan. Tokyo and the surrounding Kanto Plain sit atop geologically unstable ground. Devastating earthquakes have hit Tokyo on an average of every 60 to 70 years. The last was in

LEFT: the Tokyo Stock Exchange, and pondering future options near the Imperial Palace. **ABOVE:** collapsed tracks from the 1995 Kobe earthquake.

TOKYO'S NEXT EARTHQUAKE

Government studies in the 1990s estimated that there would be around 10,000 deaths and over half a million buildings destroyed in Tokyo if the 1923 earthquake were repeated today. Casualty estimates did not take into account subways. Three million people move in and out of Tokyo daily, mostly by train and subway, and should tunnels collapse, deaths in subways could reach tens of thousands alone. The Kobe quake was considerably more powerful than the 1923 earthquake that destroyed Tokyo. Official estimates have since been amended. Should a Kobe-strength earthquake hit Tokyo, casualties could approach 100,000.

The Great Hanshin Earthquake, as it has been named, killed more than 6,000 people and left 300,000 homeless. Fires from igniting gas mains (said to be earthquake-proof) incinerated entire neighbourhoods of poorly constructed residences; elevated expressways and *shinkansen* rails toppled over like putty. Subway tunnels collapsed. Moreover, the local and national government response was nothing short of inept and irresponsible. In the days that followed, the Japanese people were shocked by their government's inability to respond. One wonders what might happen in Tokyo should a similar 7.2-Richter scale earthquake hit it.

Two months after the Kobe earthquake, another event decimated Japanese confidence. In the heart of Tokyo, in the centre of the government district, 12 people died and thousands were injured when the Tokyo subway system was flooded with sarin, a lethal nerve gas. It was rush-hour, and the prime target was Kasumigaseki Station, *the* subway stop for offices of the national government and parliament. The effect on the Japanese psyche cannot be described. The Japanese have long prided themselves on having perhaps the safest nation in the world (and it remains so), and that Japanese could not engage in lethal terrorism against other Japanese. But the nerve-gas attack had

been seemingly spontaneous and random – the perfect terrorist attack. In the days that followed, the chief of the National Police Agency was shot in front of his Tokyo home. Mysterious fumes sickened people at Yokohama Station and in nearby department stores. Shinjuku Station was literally seconds away from the release of enough hydrocyanic gas to kill 10,000 people. (A passer-by found the gas package in a restroom. It was rush-hour.)

The sarin gas attack – and other deadly deeds uncovered by investigators – were traced to a religious cult, Aum Shinrikyo, led by a nearly blind self-proclaimed prophet. On the day that its guru leader was arrested at the cult's main compound near Mt Fuji (he was hiding in a secret compartment), a parcel addressed to the governor of Tokyo exploded; the hand of the governor's aide was blown apart.

Persistent doldrums

In late 1998 the International Monetary Fund declared that the most significant risk to the world's economy (Asia's economic collapse had nurtured fears of a world-wide depression) was Japan's inability to resolve its own economic doldrums. Bad debts at the country's banks amounted to nearly 30 per cent of the nation's GDP. This is not to suggest that the Japanese people themselves were suffering greatly; in fact, most hardly noticed any difference in their daily lives. But traditions of life-long employment and unfettered national growth evaporated, and public cynicism towards politicians – and towards bureaucrats who had long masked the country's problems – increased. In a switch, American and European companies returned to Tokyo and Japan to buy up property and increase their market share of banking and other financial services.

Bureaucratic and political inertia failed to display domestic and regional leadership to put the world's second-largest economy back on track, especially considering that other Asian countries, whose economies and currencies had nearly collapsed in the late 1990s, looked to Japan as an engine of economic revival. Yet there were hints that even bureaucrats were willing to restructure how things are done, as the Meiji Restoration had done earlier. ❏

LEFT: female construction worker in Tokyo.
RIGHT: young businessman with a purpose.

A NATION OF ISLANDS

An archipelago formed by the meeting of tectonic plates, Japan's thousands of islands are often rugged and violent, accented by soothing hot springs

Nihon-retto, the islands of the Japanese archipelago, were formed from the tears of a goddess. Where each tear fell into the Pacific there arose an island to take its place. So goes the legend. But no less poetic – and dramatic – is the scientific view of the origins of this huge archipelago that stretches from the subtropical waters of Okinawa – not far from Taiwan – to the frozen wastes of northern Hokkaido. The islands were born of massive crustal forces acting deep underground and shaped by volcanoes spitting out mountains of lava. The results seen today are impressive. Japan has long been regarded as one of the more scenic places on the planet, with snow-capped mountain ranges and 27,000 km (16,800 miles) of indented coastline.

The archipelago consists of four main islands – Kyushu, Shikoku, Honshu and Hokkaido – and about 3,900 smaller islands extending from southwest to northeast over a distance of 3,800 km (2,400 miles) off the east coast of Asia. Honshu is by far the largest and most populous of all the islands. The main islands are noted for their rugged terrain, with 70 to 80 percent of the country being extremely mountainous. Most of the mountains were uplifted over millions of years as the oceanic crust of the Pacific collided with the continental plate of Asia. The oceanic crust submerged beneath the thicker continental crust, buckling the edge of it and forcing up the mountain chains that form the backbone of the Japanese archipelago and that of the Philippines to the south.

Other singular peaks in Japan – including Fuji, the highest – are volcanic in origin. They were formed from molten lava that originated far below the earth's surface as the oceanic crust sank into the superheated depths of the upper mantle. The molten rock was forced up through fissures and faults, exploding onto the surface. Weather and glacial action did the rest.

PRECEDING PAGES: autumn snow in Hokkaido; Sakura-jima volcano, Kyushu. **LEFT:** Cape Sata, southernmost point of Kyushu. **RIGHT:** Mt Fuji.

Volcanoes and earthquakes

One of the attractions of a visit to Japan is the possibility of seeing these geological forces in action. About 60 of Japan's 186 volcanoes are still active in geological terms, and occasionally they make their presence felt. Mihara on Oshima, one of the isles of Izu near Tokyo and

GEOGRAPHY IN JAPANESE	
Japan: *Nihon*	village: *-mura*
world: *sekai*	city ward: *-ku*
country: *kuni*	lake: *-ko*
island: *-shima*	pond: *-ike*
mountain: *-yama*	river: *-kawa*
volcano: *-dake*	bay/gulf: *-wan*
valley: *-tani*	forest: *-shinrin*
cape: *-misaki*	hot spring: *onsen*
peninsula: *-hanto*	north: *kita*
prefecture: *-ken*	south: *minami*
city: *-shi*	east: *higashi*
town: *-machi*	west: *nishi*

part of Metropolitan Tokyo, exploded as recently as 1986, forcing thousands of residents to evacuate the island. A few years later, Unzen-dake on Kyushu violently erupted and devastated hundreds of kilometres of agricultural land. Sakura-jima, also on Kyushu and just a few kilometres from the city of Kagoshima, regularly spews ash – and an occasional boulder the size of a Honda – onto the city.

Earthquakes are far more frequent than volcanic eruptions, especially around the more seismologically active areas near Tokyo. They are also a more serious threat and the Japanese government currently spends billions of yen

Despite the dominance of mountains in these islands, the Japanese are not a mountain people, preferring instead to squeeze onto the coastal plains or into the valleys of the interior. Thus separated from each other by mountains, which once took days to traverse, the populated areas tended to develop independently with distinct dialects and other social peculiarities; some local dialects, such as in Tohoku or Kyushu, are unintelligible to other Japanese. At the same time, isolation and efficient use of land meant that agriculture and communications evolved early in the country's history.

The highest non-volcanic peaks are in the so-

annually on earthquake detection – not that it works particularly well. Complacency is a common problem anywhere and certainly was in Kobe, which had been declared to be outside of any significant earthquake zone. Nevertheless, in 1995 a massive quake hit the city, killing 6,000 people and toppling high-rises.

Most Japanese tend not to dwell on the morbid aspects of the islands' geological activity, preferring to enjoy its pleasures instead. *Onsen*, or hot springs, are a tangible result of the massive quantities of heat released underground. For centuries hot springs have occupied a special place in Japanese culture until the onsens' pleasures have become a national past-time.

called Japan Alps of central Honshu. Many of the landforms in these mountain ranges were sculpted by glaciers during an ice age more than 27,000 years ago. Cirques, or depressions left where the glaciers formed, are still a common sight on some higher slopes. Debris brought down by melting ice can also be seen in lower regions.

Fauna and flora

To the Japanese, people are a part of nature and therefore anything people have constructed is considered part of the environment. A Japanese can look upon a garden – molded, cut, sculptured, and trimmed to perfect proportions

– and still see it as a perfect expression of the natural order, not something artificial.

The result of this philosophy has been disastrous for the wildlife and ecosystems of Japan. The crested ibis, for example, once considered to be a representative bird of Japan and common throughout the archipelago 100 years ago, is reduced today to less than a dozen individuals. The Japanese crane (*tancho*) is also close to extinction, though the bird was once common in Hokkaido. Fish such as salmon and trout are

sharply reduced since the 1950s. During the winter months, macaca in Nagano and Hokkaido take to bathing in local hot springs.

In the far south of Japan, the islands of Okinawa have a distinctive fauna and flora of their own. Here, the natural forests are subtropical, but many of the indigenous species of fauna have now become rare or even extinct. The most spectacular characteristic of these islands is the marine life. Most of the islands are surrounded by coral, home to a rich and colourful variety of warm-

no longer able to survive in Japan's polluted rivers and lakes. Brown bears have been hunted almost to extinction, and only recently have hunting laws been amended and the animal recognised as an endangered species.

Of the other land mammals, the Japanese monkey, or *macaca*, is by far the most common in Japan. Originally a creature of the tropical rain forests, the macaca has adapted to the more temperate climates of these islands and can now be found throughout Kyushu, Shikoku and Honshu, although its numbers have been

water fish. Yet once again the rapid growth of the tourist and leisure industry – especially that of scuba diving – has led to the destruction of much of this natural coral.

In Hokkaido, the greater availability of space and natural moorland vegetation has led to the growth of the cattle and dairy industries. Meat is gradually becoming a more important part of the Japanese diet, just as rice is declining in popularity. In a sense, this is symptomatic of the way Japanese culture is changing over the years. Younger generations are gradually turning away from the fish-and-rice diet to eat more meat and bread as Japan becomes more affluent, urbanised, and Western in outlook.

LEFT: summit of Kyushu's Sakura-jima. **ABOVE:** protective barriers on Sakura-jima, and hot spring.

The climate

As any visitor will soon discover, an obsessive past-time with Japanese is talking – or listening – about the weather. As a matter of routine, people nearly always greet each other by commenting on the weather, and the changing seasons still attract an unwarranted amount of attention by the television and print media in what is, after all, a largely urban society. If the blooming of the plum trees or cherry blossoms is a few days late this year, it will be a lead story on the news.

The two extremities of Japan, from the coral reefs of Okinawa to the ice floes of northern

Hokkaido, are in very dissimilar climatic zones. Because of the high mountain ranges running along the spine of Honshu, there are also major climatic differences between the Sea of Japan coast and the Pacific Ocean coast.

In the northern hemisphere, Japan's seasons are, of course, similar to those of Europe and North America. The coldest months are December through February, when the Sea of Japan sides of Hokkaido and Honshu experience heavy falls of snow as the cold air from Siberia picks up moisture over the Sea of Japan. The Pacific Ocean side, by contrast, is very dry during the winter months. This is accentuated in Tokyo by urban growth, which has tended to reduce evaporation and therefore is the cause of a further drop in winter precipitation. Winter water shortages are now becoming a serious problem in the capital.

The southern areas of Kyushu and Okinawa have a relatively mild winter and are the first to experience the coming of spring. This manifests itself with the flowering of the cherry blossom – *sakura* – an event which the Japanese like to celebrate with a festival called *hanami*. Like the weather, the blossoming of sakura (and the autumn changing of leaves) is followed in the national media like the advance of an attacking army. The cherry trees flower in Kyushu towards the end of March; the phenomenon moves northward, finally reaching Hokkaido about the second week in May.

Alas, the burst of spring that follows is all too short. Soon after the cherry blossoms have fallen, about a week after they open, they are blown around by strong, southerly winds that bring with them occasional rain and precede the start of *tsuyu*, the rainy season. Temperatures rise quickly, and continuous but moderate rains begin to fall about two months after the end of the cherry-blossom season. (The Japanese are very definitive about their seasons. A weather forecaster once announced on television: "The rain you are now experiencing is not the rainy-season rain – the rainy season will start as soon as this rain finishes".)

Once again, the central mountains of Japan define the boundaries of the rain fronts. On the Pacific Ocean coast of Honshu, the tsuyu rain is soft and drizzly. Further south and on the Japan Sea coast, it is hard and much more tropical in nature. In the southern areas, especially, the rain is often accompanied by typhoons. Hokkaido,

TYPHOONS

Generally three or four typhoons hit Japan during the season, smaller ones in August building up to larger ones in September. The southern or Pacific side of Japan bears the brunt of these ferocious winds, which are quite capable of knocking down houses and wrecking ships. Fortunately for Japan, however, most typhoons have expended their energy in the Philippines or Taiwan before reaching the archipelago. While more frequent than Atlantic hurricanes or Indian Ocean cyclones, the Asian typhoons are also considerably smaller in size and strength. The Japanese don't use names for typhoons, just numbers.

however, has a very indistinct rainy season. The rains ease around late June on the Pacific Ocean side and make way for the hot, humid summer. Temperatures reach a peak in August, when many city dwellers escape to the cool comfort of the mountains. Nonetheless, the city of Yamagata, which is buried under one metre of snow in the winter, once recorded Japan's highest summertime temperature: 41°C (105°F).

The warm body of water around Japan causes the heat of summer to linger into September, with occasional balmy days in October. But as the warm air mass moves south, the rains return on the backs of devastating typhoons.

main islands. Yet despite a soaring demand for timber – used in the construction industry and for paper and disposable chopsticks – domestic production has actually fallen. The Japanese prefer to buy cheap, imported timber from the tropical rain forests of Southeast Asia, a practice that is causing considerable concern among many environmentalists as the rain forests of Borneo and Burma, and until recently Thailand, are being reduced to barren slopes.

Fishing is another rural occupation that has declined in activity, mainly because of a decline in fish stocks as a result of over exploitation. Japanese fleets now operate in international

Natural resources

There are coal mines in Hokkaido and Kyushu, but coal production peaked in 1941 and many coal-mining communities are now in serious decline. Nearly all of Japan's other raw materials, such as oil, minerals and metal ores, are imported. Timber is one resource Japan has in abundance, as most of the country's mountains are covered in natural or plantation forest. The natural cover varies from subarctic conifers in Hokkaido to deciduous and evergreen temperate broad-leafed trees throughout the other three

LEFT: rice field near Kyoto. ABOVE: autumn harvest of vegetables in northeastern Hokkaido.

waters far away from home, and ports that once supported fishing fleets are turning towards other endeavours. One of the most lucrative of these is tourism. As the urban Japanese become more affluent and seek recreation outside the cities, ports and harbours are becoming leisure marinas, hotels and resorts are springing up all over the countryside, and mountains are being levelled in order to make way for golf courses. Yet, to Westerners, there is a paradox with the Japanese approach to ecology. It has been one of the proud boasts of Japanese that they live close to and in harmony with nature – a strong theme in Japanese poetry and reflected in the Japanese preoccupation with the weather.

Urban zones

By far the largest of Japan's few flat spaces is the Kanto Plain, an area centred on Tokyo Bay and formed by a build-up of sediments resulting from Ice Age-induced changes in sea level. Other extensive areas of flat land occur in the Tohoku region, Hokkaido, and along the Nagoya–Osaka industrial belt.

Such is the concentration of resources in these plains that most of Japan's people, factories, farmland, housing, and public facilities are all crowded onto approximately 20 percent of Japan's total land area. Thus, very little of what one might call countryside exists on the plains.

Cities, towns and villages tend to merge into an indistinct urban blur that stretches endlessly across the flat land, with fields and farms dotted in between. In general, the plains are monochromatic, congested, and less than aesthetic.

The main industrial regions are the Kanto and Kansai areas, centring on Tokyo and Osaka, respectively. The Kanto area alone produces nearly a third of Japan's entire gross domestic product. If it were an independent nation, it would produce more goods and services than Great Britain.

Once again, it is the Kanto region and Tokyo in particular that has benefited from Japan's prosperity since World War II. Metropolitan Tokyo now has a nominal population of more than 10 million, but in fact the city spreads beyond its political boundaries north, south and west to form a massive urban complex that stretches across the entire Kanto Plain. The actual population of this megalopolis is estimated at around 30 million people.

Metropolitan Tokyo and Yokohama are the first and second cities of Japan, respectively. Third in size is Osaka, with a population of 3.2 million, followed by Nagoya with a little over 2 million. These cities have experienced phenomenal growth since World War II as Japan's urban industrialisation and rural mechanisation drew people off the farms and into the cities.

Many rural communities are now suffering from an increasingly aged population, and some have become virtual ghost towns as young people have literally fled the rural lifestyle. The situation is serious. A shortage of women in the countryside results in male farmers going on organised urban field trips in search of mates wanting to escape the city.

This demographic problem is not one that will in the future be restricted to the countryside. Japan as a whole has one of the slowest population-growth rates in the world, at less than one percent annually, and many analysts believe that the problem of an aging population will, more than anything else, eventually lead to Japan's demise as a world economic leader as the economy shifts to support a population with at least 25 percent of it in retirement.

The reasons for this low growth rate are not hard to find. The average Japanese enjoys the longest life expectancy in the world. But the overcrowded condition of the cities, which forces couples to live in cramped two- or three-room apartments and often with parents, is not conducive to large families, nor are the phenomenal costs of education and urban life. The alternative – the countryside – lacks appeal and job opportunity. Farming on the typically garden-size Japanese farms is amazingly inefficient and backward, made profitable only by heavy and politically motivated subsidies from the government. Unlike most other modern, industrial nations, Japan has few natural resources and depends heavily upon manufacturing for wealth and employment. ❏

LEFT: urban congestion in central Tokyo lacks aesthetic appeal. **RIGHT:** first snow in northern Hokkaido.

BAMBOO: ITS UTILITY STEMS FROM UBIQUITY

Typically overlooked because of its simple form and subtle intrusions, for centuries bamboo has provided Japan with functional utility and poetry.

As elsewhere in Asia, in Japan bamboo is ubiquitous to the point of often not being noticed. But there it is, as an ornament in a restaurant, scaffolding on the side of a building, a rustle in the wind. Its utility is simply phenomenal.

There are up to 1,000 species of bamboo, though even botanists are not sure and the venerable *Encyclopedia Britannica* offers that "many names are synonymous and thus not considered legitimate".

The smallest species of bamboo reaches just 10 to 15 centimetres (4–6 in) in height, while the tallest can soar to more than 40 metres (130 ft). In some species, growth of the main stalk can be as much as 30 centimetres (1 ft) daily. The recordholder is a Japanese species that sometimes grows 1.2 metres (4 ft) in a 24-hour period.

A giant member of the grass family (subfamily *Bambusoideae*, family *Poaceae*), bamboo is found in most tropical and subtropical regions, extending into the mild temperate zones. The largest number of species are found in East and Southeast Asia, and on islands in the Pacific and Indian oceans.

Where bamboo does grow, other plants are rarely found beneath the clusters of bamboo plants. The bamboo plant is long-living, flowering and producing seeds after 12 to 120 years of growth – just once in its lifetime. In the late 1990s, scientists shortened the flowering period of some species to just three months.

◁ **WOVEN FORM**
Its leaves are often used for woven purposes, as is the bamboo's stem when split into thin slats.

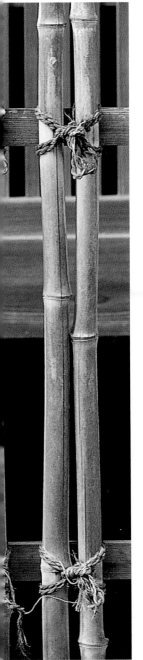

△ STRENGTH IN NUMBERS

Uniformity of shape and consistency in straightness allows the bamboo's stem to be combined into strong fences and walls.

◁ GARDENS

Outdoor gardens – both for walking and viewing – use bamboo for both flora and for structural purposes, such as fence railings and even small bridges.

△ BAMBOO IS IT

If not soaked in water first, bamboo can decay quickly after cutting. Treated, some bamboo is twice as strong as cement.

▽ TO CLIMB UPON

The vertical and cylindrical shape of bamboo, strengthened by joints along its length, make it a natural material for ladders.

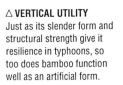

△ VERTICAL UTILITY

Just as its slender form and structural strength give it resilience in typhoons, so too does bamboo function well as an artificial form.

UNIVERSAL PLANT IN ART AND LIFE

Images of bamboo plants appear in numerous, ancient forms of Asian art, whether the scrolls of old China or the gilded screens of medieval Japan. Its stem and leaves are natural forms for the calligrapher's brush and black ink, and its moodiness and wistfulness have long tempted the poets, such as Japan's Basho Matsuo, the wandering lyricist.

On more pragmatic levels, bamboo is the most utilised plant in Asia: seeds are used as grain, young shoots are integrated into cuisine. In the joints of some species is found a type of silica – tabasheer – used in Asia as a medicine. Recently, Japanese scientists have uncovered the extract of pulverised bamboo bark that preserves food by preventing bacterial growth; in fact, Asians have been wrapping food in bamboo for centuries

Woodwind and percussion instruments are crafted from its stem and its fibres are pounded into fine paper. Lashed bamboo scaffolding buttresses tall buildings under modern construction.

THE JAPANESE PEOPLE

One of the most homogeneous societies in the world, Japan is a place of rather definitive rules of behaviour and some unique ways of engaging life

Of whatever size or purpose, the group defines for the Japanese a person's individual purpose and function. And the group known as the Japanese – *nihon-jin,* or if especially nationalistic, *nippon-jin* – is the mother of all groups. Not exactly an irreverent comment, given that Amaterasu Omikami, or Sun Goddess, is the mythological foremother of the Japanese themselves. Television commentators and politicians repeatedly refer to *ware-ware Nippon-jin,* or "we Japanese" and the implicit definition of what "we Japanese" are or aren't, do or don't do, believe or don't believe. The compulsion to define identity even shows up in advertising.

"Don't understand us too quickly," the Japanese will warn visitors, who are by definition outside of any group of which the Japanese feel themselves a part. Indeed, Japanese often seem to prefer that foreigners not understand too much about them at all, and there can be a certain pride amongst Japanese that outsiders simply don't understand something that is Japanese simply because foreigners are not Japanese.

Origins

The Japanese sense of uniqueness extends down to a basic identity of a race and culture distinct from others – if not superior. But the objective evidence strongly points to origins from the mainland.

From the third century BC, waves of human migration from the Asian continent entered the Japanese archipelago, bringing along rice cultivation (including the use of tools), metallurgy, and different social structures. These migrations are now considered to have brought the ancestors of today's Japanese people, the Yamato, who displaced and pushed the resident – and decidedly different – Jomon population into the northern regions or else into other less desirable areas of the archipelago.

PRECEDING PAGES: shellfish harvesting near Sendai. **LEFT:** proud yam harvesters, Kyushu. **RIGHT:** smiles at Kyoto temple during *shichi-go-san.*

Theories regarding the racial origins of the Japanese cite both the north and the south – Manchuria and Siberia, and the South China or Indochina regions – as likely possibilities. Students of the subject differ as to which origin to favour. The southern physical type is, of course, the Malay; the northern type is the Mongolian.

Today, both north and south Asia are considered equally valid as likely origins of the Japanese. Still, the precise configuration of the migrations and the cultural traits associated with areas of origin are subject to argument. (Toss in, too, other legitimate theories about migrations from Polynesia or Micronesia.)

There was substantial human immigration later – in addition to cultural and artistic influences – from the Korean peninsula, a point vehemently denied by Japanese nationalists and racial purists despite the overwhelming archaeological and anthropological evidence. Whereas archaeology in many countries is considered the most neutral of disciplines, without political overtones of any kind, in Japan it is rife with factions and rivalries. One group of "experts" in Japan has steadfastly refuted and rejected most modern, scientific dating methods, particularly when they are used to authenticate theories proposing a Japan–Korea connection.

(Some observers have dared to suggest that Japan's brutal occupation of Korea from 1910 through 1945 was an attempt to erase any historical Korean link – the Japanese forced Koreans to take Japanese names, speak only Japanese, and tens of thousands of Koreans were brought to Japan as slaves to work in mines and factories. Even today, third-genera-

tion descendants of those imported Koreans are denied the rights of Japanese citizenship, even though they and their parents were born and raised in Japan. The possibility of Korean ancestry, uncovered after researching mandatory family registries kept by regional governments, has spoiled marriage plans on more than isolated occasions.)

In any case, it may also be possible that the Korean and Japanese languages were mutually understandable, if not identical, some 2,000 years ago and that the people on the Korean peninsula and the Japanese archipelago may have approached a common culture.

THE AINU

Today with a population of less than 20,000, the Ainu people of Hokkaido were early inhabitants of Hokkaido and also northern Honshu. An enigma is their origins; it was once thought that they were of Caucasian heritage, but blood and skeletal research points most probably to connections with Siberia's Uralic population.

Today there are few speakers of Ainu, which has much in common with other northern Asian languages and also with languages of Southeast Asia and some Pacific cultures. Traditional Ainu culture was one of hunting and gathering. Bears and salmon had an especially sacred place in Ainu traditions.

Unique or arrogant?

Perhaps the most substantial insulator of Japanese from the outside is the modern language, spoken only in the islands. In fact, the grammar and syntax are considerably easier than most germanic or romance languages. The Japanese will retort, however, that it is undoubtedly one of the world's most difficult. The language in fact isn't, but the context of usage can be confusing and difficult for those not brought up within the Japanese culture.

There is much in the Japanese language that buttresses a fundamental notion. There is an undercurrent in Japanese thinking and in Japanese traditions that all things Japanese, including the race, are "special", if not unique, among the world's things. And most Japanese certainly believe that outsiders will never be able to fully appreciate, much less understand, the distinctions and nuances of *being* Japanese and of Japanese ways.

Stay in Japan long enough, listen to the conversation and media, and it seems that only Japan has earthquakes, typhoons, tasty rice, misery, hot weather, bad memories of war, trees that change colour in autumn, snowfall, and fast trains. When French ski manufacturers first tried to export skis to Japan several decades ago, the Japanese government declared the skis

Living on egg shells

In a country where physical crowding and complex interpersonal relationships have shaped the language and social manners over the centuries, even the slightest chance of offending, disappointing, or inconveniencing another person is couched in a shower of soft words, bows, and grave smiles. (Or worse, giggles, a sure signal of acute embarrassment or being uncomfortable.) That foreigners have sometimes stereotyped Japanese behaviour as insincere is, to the Japanese, simply ignorant and hurtful.

Consider the observations of one Russian journalist: "From generation to generation, the

unsuitable for the special and unique Japanese snow. Later, in the late 1980s when American beef producers were trying to open the Japanese market, the agriculture ministry argued that only Japanese beef was suitable for the special and unique digestive systems of the Japanese people. In the 1990s, respected university researchers claimed that the Japanese were genetically unique in their ability to appreciate to the fullest the sounds of nature like crickets and waterfalls.

LEFT: the businessman (*sarariman*) often spends long hours after work continuing the office bonding.
ABOVE: morning trot in Fukuoka.

Japanese have become accustomed to beating about the bush in order to avoid open conflicts of opinion and direct assertions that might hurt someone's feelings... The ability to express thoughts clearly, accurately and in a straight-line fashion," continues the Russian with marvellous understatement, "corresponds very little with the Japanese understanding of courtesy".

Indeed, the Japanese language is excruciatingly indirect to foreigners, requiring a finesse in extracting the proper message. Raised in the social and cultural context, the Japanese easily read between the lines.

Sometimes the Japanese are able to use this to their advantage. Notable both for the linguistic hedging and for the insight into Japanese thinking is the difference of how Japan and the rest of Asia, if not the world, remember World War II. Recent prime ministers have made efforts to address the past despite the vociferous views of right-wing politicians, nationalists, and university scholars to the contrary. Yet the linguistic nuances, when properly translated and understood, reveal not the expected apology as it first seems to be when translated from Japanese, but rather a promise of "reflection" or "remorse concerning unfortunate events", hardly an admission of wrong action or sincere apology.

Obligations

If apologies are linguistic puzzles, other expressions of social necessity too are interesting, if not curious. Strangely, the very word for "thank you" – *arigato* – literally means "You put me in a difficult position". *Oki no doku,* which is an expression of sympathy, means "poisonous feeling". And who would think of expressing regret or apology with *sumimasen,* which in strictly literal translation means "This situation or inconvenience will never end"?

Then there is that virtually untranslatable word, *giri.* To violate it is simply unthinkable. Giri is often translated as a sense of duty and

LANGUAGE IN SEX AND SOCIETY

The Japanese *keigo,* or polite language, is a hold-over from the structured class system of feudal times when politeness was reinforced with a sword. In the present century, keigo has been preserved as a key element in the deeply rooted Japanese tradition of deference to one's superiors and of courtesy to guests.

Proper speech is a source of pride for most Japanese and the use of keigo can be an art in itself. Moreover, simply shifting the politeness level up a notch – or down – can have the effect of sarcasm or insult. (The younger urban generation, however, appears keen in dropping some of the complicated formal constructions.)

Perplexing to outsiders are the distinctions between the talk of males and females. Consider the first-person pronoun. Men have the option of several forms, the use of each dependent upon the situation and the people involved: *watakushi, watashi, boku,* or *ore,* from most polite to exceedingly casual. Women, of course, have fewer options. Modulation and tone of voice also tend to vary between the sexes. Men try to affect a deep rumble, which can approach theatrical proportions. Women often tend to inflect a high, nasalised pitch, said to be appealing and sexy to men. (Japanese women usually drop their voice to normal pitch when speaking a second language, however.)

honour, but such a definition ignores the subtle communal and personal responsibilities behind giri. In Japan, there are unspoken responsibilities inherent by acceptance and participation within a group, whether in a friendship or with coworkers in an office, or in the sharing of communal village life. When the responsibility beckons, and the member of any group can easily recognise it without articulating it, the individual must meet and honour that responsibility while putting aside one's work or personal desires.

SUICIDE RATES

Japan's suicide rate is 17.2 deaths per 100,000 people annually, higher than the United States (12) and England (7.5) but notably lower than Finland (27.3).

understand the intrinsic depth of giri in the lives of Japanese. Not only is giri an obligation to another, but it includes an obligation to accept responsibility, if not shame, for an action committed by a distant relative or coworker – all members of a person's various social and professional groups.

Family values

No doubt there's a proverb somewhere saying that obligation, like charity, begins at home. It's true, for example, that in Japan the eldest child (once only the male but

Giri is the theme of many tragedies in Japanese literature and drama. A plot might turn on a daughter's obligation to put aside *ninjo,* or human feeling, and marry someone of her parents' choosing. If unable to reconcile her own desires with the obligations of giri to her parents, suicide is an accepted recourse. Of course, such recourse is rare today, but it still occasionally happens.

Westerners may express an appreciation of what they think giri entails, but rarely do they

---

LEFT: Shinto priests are important to the village.
ABOVE: young couple on their way to a wedding party in Tokyo's fancy Ginza district.

now the female as well) is expected to care for aged parents. Likewise, it is still true that the estate, if any, of a deceased parent automatically passes to the eldest child. In fact, these mutual obligations were once inviolable. Today, however, disputes over care for the aged and for inheritance of wealth are increasingly common and often decided in favour not of the parents or children, but of the national government because of prohibitively high inheritance taxes.

Often cited as the core of Japan's traditional social stability, extended families are nowadays as far flung from the original homestead as education, job opportunities, and jet planes can take them. And although nostalgia for the hometown and simpler living have taken on a trendy air in recent years, especially as affluence spreads, the urban family is increasingly defining the contours of Japanese life. On the surface, the family appears both paternal (the man is nominally the household head) and maternal (as women still control the household budget and child rearing). More opportunities for women in business, however, along with increased affluence and broader appetites for the good life, are slowly challenging this status quo. But the inertia to

XED-OUT EX

Batsu-ichi ("one X") is a nickname for those who are divorced. When a person gets divorced, an X is put through the spouse's name in the government's family registry.

eventually become fond of each other and maybe become good friends. The wife, having severed the ties to her own family through marriage, adhered to the customs and practices of her husband's family. After all, throughout her upbringing, she had been taught that a woman found her greatest fulfilment in marriage. The mother-in-law – and often sisters-in-law – frequently added to the wife's burdens by complaining about her shortcomings. And when the mother-in-law grew feeble, the wife would take care of her.

any social change is considerable and difficult to alter.

In the Japan of pre-World War II, a young man often got married about the time his parents reminded him that he had reached the *tekireiki*, or appropriate marriageable age. His parents would take an active role in the selection of his bride, making sure she bore the markings of a good wife, wise mother, and self-sacrificing daughter-in-law. They interviewed the woman's parents. Even birth records were checked (and often still are), assuring that the woman's family tree had no bad apples or embarrassing branches. Love rarely entered the picture. Parents knew that the couple would

Despite the hardships, the wife generally chose to stay married. To divorce meant she had to face the censure – blame for the marital break-up was all hers – of her own family and that of the community.

The traditional wife follows a pattern that her grandmother followed in the prewar years. Getting up earlier than her husband and children, she prepares the breakfasts and makes sure everyone gets off to work or school on time. During the day, she does the housework, goes shopping, and manages the daily household accounts. Occasionally, she takes part in activities of the neighbourhood association or of her children's school. She may also enjoy leisure activities such as learning a foreign language.

At night, she and the children will eat together, since her husband comes home much later in the evening. Upon his return, she will serve him (and his relatives, if present) his dinner and sit with him while he eats. The wife knows better than to discuss family matters at those times. She waits until the weekends or when he appears less drained.

While the above is not as common or automatic as before, it is still a marital paradigm in both cities and rural areas. In many marriages today, the husband still maintains a higher status and exercises greater authority in the family

wives file for divorce when husbands retire from their jobs, demanding half of the husband's severance pay.

Some couples divorce before they even get started on a proper married life. It's called a Narita Divorce. Modern Japanese women have usually spent more time travelling overseas than their new husbands, who may never have been outside of Japan because of the emphasis on career. Their first jaunt overseas, perhaps a honeymoon, is ripe with tension and ends in disaster because the woman is more self-reliant than the man. After returning home to Narita, Tokyo's international airport, they divorce.

by virtue of being the sole provider. He shows little inclination in helping around the house or taking care of the children, except when it suits him. Yet some husbands, like their wives, have been exposed to Western lifestyles and trends and make an effort at being liberated men in the Western sense, cultural biases aside.

Although comparatively low, rising divorce rates reflect the growing desire of spouses, particularly wives, to exert personal aspirations and concerns over those of the family. Some

LEFT: mother and child are rarely separated in rural Japan. **ABOVE:** boys reading popular *manga*, or comic books, and concerned girl in trendy Harajuku, Tokyo.

BOTTLED ENERGY

Japanese men – and increasingly women – have a number of ways to sustain energy. Traditionally, for example, grilled eel is eaten during the heat of summer. But for those on the move, and in Tokyo there are many, small amber bottles of *eiyo dorinkku*, or nutrition drink, are consumed several times a day. It is believed that they help the businessman handle the long commutes, long work days, and long evenings out with the boys or boss. Of questionable effectiveness, the drinks can include vitamins, ginseng, caffeine, sugar, Chinese herbs, and dehydrated snake. Even Coca-Cola offers a concoction, called Real Gold.

Education

In the 6th century Japan adopted major elements of Chinese culture, including Chinese ideographs, Buddhism, and Confucianism, not to mention a heavily bureaucratic system of government that persists today. Education was based on the meritocratic selection of talented individuals, later to be bureaucrats, who would then be taught to read and write the *Analects* of Confucius and works related to Buddhism. This Chinese system of education and civil service was absorbed within Japanese society.

With the rise of the Tokugawa clan to power in 1603, the pursuit of Western knowledge was strictly limited and controlled, and the study of Buddhist works declined in favour of Confucian ethics. Both actions were in part due to difficulties the shoguns had with religiously motivated rivals for political power, particularly around Kyoto. More than one activist Buddhist temple was torched and the monks scattered to the winds by the shogun's samurai.

During the feudal period, education was available to common people in *terakoya*. (*Tera* means temple and *koya* refers to a small room.) These one-room temple schools offered the masses instruction in the written language and certain practical subjects, such as the use of the

THE OLDEST SOCIETY IN HUMAN HISTORY?

In 1998, the number of Japanese older than 100 reached over 10,000. About 80 percent of those were women. In 1965, there were only 150 Japanese centenarians; in 1993, there were 5,000. Japanese are living longer and having fewer children, and the skewed demographics are giving government planners considerable worries. The birth rate of 1.4 per woman is resulting in Japan becoming one of the world's oldest societies. The median age is around 40, matched in the world only by Germany. Japan's 65-plus generation, now at 15 percent of the population, will reach 25 percent by 2020. In contrast, that of the U.S. will reach only 17 percent by 2020.

Of concern is the cost of providing retirement pensions and old-age benefits. It is estimated that to maintain the Japanese pension system, over the next 20 years it will be necessary to double basic income taxes. And as the population ages, the savings rate will drop, depleting the government's largest source of operating capital.

Said one demographer: "There is a rapid aging process going on in Japan. Japan has gone from being a very youthful society in the 1960s to one of the world's oldest societies in the 1990s... (By 2015) Japan will rank by itself. Its median age will have risen to 45... Japan will be the oldest society in the history of mankind."

abacus and elementary arithmetic. Texts were similar to the Chinese classics used by the samurai. Many of the teachers were monks.

Defeat in 1945 brought to Japan a total reformation of the educational system. The new model was essentially American in structure: six years of elementary school, three years of junior high school, and three years of high school. The first nine years were compulsory.

Approximately 2 kilometres northeast of Tokyo's central government district, Kasumi-

EASY U.

Entrance into the university is the start of the student's easy life. Unlike the high-school years, little out-of-class study is required or even expected in the university.

higher education, Tokyo University, or more commonly in Japanese, Todai. A degree from here, regardless of one's academic success within, is a definite guarantee of one's prestigious employment. One only has to gain admission and attend for the job offers to arrive.

Japanese social institutions in general, and schools in particular, are arranged hierarchically in terms of their ability to bestow economic and social status. No institution ranks higher in this regard than Tokyo University. (The other two

gaseki, stands a red, double-doored wooden gate roofed with gray slate tiles. A low, amber-hued brick wall stretches northeast and south-west from the gate, hiding much of what lies beyond from the casual gaze of people passing by on the busy thoroughfare outside the wall. The upper stories of a number of buildings – some obviously post-1945, others from previous decades – can just be glimpsed among the trees that line the inner edge of the wall. The gate is called Aka-mon (Red Gate) and it stands at the entrance of Japan's premier institution of

heavyweights are Keio University and Waseda University, both also in Tokyo.) Since its founding in 1877, Tokyo University has supplied most of the nation's political leaders and career bureaucrats, as well as the largest number of presidents of companies listed on the Tokyo Stock Exchange. The awe with which the Aka-mon is regarded is illustrated in tales of ambitious and kimono-clad mothers taking their five-year-olds to visit the gate before packing them off to their first day at school, seeking to impress upon the youngster *the* goal for the next 15 years of life.

Entrance to higher education is determined by dreaded examinations, which are adminis-

---

LEFT: fishing experts untangling a line in Fukuoka.
ABOVE: high-school students on a Kyoto excursion.

tered by the individual universities; for each school applied to for admission, a complete set of entrance exams must be endured. There is no universal university admissions exam. The more prestigious a school is, the greater the number of applicants seeking admission and the more difficult the examination.

To help them reach the goal of passing the examinations, parents will budget a considerable amount of their monthly income to send children to *juku,* or private cram schools that are a multibillion-yen business. For the most disciplined of students, every night and weekend is spent at juku having their brains crammed with exam-passing information. It is all learned by rote and not deduction.

There is no doubt that the Japanese are united in a consensus that education is essential for social cohesion, economic prosperity, and prestige in the international arena. Unfortunately, both in the primary and university levels, form and rote usually take precedence over function and knowledge. Students are taught not analysis and discourse, but rather only the information needed to pass exams for entrance into the next level of their schooling. There are exams for primary school, middle school, and high school. And there are the exams for the university, the whole point of life up to this point.

Perhaps, more importantly, schools reform undisciplined brats (before starting school for the first time, children are often allowed to be especially unruly, the parents knowing it will be moderated in school) into socially predictable and socially responsible persons. The schools pound down the nail that sticks out. From the earliest days of school, the educational system focuses on developing such basic Japanese values as harmonious relations with others and establishing group identity through membership in a limited number of social and vocational groups.

Education is respected in Japan, and so are educators. In fact, the honourific for teacher – *sensei,* as in Nakamura-sensei – is the same as for physicians. Unfortunately, the responsibility and professional pressure is considerable upon teachers, especially at the high-school level when students are preparing for their university exams. Holidays are rare for the teachers.

Even the Japanese themselves admit their educational system's shortcomings. The excessive emphasis on entrance examinations is a cause of much national concern and debate. Because of the emphasis on conformity and passing exams, students lack initiative and creative abilities. As a result, Japanese corporations, for example, must go to North America and Europe for original research-and-development work. Reforms are being considered. The rigidity of formal education and the alienation of numbers of young people, along with increased awareness of violence in the schools and bullying of pupils, are also concerns. ❑

TEENAGE TREND THINKERS

Whether regarding hair gel or soft drinks made with fermented milk, high-school girls are found to be highly articulate in expressing likes and dislikes (unlike boys), and for predicting trends. Corporations – both Japanese and foreign (including Coca-Cola and Procter & Gamble) – spend considerable time and money to cultivate the girls' opinions about snack foods, prime-time TV dramas, and cosmetics. "We love their brutal honesty and keen observant eye for details," says a Coke representative. A cosmetics company representative notes that Japanese girls are "extremely honest", lacking the reserved modesty of their elders.

LEFT: Meiji-era school boys. **RIGHT:** a father takes care of his daughter's fishing line, Tokyo Bay.

RELIGION

To the outsider, the adaptability of worship and philosophy seems contradictory and diffused. To the Japanese, beliefs are pragmatic and without hypocrisy

Polls asking Japanese in which religion they believe consistently yield results that total well over 100 percent – most say they are followers of both Shinto and Buddhism. The average Japanese thinks nothing of marrying at a Shinto shrine, burying loved ones in a Buddhist cemetery, or boisterously celebrating Christmas. Although the devout Christian or Muslim – each with a monotheistic god demanding unswerving fidelity – might find this religious promiscuity hard to fathom, the typical Japanese sees no contradiction. Ask a Japanese how many gods there are and the answer may be one or one thousand. Ask about the nature of the *kamisama*, or deities, that are worshiped and a confused silence may result.

There is no Japanese equivalent of the Bible or Koran, unless one counts the *Kojiki* (*Record of Ancient Matters*), which describes the mythological origins of the Japanese. Even the most ardent ultranationalist, however, does not completely accept the 8th-century chronicle as divine writ.

Traditionally, nearly every home once was equipped with a *kamidana,* a god-shelf with Shinto symbols, or else a *butsudan,* a Buddhist household altar containing memorials for the family's ancestors before which offerings of flowers, food, drink, or incense are made daily. Most homes had both, and many still do. Likewise, people passing by any of the thousands of Shinto shrines or Buddhist temples throughout the country today still tend to drop in for a brief devotion before going on their busy way again.

It is hard to attribute all this to simple custom. The Japanese definitely seem to have a sense of religious piety and spiritual yearning, although it is far different from that in the West. The main difference seems to be that the line between the sacred and the profane is much less clearly drawn in Japan. In many ways, community life and religion are one and the same.

Similarly, the distinction between good and bad, or sinful and righteous, is less clear in Japanese society. It is said that the West considers most things as black or white; in Japan, as elsewhere in Asia, there is a lot of gray.

First-time visitors to Japan are apt to overlook the important role that religion continues

to play in the daily lives of the Japanese. In rushing from one temple to the next, visitors more often than not miss that little Shinto shrine perched on the top of a department store or between looming office buildings, or the purification-cum-exorcism being conducted by a Shinto priest at a new convenience store.

Shintoism

A basic understanding of the Japanese religious sensibility must begin with Shinto – not a "national religion" in any current official sense (although it once was zealously nationalistic), but rather one that influences virtually every aspect of Japanese culture and society. It is hard

PRECEDING PAGES: Shinto shrine, marked by a *torii,* in Hokkaido. **LEFT:** Shinto priest reciting prayers to deities. **RIGHT:** Buddhist tomb in northern Hokkaido.

to give any simple definition of Shinto (lit. way of the gods, or *kami*), since it is not a systematised set of beliefs. There is no dogmatic set of rules nor any holy script. The term *shinto* was not even invented until after the introduction of Buddhism, a date traditionally given as AD 552, and then only as a way of contrasting the native beliefs with that imported faith.

In general, it can be said that Shinto shares with many other animistic beliefs the truth that all natural objects and phenomena possess a

NO IMAGES

Prior to the arrival of Buddhism in the 6th century, Shintoism lacked artistic or literary representation of beliefs and myths, and so it had no defined pantheon of deities.

– the sun goddess, she who ruled the heavens – as the ancestress of the imperial family, if not all the Japanese people.

The *Kojiki* is basically a justification for the Yamato conquest of the "Middle Land Where Reeds Grow Luxuriously" and their rule over other apparently related groups, such as the inhabitants of Izumo on the Japan Sea, who were said to be descendants of Amaterasu's brother, the rowdy storm god Susanoo no Mikoto.

It should be recognised that the term *kami*,

spiritual side. It is this animism – mixed with ancestor worship, a shared trait with Buddhism – that characterises Shinto. A tree, for example, was revered by the ancient Japanese as a source of food in nuts and fruit, of warmth in firewood, of shelter, and even of clothing. For that reason, when a great tree was felled to provide wood for the Buddhist temple complexes at Nara or Kyoto, it was not used for several years in order to give the spirit within time to safely depart. Mountains, forests, and even the oceans were also revered.

As for ancestor worship, the Yamato "race" always believed that it had descended from heaven and so worshiped Amaterasu Omikami

although usually translated as "god", is quite different from the Western concept of divinity. The classic definition, as originally understood in Japan, was made by the 18th-century scholar Moto-ori Norinaga: "Anything whatsoever which was outside the ordinary, which possessed superior power, or which was awe-inspiring, was called kami".

That goes for people, too. Today, in Japan one often hears expressions like "the god of baseball" or "the god of management". These expressions are not intended to be taken entirely tongue-in-cheek. Japanese, at least subconsciously, still believe that their land and its air is filled with kamisama of all kinds.

In ancient Shinto there was also a belief in a kind of soul – *tamashii* – that lived on after death. An unrefined form of ancestor worship also existed, remnants of which can be seen in the observances of the spring and autumn equinoxes. It can also be seen in the Obon festivities in early autumn, which, although primarily Buddhist in other parts of Asia, has both Shinto and Buddhist overtones in Japan.

Primitive Shintoism had concepts of heaven and hell as well, although they were hazily conceived at best. To use electricity as an analogy, you might say this world is plus, while the afterworld is minus. There was no concept of sin nor of divine retribution nor of absolution for offenses committed. Just about the worst thing that could happen was the pollution of a ritual. Otherwise, as far as the afterlife was concerned, it was commonly thought that the dead would eventually be reborn into this world, just as spring returns after winter.

The aforementioned plus-minus concept in Shintoism suggests an affinity with Daoism and indicates that the basis of the religion arose in China or even Korea. In fact, however, not much is known about the origins of Shinto; elements seem also to have come from Southeast Asia and even Polynesia.

Some experts feel that prehistoric beliefs from as far back as the Jomon culture also have survived in Shinto beliefs. They look to remnants of the original beliefs of the Ainu, the indigenous people of Hokkaido, and to the still-surviving Okinawan religion for evidence of this. Specifically, the Ainu creation myth, as well as that found in Okinawa's *Omoro Soshi*, which was compiled in the mid-16th century, have some interesting parallels to the ostensibly Shinto tale told in the *Kojiki*.

There are 13 mainstream Shinto sects and numerous subsects in Japan today, but since the American occupation following World War II, they have not been controlled by the government. In fact, it was only during the period from the Meiji Restoration of 1868 through the end of World War II that the government took any direct part in Shinto.

It was during the Meiji Restoration that the government introduced *kokka* (national) Shinto as a political tool for controlling the people

through the policy of *saisei it'chi* – the "unity of rites and politics". Although the emperor was said in the Meiji constitution to be "sacred and inviolable", the nature of his sacredness was never officially defined.

The most common interpretation, however, was that through prayer the emperor became one with his divine ancestor Amaterasu and the other gods and could therefore intercede on behalf of his people.

Several shrines were established by the national government for various purposes as "national" shrines, including Yasukuni-jinja in Tokyo (*see box below*) and the impressive

CONTROVERSIAL WORSHIP

Yasukuni-jinja, a large and controversial Shinto shrine just north of the Imperial Palace in central Tokyo, is an example (and a particularly notorious one) of the national shrines set up by the government authorities before World War II. It is here that the spirits of every soldier who has died in the name of the emperor since 1853 are enshrined (including war criminals executed by the Allies after World War II). Visits made here – official or not – by the prime minister and members of government are usually done to appease right-wing nationalists and are vociferously denounced by neighbouring countries such as China and South Korea.

LEFT: purification at Heian-jingu, in Kyoto.
RIGHT: ringing the bell announces one to the gods.

Meiji-jingu, to the north of Shibuya in Tokyo, whose majestic architecture and impressive presentation, including the towering *torii* gates, reminds the traveller that Emperor Meiji, enshrined within, was thought of as divine.

In fact, none of the national shrines – state inventions all – has much to do with traditional beliefs found within Shintoism. Dismissing the national shrines as unimportant in the modern scheme of things, however, would be a sociological, if not religious and political, mistake.

VISUAL DEITIES

Under the influence of Buddhism and its vivid visual expression, Shintoism's pantheon of deities gradually became tangible.

with through entry into the blissful state of *nirvana,* or Buddhahood. Buddha's followers came to believe that one who really knows the truth lives the life of truth and thus becomes truth itself. By overcoming all the conflicts of the ego, one can attain a universal, cosmic harmony with all.

Mahayana, meaning Greater Vehicle, was the form of Buddhism that became established throughout most of East Asia. It holds that every being, sentient or non-sentient, shares a basic spiritual communion and that all are even-

Buddhism

The traditionally accepted date for Buddhism to have arrived in Japan is AD 552. While this may be true, it wasn't until centuries later that it ceased to be the exclusive province of aristocrats. This is somewhat ironic in view of the beliefs of the religion's founder, Sakyamuni – born a prince in eastern India (now part of Nepal) around 500 BC – who advocated a middle way between indulgence and asceticism.

The Buddha, as he came to be known (though this is a misnomer), blamed all the world's pain and discontent on desire and claimed that through right living, desire could be negated and the "self" totally done away

tually destined for Buddhahood. Although all beings are separate in appearance, they are one and the same in reality. Every person's present situation is determined by past deeds, Buddhists believe. This is the principle of *karma.*

Since the main Mahayana sutras only appeared around 100 BC, it is not known how closely they reflect the original thoughts of the Buddha. But by the time it reached Japan's shores through China, Buddhism had changed tremendously from Sakyamuni's simple message. It was to undergo even more radical change when it encountered the beliefs held in the Japanese archipelago.

As early as the 6th century, for example,

Shrines and Temples

S hrines are of the Shinto religion, and the names of shrines often end in the suffixes -gu, -jinja or -jingu. Temples, on the other hand, are Buddhist and usually end with -ji, -tera or -dera. Quite often, both temples and shrines will be found side by side, or a temple or shrine will have an adjunct complementary opposite on the same sacred grounds.

Shinto shrines

The thousands of Shinto shrines in Japan vary in size from tiny roadside boxes to large compounds such as the Grand Shrines at Ise and the Tosho-gu at Nikko. But nearly all share certain features.

First, there is at least one *torii*, shaped somewhat like the Greek letter *pi*. This gateway may have evolved from a bird's perch – a certain kind of bird having been a religious symbol in many animistic cults – and it may be made of wood, stone, metal, or even concrete. Like the *shimenawa* (sacred straw festoon), zigzag cuts of white paper, mounts of salt, and cleanly-swept gravel, the torii serves to mark off areas considered sacred from those thought profane.

Often the largest building of the shrine is the inner sanctum called the *honden*. This is the main dwelling of the deity. It is usually elevated above the other buildings and reached by a staircase. It is likely to be off-limits to visitors, but other than a mirror or, on rare occasions, an image, there is little to see inside. These objects, by the way, are the *mitama-shiro* or *go-shintai*, serving as spirit substitutes for the deity (*kami*) being worshiped. In front of the honden is the often quite spacious *haiden* or worship hall, used for ritual ceremonies. Usually this structure is merely a roof supported by pillars and open on all sides.

There are no elaborate rituals or prescribed procedures involved in worshipping at a shrine. On entering the grounds there is a stone water basin, often with ladles balanced across it. One rinses mouth and hands in preparation for approaching the deity. It is customary to toss a small offering into the cashbox at the foot of the haiden before sounding the shaker to attract the attention of the god. Most devout worshippers also clap their hands twice, making doubly sure the god is listening. Then, a deep bow is performed and held while the prayer is offered.

During *matsuri*, or festivals, the gods are taken out for rollicking rides through the streets in *mikoshi* (portable shrines) by energetic bearers so as to bring the blessings of the *kamisama* to all the community. (This is one of the few times when Japanese collectively shed social inhibitions and turn quite rowdy.)

Buddhist temples

Under the Tokugawa shogunate, Japanese Buddhism lost much of its vigour, leading cynics to charge that priests were good for nothing else but buying people. An exaggeration, no doubt, but crematoriums still provide a good part of the income for most temples. The main building (*hondo*), library

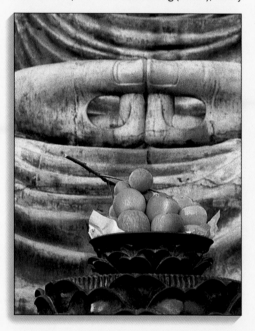

(*bunko*), bell tower (*shoro*), and other buildings of a temple complex can be exquisite architectural creations. But the one most easily admired is the pagoda, or *to*. The form in Japan is the result of evolution from the dome-shaped stupa (thought to represent an upside-down rice bowl), in which the bones of the Buddha and Buddhist saints were buried in India.

Images found in temples include Nyorai (Tathagata) Buddhas, such as Sakyamuni after Enlightenment and Maitreya (Miroku) or Future Buddhas, distinguished by a pose with one leg crossed over the other. Others include the *nio*, fierce-looking images flanking gates to many temples and derived from the Hindu gods Brahma and Indra. ❑

ART AND CRAFTS

With an aesthetic that goes back scores of centuries, Japan's art and crafts

of today retain the depth and layers of history, culture and outlook

The earliest preserved and distinctly Japanese works of art are those of the late Yayoi Period (300 BC–AD 300). These were small, tubular clay figurines called *haniwa*, some of which were set up like fences around imperial mausolea. Whatever their purpose may have been – substitutes for people buried alive in the tombs or magical instruments to ward off evil spirits or bandits – their immediate interest lies in their utter simplicity and charm.

Although many of them are only cylinders, some of the haniwa (and there are hundreds) are figures of men and women (*see picture on page 24*), horses, monkeys, and birds. Most are very simple with only a few details of decoration – perhaps a sword or a necklace. They have large hollow spaces for the mouth and eyes, which prevented them from cracking when being fired and which adds not only to their charm, but to their mystery, too. Who are they? What are they saying? Some emotion or song seems to have been eternally suspended here, and while the will to know them may be strong, the recognition of the eternally human, of the eternally here and now, is more compelling.

Aesthetic impulses

The haniwa figures are also important for another reason. We find in them – at the very beginning of the culture – many of the salient characteristics of almost all Japanese art. The haniwa are, so to speak, decorative. They are very much in this world, regardless of how much they may evoke the next. They are narrational – we want to create stories for them. As still in time as they are, we imagine a time before and after their eyes and mouths opened. And with their soft modelling and indolent lines they are recognisably human. These figures are not gods or angels: they smile, they shout, they gaze. In fact, there is little that is abstract about them. This is an "art of the real", which does

not eliminate the fantastic or even the artificial.

It is easy to see that the haniwa possess a beauty that seems almost uncannily to come from a natural aesthetic impulse. They occur during a lull in Japanese absorption of outside influences at a time when Japanese culture was developing its own native hues. It is possible

to draw a parallel with another art: the haniwa are to later art what the slightly later poetry of the *Manyoshu* (compiled in AD 759) is in purity of diction and sentiment.

Decorative, narrative, human. The decorative extends from modest fence posts to elaborately gilded, painted screens and walls in palaces and castles, to pin-ups in a swordsmith's shop. The narrational can range from rolls and rolls of scrolls illustrating one of the world's biggest (and greatest) novels – *Genji Monogatari,* or *Tale of Genji* – to a single illustration of a young boy playing a flute before a warrior. As for the human, Japanese art embraces everything, from demons to gods to people.

PRECEDING PAGES: Buddhist scriptures from the Heian Period. **LEFT:** from the *Lotus Sutra:* a hermit reciting a sutra. **RIGHT:** *Maple Viewers,* Muromachi Period.

Nara and Kamakura sculpture

Before the Nara Period, there are some superb examples of sculpture (such as the Kuze Kannon and the Kudara Kannon, both at Horyu-ji in Nara). To recommend only one, mention must be made of the Miroku at Koryu-ji, in Kyoto. This is a delicately carved wooden statue of the Buddha of the Future. The young person (gender is blurred in Buddhist art, but one assumes the figure is of a boy) has one leg crossed over the other, his chin rests on a couple of extended fingers, and one detects the slightest hint of the most gracious, lyrical smile imaginable. The Miroku is a hint of the greatness to come.

In the Nara Period (646–794), with Japan's full-scale welcome of things Chinese, the native response to the real is fused with its spiritual aspirations without ever abandoning the former. Work is done in wood, clay, bronze, or by using the curious technique of hollow lacquer.

There are some fine early pieces to be seen in the Yakushi-ji, in Nara, but visits must especially be made to the Kofuku-ji and the Todai-ji to see some of the world's masterpieces of sculptures. There, one can see numerous sculptures of the Buddha, of guardian deities, and of monks. There is, for example, the somewhat awkwardly-modelled, three-headed, six-armed Ashura, a young demon (demoness?) that has all the charms of a sensitive youth.

All of these sculptures – gods and humans alike – are spiritually powerful because they are so real. (They were probably based on real models.) And though it cannot now be seen, they were originally coloured. The patinas of age may lend them a spiritual depth, but one should not forget their original splendour. While the Buddha and some of the deities are ruled by convention (the beatific smile, various hand gestures for the former, terrifying gazes for the latter), the portraits of the blind monk Ganjin (Toshodai-ji) and of the Buddha's disciples (Kofuku-ji) are utterly remarkable for the realism of their portraiture.

It was also during this time that the 16-metre-high (52 ft) bronze Daibutsu (Great Buddha) in Nara was created. It is a sorry sight from what it must have originally looked like, housed as it is now in a much smaller hall and worn by age. It was originally gilded with bronze and incised with designs that can now only be barely discerned on some of the lotus petals upon which the figure sits. This is the great

tourist attraction at Todai-ji that should not be missed. The other Nara temples already mentioned are also worth visiting if one wants to look at the true genius of Japanese sculpture.

The Nara Period ended with the move of capital to Kyoto. With that – the beginning of the Heian Period (794–1185) – Japanese sculpture declined as other arts ascended and did not revive until the Kamakura Period several centuries later.

While Nara Period sculpture was both human and ideal, that of the Kamakura Period was wholly human, passionate, personal, and emotional. For example, the Kamakura Period

(1185–1336) produced more portraits of monks and of demons (warriors, really) than of aloof gods. Many of these (including of the priests Muchaku and Seshin, and of the Kongoo Rikishi, the Guardians of the Law), fortunately, can also be seen in Todai-ji and Kofuku-ji in Nara. The Kamakura Period also produced its Daibutsu, which, though somewhat smaller than that in Nara, is equally affecting. Now sitting uncovered in the Kamakura hills, its impressiveness has been enhanced by time.

Painting

In the Heian Period, life itself became an art, and works of art became its decorative attendant. Kyoto's Byodo-in may have been meant as a model of the next world, but it only showed that life in this one was already exquisite. (One last note on sculpture: when visiting the Byodo-in in Kyoto, do not miss out on the many small, elegant *bodhisattva* musicians floating around the larger statue of the Byodo-in Buddha.)

Japanese painting had long existed, but it had not flowered into great sophistication, particularly in the form of long, rolled, and hand-held scrolls. These paintings, or sentimental tales collected in the *Heike Monogatari* and other stories (as Western artisans drew on Homer and Virgil). The scrolls are easy to follow and with their delicacy of line reveal the Japanese gift of design. With the Genji scroll are the conventions of the removed roof, the "dash for the eye and a hook for the nose", and the floating, golden clouds that rhythmically lead the eye from scene to scene. It is a splendid example of the modern Japanese graphic sensibility in many media.

GENJI'S LOVES

Tale of Genji, the masterpiece of Japanese literature, was written by the daughter of a courtier around 1010. It is about Genji, a Heian-Period courtier, and his pursuit of the art of love.

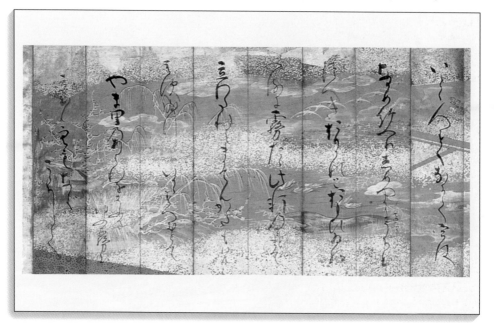

known as *Yamato-e*, might depict the changing seasons, famous beauty spots, or illustrate well-known stories. The best Yamato-e were of the latter type and depicted popular legends, warrior tales, or works of great literature such as the *Ise Monogatari* and *Genji Monogatari*, or the *Tale of Genji*. The popular legends might include a satirical look at pompous officials turned into battling frogs and rabbits, or a man who can't stop farting, or a look into the punishments that await evil-doers in hell. Post-Heian warrior tales drew on the many heroic

In the Kamakura Period, war and religion came together. This was the great period of Zen art, when *suiboku* (water-ink, or painting with black *sumi* ink) comes to the fore. One of the world's masterpieces of *suiboku-ga* can be seen in the National Museum in Tokyo: Sesshu's *Winter Landscape*, a bold landscape of a traveller dwarfed by nature, a lonely town and mountain all around, and a vertical streak of ink that cuts the sky. Another of his masterpieces, *View of Amanohashi-Date*, is in Kyoto's National Museum. Due to the sense of composition and the moods he evokes, Sesshu seems at times to be a contemporary artist. In fact, he died in 1506 at the age of 86.

LEFT: Nara-Period standing *bodhisattva.*
ABOVE: excerpts from *Tale of Genji*, 17th century.

In addition to calligraphy, suiboku-ga includes portraiture and landscape. An example of the principal "the line is the man himself" in portraiture is the stark portrait of the priest Ikkyu, in the National Museum in Tokyo.

In suiboku landscapes, the emphasis is again on the real and on the visually pleasurable (Japanese landscape is rarely as profoundly mystical as that of Chinese), and quite often also on the grotesque, the curious, and the purely fantastic.

The Momoyama Period (late 16th century) is

UKIYO-E INFLUENCE

Japanese *ukiyo-e* prints were exhibited in Paris, London, and Philadelphia in the 1800s, influencing the work of Whistler, van Gogh, Degas, and Monet.

Period art, however, is of brilliance and gold, as one can see in the Jodan-no-ma and other ceremonial halls in the Nijo Castle in Kyoto, with its painted walls and gilded ceilings, or also at nearby Nishi Hongan-ji, to the south of Nijo Castle, in the rather expansive *taimensho* (audience hall) and *Konoma* (stork room).

Floating world

The Edo Period (1603–1868) is the great age of popular art, even though much great decorative art was being made for the aristocracy or

Japan's age of Baroque splendour when, as one scholar says, "The simper of the late Ashikaga court went down before the swagger of men like Nobunaga". It is the one of the high points of Japan's decorative genius. The Momoyama Period is filled with gold and silver, with very bright, flat colours (no shading or outlining), and embellished with lush scenes painted on screens and walls of flower-viewing parties, lovely women, and sightseeing spots.

This is not to imply that monochrome was abandoned during Momoyama. Far from it: there was a great deal of superb *sumi-e* (ink picture) screens and paintings done at this time. The overwhelming impression of Momoyama-

the military classes, especially by Koetsu, Sotatsu, and Korin. The latter's gorgeous *Irises* – all violet and gold – is an excellent example of the period art and can be seen at the Nezu Museum of Art in Tokyo.

In the rigid society of the Edo Period, the artisan was the third of the four social classes, one step above the merchant, who was at the bottom (in theory but increasingly at the top, in practice). This was the age of the unknown craftsman, whose tools, hands, and skills were part of a tradition and who learned techniques as an apprentice. The merchant class, however, was developing its own pleasures in fiction, drama (*kabuki*), and art, and mass appeal soon became more important than ever before in most of the disciplines.

The art most associated with Edo Tokyo is *ukiyo-e* (lit. pictures of the floating world). Once again, the sublunary, fleshy human existence was a key element. Although woodblock printing had been used to reproduce sutras, for example, the technique first began to be used in a more popular vein in the early 18th century. At first, the prints were either monochromatic or hand-coloured with an orange-red. In time, two colours were used, then four, and so on.

Notable artists included Hiroshige Ando, Utamaro Kitagawa, and Hokusai. Although the chrome printing in ukiyo-e, a number of "genres" became established. There were, for example, portraits of prostitutes (*bijin ga*), kabuki actors in famous roles, the ever-present scenes of renowned places, and of plant and animal life. Suffice it to say that ukiyo-e is one of the world's great graphic art forms and in more ways than one. For example, the charmingly named *shunga* (lit. spring pictures) represent pornographic art of stupendous imagination and comprised a large part of every ukiyo-e artist's *oeuvre*. Ironically, shunga cannot be seen in Japan (too pornographic, but considerably tamer than what's found in magazines).

names of hundreds of ukiyo-e artists are known, it should be remembered that the production of these prints was a cooperative effort between many highly-skilled people. There was the artist who created the design and suggested the print's colours, the carvers of the many blocks, the actual printers, and finally the publishers who financed and distributed them.

Early ukiyo-e, especially those by the first great master, Moronobu, are usually portraits of prostitutes from the Yoshiwara district of old Edo or else illustrations for books. With poly-

LEFT: *ukiyo-e* of Mt Fuji by Hokusai, Edo Period.
ABOVE: *shunga* erotic woodblock print.

LACQUERWARE

Japanese lacquer (*urushi*) is the sap of a certain tree (*Rhus verniciflua*) that has been refined and which may have pigment added. It has been used as a decorative coating on wood, leather, and cloth for 1,500 years, but the earliest-known examples of lacquer in Japan – red and black lacquered earthenware pots – date back 4,000 years. Lacquerware (*nurimono*) is a community craft – no one person can do all of the 50 steps involved in the plain coating on a wooden bowl. Decoration may involve another 30. The most common Japanese examples of lacquerware are food bowls and serving trays – tableware known as *shikki*.

The Japanese have never considered ukiyo-e to be "art". It was a publishing form and not art until foreigners started collecting them. Only in the past few decades have Japanese collectors begun to realise the value of ukiyo-e. Yet the influence on Western artists has been considerable, especially amongst the Impressionists of the late 19th century. Felix Bracquemond fuelled the increasing interest in Japanese art – *Japonisme* – when he started distributing copies of Hokusai's sketches. Soon Manet, Zola, Whistler, Degas, and Monet were both collecting ukiyo-e and adopting ukiyo-e motifs and themes in their own works.

Ceramics

Japan is a treasure house of ceramic techniques, a craft that has attracted many students from abroad over the years. There are famous and numerous wares (*yaki*), the names of which have a certain amount of currency in antique and crafts circles throughout the world. In general, pottery in Japan is stoneware or porcelain, that is, high-fired wares.

Earthenware and low-fired pottery are found in small quantities, usually in the form of humble utensils, in *Raku-yaki* – a rustic style produced by hand and without the use of a potter's wheel – and in some of the enamelled wares of Kyoto and Satsuma, in southern Kyushu.

There are a number of unglazed wares, of which the most famous is Bizen, made from hard clay and with a bronze-like texture after firing. Traditional glazes are mainly iron glazes (ash glazes), though feld spathic glazes are used in some wares. The palette of the traditional folk potter is thus usually browns and black. Green from copper and iron, and a milky, streaked blue glaze made with rice-bran ash, are also found. Saturated iron glaze in thick application results in the deep-black *temmoku*; when thin, the same glaze fires a persimmon ocher. Stonewares also show iron and cobalt-blue underglaze decoration.

Porcelains are decorated with underglaze cobalt and overglaze enamels. The decorated porcelains produced by numerous kilns in the Arita area of northern Kyushu, shipped from the port of Imari from the 17th to the 19th century, are still avidly sought and collected by antique collectors, as is the Kutani porcelain of the Kanazawa area.

The porcelain industry still thrives, and much of it is hand-painted, though modern transfer processes are able to capture all the shades and nuances of hand-painted wares.

Textiles

This craft includes weaving and dyeing, as well as braiding (*kumihimo*) and quilting (*sashiko*). Japan is a vast storehouse of textile techniques, one that Western craftspeople have yet to tap.

Of course, silks are the most famous and highly refined of Japanese textiles. The glorious brocades used in *noh* drama costumes and in the apparel of the aristocracy and high clergy of bygone ages are among the highest achievements of textile art anywhere, as are the more humble but lyrical *tsujigahana* "tie-dyed" silks of the 16th century.

Japanese folk textiles are a world unto themselves. Cotton, hemp, and ramie are the most common fibres, but the bark fibres of the *shina* tree, *kuzu* (kudzu), paper mulberry, plantain (in Okinawa), and other fibres were used in remote mountain areas. Indigo is the predominant colour, and the *ikat* technique (known as *kasuri*) is the most popular for work clothes, quilt covers, and the like. These white-on-blue textiles are durable and long-lasting. ❑

LEFT: 16th-century silk *noh* costume. **RIGHT:** *Fugen Bosatsu*, a silk painting from the Heian Period.

THE PERFORMING ARTS

Most of Japan's traditional performing arts look and sound otherworldly, if not sacred, to outsiders. Yet some were designed to entertain commoners

For many of the traditional Japanese performing arts, the distinction between dance and drama is tenuous. Most traditional Japanese drama forms today developed out of some form of dance, and all, accordingly, employ musical accompaniment. Several of the forms also involve vocal disciplines to some extent, but not enough to qualify as opera.

There are five major traditional performing-art forms in Japan: *bugaku, noh, kyogen, bunraku,* and *kabuki.* Only bugaku, noh and kyogen could be called classical – all are tightly contained and formal entertainments performed originally for the aristocracy. Both bunraku and kabuki are traditional stage arts but derived out of the vigorous common-folk culture of the Edo Period. Another form, *kagura,* needs to be mentioned as well. Although it falls within what could be called folk drama, there is no single form of kagura. Rather, these offertory dance-drama-story-religious performances, held on festival days before the deity, all differ greatly throughout the country, involving anything from religious mystery to heroic epics, to bawdy buffoonery and symbolic sexual enactments – or a combination of all these elements.

Bugaku

What the ancient indigenous dance and drama forms in Japan were is not known. There certainly must have been such expression before the cultural imports from the Asian mainland. During the 7th and 8th centuries, mainland culture from both Korea and China dominated the life of the archipelago's imperial court.

In AD 702, the court established a court music bureau to record, preserve, and perform the continental music forms (*gagaku*) and dance (bugaku). Influences included not only dance from China and Korea, but also from India and Southeast Asia. These dances are so highly stylised and abstract that there is little or no

sense of story or dramatic event. The choreography is very rigid and is usually symmetrical, since the dances are most often performed by two pairs of dancers. (An almost identical music-and-dance form is found in Korea.)

The bugaku stage is a raised platform erected outdoors, independent of other structures and

ascended by steps at the front and back. The performance area is floored with green silk, the stairs are lacquered black, and the surrounding railings and posts are in cinnabar lacquer. Given that the bugaku repertoire has been preserved for almost 15 centuries, it is amazing to consider that about 60 different dances are known and performed today. These dances are categorised into "right" and "left", as was the custom in China. Left dances are slow, flowing and graceful, while right dances are relatively more humourous and spirited.

Masks are often part of a bugaku dance. Those used for the dances still performed, and many of those preserved in temples and other

PRECEDING PAGES: *kabuki* actor warms up, Tokyo. **LEFT:** the classic image of an 18th-century male *kabuki* performer. **RIGHT:** *noh* performer.

repositories (though the dances associated with them are no longer performed), closely resemble some of the masks employed in religious performances in Bhutan.

Bugaku is further classified into four categories: ceremonial, military, "running", and children's dances. The Imperial Household Agency – keeper and administrator of the imperial family – maintains a bugaku section for the preservation and performance of this ancient form; performances are held at certain times of year. Furthermore, some shrines and temples have kept up bugaku performances as part of festival and other yearly observances.

Noh and kyogen

What is called noh drama today dates from the early part of the 15th century. As an art form, its high degree of stylisation, lack of overt action, and monotonous-sounding vocal declamation (*utai*, a cross between chanting and dramatic narrative) makes it a distinctly acquired taste. It is admired by many in Japan, but its hardcore devotees are few. Still, it is performed.

Such terms as classic dignity, grace, and symbolism are used to describe the noh drama. It is said to have been developed from a dance-drama form called *sarugaku*. Little is known about sarugaku. There is evidence that would

THOUSAND-YEAR-OLD MUSIC

There are solo or small-ensemble musical forms, particularly those featuring the harp-like *koto*, *shakuhachi* bamboo flute, *samisen*, and the numerous *taiko* (drum) and *minon* (folk singing) troupes. But the most authentic (if not typical) form of Japanese music performed apart from drama or dance is *gagaku* (lit. elegant music). It is a kind of orchestral music developed in the 9th century and little changed since.

Quite unlike the popular entertainments described elsewhere, gagaku was strictly court music, almost never performed in public before World War II, and only occasionally now.

It employs esoteric instruments resembling – sometimes identical to – those used in India and China long before high-tech instruments such as the koto or the *sitar* were developed. These include drums, nose-flutes, and bowed, single-stringed droners. Together with a slow, "courtly" tempo, gagaku is ideal for (and to most Japanese ears, synonymous with) funeral music. In fact, probably the first and only time the Japanese public has heard it in recent times was during the televised funeral of Emperor Showa (Hirohito) in 1989. Devotees find tremendous excitement in gagaku's extended, soulful sounds and unrelieved tensions.

categorise it in the same way as kagura – a calling-down into physical manifestation and an offering to a deity or deities. Also, it seems there were wandering troupes who performed sarugaku. Considered part of the noh repertoire, the sprightly dance *sanbaso* is performed by tradition as part of the rituals to invoke a felicitous beginning, such as for the upcoming New Year or for a new company.

Whatever its origins, noh was perfected by Kan'ami Kiyotsugu (1333–84) and his son,

NOH RELEASE

Noh's thematic undercurrent was one of nonattachment in which restless spirits relive passions or violence of previous lives, seeking to free themselves from the memory of former attachments.

Masks, highly stylised sets and props (when such things do appear), a tightly-controlled style of movement, a voice style that projects and declaims but does not entice, and musical accompaniment – *hayashi* – of a few types of drum and a piercing fife mean that this form of play relies mostly on imagery and symbolism for its dramatic impact. In contrast to the sparse and uncluttered form of drama, the textiles used for noh costumes are the diametric opposite. The world's most opulent and gor-

Zeami Motokiyo, who were playwrights, actors, and aesthetic theorists of the highest level. They created about one-third of the 240 noh plays known today. Zeami's writings of the aesthetics of the theatre remain as some of the most profound thinking on the subject.

Buddhism had a profound influence on the content and dramatic structure of noh. The veil of "illusion" that we perceive as everyday "reality" is, in a sense, pierced momentarily by noh to expose something more basic, something that subsumes the senses.

LEFT: the *samisen* entered Japan from Okinawa in the 16th century. ABOVE: *noh* stages are minimal.

geous gold and silver and polychrome brocades are what the noh actor wears on stage. And noh masks are an art form by themselves.

As with Greek drama, the heavy and sober noh is performed in tandem with the light farces of kyogen (lit. crazy words), itself thought to reflect more directly the sarugaku antecedents it shares with noh. Although the dramatic methods share something with noh, kyogen does not use masks and is more direct and active. Traditionally, it is performed during intermissions of a noh performance, but today it is often performed by itself. These farces are both part of and independent of noh – light-hearted, dealing with nonsense, and simple.

Bunraku

Japan's glorious puppet drama is a combination of three elements, which, about 400 years ago, fused into a composite: *samisen* music, puppetry techniques, and a form of narrative or epic-chanting called *joruri*. The result is bunraku, the puppet drama that is considered to be an equal with live-stage theatre performance. Although bunraku developed and matured in the two centuries after its creation, the origin of the puppetry techniques used is still shrouded in mystery. There are folk-puppet dramas scattered throughout Japan, but the centre of bunraku puppet drama is in Osaka.

The samisen (a banjo-like instrument usually pronounced *shami-sen*) entered Japan from the kingdom of the Ryukyus (now known as Okinawa) sometime in the 16th century and was adapted and spread throughout the country very quickly. Although the instrument only has three strings, music produced by the samisen has great versatility and, in particular, lends itself well to dramatic emphasis.

Bunraku puppets (*ningyo*) are manipulated directly by hand and are quite large – it takes three men to handle one of the major puppets in a play. The skills involved in manipulation of bunraku puppets are considerable. The narrative style derives from classic epics of heroism

chanted to accompaniment of the *biwa*, a form of lute that made its way to Japan from central Asia at an early date. Although there may be more than one samisen to give musical density to the accompaniment, there is only one chanter. He uses different tones of voice to distinguish male from female characters, young from old, good from bad. Accent and intonation convey nuances of feeling and indicate shifts of scene.

While bunraku and kabuki share many traits and have some plays in common, bunraku is the older of the two and it was kabuki that adopted elements of the puppet drama. The important point is that both bunraku and kabuki are popular theatre. Bunraku was for townspeople and intended as popular entertainment, much like Shakespeare's plays in his own day.

Kabuki

Plays for kabuki are still being written. Not many, granted, but the genre is alive, and like bunraku it is not "classical". Kabuki is the equivalent of cabaret spectacular, soap opera, morality play, religious pageant, and tear-jerker. It is music and dance and story and colour and pathos and farce and everything any theatregoer could want.

The highly stylised language of kabuki, the poses and posturing and eye-crossing for dramatic emphasis, the swashbuckling and acrobatics and flashy exits, instant costume changes and magic transformations – all are part of the fun. Any visitor who goes expecting to see "classic theatre" is in for a dull time.

Kabuki originated in the early years of the 17th century with a troupe of women who performed what seems to have been a kind of dance, based on a dance performed at Buddhist festivals, and perhaps comic skits as well on the river bank at Kyoto. Whether there was anything untoward in this performance probably will never be known, but the shogunal authorities seemed to think there was and so in 1629 they banned women from appearing on stage. Male performers took their place, and to this day all kabuki performers are men; the discipline of the actor who takes female parts (*onnagata*) is particularly rigorous.

The female troupes were supplanted in short order by itinerant troupes of young men, who too got into trouble with the authorities. These were disbanded and the permanent theatre companies then developed in Kyoto, Osaka, and Edo (now Tokyo) after the middle of the 17th century. Kabuki soon became the Edo Period's most popular entertainment.

The production of a kabuki play involves strict conventions: gestures and other movements, colours, props, costumes, wigs, and makeup. Even the types of textiles used for costumes are determined. (But there are places in a play left for spontaneous ad-libs.) The audience directs much attention to the performer or performers. The story is secondary

KABUKI REPERTOIRE

There are some 240 plays in the kabuki repertoire of *jidai-mono*, or historical events and episodes, and *sewa-mono*, which deals with the lives of townspeople.

The kabuki stage has a number of unique features. The most striking is the walkway that extends from the stage to the doors at the rear of the theatre at stage level. Actors enter and exit at this stage extension (*hanamichi*, or flower path), and it is sometimes used as a venue of action. Another is the draw curtain, decorated in vertical stripes of black, green and persimmon, opened from stage right to left. The kabuki theatre also featured a revolving stage long before the concept arose in Europe.

and it will be well-known anyway. Kabuki devotees want to see favourite stars in familiar roles. Indeed, kabuki has been actor-centred since its beginning.

Training of a kabuki actor starts at about the age of three, when children are left by their actor-parents backstage. The children internalise the ambiance and the music's rhythms. With this kind of training, kabuki literally becomes part of one's core early on. This facilitates the years of rigorous apprenticeship and training that every kabuki actor must undergo.

LEFT: *bunraku* puppet and puppeteer. **ABOVE:** *ukiyo-e* print of *kabuki* backstage, and kabuki performance.

Both noh and kabuki show no clear-cut distinction between dance forms and stage movements. Still, kabuki's grandiloquent gestures are a far cry from the austere containment of noh. The kabuki technique called *mie* illustrates the formalised beauty of performance. A mie occurs at certain climactic moments when the starring actor, projecting dramatic energy at top output, freezes into a statuesque pose with rigid stare and eyes crossed to emphasise a dramatic peak of intense emotional power. Glorious overkill, indeed. At such (and other) high points of a performance, shouts will ring out from the audience – the Japanese equivalent of "Do it, Eiho!" or "Kill 'em dead, Masayuki!" ❑

THE CINEMA OF JAPAN

Japanese cinema has always refused to embrace the values of Hollywood.

In doing so, it has produced some of the world's most aesthetic and powerful films

The Japanese cinema has been pronounced dead so many times over the past few years – perhaps most often by Japanese critics and filmmakers – that its stubborn survival, if not full resurrection, comes as a relief. Just when it seemed that Japanese audiences had turned away from domestic product dealing

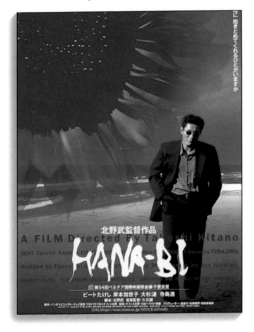

with their country's amazing history, along came *Mononoke Hime* (*Princess Mononoke*) from Miyazaki Hayao, which smashed the previous all-time box-office record held by *E.T.* until *Titanic* came along. What was so heartening about the success of the Miyazaki film was that Japanese were indeed interested – in huge numbers – to see an epic historical fantasy about Japanese history, set in an ancient time filled with gods and demons, an era in which men and animals could still verbally communicate with each other. *Mononoke Hime* is a cartoon, or more accurately, *anime*, which has always been taken more seriously in Japan than in the West. (*See story on page 109.*)

A difference in technique

Dramatically, the classic three-act structure of Hollywood holds little place in Japanese cinema. Character and mood, rather than plot, are what propel many of its best films. Stories often trail off by movie's end without a "proper" ending, storylines (especially in *jidai-geki*, or historical dramas) can be unbelievably convoluted and confusing, even to the most ardent devotees, and most Japanese films move at a considerably slower pace.

In a typical Japanese movie, dynamic action stands in contrast to long, sustained scenes of inactive dialogue, or just silence. The fundamental reason for this is that when engaging in conversation, the Japanese usually sit at *tatami*-mat level, stationary, without the pacing and arm-flailing associated with Western conversation. The Japanese are also tremendously influenced by Zen Buddhist culture, whether consciously or not. Thus, directors not only take the time to smell the roses but to plant them, nurture them, and then watch them grow, quietly. Landscape and atmosphere also play enormous roles in Japanese cinema, perhaps tied into the other major religion of the country, the pantheistic Shintoism. Floating mists, drops of water slowly falling into a stream, the soft, sad sound of cherry blossoms falling on an April day – all familiar to Japanese audiences and alien to the rest of us.

Of course, it must also be said that such mass-market genres as *kaiju* (giant monster) and contemporary *yakuza* (gangster) movies are often just as breathlessly mounted as the latest dunder-headed Steven Seagal action flick.

There's also considerably more space in Japanese cinema for morally dubious protagonists, since in both the Shinto and Buddhist traditions life is a balance between forces of good and evil, with both necessary to maintain life as we know it. Thus, a cold-blooded killer like the *ronin* (masterless samurai) Ogami Ito, who roams Japan with his tiny son Daigoro in a bamboo baby cart, dispatching others by decapitation and disembowelment in the popular

Sword of Vengeance series of films, would absolutely baffle most Western audiences. Is he a good guy or a bad guy? Is he wearing a black hat or a white hat? The answer is both. And the dirty, amoral bodyguard portrayed by Mifune Toshiro in both *Yojimbo* and *Sanjuro* would also fit this bill quite beautifully. He was the prototype for Clint Eastwood's man with no name in Sergio Leone's operatic spaghetti Westerns *A Fistful of Dollars* (a remake of *Yojimbo*) and *The Good, the Bad and the Ugly.*

But what really makes Japanese film special isn't so much the bloodshed and ultra-violence, but rather the profound humanism and com-

three major studios still surviving – Toho, Shochiku and Toei – barely crank out enough domestic films in a year to fill a couple of the multiplexes that are suddenly springing up. But it's not over yet.

The death of Kurosawa Akira in 1998 was a particular blow. "Sensei", as he became known, almost single-handedly put Japanese film on the international map with *Rashomon*, which won top prize at the 1951 Venice Film Festival. His rising and falling fortunes over the next half century were emblematic of the Japanese industry itself. Endlessly frustrated by unreceptive Japanese studios and aborted projects,

passion ranging through its entire history. One would have to look deeply into other international cinemas to find efforts as profound as Kurosawa's *Ikiru* and *Ran*, Ozu's *Tokyo Story*, Kinoshita Keisuke's *Twenty-Four Eyes* or Mizoguchi's *The Life of Oharu.*

Age matters not

The great, golden age of Japanese film, which lasted from the postwar 1950s until the late 1960s when the burgeoning availability of television laid it to waste, is certainly gone. The

Kurosawa attempted suicide after a box-office failure in 1970. Yet he would go on to make five more films, at least two of which – *Kagemusha* and particularly *Ran* – would be counted among his greatest works. However, Kurosawa repeatedly had to turn to outside of Japan and Francis Ford Coppola, George Lucas, Steven Spielberg, and Serge Silberman for support.

Kurosawa's passing notwithstanding, it's heartening that some elders are still working. Most notable is Imamura Shohei, who in the late 1990s and in his seventies had two consecutive films in competition at the Cannes Film Festival: *The Eel*, which shared grand prize, and the 1998 opus *Dr. Akagi.*

LEFT: poster for Beat Takeshi's 1997 *Hana-Bi (Fireworks).* **ABOVE:** the great Mifune Toshiro in *Yojimbo.*

Japanese film suffered a shocking and unexpected blow by the still inexplicable 1997 suicide-by-scandal of Itami Juzo. (A tabloid newspaper was about to reveal a supposed relationship between the filmmaker and a younger woman.) Itami was responsible for some marvellously smart and funny dissections of contemporary life, all of them starring his wife, Miyamoto Nobuko: *The Funeral, Tampopo,* and the societal exposes of the two *Taxing Woman* films.

Another shock to the system – quite literally – was the 1996 death of actor Atsumi Kiyoshi, Japan's beloved Tora-san. Don't underestimate the impact of this character on the national consciousness (or Shochiku's box office take). Over the span of nearly 30 years and 47 films, this itinerant amulet seller was to Japan what Chaplin's Little Tramp was to the world during the Silent Era, only more so. Within the restrictive, often suffocating bounds of Japanese society, Tora-san's gypsy-like existence had strong appeal to the millions of train-riding, 9-to-5 businessmen, and his endlessly disappointing romances held women in thrall.

Bright lights, new generation

Although filmmaking styles have been altered for scaled-down financial resources and changing audience tastes, there's much to recommend in Japan's younger generation of filmmakers. Suo Masayuki's delightful *Shall We Dance?* was the highest-grossing foreign-language film ever to play in U.S. movie theatres and would undoubtedly have won the Oscar for foreign films had it not been disqualified by one of the Academy's innumerable arcane rules.

The anarchic, dark, violent and often funny ruminations by "Beat" Kitano Takeshi – a tremendously successful and popular comedian, actor, game-show host, raconteur and moviemaker – have won international acclaim, particularly his most recent effort, the alternately tender and cataclysmic *Hana-Bi (Fireworks)*. And the first two films from Takenaka Naoto (who as an actor was seen as the wig-wearing Latin dance fanatic in *Shall We Dance?*) made a good impression: the wry and laconic *119* and *Tokyo Biyuri*, the moving but unsentimental film about the difficult relationship between a photographer and his mentally unbalanced wife.

> **FOREIGN AMBIENCE**
>
> American-style multiplexes didn't appear in Japan until the late 1990s. Previously, theatres were single-screen, with inferior projection and sound systems and run-down seats and interiors.

One step forward, two back

Curiously enough – although not so curiously, if one looks back to what occurred in the United States during the Great Depression – Japan's economic downturn of the 1990s produced greater box-office revenues. As industry after industry reported dismal earnings, the business doing best was the movie business. Much of this can be attributed to foreign films such as *Titanic,* which in Japan accounted for more than 70 percent of the revenues of foreign films. Still, domestic product was also on the rise.

Elsewhere there was scrutiny and criticism from the Japanese and international media with another film, *Unmei no Toki (Pride)*, a big-budget, nationalistic biopic from director Ito Shunya that sympathetically portrayed Japan's wartime prime minister, Gen. Tojo Hideki. A storm of controversy erupted around the region upon the film's release, Asians incensed that the man generally considered to be the prime instigator of Japanese Asian aggression – and the one responsible for what has become known as the Rape of Nanjing, in China – was actually depicted in the film to be battling for Asian interests against Western imperialism. *Pride* actually received a decent notice in *Daily Variety,* the primary American entertainment trade publication: "powerful, controversial, revisionist courtroom drama... [the film's] different spin on famous events of the Pacific war is at times quite disturbing but is nonetheless fascinating and makes for most effective drama". *Pride* was made for a huge (by Japanese standards) $11 million and starred the highly respected film and television actor Tsugawa Masahiko as Tojo.

Japanese films about World War II have always veered wildly between the powerfully pacifistic (Ichikawa Kon's harsh *Fires on the Plain* and the stunningly emotional *The Burmese Harp,* also directed by Ichikawa) and jingoistic flag waving. Often, war films try to have it both ways, especially in recent war movies in which popular teen idols, male and female, are cast in primary roles and then killed off tragically, much to the despair and tears of the young audiences. ❑

RIGHT: *Mononoke Hime,* or *Princess Mononoke.*

Anime

Sailor Moon. Dragonball Z. Doraemon. Pokemon. Evangelion. Gundam. Urusei Yatsura. Aeon Flux. My Neighbour Totoro. Akira. The Ghost in the Shell. Princess Mononoke... The Diary of Anne Frank?

Welcome to the fantastic, bizarre, beautiful, grotesque, and always surprising world of *anime*, a cartoon universe quite peculiar to the Japanese imagination but now accepted worldwide by legions of often fanatical admirers. Born of *manga* – the thick comic books read by young and old in Japan – these feature-film and television cartoons are quite a stunning detour from the animated fare that most Westerners are raised upon.

In most of the world, cartoons are almost entirely the domain of the very young, and Japan certainly pays attention to that audience with several anime aimed squarely at children. The problem (for some Westerners and concerned Japanese parents as well) is that even the kid's anime is so visually frenetic that it makes good ol' Looney Tunes seem mellow by comparison.

As for the more adult fare... Well, here's where the cultural differences between East and West are quite clear. Ultra-violence, raw sexuality and nudity, visionary and often apocalyptic views of the future, and extreme graphic style are the hallmarks of this genre, with most efforts falling into the science-fiction category. The better examples of these are truly stunning and original, such as Otomo Katsuhiro's 1989 classic *Akira* and, more recently, Oshii Mamoru's *The Ghost in the Shell*.

But there's an alternative to the endless parade of animated juggernauts and bare breasts – and his name is Miyazaki Hayao. A virtual font of creativity, Miyazaki heads the famed Studio Ghibli, which has been responsible for what many would consider to be the finest anime to emerge from Japan. Miyazaki got his start in television anime, directing a gigantically popular multi-part version of *Heidi* before moving into features with *The Castle of Cagliostro*, based on a popular James Bondian character known as Lupin the Third. Since then, his films as director have included such fanciful, haunting, and often humourous fantasy efforts as *Nausicaa of the Valley of the Wind*, *Laputa – The Castle in the Sky, Porco Rosso, My Neighbour Totoro, Kiki's Delivery Service,* and most recently, the gigantic box-office hit *Mononoke Hime,* or *Princess Mononoke.* (*See picture above.*)

In addition to his penchant for pure entertainment, Miyazaki's concerns are also ecological and spiritual in a deeply Japanese way. Shinto, the indigenous pantheistic religion of the nation, strongly informs *Princess Mononoke* – a complex story that is essentially about the inevitable clash between humans and the deities of nature, in this case giant versions of boars and wolves endowed with the power of language – and the remarkable *Heise Tanuki Gassen Pompoko* (supervised by Miyazaki but directed by Ghibli's Takahata Isao), which is about raccoons fighting the destruction of their forest home in what would later become the Tokyo suburb of Tama.

It's not too surprising that Miyazaki Hayao, often referred to as the Walt Disney of Japan, was finally discovered by Hollywood when the Walt Disney Company bought theatrical rights for *Princess Mononoke* and also made a deal to distribute on video several of Studio Ghibli's previous efforts.

There are other fine examples of ambitious anime that defy the supercharged sci-fi traditions, including of all things a very respectable 1995 two-hour version of *The Diary of Anne Frank*. While making the story palatable for a young audience, this film powerfully drove home the real-life drama against beautifully drawn backgrounds of 1940s Amsterdam and a score by Michael Nyman, who wrote the music for *The Piano*. ❏

TRADITIONAL ARCHITECTURE

With its post-and-beam construction, traditional Japanese architecture allowed flexibility with interior space and the art presented within it

What kind of house would one build in Japan if one knew it might be blown away by winds or fall apart by movements of the earth? Besides typhoons and earthquakes, Japan also has severe rains, which often cause flooding and landslides. How would one make a palace or temple or hall, a farmhouse, or a gate to survive such destructive forces? These questions had to be faced by the designers of buildings in Japan's remote past and are still faced today.

The fact that Japan has the world's oldest wooden buildings (Horyu-ji, built about AD 670) and the world's largest wooden structure (at Todai-ji, some 50 metres (165 ft) high and said to have been rebuilt at only two-thirds its original size) seems to argue that the architectural system adopted by the Japanese was at least partially successful in creating structures to last. On the other hand, at least in contemporary times, the devastation of the 1995 Kobe earthquake – thousands of homes, office buildings, and expressways simply collapsed, while thousands more burned down in a matter of seconds – suggests otherwise. Indeed, rather than wind, earth and water, it is fire that is the greatest destroyer of buildings in Japan.

In any case, Japanese architecture has influenced architectural design throughout the world. Its concepts of fluidity, modularity, utilisation of limited space, and use of light and shadow have a great power and appeal, both aesthetically and as solutions to architectural problems in contemporary times.

Whatever factors determined how buildings were built in Japan – survival, tradition, aesthetics – some common characteristics can be found that define the tradition of Japanese architecture. Given the great range of climates and the complex topography of the archipelago, the persistence of such common architectural features is truly remarkable.

PRECEDING PAGES: open verandas unite inside and outside. **LEFT:** traditional tools in use on a new shrine. **RIGHT:** imperial visit to Tokyo's Yasukuni Shrine.

Historical summary

The oldest Japanese dwellings are the pit houses of the neolithic Jomon culture, but the oldest structure to which the term "architecture" might be applied are the Grand Shrines of Ise. (*See page 283.*) First completed in the 5th century, the shrines have been ritually

rebuilt 60 times every 20 years. Each rebuilding takes years to accomplish, starting with the cutting of special cypress trees deep in the mountains, and it involves special carpentry techniques as well as time-honoured rituals. The disappearance of carpenters with the necessary skills and the enormous cost of the project have resulted in the prediction that the 1993 rebuilding may have been the final.

The introduction of Buddhism to Japan in AD 552 brought with it, in one sweep, many cultural and technical features, not the least of which was architecture in the continental manner. It is said that Korean builders came over to Japan and either built or supervised the building of the Horyu-ji (AD 607). The foundations of the vast temple that was the prototype of Horyu-ji can be seen in Kyongju, South Korea.

In the 7th century at the capital in Nara, Chinese architectural influence became quite obvious, not only in the structures themselves, but in the adoption of the north–south grid plan of the capital, based on the layout of the Chinese capital. At this time, both secular and sacred architecture was essentially the same, and palaces were often rededicated as temples. Both

When the imperial court at Kyoto lost the reins of power to the military government of the shogunate, located far to the west in Kamakura, the open and vulnerable *shinden* style was supplanted by a type of residential building more easily defended. This warrior style (*bukke-zukuri*) placed a number of rooms under one roof or a series of conjoined roofs and was surrounded by a defensive device such as a fence, wall, or moat, with guard towers and gates. Tiled roofs gave way to either shingled or

displayed red-lacquered columns and green roofs with pronounced upswinging curves in the eaves. Roofs were tiled.

The mutability of residence and temple held true in the subsequent Heian Period as well, as evidenced by the villa of the nobleman Fujiwara no Yorimichi (990–1074), which became the Phoenix Hall of Byodo-in, in Uji near Kyoto. The graceful *shinden-zukuri* style of this structure, utilised for the residences of Heian court nobles, is characterised by rectangular structures in symmetrical arrangement and linked by long corridors. The layout of Kyoto's Old Imperial Palace is similar, though it is a replica of this style.

thatched roofs. This period also saw the importation of Chinese Song-dynasty architectural styles for temples, particularly the so-called Zen style, which is characterised by shingled roofs, pillars set on carved stone plinths, and the "hidden roof" system developed in Japan, among other features.

In the subsequent Muromachi Period, which saw the purest expression of feudal government and its breakup into the Age of Warring States (15th century), Zen Buddhist influence transformed the warrior style into the *shoin* style. This at first was little more than the addition of a small reading or waiting room (*shoin*), with a deep sill that could be used as a desk and dec-

the single most noteworthy aspect of Japanese buildings. Interior spaces were partitioned so that rooms could be combined or contracted. The former was accomplished through the use of sliding and removable door panels. A room could be divided by decorative standing screens, especially those with gold backgrounds to act as a reflective surface and bring light into gloomy castle or palace interiors. Corridor width was the necessary width for two people with serving trays to pass one another.

AMBIENCE COUNTS

A Japanese ceramic bowl and a kimono are very different when seen in a traditional Japanese room and in a room with plaster walls and glass windows.

Since the floors of traditional Japanese buildings are generally raised, house floor and ground surface are not contiguous (except in the case of the packed-earth *doma*, the work and implement storage area of a farmhouse). In effect, this means that the indoor-outdoor fluidity is mainly visual and for circulation of air, not for movement of people in and out.

In rural areas, the veranda, when open, becomes a place to sit and have a good gossip with a neighbour or friend.

Inside is outside

Also, in this approach, the distinction between wall and door often disappears. This applies to outside walls – the "boundary" between interior and exterior – as well. Outside walls are often nothing more than a series of sliding wooden panels that can be easily removed, thus eliminating the solid border between inside and outside, a feature very much welcomed in Japan's humid summer. The veranda thus becomes a transitional space connecting interior with exterior of the building.

LEFT: traditional design of Kyoto's Nazen-ji. **ABOVE:** Karatsu-jo in Kyushu, and Kyoto's Heian-jingu.

The ability to open up a house interior completely to external vistas led to the development of a heightened sensitivity to such vistas and to their manipulation. Or perhaps it was a desire to view nature that led to the ability to remove the outer partitions of a house. Whatever the origin, the juxtaposition of building and nature without a clear dividing line is one origin of the Japanese garden – a manipulated or totally artificial vista, grand or miniature, "natural" or stylised and symbolic. The Japanese garden is an artifact open to the sun and rain, but clearly made to be seen and appreciated from within a building. Gardens for walking exist but are rather exceptional and usually public.

The materials used in traditional Japanese room interiors are few and limited, reflecting an ambivalence between interior and exterior, or perhaps a pleasure in harmonising rather than sharply demarking interior and exterior. Sliding door panels are either translucent *shoji* or the heavier, opaque *fusuma* paper screens, or of wood. Floors are of thick, resilient straw mats surfaced with woven reed (*tatami* mats), or of plain wood.

Supportive wooden posts remain exposed, and ceilings are generally of wood or of woven materials of various kinds. Wooden surfaces remain unpainted (a fact that received little

understanding from the postwar American occupation forces housed in requisitioned private homes). In the few areas of the country where wooden architectural surfaces are lacquered, the lacquer enhances the material, letting it speak; covering it is "cheap".

Because of the generous eaves of Japanese buildings, interiors tend to be dark and often enough may be gloomy. The use of translucent paper shoji screens to diffuse soft light helps, but the soft, natural colours of the room materials generally absorb rather than reflect light. The colours, lighting and textures of traditional Japanese rooms influenced the qualities of all objects to be used in them, including clothing.

The artistic unity or harmony of a building extends to its properties as well. Master carpenters, who were both the architects and the builders of traditional buildings, developed aesthetic proportions that applied to all elements of a single structure, as well as to individual buildings in a complex. There are special and very sophisticated traditional carpenter's measures that apply this system of aesthetic proportion to buildings under construction.

And finally, Japanese architecture is united in the display of an astonishing degree of contrast and variety. The earth's oldest wooden buildings exist not too far from the Ise shrines, whose immortality is defined by their being ritually rebuilt exactly as the original every 20 years. Thus, the shrine is both ancient and new at the same time. Tiny tea houses and the world's biggest wooden building both show an equally awesome skill in building, but of varying scales and degrees.

Gardens are contrived to draw in the vistas of distant mountains within their boundaries. Tiny "dry landscape" gardens – or rock gardens – may display such symbolic potency that they are both big and small at the same time – and then ... ceases to have significant meaning to the viewer.

Some of the finest tea house. whose total lack of surface ornament is itself a pure, ... mental statement – were built at roughly the same time as the Tosho-gu in Nikko, whose detail and colour-crammed surfaces display a naive delight in complexity and brightness, and which seems to go so far beyond mere clutter as to define a new set of principles. Both the tea house and the ornate shrines, temples, and palaces shout out that they were built by skilled artists, the former emphasising taste but as a tool to contemplation and quiet, while the latter's primary message is loud flaunting of skill, effort, money and power.

Historically, Japanese architecture shows a dialectic between imported, continental styles (mainly from China, but with some also from the Korean peninsula) and native Japanese styles. The borrowed styles from China and the Korean peninsula were constantly modified, adapted, and made into something clearly Japanese in taste. ❏

LEFT: each of Kinkaku-ji's levels is a different architectural style. **RIGHT:** three-tiered pagoda in Kyoto.

SUMO AND STRIKES

The two most popular sports are sumo and baseball, one indigenous to the archipelago and the other introduced from abroad. Both are fanatically followed

Baseball and *sumo* are the two perennial spectator sports in Japan. In the early 1990s, professional soccer was introduced under the excessively hyped "J-League" banner. For the first couple of years, it seemed the Japanese couldn't get enough of J-League or its stars, both Japanese and imported foreigners. But attendance slumped after a couple of years, as did all the breathless enthusiasm, and wags are speculating as to if J-League was simply a fad or will have staying power.

Participatory sports are few within Tokyo. It's just too expensive. Golf, the world knows, is fanatically popular in Japan, but only the rich can afford to play a proper round of golf in Japan; the rest stand in cubicles at driving ranges and hit balls towards distant nets. Skiing is a fashionable sport and Japan has the mountains. But like most activities in which the Japanese engage, there are crowds and blaring loudspeakers everywhere, even on the slopes, which leaves skiing in Japan less than satisfying. (An alternative, of course, is the year-round refrigerated ski slope in a long and inclined enclosed tunnel, looking like an odd industrial "thing," just north of Tokyo.)

In this chapter, we'll look at sumo and baseball. Although baseball is truly the athletic obsession of Japan, occupying much more of the time and energy of the country's young athletes, sumo (pronounced *s'mo*) remains the "official" national sport. This is fitting, partly because of its history that dates back as far as the third century, and too for its hoary, quasi-religious ritualism – but mostly because, in Japan, it's a more exciting sport.

Sumo

Some people say sumo is the national sport, some say it's the national spirit. Sumo wrestlers, or *rikishi,* would probably say it's a long, hard grind to fleeting glory.

PRECEDING PAGES: two *rikishi* duel in the *dohyo.*
LEFT: Little League baseball is serious sport in Japan.
RIGHT: pre-tournament sumo purification ritual.

Sumo as court entertainment dates back to the 8th century, when wrestlers drawn from army ranks fought to amuse the imperial court in Kyoto. It evolved over the years, mainly as gladiatorial entertainment. Sumo was formalised as a sport during the 17th century, with matches held on the grounds of Shinto shrines.

The parades, costumes, and rituals of today preserve a long tradition.

There was a period in the heady, decadent days of the Edo Period when there was women's sumo as well. At first they appeared just in loincloths like the men, but eventually the law made them cover up; the engravers of popular woodblock *ukiyo-e* prints had to oblige by adding vests to cover breasts.

Traditionally, however, women are not allowed to step foot in the ring, called a *dohyo.* This discrimination was challenged in 1990 when Chief Cabinet Secretary Mayumi Moriyama, a woman, expressed a wish to present the Prime Minister's Cup to the tournament winner. She was turned down by the conservative and definitely male sumo association and withdrew her request.

Sumo is a fascinating phenomenon because it involves so many different things: physical strength, centuries-old ritual, a complicated code of behaviour, religious overtones, a daunting hierarchy system, and feudalistic training regimes. It's a long physical and emotional climb to the top, with little sleep, lots of dirt and sweat, constant humiliation, cooking, running errands and

DOHYO DUO DUEL

The wrestler's goal is to force his opponent to touch the *dohyo*'s surface with anything but the feet or set foot out of the ring. The average bout lasts six seconds.

tember. Each rikishi fights one match daily for the two weeks. Winning a tournament heaps upon the tournament champion an Emperor's Cup, a significant amount of cash, and sumo-sized awards of beef, a few tons of rice... in fact, enough commodities of all kinds to keep a "stable" of hearty wrestlers and their hangers-on flatulent for years.

In the old days it was possible to rub shoulders with the wrestlers outside the tournament halls, watch them exercising in the car park, and peep into the dressing rooms

scrubbing backs, and the awesome task of accompanying 200-kilogram (450 lb) senior wrestlers to the restroom – all for just bed and board. Only those at the top receive a salary.

The goal of newcomers to the sport is to one day reach proper *sekitori* status – to be in the top 50 or so wrestlers out of the more than 600 wrestlers. Doing so means a fancy top-knot, assistants, and a salary. Only one or two of those 50 will reach the very top, that of being a grand champion, or *yokozuna*.

Six two-week tournaments are held each year, three in Tokyo's Kokugikan, in the Ryogoku area in the eastern part of the city. The Tokyo tournaments are held in January, May, and Sep-

before tournaments. All that has gone. To do that now you will have to visit the *beya,* or stables, where practice starts at the crack of dawn. Some beya require introductions to enter, others are open to the public.

Training takes place in a kind of hushed, largely humourless fashion, even though rikishi are immensely sociable off the job. Appearances to the contrary, rikishi are not slabs of flab. They are immensely strong, rigorously-trained athletes, with solid muscle often loosely covered in flab. The biggest rikishi in history (a Hawaiian named Salevaa Atisanoe, retired and now a Japanese citizen, and whose sumo name was Konishiki) reached 253 kilograms (557 lbs) before slimming down a bit for his wedding. Most grand champions, however, have ranged in weight from 110 to 150 kilograms (220–330 lbs). There are active rikishi in sumo's upper two divisions as small as 90 kilograms (198 lbs).

There are no weight divisions. During a tournament, the smallest will fight the largest. Some bouts will have a rikishi wrestling another who weighs literally twice as much. Few holds are barred, but sumo tradition frowns on below-the-waist attacks. The waist itself is wrapped in sumo's only garment, a belt called the *mawashi*. The most dignified (and probably dullest) winning technique – called *yorikiri* – requires a two-handed grip on the mawashi, which allows the winner to lift and push his opponent out.

Just as they come in all sizes, rikishi come in a range of abilities. The top sumo rank is yokozuna, or grand champion, and there are rarely more than four active yokozuna at any time. Just below is the rank of *ozeki*. Both yokozuna and ozeki retain their rank, even after a losing record (less than half of the 15 matches) in a *basho*, or tournament. After two straight basho with a losing record, however, ozeki are automatically demoted and yokozuna are pressured to retire.

The upper division of winners is called *makunouchi* (or "inside the curtain"). Here, the descending ranks below ozeki are *sekiwake*, *komusubi*, and a large group of *maegashira*, the latter being the rank-and-file wrestlers. A rikishi who achieves *kachikoshi* – at least eight wins out of the 15 bouts he must fight during a given tournament – moves automatically up the ranks; *makekoshi* (eight or more losses) on the other hand means demotion.

Baseball

A true national sport in terms of popularity and year-round interest, not to mention commercial importance, is the grand old Japanese game of baseball. It has been here since 1873 and is a major preoccupation for all ages. When American missionaries began teaching baseball to college students in Tokyo in 1912, they didn't realise how popular it was to become in Japan.

Yakyu, as baseball is technically called in Japanese (although *basuboru* is more common), rivals sumo as the national sport. The two-league professional baseball system is a money-making industry, drawing more than 15 million spectators to stadiums.

Millions more watch on national television and train commuters devour the pages of Japan's daily national sports newspapers on their way to work each morning, from April through October, for details of the previous night's baseball league action. To put it mildly, Japan is a baseball-crazy country, even more so than the United States. One essential differ-

ence between North American and Japanese baseball is that baseball players in Japan are regarded as salaried men just like anyone else and are therefore expected to train out of season as hard as they play during the April-October season. Similarly, salaries in Japan are on par with the batboys' in North America.

There are two major leagues in Japanese professional baseball, with teams owned by big companies rather than being associated with cities, although a city's name sometimes, but not necessarily, figures in the team's official name. For teams constantly on top, the advertising and promotional value for the parent company – department stores, media giants and

---

LEFT: the *dohyo* is the focus of the six annual sumo tournaments in four cities. **RIGHT:** foreign players are on nearly every team but restricted to just two.

food processing companies – is considerable.

Consider the perennially top Seibu Lions. Seibu is a corporate conglomerate. The beautiful Seibu ball park just happens to be on a Seibu railway line next to the Seibu Amusement Park. Whenever a Seibu home run is hit, the sky above the Seibu property around the ball park is lit up with fireworks. Display boards at the main Seibu train station in Ikebukuro keep commuters informed of the latest scores as they hurry past the massive Seibu department store. And inside that store – and in every other Seibu store in Japan – if the Lions have won the pennant, the team's fight-

ing-spirit song is played over and over and over, all day, on the store's public address system. Over and over and over.

Each team plays a 130-game season, as opposed to the 162-game U.S. major league schedule, with opening day the first Saturday in April and the final regular season game played in mid-October. The winners of each league pennant meet in Japan's version of the World Series, the best-of-seven Japan Series beginning the third week of October.

The Japanese rule allowing *gaijin* players in its pro leagues is one of the most interesting aspects of the system. Each Japanese team can list three foreign players on its 60-man roster,

which includes the "major league" team and one farm team. There are critics who believe the teams should be allowed to employ as many foreigners as they wish and that the limitation rule should be abolished. Others have said gaijin players are not good for Japanese baseball and should be banned.

Most, however, feel the situation is fine as is, since the colourful American players with their quirks – and occasional outbursts – make the Japanese game that much more interesting; the limit does, nonetheless, allow baseball in Japan to keep its identity as Japanese. Since the two-league system was begun in 1950, more than 300 foreign players have appeared in the Japanese leagues – some great, some mediocre, some who simply could not adjust to living in Japan or playing Japanese baseball.

Excessive, year-round workouts (including on the day of games) is the biggest gripe of American players who come and try their hand at the Japanese version (same rules, different attitudes): they all maintain that a short preseason training period and the regular season games are enough for anyone, and that professionals shouldn't need to practice techniques all winter long. The contrary argument is that Americans on salaries larger than their Japanese counterparts should play the game the Japanese way if they're on a Japanese team.

Of how many foreigners should be permitted to play on Japanese teams, the debate remains unsettled. However, now that the Japanese are showing more power and speed – if not the sheer physical size – in the game, the chances of them becoming more active on the international baseball scene are good. In 1995, a Japanese player, Nomo Hideo, became a national sensation when he joined the Los Angeles Dodgers as a pitcher, becoming a top pitcher in "American" baseball.

The rules of Japanese baseball are generally the same as for those of its North American counterpart. There are, however, several peculiarities – the ball-strike count is reversed in Japan, making a full count 2-3, rather than 3-2.

Teams have their own rooting sections, with trumpets, drums and tambourines, headed by cheerleaders paid by the team. The resulting din shatters the eardrums. ❏

LEFT: the Seibu Lions are a favourite of Japanese baseball fans. **RIGHT:** young student of *kendo*.

The Martial Arts

A general term for various types of fighting arts that originated in the Orient, most martial arts practiced today came from China, Japan, and Korea. They all share common techniques, but there is no one superior style.

Two major martial arts evolved in Japan, the *bujutsu*, or ancient martial arts, and the *budo*, or new martial ways. Both are based on spiritual concepts embodied in Zen Buddhism. Bujutsu emphasises combat and willingness to face death as a matter of honour. It contains the philosophy and techniques of the samurai warriors and includes such arts as *jujutsu* and *karate-jutsu*. Budo, which started during the late 1800s, focuses on moral and aesthetic development. *Karate-do, judo,* and *aikido* are all forms of budo.

Most of the martial arts end in the suffix *-do*, usually translated as "way" or "path". Thus, *kendo* is the way of the sword. *Do* is also the root of *dojo*, the place where one studies and practices a martial art, and in budo.

The original form of **judo**, called *jujutsu*, was developed in the Edo Period (1603–1868). It was made up of different systems of fighting and defence, primarily without weapons, against either an armed or bare-handed opponent on the battlefield. The basic principle of the judo technique is to utilise the strength of the opponent to one's own advantage. It is because of this that a person of weaker physique can win over a stronger opponent. The best known judo hall in Japan is the Kodokan in Tokyo, where one can observe judoists practicing in early evenings.

Karate, meaning "empty hand" in Japanese, is a form of unarmed combat in which a person kicks or strikes with the hands, elbows, knees, or feet. In Japan, karate developed around the 1600s on the island of Okinawa. A Japanese clan had conquered the island and passed a strict law banning the ownership of weapons. As a result, the Okinawans – racially and culturally different from the Japanese – developed many of the unarmed techniques of modern karate.

Aikido is a system of pure self-defence derived from the traditional weaponless fighting techniques of jujutsu and its use of immobilising holds and twisting throws, whereby an attacker's own momentum and strength are made to work against him. Since aikido is primarily a self-defence system and does not require great physical strength, it has attracted many women and elderly practitioners. By meeting, rather than blocking, a blow, one can redirect the flow of the opponent's *ki* (often translated as "mind" or "positive energy force"), dissipate it, and, through joint manipulation, turn it against the opponent until he or she is thrown or pinned down.

Kendo ("the way of the sword") is Japanese fencing based on the techniques of the samurai two-handed sword. Kendo is a relatively recent term that implies spiritual discipline as well as fencing technique. It is taught to most upper-level school children. (At the end of World War II, the U.S. occupation authorities banned kendo on the basis of

its use before the war to cultivate militarism. But in 1957, the practice of kendo was returned to Japanese middle schools.)

Another martial art form that developed in Japan is **ninjutsu**, which means "the art of stealing in", or espionage. People who practice ninjutsu are called *ninja*. Mountain mystics developed ninjutsu in the late 1200s. At that time, ninja were masters at all forms of armed and unarmed combat, assassination, and in the skillful use of disguises, bombs, and poisons.

Although the rulers of Japan banned ninjutsu in the 1600s, the ninja practiced it secretly and preserved its techniques. Today, ninja is a traditional martial art with a nonviolent philosophy. ❑

RIKISHI: LIFE ON THE BOTTOM AND ON TOP

Not only is the rikishi's training one of harsh days and a long apprenticeship, but competition at the top is without weight classes or handicaps.

In sumo, life is best at the top. Only when a *rikishi*, or wrestler, makes it to the top ranks of *ozeki* or *yokozuna* (grand champion, the highest rank and rarely achieved) does life become easy. Those in the lower ranks become the ozeki's or yokozuna's servants and valets, doing nearly everything from running errands to scrubbing backs.

In most *beya* – the so-called stables in which wrestlers live a communal lifestyle with other rikishi – the day typically begins at 6am with practice, not breakfast. Harsh and tedious exercises work to develop the wrestlers' flexibility and strength, followed by repetitive practice matches amongst the beya's wrestlers (the only time they wrestle one another, as wrestlers of the same beya don't compete during actual tournaments). Practice ends around noon, when the wrestlers bathe. Then the high-ranked wrestlers sit down to the day's first meal, served by the lower-ranked wrestlers. The food staple of the stable is *chankonabe*, a high-calorie, nutritious stew of chicken, fish, *miso*, or beef, to mention just a few of the possibilities. Side dishes of fried chicken, steak, and bowls of rice – and even salads – fill out the meal.

Financially, rikishi can be divided into two groups: those who earn a salary and those who don't. Lower-ranked wrestlers, considered apprentices, receive no salary, although they earn a small tournament bonus (and food and lodging are provided). When a wrestler reaches the *juryo* level, he becomes a *sekitori*, or ranked wrestler, and so worthy of a salary of at least US$7,000 a month. An ozeki receives at least $16,000 monthly, and a yokozuna, $20,000. The winner of one of six annual tournaments receives $100,000.

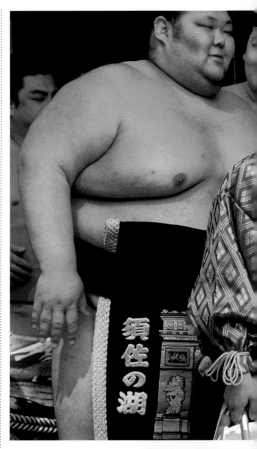

△ **THE GYOJI**
The referee of a sumo match is the *gyoji*, who shouts encouragement during matches.

▽ **MAWASHI**
The *mawashi*, or belt, is a single fabric 10 m (30 ft) long and often used to toss out one's opponent.

AN ANCIENT SHINTO SPORT

Sumo has been around for at least 2,000 years. Japanese mythology relates an episode in which the destiny of the Japanese islands was once determined by the outcome of a sumo match between two gods. The victorious god started the Yamato imperial line.

While wrestling has always existed in nearly every culture, the origins of sumo as we know it were founded on Shinto rituals. Shrines were the venue of matches dedicated to the gods of good harvests. In the Nara and Heian periods, sumo was a spectator sport for the imperial court, while during the militaristic Kamakura Period, sumo was part of a warrior's training. Professional sumo arose during the 1700s and is quite similar to the sumo practiced in today's matches.

Shinto rituals punctuate sumo. The stomping before a match (*shiko*) drives evil spirits from the ring (not to mention loosening the muscles) before a match. Salt is tossed into the ring for purification, as Shinto beliefs say that salt drives out evil spirits. Nearly 40 kg (90 lbs) of salt is thrown out in one tournament day.

◁ **HOPEFULS**
Sumo clubs nurture young hopefuls who might one day attain the adulation of a ranked wrestler.

▽ **IN THE RING**
The ring, made of a clay surface, is the *dohyo*, considered sacred ground and off-limits to women.

△ **TRAINING**
The wrestler undergoes years of rigorous training in the *beya,* or stable. All ranks train together.

▷ **TOP-RANKED GYOJI**
Gyoji follow a strict system of ranking. Higher-ranked gyoji wear elaborate *kimono* and *seta* (sandals) with *tabi* (Japanese-style socks).

CUISINE

The Japanese islands are home to what is probably the world's most eclectic, diverse, detailed, healthy, and aesthetically appealing cuisine

Japan is a country of regional cuisines and, too, of seasonal cuisines. In fact, sampling local dishes is a fundamental purpose of travelling for many Japanese, whether it be a local *ekiben* box-lunch bought at the train station or an exquisite dinner at a remote *ryokan*. It would be foolish for this book to try and cover the multitudinous regional and local cuisines. Even the Japanese don't try to know them all. But to sample them all, that would be a worthy life's goal.

In the cities, there are almost too many places from which to choose. Two types of places that particularly deserve attention for their pure Japanese ambience are the *izaka-ya*, or pub, often with a string of red lanterns above its door, and the *taishu-sakaba*, a much larger tavern-like establishment that may also sport red lanterns. These red lanterns (*akachochin*) signify a traditional Japanese place for eating and drinking. Specialties include Japanese-style fried fish, shellfish, broiled dishes, *tofu* (bean curd) dishes, *yakitori* (skewered and broiled meat), fried rice balls, and simple *sashimi*.

Kaiseki ryori

At least one meal in Tokyo should be *kaiseki ryori*, a centuries-old form of Japanese cuisine served at restaurants or in ryokan in several elegant courses. Ingredients depend upon the season and region, and Japanese will travel great distances to sample a regional specialty. One might spend a lifetime sampling every regional variation. (Be warned that authentic kaiseki ryori is very expensive.)

Fastidiously prepared, kaiseki ryori is so aesthetically pleasing that it's virtually an art form. (*See photograph on pages 130-31.*)

Ideally, the food's visual appeal would be heightened by a proper setting for the meal, whether in the snow-blanketed mountains or on the sea shore. Some of the better restaurants

serving kaiseki ryori have succeeded in creating exactly such an atmosphere regardless of outside environment, with brush works, flower arrangements, and views of waterfalls cascading over well-hewn rocks into placid pools. The effect elevates the senses and pleasure of kaiseki ryori.

The ingredients must be as fresh as the dawn. That's a prime requisite of good food in general, of course, together with a good recipe and a good cook. Rejoice in the fact that Japan has plenty of all three.

The taste of kaiseki ryori relies on the inherent taste of the food itself, not on additional spices or the like. Japanese cuisine focuses on flavour and its subtleties, and on the food's aesthetic presentation. Rather than create distinctive flavours for their dishes, Japanese chefs seek above all to retain the natural flavours. And rather than alter the appearance of their ingredients, they strive to enhance their visual appeal through artful arrangements.

PRECEDING PAGES: the elegance of *kaiseki ryori*.
LEFT: *ramen* noodle stand in Tokyo's Shinjuku.
RIGHT: warm welcome at a neighbourhood *sushi-ya*.

Noodles

Japanese noodles are of three main types: *soba*, *udon*, and *somen*. Made of buckwheat, soba noodles are thin and brownish, with a hearty consistency. Udon noodles, made of wheat, are usually off-white and thick to very thick. Somen noodles, also made of wheat, are as thin as vermicelli. Udon is usually eaten in hot dishes, while soba and somen may be eaten hot or cold, depending upon season.

Additionally, another type of noodle called *hiyamugi* (iced noodles) is eaten only cold. Hiyamugi is a made of the same ingredients as udon but much thinner.

THE EELS OF SUMMER

Travellers will encounter many unusual dishes in Japan. Some fit in a category that Japanese commonly refer to as stamina *ryori*, or dishes intended to raise energy levels and "staying" power. Japan and especially Tokyo can be pretty enervating, so "stamina restaurants" (and drinks) are a common phenomenon. A popular summer dish is *unagi*, or broiled eel served on rice. It's said to help one withstand the hot and humid days of the Japanese summer – *doyo no iri*. Usually served with a sweetish tare sauce, unagi is rich in vitamins E and A, and it exceeds pork and beef in protein content yet contains fewer calories.

Most common are soba, particularly delicious if not overburdened with non-buckwheat flour extender. Soba is usually served with *wasabi* (green horseradish), thinly sliced scallions, a dip made of *mirin* (sweet *sake*), and *katsuobushi* (shaved flakes of dried bonito). Soba noodles in this form, when served chilled on a *zaru*, a type of bamboo tray, are called *zarusoba* and make a delicious summer meal. Soba is extremely nutritious, the more so in proportion to its *sobako* (wheat flour) content, a rich source of vitamins B1 and C.

Another hot weather favourite – just as soba is, but entirely different – is somen, the thin and off-white wheat noodle noted for its delicate flavour and adaptability to many garnishes. Somen can be served *gomoku* ("five-flavour") style with strips of omelette, chicken, and vegetables; *gomadare* style, with eggplant, fish, and *shiso* (beefsteak plant); with fruit and hard-boiled swallow eggs; or *hiyashi* style – cold, with nothing but soy sauce containing sesame oil. As a light, refreshing treat on a hot summer day, somen may have no filling rival.

One of Japan's great cold-weather favourites is udon, a somewhat thick to very thick wheat noodle served in a hot, soy-based broth with scallions, other vegetables, and an egg. Unlike soba and somen, udon is not placed in a dip before being eaten. Udon, a real body-warmer, is appreciated for its excellent texture.

Not strictly a traditional dish, but one that is uniquely Japanese and that can be (one must admit) quite delicious, is *kare-udon*. As its name implies, it's udon served in the thick, somewhat spicy gravy that passes for curry in Japan. (Another popular curry dish is *kare-risu*, or curry rice. Look for it at large train stations.)

Unlike pasta that's turned around on a fork, Japanese noodles are sucked into the mouth with chopsticks and *slurped* down. *Noisily.* In Japan that's how you do it, unabashedly and with total commitment. Experts say the noodles taste better that way. Although essentially Chinese, so-called *ramen* noodles are eaten so obsessively in Japan that to omit mentioning them would be remiss. Ramen is served very hot in soy-flavoured broth with savoury ingredients, most typically strips of bamboo and slices of scallion and roast pork. Instant ramen is a mainstay of the home.

If short on time, drop into a stand-and-eat soba stand, a *tachiguisoba-ya*, "stand-and-eat soba". Train stations always have them and a stand will sometimes be found on the platform. Prices are very cheap, usually ranging from ¥200 or so for *kakesoba* (basic soba in broth) to somewhat higher for *tendama* (soba with raw-egg and mixed ingredients fried together, tempura-style). Priced in between are *tempura soba*, *kitsune* (with fried tofu), *tanuki* (with tempura drippings), *tsukimi* (with raw egg), *wakame* (with kelp), and countless others. At the tachiguisoba-ya's low prices, the quality usually is average, but on a cold, winter day (or night) hot soba is wonderfully warming. It's also an efficient use of commuting time.

elegance, but in a kaiten sushi-ya the uninitiated can study the sushi offerings at leisure and sample it for less cost. Then later, armed with new-found expertise, visit a proper sushi-ya.

Good sushi requires that the ingredients should be of good quality and exceedingly fresh, that the rice be properly vinegared and steamed, and that the topping should be as fresh as possible. (Thawed-out frozen fish just doesn't cut it.) Those who prefer raw fish and seafood without rice should order sashimi, served in a tray or on a plate with attention to the appearance. Often small bowls of sauce will be offered for dipping the sashimi.

Sushi and sashimi

Taste and visual pleasure converge in *sushi* and *sashimi*, both prepared with uncooked seafood. Japanese simply adore sushi and sashimi, and knowing the Western bias against raw fish or meat will often ask visitors – simply out of sheer curiosity – if they can eat one or the other.

A good sushi shop, or *sushi-ya*, can be both expensive and confounding if one doesn't know what to ask for. Try, instead, a *kaiten sushi-ya*, where small dishes of sushi pass by on a conveyor belt along the counter. It lacks a certain

LEFT: vendor of *unagi*, or eel, popular in summer.
ABOVE: counter fare can be fast and economical.

Nabemono

If hot-pot dishes are your pleasure, Japan is the place to be in autumn and winter. Every part of Japan, without exception, has its own distinctive *nabe-ryori* (pot dishes).

Nabemono are typically winter dishes and include *ishikari-nabe* (Hokkaido Prefecture), containing salmon, onions, Chinese cabbage, tofu, *konnyaku* (a jelly made of root starch), and *shungiku* (spring chrysanthemum); *hoto* (Yamanashi), with handmade udon, *daikon* (white radish), *ninjin* (carrot), *gobo* (burdock), squash, onions, Chinese cabbage and chicken; and *chiri-nabe* (Yamaguchi), containing *fugu*

(blowfish) meat, Chinese cabbage, mushrooms, tofu, and starch noodles.

Popular for a quick meal and usually available in mini-marts is Tokyo-style *oden-nabe*, a potpourri containing potatoes, tofu, konnyaku, boiled eggs, octopus, carrots, daikon, kelp, and a wide variety of other ingredients. Make a note of oden, which are often presented as pick-and-chose right next to the cash register in convenience stores like 7-11. It is one of the better winter body-warmers and a hearty dish.

To dare to suggest that these few nabe-ryori examples should be considered to the exclusion of others from around Japan would incur well-deserved censure from regions far and wide.

Bento

Like most modern countries, Japan is increasingly a land of fast-food. The traditional Japanese box lunch, *bento*, or more respectfully, *obento*, has become a form of fast-food in itself, with both convenience stores and *bento-ya* offering wide selections to take out. A bento box, flat and shallow, is used with small dividers to separate rice, pickles, and whatever else might grace the inside.

Just about anything can be used in bento, including Western imports like spaghetti, Vienna sausages, and hamburger. Schoolchildren take bento to school for lunch.

A special type of bento that has become an art in itself, not to mention a pursuit for the connoisseur, is the *ekiben* (from *eki* for train station and bento). Japan is a nation of obsessed train travellers. Of all transportation forms, the train is incontestably the most popular. Thus, some of Japan's most popular forms of food are those sold inside the stations.

Trains often make stops of just long enough duration to permit passengers to get off briefly and buy some of their favourite *meisanbutsu* (local specialties), especially the ubiquitous ekiben, to be eaten aboard the train.

Tsukemono

A Japanese meal always comes with *tsukemono*, or distinctive Japanese-style pickles. Historically, pickles probably owe their origins to the practice of pickling foods in anticipation of famines. During the Edo Period, pickles came into their own and the *tsukemono-ya* (pickle shop) emerged as a new type of business. Ingredients used in Japanese pickles vary somewhat with the seasons. Common ingredients are Chinese cabbage, bamboo, turnips, *kyuri* (Japanese cucumbers), hackberry, daikon, ginger root, *nasu* (Japanese eggplant), *udo* (a type of asparagus), *gobo*, and many others.

Tsukemono add colour to a meal and offer a wide range of textures, from *crunch* to *squish*, that might be missing from the main dishes. Pickles can serve to clear the palate for new tastes – such as in sushi, in which a bite of pickled ginger root rids the mouth of the aftertaste of an oily fish such as *aji* (mackerel) and prepares it for the delicate taste of *ebi* (prawn). ❏

LEFT: *tsukemono* (pickle) stand in Kyoto.
RIGHT: Western-style food depicted in plastic.

Odds and Ends

The Japanese dining experience involves all the senses. Unlike the fork or spoon, for example, chopsticks (*hashi*) convey to the hand a sense of tactile rapport with the food. Small soup bowls (*owan*) raised to the mouth with the free hand convey the warmth or coolness of their ingredients. The loud slurping of hot *udon* – not considered rude – imparts its own lusty ambience to a gathering.

Etiquette: One should be aware of some chopstick etiquette. Never wave chopsticks indecisively over food, considered to be bad manners. Likewise, never spear food (*sashi-bashi*) with the tips of the chopsticks. Some things may be a bit more difficult to pick up with chopsticks than others, but chopsticks are designed to pick up food, not to spear and stab. Equally forbidden is *yose-bashi*, using chopsticks to pull a dish forward. Use only hands. Do not pass food back and forth with chopsticks (*hashi-watashi*), either. The worse offense at a meal would be to stick the chopsticks into a bowl of rice so that they stand upright on their own, as this is symbolic of death.

Japanese-style soups (*suimono*) and other liquid dishes should be sipped straight from the bowl. Whereas it is altogether acceptable form in Japan to slurp noodle dishes, such as udon or ramen, it is not required nor indeed is there any reason to slurp Japanese soups. Sip them directly from the bowl without a spoon, as this the best way to savour their delicate nuances of flavour.

For dishes that are dipped in sauce, such as *tempura* and *sashimi*, hold the sauce dish with one hand and dip the food into it with the chopsticks. Soy sauce should not be splashed onto a dish. Rather, pour into the small soy sauce dish, only a little at a time and sparingly.

Unlike in the West, relatively few Japanese dishes are submerged in sauces, doused with gravy, and seasoned beyond recognition. Granted, the Japanese often splash on soy sauce as impulsively as some Westerners do catsup. Eat all the rice in the bowl, and when asking for more, take only what can be finished.

One will never see Japanese eating and walking at the same time, even for something as innocuous as an ice cream cone. Most Japanese consider it rude to walk and eat at the same time. One buys the food or snack, then finds a place to properly sit and completely finish it.

Never fill your own drinking glass. Someone else will always keep it filled. Your responsibility is not your own glass but those of others near you. Doing so helps encourage bonding and trust in the social group, whether friends or coworkers.

Economical eating: Eating can be expensive in Japan, especially if one goes to restaurants. Even the average restaurant, of whatever cuisine, can set the wallet back ¥5,000 to ¥10,000 per person, triple what one might expect to pay for similar meals in other countries.

However, many of Japan's most enjoyable and popular dishes are common and reasonably priced. Among them are such everyday dishes as *yaki-*

mono (fried dishes), *nabemono* (pot dishes), *age-mono* (deep-fat fried dishes), *nimono* (boiled dishes) and a wide variety of noodle dishes. (The suffix *-mono* can be roughly translated here as "things", as in "fried things".)

Increasingly, Japanese are buying meals at convenience stores like 7-11. Don't laugh. The competition between convenience stores is stiff and the quality of the food is excellent, made fresh daily and using only top-quality rice (Japanese are finicky about rice) for *bento* and *onigiri*, a rice ball with a filling and wrapped in dried seaweed.

Among the best bargains are *soba* restaurants and *ramen* shops. Both types of noodles usually come with meat or seafood. ❑

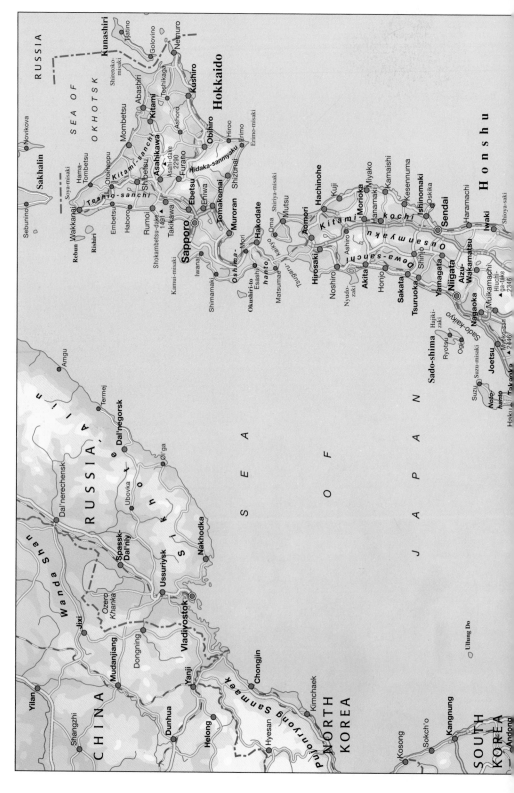

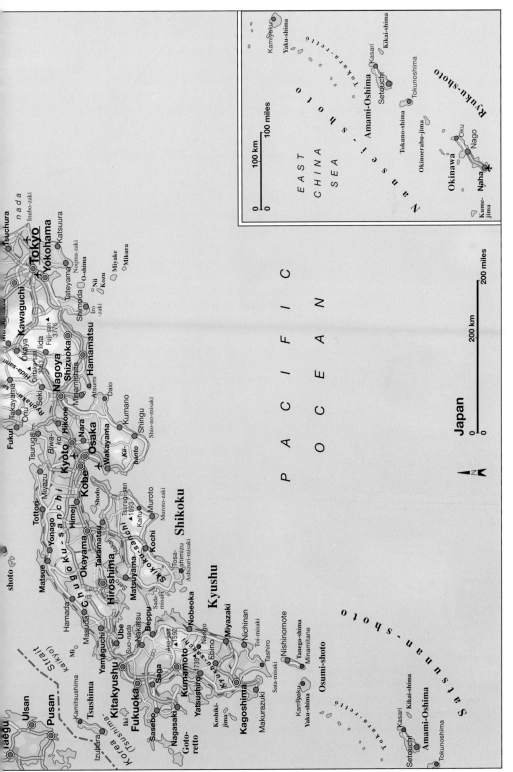

PLACES

*A comprehensive look at Japan's important destinations,
with numbered cross-references to detailed maps*

Spread like cultured pearls in the western Pacific, the islands of the Japanese archipelago lie off the coast of China, Russia and Korea. There are nearly 4,000 of these islands, strung out for over 2,800 km (1,700 miles) – from the remote mountains of the north, which look out across small stretches of water to Russian islands, to the southwest in Okinawa and nearly within sight of Taiwan. Covering 380,000 sq. km (147,000 sq. miles), Japan's land area is the size of Montana and a little larger than Italy, but twice as populous with more than 120 million residents – half the population of the United States.

The main islands of Hokkaido, Honshu, Shikoku and Kyushu are mountainous, cut through with narrow valleys. Fuji-san, the snow-capped 3,776-metre-high (12,388-ft) landmark, remains dormant and within sight of downtown Tokyo on a clear winter day. Overall, there are some 60 volcanoes in the archipelago considered to be active.

The transportation system of Japan is known throughout the world, both for its efficiency and punctuality and for its rush-hour congestion within the train. The trains will take travellers nearly anywhere on the four main islands, even to the smallest villages and with a punctuality by which to set chronometers.

The nation's capital, Tokyo, is on the main island of Honshu, which has the country's 10 largest cities, including the sprawling megalopolis of Tokyo-Kawasaki-Yokohama. The largest city outside of Honshu, Fukuoka, is far to the south on Kyushu.

It is expensive to travel within Japan. Trains aren't cheap and accommodation is costly. Indeed, it is cheaper for Japanese to take vacations in Hawaii or Sydney instead of within their own country. Yet they do travel within Japan, and they have made an art of travel that is often a bit too hierarchical and dogmatic for Westerners. Nevertheless, regardless of where one ends up, there are exquisite and delightful pleasures for the traveller, whether the *ekiben* box lunches at train stations or the precision with which a traditional *ryokan* pampers guests.

Naming conventions

Wherever possible, we use Japanese terms for geographical identifications. These appear as suffixes to the proper name. For example, Mount Fuji is referred to as Fuji-san. Mountains may also appear with other suffixes, including *-zan, -yama,* and for some active volcanoes, *-dake*. Islands are either *-shima* or *-jima*, lakes are *-ko*, and rivers are *-gawa*. Shrines are Shinto, and proper shrine names usually end in *-jinja, -jingu*, or *-gu*. Temples are Buddhist, with names usually ending in *-tera, -dera*, or *-ji*. ❏

PRECEDING PAGES: sunset along the Honshu coast near Hagi; Tokyo's Asakusa Kannon in late autumn; Tokyo's stock exchange.
LEFT: Daibutsu, the Great Buddha in Kamakura, south of Tokyo.

CENTRAL HONSHU

The central part of Honshu contains not only a region known as Chubu, but too the Kanto Region – and Tokyo

Descriptions of the Kanto region can be misleading. It is Japan's largest alluvial plain, but it is certainly not an area of wide-open spaces. None of the flat land extends far enough to offer a level, unbroken horizon. Most of Japan's longest rivers – the Tone, Naka, Ara, Tama, and Sagami – all pass through the Kanto and empty into the Pacific, but few would call these concrete-lined conduits, managed and contained into near-obscurity, rivers at all.

Kanto is home to Tokyo, perhaps the world's most populated urban area. The Kanto plain wraps itself around Tokyo and its equally-congested southern neighbours of Yokohama, Kamakura, and Izu. To the southwest are Mt Fuji (or Fuji-san) and Hakone, and to the north is Nikko. There are six large prefectures in Kanto, not including Tokyo itself, which is a self-administrating entity. The area has a total population of well over 30 million people, most of them within the greater metropolitan area of Tokyo.

The average population density of the Kanto region is approximately 15,600 persons per square kilometre, three times that of Los Angeles but not so bad in comparison with Hong Kong, Bombay, Jakarta or even Mexico City. Yet many people think that Tokyo has grown too big, and recently talk has returned to the relocation of the national government's operations elsewhere, perhaps in Sendai, to the north in the Tohoku region.

Virtually nothing of interest about the region is recorded until Minamoto Yoritomo, the first Kamakura shogun, endowed Tokyo's Asakusa-jinja with 90 acres (36 hectares) of arable land around 1180. Later, in 1456, a village called Edo (Estuary Gate) was recorded when the first Edo castle was built by a small-time *daimyo* on the site of today's Imperial Palace. In 1600, a shipwrecked Englishman became the first foreign guest at Edo, tutoring Ieyasu Tokugawa. Three years later, Ieyasu started the 250-year Tokugawa dynasty.

Like all great cities, although perhaps even more so, Edo suffered its share of natural disasters, amongst them earthquakes and the last eruption of Fuji-san, in 1707, which covered Edo with 10 cm (4 inches) of volcanic ash.

In the area known as Chubu, beyond the Kanto, Japan is both highly industrial, as in Nagoya to the southwest, and rural, such as is found in the delightful Noto Peninsula and elsewhere along the Sea of Japan coast. There are also the historical city of Kanazawa, the mountainous resort city of Nagano, and the remoteness and drumming thunder on the island of Sado. ❑

LEFT: a Kodo drummer from Sado Island performs on a large *taiko*.
PRECEDING PAGES: Mt Fuji seen on a clear day from Shinjuku, Tokyo.

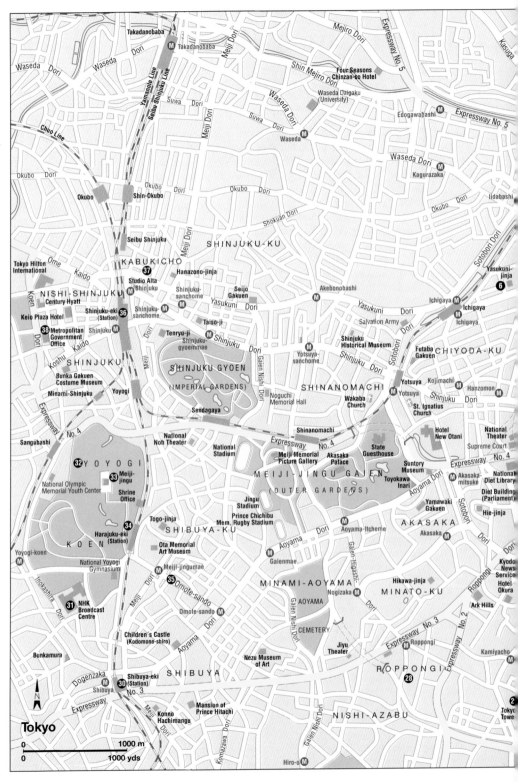

Tokyo

0   1000 m
0   1000 yds

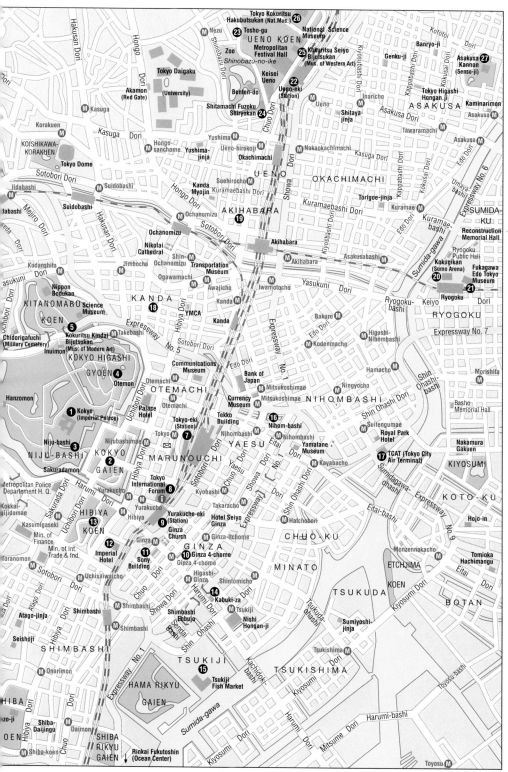

Kototoi Dori

Hakusan Dori
Hongo
Nezu
Banryo-ji

Tokyo Kokuritsu **26**
Hakubutsukan (Nat.Mus.)

Tosho-gu **23**
UENO KOEN
Genku-ji

National Science
Museum
Kappabashi Dori

Zoo
Metropolitan
Festival Hall
Kokuritsu Seiyo **25**
Bijutsukan
(Mus. of Western Art)

Kiyosubashi Dori
Kokusai Dori

Asakusa Dori
Asakusa **27**
Kannon
(Senso-ji)

Tokyo Daigaku
Shinobazu Dori
Shinobazu-no-ike

Kaminarimon

Akamon
(Red Gate)
(University)

Keisei
Ueno

Ueno-eki **22**
(Station)

Inaricho

Tokyo Higashi
Hongan-ji

Kasuga
Benten-do

Shitamachi Fuzoku
Shiryokan **24**

Chuo Dori
Ueno
Shitaya-
jinja

ASAKUSA

Korakuen
Kasuga
Dori
Yushima
Yushima-
jinja

Ueno-hirokoji
Okachimachi
Nakaokachimachi
Kasuga Dori
Kappabashi Dori
Tawaramachi

Asakusa

KOISHIKAWA-
KORAKUEN
Hongo-
sanchome

Suehirocho
UENO
OKACHIMACHI
Kuramae

Asakusa
Edo Dori

Expressway No. 6

Tokyo Dome

Iidabashi
Sotobori Dori
Suidobashi

Kanda
Myojin
Kuramaebashi Dori

Kuramaebashi Dori
Torigoe-jinja
Kuramae

Kuramae-
bashi
SUMIDA-
KU

Suidobashi

Hakusan Dori

Ochanomizu
Sotobori Dori

AKIHABARA **19**

Showa
Dori

Kiyosubashi Dori

Asakusabashi
Ryogoku
Public Hall

Reconstruction
Memorial Hall

Nikolai
Cathedral
Ochanomizu
Akihabara

Sumida-gawa

Ryogoku-
bashi
Kokugikan
(Sumo Arena) **20**

Fukagawa
Edo Tokyo
Museum

Kudanshita
Jimbocho
Shin-
Ochanomizu

KANDA
Awajicho
Iwamotocho
Yasukuni
Dori

Bakuro
Higashi-
Nihombashi
Keiyo
Ryogoku **21**

RYOGOKU

Nippon
Bodukan
Science
Museum **18**
Ogawamachi
Transportation
Museum

Kanda
YMCA
Kanda

Expressway No. 7

KITANOMARU
KOEN

Chidorigafuchi
(Military Cemetery)

Kokuritsu Kindai
Bijutsukan
(Mus. of Modern Art)
Inuimon
Takebashi

Expressway
No. 5
Kanda
Edo Dori
Kodenmacho
Hamacho
Morishita

KOEN **5**
Sotobori Dori

Hibiya
Dori

Shin
Ohashi-
bashi

KOKYO HIGASHI
GYOEN **4**
Otemon
Communications
Museum

Bank of
Japan
Ningyocho
Basho
Memorial Hall

Hanzomon
Otemachi
OTEMACHI
Mitsukoshimae
NIHOMBASHI
Shin Ohashi Dori
Nakamura
Gakuen

Kokyo
(Imperial Palace) **1**

Palace
Hotel
Currency
Museum
Mitsukoshimae
Suitengumae
Royal Park
Hotel
KIYOSUMI

Niju-bashi **3**
Nijubashimae
Tekko
Building
Nihombashi
Nihom-bashi **16**

Tokyo-eki
(Station)
Tokyo **7**
Nihombashi
Yamatane
Museum

TCAT (Tokyo City
Air Terminal) **17**

NIJU-BASHI
KOKYO
GAIEN **2**
MARUNOUCHI
YAESU
Yaesu
Kayabacho

Sumidagawa- Expressway
Sumidagawa-
ohashi
No. 9

Sakuradamon
Tokyo
International
Forum **8**
Nijubashimae
Sotobori Dori
Chuo
Dori
Showa
Dori
Shin Ohashi Dori
Eitai-bashi
KOTO-KU

Metropolitan Police
Departement H.Q.
Harumi
Dori
Yurakucho
Kyobashi
Hatchobori
Eitai

Hojo-in

Kokkai-
gijidomae

Hibiya Dori

Yurakucho-eki
(Station) **9**
Takaracho
Hotel Seiyo
Ginza
Hibiya
Ginza-Itchome
CHUO-KU
Monzennakacho
Tomioka
Hachimangu

Kasumigaseki
HIBIYA
Hibiya
Ginza
Church
Higashi-
Ginza
MINATO
ETCHIMA
Eitai
Dori

Min. of
Finance
KOEN
Ginza
GINZA
Shintomicho
TSUKUDA
KOEN
Kiyosumi Dori
BOTAN

Toranomon
Min. of Int.
Trade & Ind.
Imperial
Hotel **12**
Sony
Building **11**
Ginza 4-chome **10**
Ginza 4-chome

Uchisaiwaicho

Sumida-
ohashi

Kachidoki-
bashi

Kabuki-za **14**
Tsukiji
Nishi
Hongan-ji

Tsukuda-
ohashi
Sumiyoshi-
jinja

Atago-jinja
Shimbashi
Higashi-
Ginza

Shimbashi
Gekujo
Tsukishima
Tsukishima-
bashi

Seishoji
Shimbashi
Sendai-
bashi
Shin
Ohashi
TSUKISHIMA

SHIMBASHI
TSUKIJI **15**

Onarimon
Tsukiji
Fish Market

Shiba-
Daijingu
Daimon

Harumi
Dori

Sumida-gawa
Harumi-bashi

HAMA RIKYU
GAIEN

Kiyosumi
Mitsume Dori

SHIBA
RIKYU
GAIEN
Rinkai Fukutoshin
(Ocean Center)
Kiyosumi Dori

Toyosu

TOKYO

Vying with Mexico City as the world's largest city, the Tokyo metropolitan area and its 30 million people exist in the former capital of the shoguns – and on an earthquake zone

Map on pages 152–3

Japan has always been a country of villages. If Tokyo is Japan's biggest village – and it is by far at over 620 sq. km (240 sq. miles) and 10 million people in central Tokyo alone – then one can easily reduce Tokyo itself into a gathering of smaller villages anchored around major train stations. Indeed, these stations are helpful for understanding Tokyo's layout, which doesn't have a central urban core.

Most of Tokyo's smaller "villages" lie on a circular rail line called Yamanote-sen, or Yamanote Line. There are 29 stations on the Yamanote and it takes about an hour to make the complete loop, actually an oval in shape. Look at the layout of the Yamanote-sen, and of the placement of the stations along the way, and orientation in Tokyo becomes so much easier. The important stations on the line – and the ones with which to become most familiar – are Tokyo, Ueno, Shinjuku, and Shibuya. In the centre of the oval defined by the Yamanote-sen, a bit off-centre to the east, are the grounds of what once was the Edo castle. The Imperial Palace has replaced the castle, but the old symmetry of the castle defenses – moats and gates – are evident still today.

In all cases, most of Tokyo is accessible by one station or another, by one train or subway line, or many. Use them. They're fast, cheap and utilitarian. Just stay off the trains during rush-hour for obvious reasons. Or walk. Only then do the many of Tokyo's villages feel connected, giving a sense of the big village, of Tokyo itself.

LEFT: Harajuku's Takeshita-dori.
BELOW: back alley in Shinjuku.

Imperial Palace

In the centre of Tokyo is the **Imperial Palace**, or **Kokyo ❶**, a functional palace where the emperor and his family reside. Much of the palace grounds – including the palace itself – are closed to the public and secluded behind massive stone walls, old trees and Edo-Period moats. (The best view of the grounds is from the observation windows on the 36th floor of the Kasumigaseki Building, a tall office tower about one kilometre south of the palace and in the government district of Kasumigaseki.)

Most of the 110-hectare (270-acre) palace complex is forested or given to private gardens and small ponds. The Showa emperor (Hirohito), who reigned from 1926 until 1989, was a skilled biologist and much of the inner garden area is a nature preserve. The Imperial Palace building itself is an expansive, low building of concrete veiled with a green roof. It was completed in 1970 to replace the wooden residence destroyed in a 1945 Allied air raid.

Kokyo Gaien ❷, the palace's outer garden to the southeast, is an expansive area of green and impec-

cably sculpted pine trees planted in 1889. Directly east is Tokyo Station. Kokyo Gaien is where most tourists come for their obligatory photograph. A large, gravel-covered area leads to a famous postcard scenic – literally – of **Niju-bashi** ❸, a distinctive bridge across an inner moat and one of the most widely recognised landmarks in Japan. Tourists come here by the bus-loads for a group portrait in front of the bridge (*bashi*) and moat. Niju-bashi is both elegant and a functional entrance – the main gate – into the palace grounds, but it is definitely not open to the public, except on New Year's Day and the emperor's birthday, when the public is allowed to cross Niju-bashi and stand near the imperial residence to receive greetings from the emperor. Behind is **Fushimi-yagura**, a lookout turret of the original Edo castle. Parts of the outer grounds were unpleasant places in 1945 immediately after the Showa emperor (Hirohito) announced Japan's surrender on the radio. (In fact, it was the first time that the people had heard his voice.) Numerous loyal soldiers, refusing to admit surrender or defeat to the Allies, disembowelled themselves outside the palace.

Visitors are also permitted in the **Kokyo Higashi Gyoen** ❹, the East Imperial Garden of the palace. It is open most days and can be entered through Ote-mon, Hirakawa-mon and Kitahanebashi-mon, three of the eight gates (*mon*) into the palace grounds. Inside are remains of the defenses of Edo-jo, the shogunate's castle (*jo*), and the foundations of the castle's *donjon*, the primary lookout tower of the shogun's residence.

The castle itself, Edo-jo, was constructed of granite and basaltic rocks quarried at Izu Peninsula, a hundred kilometres south. Several thousand boats made the two-week roundtrip carrying immense stones. Off-loaded near Kanda to the north, the stones were dragged on sleds – often with seaweed laid underneath

Tokyo was the world's largest city with over 1 million people in the 17th century. Following World War II, the population was around 3 million. By 1970 it had reached 9 million.

BELOW: Niju-bashi and Fushimi-yagura.

Map on pages 152–3

for lubrication – by oxen and men provided by the shogun's warlords, always eager to impress the shogun. Half a century later, around 1640, the Edo castle was completed. But less than two decades later, it was reduced to ashes in a fire.

Covering about 2 sq. km (0.8 sq. mile), the castle's inner compound had four fortresses, or *maru*. Honmaru – or the inner citadel, and as the shogun's residence the most important maru – was also the highest. Just below Honmaru was the second fortress, Ninomaru, intended as a pleasant (but secure) place of retirement for the shogun in his twilight years. Southwest was Nishinomaru, the western fortress and where the Imperial Palace now stands. North was Kitanomaru, now a public park. Each fortress had its own defenses, which were buttressed by the adjacent fortress's defenses. In turn, the complex was protected by the moat system. Twenty-one guard towers, or *yagura*, lined the defenses; three still stand, including Fushimi-yagura near Niju-bashi. Unfortunately, today nothing substantial remains of the old Edo castle itself, except for the three turrets and the donjon foundations, not to mention the moats and gates. Nor are there surviving visual representations of the castle.

The Meiji emperor chose the shogunal castle site to be the new imperial residence and moved there in 1869 from Kyoto, the city that had been the imperial capital for more than a millennium. The new Imperial Palace was completed in 1889 of exquisitely designed wood, and the city was renamed Tokyo, or Eastern Capital. The palace has remained the residence of Japan's emperors since. (In 1945, the 1889 Meiji palace was destroyed in Allied bombing raids.)

At the northern part of the old castle grounds in **Kitanomaru-koen** is the **Kokuritsu Kindai Bijutsukan ❺** (**National Museum of Modern Art**; open Tuesday–Sunday, 10am–5pm; admission fee). The modern building displays

BELOW: painting the old castle moat.

GOJIRA VS. GODZILLA

To the Japanese, Godzilla isn't some huge, lumbering, atomic-born giant lizard. He's *their* huge, lumbering, atomic-born giant lizard. With the 22 movies since his debut in 1954's *Gojira* (a combination of the Japanese words for "gorilla" and "whale", anglicised to Godzilla for its U.S. release two years later), this monster is one of the most famous icons of postwar Japan. To some, the big-budget American version of *Godzilla* was heresy.

Still, the 1998 film did reasonably well in Japan. But reactions were less than positive. Said one Japanese: "Godzilla's personality is like the neighbourhood *oyaji* (middle-aged man) who's friendly and grumpy at the same time. Godzilla kicks down Tokyo over and over again like an oyaji kicks down a *chabudai* (low table) if he's in a bad mood." Says Eric Brevig of George Lucas's Industrial Light and Magic: "Japanese monster movies like Godzilla are charming in that there's an agreement between film-maker and audience to look past such surface flaws as the fact that the monster is obviously being played by a guy in a rubber suit, and that there are visible wires holding up the airplanes attacking him. In America, we spend a fortune erasing those seams... Time is spent making something technically perfect, but empty in terms of its soul."

excellent examples of Japan's contemporary artists, many of whom studied in Europe earlier in the 20th century, in well-presented galleries.

West from Kitanomaru-koen, Yasukuni-dori leads to **Yasukuni-jinja ❻**. What is said to be Japan's largest *torii* – eight stories high, made of high-tension steel plates and weighing 100 tons – boldly announces the shrine. Its entrance nipping the northern tip of the Imperial Palace grounds, this Shinto shrine is Japan's most controversial. Proponents say it honours those who died for Japan and the emperor; opponents say it glorifies Japanese aggression and that it honours convicted war criminals. Pinched between the two extremes are politicians, who must decide whether or not to attend annual ceremonies at the shrine. When a prime minister does visit, governments throughout Asia respond in vocal disapproval.

Yasukuni-jinja's torii *is made of steel.*

The souls of more than 2½ million Japanese soldiers killed between 1868 (the shrine was founded in 1869) and World War II are enshrined at Yasukuni (lit. peaceful country). In the shrine's archives, the names, dates, and places of death for each soldier are recorded. The **Yushukan (War Memorial Museum**; open daily 9am–5pm; admission fee), part of Yasukuni-jinja, includes samurai armour, *kamikaze* memorabilia, and a rocket-propelled kamikaze winged bomb.

Tokyo Station, Ginza, and Nihombashi

BELOW: soldiers killed in the name of the emperor are enshrined at Yasukuni-jinja.

Directly east from the Imperial Palace and Kokyo Gaien is the **Marunouchi** district, once an inlet of Tokyo Bay, its waters extending almost up to where the Palace Hotel now sits. Marunouchi is old feudal land-fill; numerous shogunate engineering projects left a lot of excavated dirt. Atop this land-fill of Marunouchi – meaning "inside the wall" of the Edo castle fortifications – an exclusive res-

idential area for Tokugawa samurai lords was created in the early 17th century. Known as Daimyo Koji, or the Little Lanes of the Great Lords, Marunouchi served not only as a buffer between the shogun's castle and the outside world of commoners but also permitted the shogun to keep an eye on his provincial warlords, whom he required to live in Edo on a rotating basis. Today it is filled with corporate headquarters and government offices.

A wide boulevard slices through these corporate buildings from the grounds of the Imperial Palace to **Tokyo-eki ❼** (**Tokyo Station**). While not Japan's busiest station – Shinjuku is quite possessive of the honour – Tokyo Station is nonetheless sizable with 19 platforms side by side, including the terminus for the *shinkansen* (lit. new trunk line), or bullet train. Deep beneath the station are additional platforms for more subway and JR lines.

The Marunouchi side of the station is fronted by the original Tokyo Station, built in 1914 of red brick in an Old World, European style. Air raids in 1945 damaged the station, taking off the top floors; renovations, finished in 1947, left it somewhat lower.

On the other side of Tokyo Station, the **Yaesu** entrance opens onto a boulevard of rather undistinguished office buildings, many of them banks and corporate headquarters. Extending from the Yaesu central exit is Yaesu-dori, which intersects the major arteries of Chuo-dori and Showa-dori, running south to Ginza and north to Ueno.

Immediately south of Tokyo Station is the **Tokyo International Forum ❽**, an echoing complex of concert and exhibition halls. There is a **Tourist Information Centre** (open Monday–Friday, 9am–5pm, Saturday, 9am–noon; tel: 03 3201 3331) here, in the basement. If expecting to travel in Japan, visit this cen-

Map on pages 152–3

Two prime ministers were assassinated in Tokyo Station during the 20th century.

BELOW: station rush hour, and the original side of Tokyo Station.

BELOW:
famous Ginza 4-chome in the rain.

tre for extensive information about Japan, whether walking tours through Tokyo or lodging in Okinawa. The staff speaks English and offers more printed information than can be stuffed into a ragged backpack. South again are elevated train tracks extending from **Yurakucho-eki ❾** (**Yurakucho Station**), constructed in 1910; the shinkansen and Yamanote-sen trains snake along the overhead tracks.

An elevated expressway over Harumi-dori defines the boundary between Ginza and Yurakucho. Towering on the opposite side of the expressway are the tall, curving exteriors of the Seibu and Hankyu department stores, anchored at the ground by a musical clock and a hard-to-miss (or ignore) police box.

Of all places in Japan, **Ginza** has perhaps the greatest name recognition in the world after Tokyo and Kyoto. During the super-heated bubble economy of the late 1980s, land in Ginza was literally priceless, the most expensive real estate anywhere and priced in square centimetres. Likewise, an evening's entertainment in the exclusive and unmarked clubs of its back alleys too seemed nearly priceless – and still is.

Ginza derives its name from *gin*, or silver. Japan once used three different coinage systems, each based upon silver, gold and copper. Tokugawa Ieyasu decided to simplify the system to only silver. In 1612, he relocated the official mint from the countryside to Ginza. Two centuries later, the mint was once again shifted, to Nihombashi, but the name of Ginza stayed.

The Mitsukoshi store anchors **Ginza 4-chome ❿**, where Chuo-dori intersects Harumi-dori, the second main avenue (*dori*). (Most Tokyo districts are subdivided into *chome*; Ginza has eight.) Chuo-dori, sometimes called Ginza-dori, is one of two main arteries through Ginza and extends northward to the east of Tokyo Station and into Nihombashi. A few blocks past the overpass sepa-

Map on pages 152–3

rating Ginza from Nihombashi and Yaesu is a monument to the original site of Ginza. Further on, numerous fashionable boutiques and galleries line the wide boulevard. Immense department stores – including Matsuya (Ginza's largest) and Mitsukoshi (founded in 1673, with the current Ginza store dating from 1930) – cascade onto the sidewalks. Ginza's potential for shopping abounds.

A popular meeting place is the **Sony Building ⑪** – note the waiting and expectant faces outside; inside are the latest in consumer electronics and a Toyota showroom. In the alleys southwest of Harumi-dori are numerous art galleries with offerings of the highest calibre. (Take the platinum card.)

Along Hibiya-dori is the towering **Imperial Hotel ⑫** (**Teikoku Hoteru**). Always a place of impeccable standards by which other hotels are measured, the first Imperial Hotel opened in 1890. Its modest structure was later replaced by a wonderful Frank Lloyd Wright design; the day after it opened to the public in 1923, the destructive Great Kanto Earthquake hit Tokyo. The hotel was one of the few structures to escape destruction. The Wright building was replaced by the modern structure in 1970. It's indeed a shame the Wright building wasn't kept in Tokyo. (It is now in Nagoya, reassembled as before.) Across from the Imperial Hotel, **Hibiya-koen ⑬** (**Hibiya Park**) was Japan's first European-style plaza, opened in 1903. It quickly became a popular venue for rallies and demonstrations against rises in rice prices during the early 1900s. A significant number of homeless people live here, though not to the degree as in Ueno-koen.

Harumi-dori extends from Hibiya-koen back down through Ginza 4-chome and Tsukiji and across the Sumida-gawa, Tokyo's barely accessible river (*gawa* or *kawa*). Along Harumi-dori, just past Showa-dori, the **Kabuki-za ⑭** is clearly a venue of *kabuki*, with performances that are nearly eternally ongoing. The

Kabuki-za.

BELOW: Ginza's Chuo-dori.

current building was constructed in 1925 in what is known as the Momoyama style, which has roots in the castles of the late 1600s.

Closer towards the Sumida-gawa is **Tsukiji** ⑮ and its wholesale fish market (*chuo oroshiuri ichiba*), where merchants arrive long before dawn to select the best of the day's fresh catch. Other produce is also auctioned here; in fact, there is a storage refrigerator here large enough to chill ten days' food supply for the entire city. Any edible creature of the sea is auctioned here. To see the best, arrive before 5 o'clock in the morning.

Tsukiji means, simply, "built land". And indeed it was Edo-Period land-fill that pushed back the shoreline of Tokyo Bay. As with Marunouchi, another land-fill area near the Imperial Palace, the newly created land was set aside for samurai estates, although of lower ranking than Marunouchi. In the mid-1800s, a part of Tsukiji was set aside for foreigners and a hotel was constructed. Apparently it was quite dapper, with more than 100 rooms and a billiards parlour; a few years later, it burned to the ground and was left that way.

Woodblock print of Nihom-bashi during the Edo Period.

Returning north to the Yaesu side of Tokyo Station, Chuo-dori crosses Nihom-bashi-gawa over **Nihom-bashi** ⑯ (**Nihon Bridge**; the Nihom/Nihon variation is a phonetic one of pronunciation, not meaning.) An infuriatingly ugly elevated Shuto Expressway directly above was erected for the 1964 Tokyo Olympics. Both the concrete-lined river and expressway diminish the significance of the original 1603 arched wooden bridge that was the centre of Edo-Period Tokyo and the zero point for the five main roads leading out of Edo to the rest of Japan. The present stone bridge, dating from 1911, retains little – if none – of its Edo-Period ambience. Still, embellishments like bronze Chinese lions and granite sidewalks distinguish this bridge from most of Tokyo's ster-

BELOW: fish market at Tsukiji.

Map on pages 152–3

ile concrete-and-steel bridges. **Nihombashi,** as the area came to be known, was a stage of gossip, announcements, and public humiliation. Murderers condemned to crucifixion were allowed an alternative, whether they liked it or not. The condemned were buried in the ground near the bridge with only neck and head exposed. Lines were drawn on the neck and two saws left on either side. Any passers-by so inclined could saw off the murderer's head. Painful, but quicker than crucifixion.

On the eastern periphery of Nihombashi, towards the Sumida-gawa, the **Tokyo City Air Terminal ⓱** (TCAT) is a downtown check-in facility for flights departing the international airport at Narita. Not only can airline and baggage check-in be done here, but clearance of immigration, too. A nonstop limousine bus goes to Narita, with minimal hassles at Narita immigration. (And the lines at Narita's immigration counters can get long.)

Haneda Airport, near downtown Tokyo, is used only for domestic flights, but some China Airlines flights use Haneda.

Kanda and Akihabara

If there is a book, however old and in whatever language, that seems unattainable, it can be found in **Kanda ⓲,** especially around the Jimbocho station. There are stores specialising in art books, second-hand books, comic books – in English, French, German, Russian... Anything and everything. The bookshops have been in Kanda since the 1880s, nearly as long as the nearby universities. Many of the early book printers established their shops in Kanda, followed later by several of the most famous publishers in Japan.

The neighbourhood of **Akihabara ⓳** epitomises the old Edo tradition of merchants or craftsmen of a particular commodity congregating together. Indeed, Akihabara is singularly devoted to the sales of electrical and electronic things.

BELOW: shop in Akihabara, and a "pencil" building making the best of space in Tokyo.

Today its prices may be the cheapest in Japan, but rarely do they beat prices of similar components for sale overseas. The only reason to buy something in Akihabara is if it's not for sale overseas. Akihabara's fame for electrical things originated shortly after World War II, when a black market for scarce electrical and radio components evolved near the station. Now, Akihabara accounts for around 10 percent of Japan's domestic electrical and electronic sales.

East of Akihabara and on the other side of the Sumida-gawa, the area known as **Ryogoku** is the site of Tokyo's sumo arena, **Kokugikan** ❷⓪. A lot of very large men live in Ryogoku – it is the home of many of the sumo *beya*, or stables, as the training centres/dormitories for the *rikishi*, or wrestlers, are called.

Behind the Kokugikan is the **Fukagawa Edo Tokyo Museum** ❷① (open Tuesday–Sunday, 10am–6pm; admission fee), a spectacular hall that encompasses a massive reconstruction of a part of *shitamachi* Edo from the 19th century. It is like walking onto the set of a samurai drama; there is even a lifelike dog relieving himself by the guard tower. Every 20 minutes, the lighting cycles through night and day. There are intricately constructed models of villages and a life-size reconstruction of Nihom-bashi, the Edo-Period bridge. It is one of the finest museums in Japan, well-planned and meticulously thought out. A hall for concerts and public performances is attached.

Ueno and Asakasa

North of Tokyo Station and Akihabara, exactly eight minutes on the Yamanote train, is **Ueno-eki** ❷② (**Ueno Station**). It's a subjective and subtle impression, but the area around the station seems somehow more down to earth, if not grittier, than other parts of urban Tokyo. It was once the commoner's part of town, in

Banners outside the Kokugikan with the names of tournament sumo wrestlers.

BELOW: Fukagawa Edo Tokyo Museum.

what was called Shitamachi. Nowadays there's an aspect of urban life around Ueno not typically noticeable in Japan – the homeless men who camp out in Ueno-koen, a tired park lacking the showcase polish expected of an urban park in one of the world's richest cities, or the foreigners on expired visas hustling passers-by with counterfeit telephone cards.

West of the station, **Ueno-koen (Ueno Park)** is nonetheless Tokyo's most distinctly "park" park: sprawling grounds with trees, flocks of scrounging pigeons, monuments and statues, homeless Japanese, a zoo (less than inspiring), a big pond with lilies and waterfowl, and national museums. It's not quite as tidy and pristine as one might expect in Japan; the park is in need of scrubbing and many more trash cans, always a scarce item in Japan.

But the park is a fine place for people-watching, especially on weekends when people take a few hours to play. In the spring, Ueno-koen is cherished amongst Japanese for its blossoming cherry trees. The idea of blossom-viewing – *hanami*, a tradition extending back centuries – seems aesthetically appealing; in fact, it is often a drunken and crowded party with few serene moments.

The **Tosho-gu** ㉓, a shrine adjacent to a five-storied pagoda, was established in 1627 (the present buildings date from a 1651 renovation) by a warlord on his own estate to honour the first Tokugawa shogunate, Tokugawa Ieyasu. The walkway to Tosho-gu (lit. Illuminator of the East) is lined with dozens of large, symbolic stone or copper free-standing lanterns, all donated by warlords from throughout the land to cultivate a little merit with the shogun. (Lanterns such as these are simply symbolic and not used for illumination.) Although not as embellished as it was in the Edo Period, the main shrine building is still a magnificent, ornate building. The outer hall features murals painted by the famous

Map on pages 152–3

TIP

Beware of illegal immigrant hustlers on the streets between Ueno Station and the Keisei Skyliner Station (with express trains to Narita). Whatever they are offering, it's fake.

BELOW: saving a place for *hanami* in Ueno Park, and Shinobazu Pond.

Edo artist Kano Tanyu. Also interesting is the Chinese-style Kara-mon, a gate decorated with dragons that are meant to be ascending to and descending from heaven. It's said that the dragons slither over to the park's pond, Shinobazu-no-ike, under the cover of night to drink.

Tokyo is short on land, and over the years there have been proposals to use Shinobazu for other purposes. Recent suggestions include building a parking garage beneath the pond; for now, the plan is just a plan.

Shinobazu-no-ike (Shinobazu Pond) was once an inlet and is now a pond (*ike*) dense with lily plants. A small peninsula juts into the pond with a Buddhist temple to Benten – a goddess of good fortune and the only female amongst the Seven Deities of Good Luck – perched on the end. A promenade follows the pond's squarish 2-km (1¼-mile) circumference. The **Shitamachi Fuzoku Shiryokan ㉔ (Shitamachi Museum**; open Tuesday–Sunday 9.30am–4.30pm; admission fee), near the pond at the park's south entrance, is a hands-on exhibit of Edo commoners' daily life in Shitamachi, as this part of Edo Tokyo was once known. (Children typically love this museum.)

The **Kokuritsu Seiyo Bijutsukan ㉕ (National Museum of Western Art**; open Tuesday–Sunday, 9.30am–5pm; admission fee) is anchored by a collection of nearly a thousand pieces, ranging from the Renaissance to the contemporary and including Gauguin, Rubens, and Jackson Pollock, not to mention several sculptures by Rodin and a sizeable collection of 19th-century French art. The **Tokyo Kokuritsu Hakubutsukan ㉖ (Tokyo National Museum**; open Tuesday–Sunday, 9am–4.30pm; admission fee) offers a superbly displayed collection of Asian art and archaeology. Holding the extensive Japanese collection, the main hall dates from 1937. Arching over the outside entrance to the museum grounds is an immense samurai-estate gate.

West of Ueno is the most prestigious of Japanese universities, **Tokyo Daigaku (Tokyo University)**, founded in 1869 and usually called Todai. Competition to

BELOW: Tokyo National Museum.

enter is fearsome, devouring the youth of many children preparing for exams.

From the mid-1800s until World War II, **Asakusa** was the centre of all fine things in Tokyo, a cultural nucleus of theatre and literature, and of cuisine and the sensual delights. Imagine today's Shibuya, Ginza, Roppongi, and Shinjuku tossed together, countrified and without the benefit of neon, fast-food, and loud-speakers. Asakusa's cultural and social flowering began with exile – first with the banishment to Asakusa of the Yoshiwara, or the licensed prostitution district (the name followed the ladies) in the 1600s, and then later with that of theatre, especially kabuki, in the 1800s.

Located to the northeast outside of the Edo gates, the Asakusa area along the Sumida-gawa became a vigorous commercial port with wharves on the Sumida's bank, including an important rice depot for the shogun.

The people of Asakusa (and of nearby Nihombashi, Kanda and Ueno) were known as Edokko, or people of Edo. Asakusa dripped with *iki*, a sense of style and urbane polish, and with *inase*, or gallantry. It was the place to be seen in Edo Tokyo, reaching a critical mass in the 1800s.

Anchoring Asakusa was **Senso-ji**, or **Asakusa Kannon** ㉗, perhaps the oldest Buddhist temple in the region and a draw for people from around Japan who brought with them spending money to make Asakusa prosper.

Old places always start with a legend. Asakusa's legend has it that Senso-ji was founded in AD 628 when two fishermen – brothers, actually – netted a small statue of Kannon, the deity of mercy. (In Buddhism, Kannon is typically male or neuter but exceedingly feminine in form and personality and often referred to in the feminine gender.) A temple was built by the village leader to house it. Around the time that the statue appeared, the legend continues, a great

Map on pages 152–3

Tokyo Daigaku, or Tokyo University.

BELOW: Senso-ji, Asakusa Kannon.

and golden dragon slithered its way down to earth from the heavens. The temple became a favourite of samurai and shoguns, and so it prospered economically and politically.

The south entrance to the temple, on Asakusa-dori, is a large gate, Kaminari-mon, or Thunder Gate, dating from 1960. (The original burned down a century before.) Here begins Nakamise-dori (lit. inside the shops), where two rows of red buildings funnel temple-goers northward through a souvenir arcade before spilling out onto the temple grounds.

In the other direction, east of Senso-ji, is the **Sumida-gawa** (**Sumida River**), which empties into Tokyo Bay. The exit for the Ginza Line, Tokyo's first subway line that opened in 1927, surfaces near the Azuma-bashi (Azuma Bridge). Just north of the bridge is **Sumida-koen**, a park intended to open up the river that passes through the old core of Tokyo.

Although the Sumida was an easily accessed and well used, if not commercially essential, river during the Edo Period and well into the early 1900s, until recently property along it was undesirable, as it was not considered a proper place in which to live.

With the lack of interest in the river, especially as its commercial and transport importance faded with industrialisation, most of the Sumida became inaccessible and hidden behind concrete. But as Japanese began travelling during the 1970s and 1980s, they returned with memories of romantic urban rivers in Europe. Only since the mid-1980s have efforts started to bring the Sumida back into the lives of Tokyo's residents. The park is a pleasant stroll, especially in spring when the cherry trees are blooming, but benches in the park are often draped with the homeless.

Schoolgirls posing at Senso-ji's south gate, Kaminari-mon.

BELOW: summer fireworks on the Sumida, and Asakusa festival.

Roppongi and Minato

In the lower middle of the oval defined by the Yamanote-sen and just to the southwest of the Imperial Palace is an area favoured by Tokyo's expatriate community: **Minato-ku**, a Tokyo ward (*ku*) made up of Aoyama, Akasaka, Roppongi, Azabu and Hiroo. The area is peppered with embassies and high-priced expatriate (and company-subsidised) housing – US$10,000 a month is not unusual – and liberally spiced with nightclubs and restaurants.

Up on a hill, **Roppongi** ❷ is the heart of the area's social life and nightlife and courting life. It crawls with both foreigners and Japanese on the prowl for the opposite sex. Its main avenues are bright and loud, the back alleys lined with drinking establishments laced by themes meant to nurture nostalgia or homesickness in strangers in a strange land. But don't confuse the activity here with the blatant sex trade of Shinjuku's Kabukicho. In Roppongi, it's only upscale food and drinks garnished by probing smiles.

Roppongi means "six trees". There may have been six trees here, perhaps pine, at one time. Another possibility for the name are the six samurai lords who had estates here during the Edo Period. Each of their names was related to trees: Aoki, or Green Tree, for example. Roppongi later became a garrison town for the Meiji government, and later, after World War II, the American army established barracks here. With a steady turnover of hormonal young soldiers, together with the embassy staffs in nearby Azabu and Akasaka, Roppongi was a natural crossroads for nightlife.

East of Roppongi along the roadway towards the Imperial Palace, the **Ark Hills** complex of offices, apartments and stores is the work of Mori Taikichiro. Riding the real estate boom of the 1970s and 1980s, he advocated urban rede-

Map on pages 152–3

BELOW: seeking a cozy evening in Roppongi.

Tower of Ark Hills, looking west towards Roppongi.

velopment and replaced some of the claustrophobic neighbourhoods of Tokyo with modern complexes. Mori made most of his US$13 billion of wealth after retiring at age 55 from academia. At his death in 1993, he owned more than 80 buildings in central Tokyo and was then considered the world's richest private citizen. Most of his buildings he named after himself, such as Mori Building 25.

Check the horizon to the south, towards the area known as Shiba: the red-and-white **Tokyo Tower ㉙** (open daily, 9am–8pm; admission fee) juts skyward, looking industrial and out of place. Finished in 1958, its primary purpose was to broadcast television signals. Subsequent lyrical allusions to the Eiffel Tower or urban elegance were fabrications of creative writing. It's an ugly projection into the skyline – 333 metres (1,093 ft) – but views from the observation deck at 250 metres (820 ft) are excellent.

Tokyo-wan (Tokyo Bay) has shrunk over the centuries from extensive land-fill. The shoguns did it for housing of their samurai, while politicians have done it in the past decades for glory and pork-barrel. In the late 1980s, grand plans were hatched to create a futuristic mini-city, **Rinkai Fukutoshin (Oceanfront Sub-city Centre)** on new land-fill, to be inaugurated during a planned 1996 international exposition. It was a massive white elephant and an obvious waste of money, and a newly elected governor of Tokyo (and former television comedian) cancelled the exposition. (Experts fear liquification of the land-fill when the next big earthquake hits Tokyo.) Still, the buildings that were completed are rather magnificent and can be seen from a monorail that leaves Shimbashi Station for the artificial islands over the **Rainbow Bridge**. In addition to hotels and office buildings, there are a ship-shaped Museum of Maritime Sciences, restaurants, and Tokyo's very own Statue of Liberty.

BELOW: Tokyo Tower from across Tokyo Bay.

Shibuya and Harajuku

Although many resident foreigners might nominate Roppongi to the east, **Shibuya** is one of the trendiest commercial neighbourhoods in Tokyo. (Roppongi caters to foreigners and has done so with style for decades. Shibuya, on the other hand, caters to Japanese youth with money to spend and style to flaunt.)

Shibuya was a rural but bustling stop along one of the great highways built during the Tokugawa years and leading from Edo Tokyo. Later, mulberry (for an abortive attempt at silk production) and tea fields surrounded Shibuya's first train station, which opened in 1885. Nearby, along the Shibuya-gawa, were mills powered by water wheels.

Several private rail lines opened in the subsequent years, each with its own station. Finally, all the stations were consolidated at the current site of **Shibuya-eki ㉚ (Shibuya Station)** in 1920. The most popular exit of Shibuya Station, opening to the northwest, is named after a hound dog. And outside of that entrance one will find a statue erected in 1964 of said dog, an Akita named Hachiko. For a rendezvous in Shibuya, Hachiko's statue is the preferred spot.

While the story of Hachiko may seem rather trite and insignificant to the Westerner, every Japanese knows the story of Hachiko, ad nauseam, from movies, television, novels, and an expanding legend that

refuses to fade into history. Stay in Tokyo long enough and the story of this dog turns increasingly tedious. Nonetheless, the story goes like this: In the 1920s, Hachiko would follow her master, a professor at the Imperial University, to the station. In the evenings, Hachiko would meet her returning master. One day, the master returned no more. He had died. Yet Hachiko waited and waited, returning night after night, year after year, until she herself died. Japanese love the story, but there are some doubts about its authenticity. Enough of Hachiko.

Beyond the Hachiko entrance is an immense intersection. Looking straight ahead, note the tall cylindrical building: the Shibuya 109 building and a good reference for orientation. The crowded road to its right leads up a gentle hill to Tokyu department store, and adjacent to it, the **Bunkamura**, a performance hall built during the roaring 1980s. Something's always going on inside – art, music, cinema, theatre – and the interior spaces are refreshing on a hot day.

At the top of the hill to the left is the huge **NHK Broadcast Centre ❸**, a 23-story building with two dozen TV studios and an equal number of radio studios. NHK is the government-run, viewer-subsidised (or taxed, more accurately – if one has a television, one must pay the NHK tax) television and radio broadcaster. In addition to two subscription satellite channels, there is the standard NHK broadcast channel and an educational channel, with dowdy professors and chalkboards and charts of chemical molecules. More than 1,500 shows are produced in the broadcast centre weekly.

Open to the public inside the centre is the **NHK Studio Park**, a well-designed introduction to television broadcasting with a number of interactive exhibits. Overhead observation windows look down upon sets for the ever-popular samurai dramas, which in fact rarely seem to be in production during visitor hours.

Map on pages 152–3

TIP

To see Japanese consumerism at its most diverse, visit Shibuya's Tokyu Hands store. Imagine something and you'll find it here – whether pots and pans, expensive leather goods, lapidary equipment and even rocks, furniture, or traditional Japanese tools for woodworking.

BELOW: Shibuya's main intersection.

Nearby **Yoyogi-koen** ㉜ served as the Olympic Village during the 1964 summer games. Previously, the area was a barracks called Washington Heights for the American army. Everything was eventually torn down, but rather than erecting something new, the site was turned into the park. It now includes a wild bird park and playground. Yoyogi gained notoriety for some of the worst free music and punkiest or Elvis-ised adolescents. Wannabe rock groups gave weekend "concerts" on a closed-off street, all playing at the same time and hoping to establish a following of adolescent girls that would cascade into Japan-wide popularity. The city government put an end to the well-planned spontaneity.

Yoyogi-koen is an extension of one of Japan's most famous Shinto shrines, **Meiji-jingu** ㉝. The shrine deifies Emperor Meiji and Empress Shoken. (Their remains, however, are in Kyoto.) The emperor, of course, was restored to rule in the 1868 Meiji Restoration when the Tokugawa shogunate collapsed. The emperor died in 1912 and the empress two years later. The original shrine, built in 1920, was destroyed during World War II; the current shrine buildings were reconstructed in 1958. The shrine itself is constructed of Japanese cypress.

The shrine's grounds cover 70 hectares (175 acres) and were a favourite retreat of the emperor. The park is populated by nearly every species of tree growing in Japan, all of the trees donations to the shrine. The long walk to the shrine passes through a tunnel of these trees and beneath three large torii gates, said to include one of the largest wooden gates in Japan: 12 metres (40 ft) high with pillars more than a metre in diameter. Cypress wood over 1,700 years old from Taiwan was used for the gate.

The entrance to Meiji-jingu is near **Harajuku-eki** ㉞ (**Harajuku Station**), architecturally interesting for a Japanese train station. Leading from the station are a number of hip and groovy avenues. (Harajuku itself was once a post station on the road from Kamakura in the less-hip 11th century.) For some reason, probably its proximity to once-outrageous Yoyogi-koen, narrow Takeshita-dori, a small side street between the station and Meiji-dori, has become a teeny-bopper avenue of shops. It lacks breathing room on weekends. (*See picture on page 154.*)

More room is found instead on the wide and upscale **Omote-sando** ㉟, a boulevard running from the southern end of Harajuku Station. Omote-sando has a European feel about it from the expansiveness of the boulevard (at least for Japan) to the zelkovea trees that line it. Even the architecture of some older buildings lends a cosmopolitan air. In summer, outdoor cafes with suave-sounding French names offer expensive coffees and draw a decidedly expensive crowd.

Shinjuku

After building Edo castle and settling down, Tokugawa Ieyasu had the **Shinjuku** area surveyed at the urging of some entrepreneurs. He then established a guard post – near today's Shinjuku 2-chome – along the Koshu Kaido, a road that led west into the mountains. Shinjuku (lit. new lodging) quickly became one of the largest urban towns in Edo, filled with shopkeepers, wholesale distributors, inns, and tea houses. Shinjuku was also known for the male sensual

Emperor Meiji was a strong supporter of adopting Western ideas and technology. He wore Western clothing and enjoyed Western food. He also composed nearly 100,000 poems in traditional style and ordered the annexation of Korea in 1910.

BELOW: shopping in trendy Harajuku.

delights, with 50 "inns" catered by "serving girls". Unlike those in Asakusa, the women of Shinjuku were without licenses and considered downscale.

In its early days, when the rail line through Shinjuku was but 21 km (13 miles) long, only about 50 people used the station at Shinjuku daily. Surrounding the wooden station was a forest of trees. The year was 1885. Nowadays, it's said by the Japanese that **Shinjuku-eki ㊱ (Shinjuku Station)** is the world's busiest train station. Maybe, maybe not, given the Japanese propensity for superlatives. Let there be no doubt, however: it is a furiously busy place – approaching 3 million people daily – and congested, and if one is unfamiliar with the station, patience can melt within minutes.

Shinjuku Station is one of the most important stations in Japan, a major transfer point for both metropolitan and regional trains and for subways. As with most large urban stations in Japan, there are multitudinous shops and restaurants filling every unused space in the multilevel labyrinth above and below ground. There are also four massive department stores within Shinjuku Station itself, two of which have their own private train lines leading from Shinjuku: Keio, with a line that opened in 1915, and Odakyu, its line beginning in 1927.

Japanese trains wait for no one. On busy lines, they are timed to the second. During Tokyo's morning rush hour that peaks around 8am, a 10-car train with 3,000 severely compressed people stops at platforms for the Chuo and Yamanote lines every 90 seconds. Unloading and boarding times included, not to mention the time needed for the white-gloved wranglers to squeeze in the last passengers, there is but a 10- to 20-second window between trains. (Evening rush hour is less congested, as it's staggered throughout afternoon and night.)

If the four department stores within the station are somehow lacking, tumble

Map on pages 152–3

Map on pages 152–3

TIP

Japanese trains during rush hour can be plagued by *chikan*, or female-body gropers. Unfortunately, cultural norms and social expectations keep women from publicly castigating the chikan. (Instead, they will endure it until the next station stop.) Western women aren't exempt.

BELOW: east side of Shinjuku Station.

Map on pages 152–3

out the station's east entrance onto Shinjuku-dori, where there are more department stores and thousands of regular stores, and tens of thousands of people. This entrance of Shinjuku Station is a popular meeting and rendezvous spot. A small open plaza tempts the idle to linger, especially when there is something to watch on the immense outside television screen at Studio Alta. If a rendezvous has fizzled or has the possibility of doing so, pretending to watch the television – with blaring sound – helps to mask humiliation.

This side of the station is a superb rambling area, which one can do for hours with little purpose. Many of those who have a purpose enter **Kabukicho** ㉟, north of Yasukuni-dori. After World War II, residents of this area sought to establish a sophisticated entertainment area of cinemas and dance halls, and perhaps most importantly, a kabuki theatre. Hence, Kabukicho (*cho* means "ward" or "district"). But somewhat optimistically, naming of the neighbourhood preceded construction of any kabuki theatre, which was never built.

The cinemas were, however, and for many years Tokyo's best cinema-viewing was in Kabukicho; European films were very popular during the 1960s, especially with intellectuals and political radicals. Eventually they moved elsewhere, leaving Kabukicho to the *yakuza*. Kabukicho is famous nowadays for its sexual entertainment, which tends towards voyeurism rather than participation.

For more stately pursuits, follow Yasukuni-dori under the tracks to the west side of Shinjuku. (One could also exit the station directly to avoid the east side altogether.) Of most immediate interest are the numerous tall buildings on this side. Much of Tokyo is either alluvial soil or land-fill, both of which are geologically unstable foundations during earthquakes. (On the east side of the Sumida River, the soil has settled up to 3 metres or more in some areas due to the lowering of the groundwater level by industrial use.)

Kabukicho is also a notorious hangout for yakuza. Many of the "hostess" bars catering to Japanese men use women from Thailand and the Philippines, often as indentured labour.

OPPOSITE: towers in west Shinjuku.
BELOW: towers of Tokyo Metropolitan Government Office.

Given the shakiness of Tokyo's land, not to mention the experience of several devastating earthquakes, tall buildings in Tokyo have been limited. But Shinjuku sits atop rather solid ground, giving architects the confidence to build what they claim are earthquake-proof buildings that utilise sophisticated techniques for stress dissipation and structure stabilisation.

The twin towers of the **Tokyo Metropolitan Government Office** ㊳ were conceived and started at the beginning of the so-called bubble economy in the 1980s. They were intended to make a statement that Tokyo was now one of the world's great and most powerful cities. (Still, only 85 percent of Tokyo residences have access to sewage systems.) Around 13,000 city employees fill the buildings each day.

At the base of the main building is the Assembly Hall, separated from the main building by a semicircular, 5,000-sq.-metre (54,000 sq. ft) public plaza. Sculptures – mostly of naked women, a popular theme for public sculptures in Japan – grace the plaza. The main building has two upper towers. Finished in 1991, these two towers are 48 floors high, or 243 metres (797 ft). At the top of both towers, on the 45th floors at 202 metres (660 ft), expansive observation decks with cafeterias offer Tokyo's finest views (open Tuesday–Friday, 9.30am–5.30pm, weekends and holidays, 9.30am–7.30pm; free). ❏

JAPAN'S TRAINS TURN TRAVEL INTO AN ART

The shinkansen, *which means "new trunk line",*
is a technological symbol of Japan to the world,
but it's not the only train plying the islands.

The French have made a gallant effort to redefine what it is to have a fast train. But the Japanese simply do it better, and have been doing it longer ever since 1959, when construction of the Tokaido *shinkansen*, or bullet train, began. Five years later, service on the Tokaido line began between Tokyo and Osaka with 60 trains daily. And while the French TGV-A set the record for the fastest conventional train at 515 kmh (322 mph), that was just once. The fastest regularly scheduled train between two station stops is the JR500-series *Nozomi* (see top-centre photo) between Osaka and Fukuoka at over 300 kmh (185 mph).

The Japanese live by the train and play by the train, literally and figuratively. The highest real-estate values are found near the train station in any city, and entire mini-cities sprout near most stations. The Japanese love their trains, whether they admit it or not, and well they should. A train will take you nearly anywhere in the islands, to the remotest cape or valley.

For the Japanese, train travel is a life experience in itself in which the journey can be more important than the destination. Families will board the train and go on outings anywhere, and a train car can take on the ambience of a social club. Some will even charter a special train with *tatami*-mat cars and go nowhere in particular, just party in locomotive style.

The Japanese like to have the biggest, smallest, or fastest thing in the world. A Japanese "maglev" train, using electromagnetic rails, has been clocked at 550 kmh (344 mph).

△TAKE ME, I'M YOURS
Since Japan National Railways was broken into five regional lines in 1987, each line has tried to outdo the others with innovative and unusual designs.

▷ **WAITING**
Except during rush hour, queues are well-behaved and lacking in any overt excitement.

▷ **HIGH-BROW ADVERTS**
With a captive audience, often with nowhere to look but up, Japan's periodicals promote their latest weekly and monthly offerings from the rafters.

A PRIMER OF AMAZING FACTS

△ **NEVER LATE OR SLOW**
Shinkansen like the JR500-series above, Japan's fastest train, have an annual schedule deviation of 36 seconds, inclusive of the typhoon season and winter.

▽ **RAIL LUNCH**
Express trains offer food and beer, while local stations offer *ekiben*, a version of the *bento* "box" lunch made of local ingredients and packaging.

◁ **MAY I ASSIST, SIR?**
Not every train requires white-gloved wranglers, but they'll be found in Tokyo's busy stations – like Shinjuku – during the rush-hour crush.

According to Japan Railways (JR), on any given day there are 8,600 people – drivers, train staff, controllers, and maintenance engineers – involved in operating the Tokaido *shinkansen* line between Tokyo and Osaka. Each train carries 6.2 tons of water for drinking and flushing toilets, and each 16-car train carrying 1,300 passengers is 400 metres (1,300 ft) long.

Each 16-car train also requires 40 motors generating 12 megawatts to move it through the 66 tunnels that the shinkansen uses between Tokyo and Osaka. The longest of these is 8 km (5 miles) long. On the other hand, the shortest tunnel is but 30 metres (100 ft) long.

When the shinkansen is travelling at 270 kph (170 mph), it will take a little over 5 km (3 miles) to come to a complete stop. The strengthened glass in the windscreen of the shinkansen engine is 22 mm (0.9 in) thick, while the passenger windows are triple-glazed, with two outer layers of hardened glass and a 5 mm-thick inner pane separated from the outer panes by an air gap. It's a hardy train, indeed.

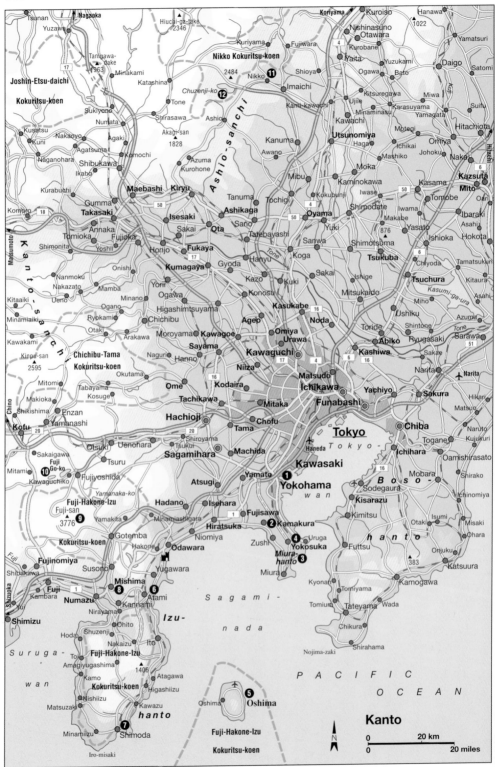

Kanto

0   20 km

0   20 miles

SOUTH OF TOKYO

Trains make travel outside of Tokyo easy. To the south are Yokohama, Kamakura, and the peninsulas of Miura and Izu, where hot springs are nurtured by the same fault that threatens Tokyo

Map on page 182

Tokyo

The very sound of **Yokohama ❶** is somehow exotic. And although the city today is both an integral part of the Greater Tokyo area and a major urban centre in its own right, Yokohama has a distinctive personality and even a mystique, much of it stemming from its vital role as one of the greatest international seaports of the Far East.

When Commodore Matthew Perry and his armada arrived in 1853, Yokohama was just a poor fishing village next to a smelly swamp. Under the terms of a treaty negotiated in 1858 by the first U.S. envoy to Japan, Townsend Harris, the port of Kanagawa, located on the Tokaido (the East Sea Road between Edo Tokyo and Kyoto), was to be opened to foreign settlement. But given its proximity to the important Tokaido, the shogunate reconsidered and built an artificial island on the mud flats of Yokohama instead for the foreigners.

That attempt to segregate the "red-haired barbarians" proved fortuitous for all concerned, since Yokohama's superb natural harbour helped international trade to flourish. The wild, early days of the predominantly male community centred around such recreational facilities as Dirty Village, the incomparable Gankiro Teahouse, and the local race track. Periodic attacks by sword-wielding, xenophobic *samurai* added to the lively atmosphere.

Eventually, foreign garrisons were brought in and the merchants could concentrate in a more sedate environment. Honcho-dori became the centre of commercial activities, and the wide street is still bracketed with banks and office buildings. With a population of more than 3 million, Yokohama is second in size only to Tokyo.

Happily, however, many of those areas worthy of exploring are concentrated in a relatively small area and can be covered for the most part by foot. Another aspect that makes Yokohama – only a 30-minute train ride from Tokyo – alluring is that its broad, relatively uncrowded streets (except on weekends) and laidback atmosphere provide a perfect antidote for Tokyo's claustrophobia and frantic pace.

Start a walking tour of central Yokohama at **Sakuragicho-eki (Sakuragicho Station)**, which is the terminus for the Toyoko Line originating at Tokyo's Shibuya Station. Sakuragicho was also the last stop on Japan's first railroad, which began service to Shimbashi in Tokyo in 1872. Other ways to get here from Tokyo are aboard the JR Yokosuka or Tokaido lines from Tokyo Station, or the Keihin-Kyuko Line from Shinagawa Station. In both cases, you have to transfer onto the Negishi Line at Yokohama Station.

Central Yokohama is now dominated by the mas-

PRECEDING PAGES: Mt Fuji and bullet train; atop Mt Fuji. **BELOW:** Yokohama's modern port.

Steamship berthed at Yokohama, 1930s.

sive **Minato Mirai 21** shopping and leisure complex, between Sakuragicho Station and the ocean. Trumpeted as the last great Japanese mega-complex to be constructed before the millennium (and after the economic meltdown in the 1990s), its 190 sq. km (75 sq. miles) is dominated by the 73-story **Landmark Tower**, Japan's tallest building at 296 metres (970 ft) and having one of the highest observatory decks (open daily, 10am–9pm; admission fee) – on the 69th floor – in Japan. Other buildings of note are the Yokohama Grand Inter-Continental Hotel, strikingly designed to resemble a sail, and the **Maritime Museum** (Tuesday–Sunday, 10am–5pm; admission fee). The *Nippon Maru*, a traditional sailing ship, is anchored nearby. The **Yokohama Museum of Art** (open Friday–Wednesday, 10am–5pm; admission fee) has an excellent collection of 19th- and 20th-century paintings and modernist sculptures. Also part of Minato Mirai 21 is what's claimed to be the world's largest Ferris wheel.

On the southeast side of the Oka-gawa, a stream that bisects Yokohama, from Sakuragicho Station is an area of old government buildings, banks, and the like. Further on is a tree-lined street with red-brick sidewalks: Bashamichi-dori (Street of Horse Carriages). Here is the **Kanagawa Prefectural Museum**. The building, built in 1904, was formerly the head office of a bank. As one of the best surviving examples of the city's old commercial architecture, it has been designated a so-called Important Cultural Property by the national government.

In the same neighbourhood are the stately Yokohama Banker's Club and on the right, four blocks down, the lovely red-brick Yokohama Port Opening Memorial Hall, which miraculously survived the Great Kanto Earthquake of 1923 and the bombings of World War II. Also in the area are numerous offices for the prefectural government.

BELOW:
harbour from
Yamashita Park.

This district is sometimes called the Bund and its oldest buildings have a distinctly European look, something shared with buildings along the Bund in Shanghai, built about the same time.

The **Yokohama Archives of History**, on the site of the former British consulate, houses a museum with various exhibits about Yokohama's fascinating history and a library with related audio-visual materials. Across the boulevard is the **Silk Centre**, with a delightful museum on the history of that mysterious fabric; at one time, Yokohama owed its prosperity primarily to silk, in which the local Indian community was intimately involved.

Yamashita-koen (Yamashita Park) is well worth a visit for the people-watching, although the park itself is rather undistinguished. Among the attractions at the park are the "Girl with the Red Shoes", a statue dedicated to international friendship among children. If serendipity brings you here on a clear summer night, a rock band is liable to be wailing away on a temporary stage several hundred feet offshore. The former passenger liner and hospital ship *Hikawa Maru* is permanently moored here and can be visited. Conveniently, there is a beer garden on deck, and boat tours of the harbour leave from next to the ship. Occasionally, distinguished visitors such as the *Queen Elizabeth II* are also to be found in port. A little bit farther down the same road is the New Grand Hotel, which, although slightly down at the heel, is still a civic institution and the best spot for a break over coffee and cake. Next to it is the somewhat garish 106-metre (348-ft) **Marine Tower** and a doll museum.

On public holidays, the aquarium at **Yokohama Hakkeijima Sea Paradise** is as crowded as a sardine can. Aquariums abound in Japan, and this is one of the finest in the country. Nearby are a 1.2-km-long roller coaster and the Blue

Map on page 182

Unfortunately, like many of Japan's urban public spaces, Yokohama Park often has a run-down and unkempt appearance.

BELOW: Yokohama's Marine Tower.

PERRY'S ARRIVAL

More than two centuries of isolation evaporated in 1853 when Matthew Perry, a U.S. naval officer, sailed an expedition of four ships into Uraga, near Yokosuka. His sole mission was to force Japan into trade and diplomacy with the U.S., which then became an equal with Britain, France and Russia in East Asia.

He refused Japanese demands to leave and insisted that he be received. Mindful of China's recent defeat in the Opium Wars, the Japanese agreed as a stall for time while improving their defenses. In 1854 Perry reappeared in Tokyo Bay with nine ships to conclude a first treaty, which included a U.S. consul in Japan and trade rights. Soon other countries demanded treaties, which the shogun realised he could not refuse. This weakness helped the collapse of the shogunate system.

Perry later advocated a network of Pacific bases, but the U.S. government waited over 50 years before doing so.

TIP

Yokohama and
Kamakura are easily
accessible from Tokyo
Station on the same
train, the Yokosuka
Line. Yokohama is
exactly 30 minutes
from Tokyo, Kamakura
just 1 hour.

Drop – a 107-metre (350 ft), 125-kph (80 mph) chair-drop that is, according to yet another Japanese superlative, the highest in the world. "You can't stop screaming!" demands the brochure.

No visit to Yokohama would be complete without a meal in **Chukagai**, Yokohama's Chinatown. This dozen or so blocks is the largest Chinatown in Japan and is nearly as old as the port. The area within its five old gates accounts for 90 percent of the former foreign settlement. Chinatown also takes pride in the historical role it had in providing staunch support to Sun Yat-sen when he was here in exile trying to rally support for revolution on the Chinese mainland.

On days when a baseball game is on at nearby Yokohama Stadium, the area is visited by more than 200,000 people, the majority intent on dining at one of the approximately 150 local restaurants. Most also sneak in at least a peak at the exotic shops selling imported Chinese sweets and sundries from elsewhere in Asia. There are also many herbal medicine and tea shops. Although in most Chinatowns, from San Francisco to London, restaurants prepare food for Chinese tastes, in Yokohama everything is adjusted to Japanese taste buds, with a tad of French influence. (Top chefs recruited from Hong Kong and Taiwan have to be deprogrammed to prepare Chinese food in Japan.)

Back in the old days, the waterfront Bund often stood in contrast to the **Bluff**, or **Yamate Heights**, where the leading foreign merchants lived in palatial homes. Nanmon-dori in Chinatown was the central street that ran through the international settlement and connected the two. It became a local tradition – known as Zondag, from the Dutch word for leisure – that on every Sunday the flags of the many nations were flown and brass bands strutted down the road.

There is a foreign cemetery (*gaijin bochi*) where around 4,200 foreigners

BELOW: Victorian
house in Yamate
Heights, and the
city's Chinatown.

from 40 countries are buried. The adjacent Yamate Museum, with quaint displays on the life of early foreign residents, sits near where one of Japan's earliest breweries was located.

Motomachi, a popular shopping street just below the Bluff and slightly inland from Yamashita-koen, means "original town". This is somewhat of a misnomer because the area was developed long after Yokohama itself was established. Still, Motomachi, adjacent as it was to the foreign district (now Chinatown), has played an important role in the city's history by serving the needs of foreign vessels and their crews visiting the port. Motomachi's legacy of "foreignness" led to its revival in the 1960s and 1970s as a centre of trendy boutiques and a few flashy discotheques. However, the focus of fashion in Yokohama has shifted to Isezakicho, south of Kannai Station, and to the big department stores around Yokohama Station.

Kamakura

Cradled in a spectacular natural amphitheatre, **Kamakura ❷** is surrounded on three sides by wooded mountains and on the fourth by the blue Pacific. For roughly 150 years – from 1192, when Minamoto Yoritomo made it the headquarters of the first shogunate, until 1333, when imperial forces breached its seven "impregnable" passes and annihilated the defenders – Kamakura was the de facto political and cultural capital of Japan. During those years, the military administration based here built impressive temples and commissioned notable works of art, a great deal of it Zen-influenced. Despite the endemic violence of Japan's middle ages, most survived and can be viewed today.

It is a pity that the majority of visitors spend only a day or two in Kamakura, since it is best appreciated leisurely with visits to famous historical sites – there are 65 Buddhist temples and 19 Shinto shrines – interspersed with walks through the quiet, surrounding hills. Kamakura is only an hour from Tokyo Station and 30 minutes from Yokohama on the JR Yokosuka Line. For that reason, much of it resembles an open-air madhouse on weekends, a time when it is highly recommended for the traveller to be elsewhere.

Visitors customarily begin their sightseeing from **Kamakura-eki ❹** (**Kamakura Station**). In addition to the main rail line, there is a private electric-trolley line, the delightful Enoden (Enoshima Dentetsu). The Enoden, which began operations in 1902, plies a meandering route with some wonderful views between Kamakura and Fujisawa, with 13 stops in between. For about half its 10 km (6 miles) length, the cars run along the ocean. When the trains are not crowded, the conductors allow surfers to bring their boards aboard. Unfortunately, delightful old cars have been replaced with modern ones. If time permits, take the Enoden the entire length.

Hop off the Enoden at Hase, the station closest to the **Daibutsu ❸** (**Great Buddha**). A road leads to the statue. In the hills to the left and along the way are **Goryo-jinja** (next to the Enoden tracks), which holds a unique festival every 18 September with humourous characters sporting macabre masks; **Hase-dera**, a

Maps on pages 182, 188

BELOW: bamboo grove in Kamakura.

temple with a 9-metre (30 ft), 11-headed Hase Kannon statue, along with thousands of small *jiso* statues decked out in colourful bibs and bonnets and dedicated to lost babies (mostly due to abortion); and **Kosoku-ji**, a temple known for its collection associated with the priest Nichiren. On a knoll to the right of the approach to the Buddha is the 1,200-year-old **Amanawa Myojin**. Dedicated to the Sun Goddess, Amaterasu Omikami, the shrine offers majestic views.

Even first-time visitors to Japan have no doubt seen photos of Daibutsu, the Great Buddha. But if not, there's little chance of missing the colossus. At 11 metres (40 ft) in height – minus the pedestal – and weighing 93 tons, this representation of the compassionate Amida is unlikely to get lost in crowds posing for pictures below. The features of the statue were purposely designed out of proportion when it was cast in 1252 so that the proper proportions come together when one is standing 4 to 5 metres (15 ft) in front of the statue. For a fee, crawl around inside the statue.

Astonishingly, the Great Buddha has survived the onslaughts of earthquakes, typhoons, and tsunami, like the one in 1495 that ripped away the wooden building that once enclosed it.

On the east side of Kamakura Station is **Wakamiya-oji C**, a broad boulevard that begins at the beach and heads inland under three massive *torii* archways to the Tsurugaoka Hachiman-gu. Parallel to Wakamiya-oji is **Kamachi-dori**, Kamakura's modest answer to the Ginza and with little elbow room on weekends. The area abounds with all kinds of trendy shops and eating places, and many of the Japanese-style restaurants here and elsewhere in the city have incorporated Zen principles of cooking.

Along Kamachi-dori and especially on some of the side alleys, craft shops

TIP

On weekends during the summer, Kamakura is elbow to elbow with people. Unless crowds bring you joy, you will have little fun trying to shop and sightsee.

BELOW: Daibutsu.

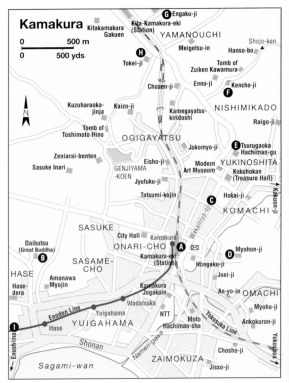

encourage serious browsing. Kamakura is most famous for *Kamakura-bori* (lacquerware), which originated in the area in the 13th century for the production of utensils used in religious ceremonies. Unlike the traditional Chinese lacquerware from which it drew its inspiration, one starts Kamakura-bori by carving the design first and then applying the lacquer. Like fine wine, Kamakura-bori improves with age, taking on richer and subtler hues and lustre. Learn more about this art at the **Kamakura-bori Kaikan**, on the right as you start up Wakamiya-oji from the train station towards Tsurugaoka Hachiman-gu.

The area due east of Kamakura Station, on the other side of Wakamiya-oji, is largely the province of temples of the Nichiren sect. Although most foreigners have heard of Zen, few know much about Nichiren (1222–82) and his teachings, despite the fact that the iconoclast priest founded the only true Japanese Buddhist sect. Nichiren was an imposing personality who in his lifetime was nearly executed, exiled twice, and set upon by mobs on more than one occasion, and who continues to generate feelings of both respect and disdain centuries after his death. Nichiren's importance in political (as opposed to religious) history lies in his prediction of the Mongol invasion as divine punishment for the failure of the authorities to accept his arguments. The irascible Nichiren seems to have been quite put out that the Mongols did not actually conquer the country.

The temples of **Myohon-ji ⓓ**, **Hongaku-ji**, **Chosho-ji**, **Myoho-ji**, and **Ankokuron-ji** are all Nichiren temples and are worth a visit. The Myohon-ji, for example, although only 10 minutes from the station, seems a world apart.

At the top end of Wakamiya-oji, the approach into **Tsurugaoka Hachiman-gu ⓔ** crosses a steep, red, half-moon bridge that separates the Gempei Ponds. The name Gempei refers to the Minamoto (Genji) and Taira (Heike) clans,

Map on page 188

Zen and Nichiren forms of Buddhism reflect the removal of boundaries between Buddhism and Shinto, with Shinto the realm of daily life and Buddhism of the afterlife.

BELOW: main temple building at Hachiman-gu.

Minamoto Yoritomo.

which fought to the end in the samurai power struggle known as the Gempei War. The three islands on the right – the Genji side – signify the Chinese character for birth, symbolising the victory of Yoritomo and his followers, while the four in the Heike pond stand for the death of the rival Taira. Yoritomo's indomitable wife, Masako, who ironically was of Taira blood, apparently built the pond to rub in her husband's victory over the ill-fated heirs of Taira.

Behind the Heike Pond is the Kanagawa Prefectural Museum of Modern Art, and a little past the Genji Pond is the modern and disaster-proof (from earthquakes, for example) **Kokuhokan (National Treasure Hall**; open Tuesday–Sunday, 9am–4pm; admission fee). Each month the Kokuhokan teasingly changes the limited displays of the 2,000 treasures from the temples of Kamakura that are in its possession. Still, whatever is being shown at any given moment should be stimulating for those interested in Buddhist art. (Incidentally, the Kokuhokan building is a copy of the Shoso-in repository in Nara.)

Continuing up towards the main shrine, cross a 25-metre (80-ft) dirt track, along which every 16 September mounted archers gallop and unloosen their arrows at targets in the ancient samurai ritual of *yabusame*. Next is an open area below the steps to the *hongu*, or shrine hall. Here is the red stage upon which Shizuka, Yoritomo's paramour, danced defiantly at the order of his vengeful older half-brother, using the occasion to sing the praises of her lover. The pregnant girl's courage sent Yoritomo into a furious and vengeful rage, and although he spared her life, he executed her son.

Just past the stage on the left of the steps is a huge gingko tree measuring 8 metres (26 ft) around and reputed to be 1,000 years old. It was near here, in 1219, that Yoritomo's second son, Sanetomo, at 26 years old already an accomplished poet, was assassinated by his own nephew. Thus came to an end Yoritomo's line; thereafter, the shogunate was controlled by Masako's family, the Hojo, through a regency.

BELOW: in the hills above Kamakura.

Tsurugaoka Hachiman-gu's prominence on the top of Stork Mountain and the shrine's dedication to Hachiman, the god of war and tutelary deity of the Minamoto, made it the central point of reference for the numerous offices of the military government situated below. Actually, the shrine was founded way back in 1063 by one of Yoritomo's ancestors. Yoritomo's very unpretentious tomb is to be found off to the right of the shrine near a hill. It is an austere grave befitting a samurai, unlike the monstrous mausoleums for the Tokugawa shoguns at Nikko, which look as if they were built for *mafioso* dons.

Two isolated temples of great interest and few crowds are the **Kakuon-ji**, back in the hills behind Yoritomo's tomb, and the **Zuisen-ji**, considerably to the east. The former was founded in 1296. Its Buddha hall, dating to 1354, houses a beautiful Yakushi Nyorai flanked by guardians representing the sun and moon, as well as a shrine to the Black Jizo, whose indelible colour results from its constantly being scorched by the flames of hell in its efforts to save souls. Access to this temple is strictly controlled. Zuisen-ji has a Zen rock-and-water garden designed by its founder, the monk Muso Kokushi.

Another spot to visit that is not so far off the beaten track, but which is nevertheless largely missed by the tourist packs, is so-called **Harakiri Cave**, a 20-minute walk to the northeast of Kamakura Station past the shallow, meandering Nameri-gawa. In 1333, in what was then a temple called Tosho-ji, the last Kamakura regent, who had been scorned for his patronage of dogfights, died by his own hand while surrounded by more than 800 of his cornered followers.

North of Tsurugaoka Hachiman-gu is **Kencho-ji** , established in 1253 and perhaps Kamakura's most significant Zen temple. Before fires in the 1300s and 1400s razed the temple, Kencho-ji had 49 sub-temples. To the right of the main gate, San-mon, is the temple's bell (*bonsho*), cast in 1255 and inscribed by the temple's first abbot, a priest from China. The large juniper trees beyond the main gate are said to have been planted by the Chinese priest. The *Butsu-den* (Buddha hall) has a floor of stone rather than the more traditional *tatami*.

To the north is the station at **Kita Kamakura (North Kamakura)**, the first stop beyond Kamakura towards Tokyo. West of the station is **Engaku-ji** , which dates from the late 13th century and was intended for the souls of those killed during the unsuccessful Mongol invasion the previous year. After the main gate and on the right are steps to a 2.5-metre-high (8-ft) bell cast in 1301, the largest temple bell in Kamakura. The bell's sound, it is said, guides souls that have been spared by the king of hell back to earth and the living. Engaku-ji's Butsu-den dates from 1964 and has been rebuilt numerous times over the centuries after fires and earthquakes.

Not far from Engaku-ji and on the main road across the tracks between Kita Kamakura and downtown Kamakura is **Tokei-ji** , which can be seen from Engaku-ji's bell tower. Begun in the 1280s as a nunnery, Tokei-ji became noted

Map on page 188

TIP

The hills above Kamakura are laced with hiking trails good for an hour or a day of rambling. To find them, just follow a Japanese seemingly dressed for a hike in the Swiss Alps

BELOW: *jizo* images at a temple.

as a refuge for abused wives. Women who found sanctuary here worked as lay helpers for three years, during which time they were safe from husbands. At the end of the three years, the women were released from marriage.

Enoshima

The wooded islet of **Enoshima** ❶ (**Bay Island**) is one of those spots that few Japanese these days would think of recommending to visitors for a daytrip. In the good old days before the popularity of off-road vehicles and windsurfing, Enoshima was one of the places to visit from Tokyo, at least until Disneyland and other theme parks arose. But it has many attractions in any weather and is easily reached either from Shinjuku in Tokyo on the private Odayku Line (a pleasant 75-minute ride), or from Kamakura on the quaint and rattling Enoden railway. As always, avoid weekends and holidays.

The island, about 2 km in circumference, is a wooded hill surrounded by rocky beaches and cliffs. But these days it hardly deserves the name of island: the 600-metre-long (2,000-ft) Benten Bridge, which connects Enoshima to the bright lights of the beach at Katase and the adjacent resort town, has gradually turned into a major causeway. The usually crowded beaches of Shichirigahama and Miami stretch far to the east and west. Still, access on foot or by car is simple, and there is plenty of parking space at the foot of the hill. Just beyond where the causeway meets the island is the yacht harbour, constructed for the Summer Olympics in 1964.

The ascent of the hill begins at the end of Benten Bridge along a narrow street crammed with restaurants and souvenir shops. Genuine crafts nestle next to plastic octopi. This narrow street leads up to the start of a series of covered

Not only are there appropriate clothes and tools for every activity in Japan, but there are definite times when sports can, and cannot, be undertaken. The first of September is the end of summer and thus the end of ocean swimming, even if summer's heat still lingers.

BELOW: beach at Enoshima.

Map
on page
182

escalators, which make the upward progress simple. First stop is the charming **Enoshima-jinja**, built in 1182 and dedicated to Benten, the goddess of fortune. Her naked statue used to reside in a cave on the far side, but fears for her safety led to a place in the shrine itself.

And on top are tropical plants, greenhouses, a small zoo, game machines, miniature trains, a short go-cart track, and restaurants and patios providing views of the ocean – everything one needs for a less-than-quiet and fussy get-away. An observation tower, 50 metres (160 ft) high and accessible by elevator, gives more exposed views.

The more spiritually minded might like to visit the famous **Ryuko-ji**, a temple near the station that features a fine pagoda, albeit one of the 20th century. The temple is dedicated to Nichiren, founder of the only genuinely Japanese sect of Buddhism. It was here that Nichiren was saved from execution by a timely stroke of lightning that hit the uplifted blade of the executioner's sword.

Miura Peninsula

During the 19th century, the *ukiyo-e* (woodblock) artist Hiroshige Ando stood on the beach at **Akiya**, on the west coast of **Miura-hanto** ❸ (**Miura Peninsula**), and looked out across the sea. In the foreground were the impressive rocks of Tateishi, with black-eared kites soaring on the evening breeze, and on the horizon Fuji-san was outlined 80 km (50 miles) away against a sunset. He immortalised the view with his chisel in a well-known print.

There have been many changes at Akiya and on Miura Peninsula itself, especially during the 1980s when the apartment blocks and weekend homes began to sprout, and when the newly affluent youth of Tokyo and Yokohama discovered that a daytrip round the peninsula was a perfect way to indulge in *doraibingu*, the Japanese pronunciation of the English word "driving", especially bumper-to-bumper doraibingu on the weekends.

Over on the east side of Miuri-hanto is the city of **Yokosuka** ❹, anchored by a large American naval base for the Seventh Fleet. Like Yokohama, Yokosuka's history is bound up with Japan's less-than-voluntary opening to the world in the mid-1800s. Yokosuka has close associations with Will Adams (Miura Anjin in Japanese), the English pilot who was advisor to Tokugawa Ieyasu, the shogun of the contemporary popular book *Shogun*. Adams is buried in Tsukayama-koen. Just to the south is the port of Uraga, where Commodore Perry anchored in 1853, and Kurihama. Yokosuka also features Admiral Togo's flagship in the 1905 Russo-Japanese War.

The gray, volcanic-sand beaches may not quite be Maui, but the many little inlets all down the west coast from Zushi provide safe swimming with refreshment stands and changing facilities throughout the summer. Most beaches have windsurfing facilities and there are several yachting harbours and marinas.

Down the coast are rocky outcroppings and a view towards **Oshima** ❺, an island that's part of Metropolitan Tokyo and with an active volcano, and **Ito**, on Izu-hanto, where an underwater eruption in 1989 gave false hope of extending Japan's limited land area.

BELOW: sunset at Akiya, Miura-hanto.

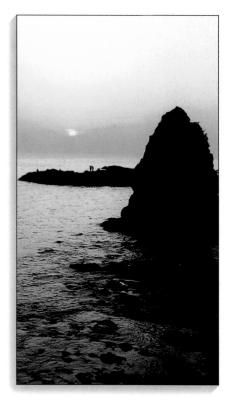

Map
on page
182

TIP

In the middle of May, Shimoda celebrates the Kurofune Matsuri (Black Ship Festival) in commemoration of Perry's landing and with ceremonies, parades, and of course fireworks.

OPPOSITE: Mt Fuji on a good day.
BELOW: souvenirs for sale near the summit of Mt Fuji.

Izu Peninsula

Extending into the Pacific between Sagami and Sugura bays is **Izu-hanto** (**Izu Peninsula**), 60 km (40 miles) long and 30 km (20 miles) wide and where countless bays, beaches, and *onsen* (hot springs) meld with a very inviting climate to give Izu its reputation as a resort for all seasons. Seafood is excellent here, too. Trains run only along the eastern coast, however.

Eastern Izu begins at **Atami ❻**, a hot spring dating back more than a thousand years. During the Edo Period, the shogun had its waters brought to the Edo palace so he could enjoy a relaxing bath. Today, Atami is a lively and even bawdy town offering reasonably sophisticated nightlife and numerous recreational facilities. Access from both Tokyo and Osaka is easy via the *shinkansen*, which stops at Atami. The MOA **Art Museum** (open Friday–Wednesday, 9.30am–4pm; admission fee), located above the train station, boasts a fine collection of *ukiyo-e* (woodblock prints), ceramics, and lacquer works, many of which have been designated as National Treasures and Important Cultural Properties by the national government.

Those travellers who have read James Clavell's *Shogun* may recognise **Ito**, south of Atami on the eastern coast of Izu-hanto, as the temporary abode of the shipwrecked Englishman who – so serendipitously, at least in Clavell's version – ingratiated himself into Japanese affairs. Today it is a popular hot-spring resort, punctuated by the Kawana resort complex in the south part of the city. The **Ikeda Art Museum** offers some 600 paintings and sculptures by Matisse, Picasso, Chagall, Dali, and other masters. South is another hot-spring outpost, **Atagawa**, noted for **Atagawa Banana-Wanien (Banana and Crocodile Park)**.

Shimoda ❼ is a somewhat sleepy resort city at the southern terminus of the rail line. A fine view of **Iro-misaki (Cape Iro)** to the south can be had from the top of **Nesugata-yama**, three minutes by cable car from Shimoda Station. The view includes volcanically active Oshima, an island to the east and part of Metropolitan Tokyo.

The first U.S. consul general to Japan, Townsend Harris, was based here, arriving in 1856. This was the first permanent foreign consulate in Japan, chosen by the shogun in part for its remoteness and thus its distance from centres of power. A monument in **Shimoda-koen (Shimoda Park)** commemorates the occasion. The friendship treaty between Japan and the U.S. was signed at **Ryosen-ji** in 1854.

Central Izu is the cultural heart of the peninsula. The **Taisha-jinja** in **Mishima ❽** is revered as Izu's first shrine; its treasure hall keeps documents of the first Kamakura shogun as well as swords and other artifacts. The Egawa house in **Nirama** is the oldest private dwelling in Japan. **Shuzen-ji**, along the Katsura-gawa, sprang up around a temple founded by the monk Kobo Daishi; this quiet hot-spring town became a favourite hideaway for Japan's great literary talents such as Natsume Soseki, Nobel prizewinner Kawabata Yasunari, and Kido Okamoto.

The west coast is less visited by tourists, for unlike the east it has no train service. Still, resort towns such as **Toi** are interesting and reputedly have the best hot springs in this part of the country. ❑

Fuji and Hakone

The region around **Fuji-san** ❾ (**Mt Fuji** but never Mt. Fuji-san) has been the inspiration for the works of many of Japan's most celebrated writers, poets and artists. It would be hard to find a mountain more highly praised for its beauty than Fuji-san or a lake more often photographed than Hakone's **Ashi-ko**. Most of the region is designated a "national park", but due to Japan's rather weak laws protecting and restricting commercial exploitation of such assets, one can often consider a national park to be a "nature" amusement park.

Sweeping up from the Pacific to form a nearly perfect symmetrical cone 3,776 metres (12,388 ft) above sea level, the elegantly shaped Fuji-san watches over Japan. Fuji's last eruption in 1707 covered Edo-Period Tokyo, some 100 km (60 miles) away, with ash. Like many natural monuments held to be sacred and imbued with a living spirit, Fuji-san was off-limits to women for many centuries. It was not until 1867, when an Englishwoman boldly scaled the mountain, that there is any record of a woman climbing the peak. Today, half of the 400,000 annual hikers are women.

Although climbers are known to set out to challenge the mountain throughout the year, the "official" climbing season for Fuji-san begins on 1 July and ends on 31 August. The mountain huts and services found along the trails to Fuji's peak are open only then. Expect thick crowds and a distinctly commercial atmosphere, not only around the facilities but along the entire trail to the top.

For those who wish to see the rising sun from Fuji's peak, start in the afternoon, stay overnight (forget sleeping – it's noisy) at one of the cabins near the top, and make the remaining climb while the sky is still dark. The other option is to climb through the night. The trails are well travelled and are hard to miss, especially as there'll be a continual line of people on the trail.

Fuji Go-ko ❿ (**Fuji Five Lakes**) skirts the northern base of Fuji-san as a year-round resort, probably more than most visitors seeking Japan's sacred mountain would expect or want. From east to west, the lakes are Yamanaka, Kawaguchi, Sai, Shoji, and Motosu. (A -ko added to the end of these names signifies "lake".)

Yamanaka-ko, which is the largest in the group, and the picturesque Kawaguchi-ko are the most frequented of the five, but some of the best spots are hidden near the smaller and more secluded Motosu-ko, Shoji-ko and Sai-ko. Some recommended visits include the Narusawa Ice Cave and Fugaku Wind Cave, both formed by the volcanic activities of one of Fuji's early eruptions.

Hakone is set against the backdrop of Fuji-san and has long been a popular place for rest and recreation. Hakone's 16 hot springs are nestled in a shallow ravine where the Hayakawa and Sukumo rivers flow together. The inns here have natural mineral baths. If on a daytrip, the Tenzan public bath provides a hot-spring treat for just a few hundred yen. Miyanoshita is the oldest and the most thriving of the spa towns.

Note: The area around Mt Fuji is probably the most popular in Japan. As such, it can be highly commercial and very crowded. ❏

Map
on page
182

NIKKO

Known as much for its autumn splendour as for its Buddhist temples embellished with carvings and details, Nikko is less than two hours away from the claustrophobia of metropolitan Tokyo

After learning that the main attraction at Nikko, a temple called Tosho-gu, comprises 42 structures and that 29 of these are embellished with some sort of carving – 5,147 in all, according to a six-year-long survey concluded in 1991 – more than a few travellers begin to realise that they've allotted too little time for Nikko.

The small city of **Nikko ⓫** itself is of little interest, serving merely as a commercial anchor to the splendours that decorate the nearby hillsides and plateau across the river to the west from the main railway stations. The Tobu train arrives in exactly (and a watch can be set by it) 101 minutes after departing Tokyo's Ueno Station, a fact that the railway's advertising department has made a catch-phrase for years.

How this region – once a several-day trek from the shogunate's capital in Edo (present-day Tokyo) – was chosen as the site of Tokugawa Ieyasu's mausoleum is a story in itself. True, Nikko forms a sort of crown at the northern perimeter of the great Kanto Plain, of which Edo was the centre. However, Ieyasu was from Kansai, not Kanto, and he had established his capital in Kanto primarily to distance himself from the imperial forces in Kansai's Kyoto, forces he had vanquished to seize power in the first place.

Still, Ieyasu's grandson Iemitsu (1604–51) set in motion the process that turned this once out-of-the-way region into Tokugawa territory about 20 years after Ieyasu's death. In fact, Iemitsu himself and his successor Ietsuna – and the Tokugawa shoguns and princes for the next 250 years – made at least three annual pilgrimages to the site to pay tribute to the founder of the dynasty that kept Japan and its people isolated from the outside world.

Through the gates

Ironically, however, given the Tokugawa aversion to things from outside Japan, many of the 5,000-odd carvings at **Tosho-gu** depict things foreign. The façade of the main shrine, for example, features carvings of three Chinese men, said to represent important figures of that country who, having turned down their chances to be kings or emperors, became folk heroes. Perhaps the carvings are meant to convey the fallacy that Ieyasu came to power only after the Toyotomi emperor had voluntarily abdicated in his favour.

Most ironic of all – and most hypocritical, considering its importance in the annals of Japanese art – is the famous, not to say fabulous, **Yomei-mon**, the gate beyond which only the highest-ranking samurai could pass into the inner sanctum of the shrine, and then only after laying aside their swords. This gate is a

BELOW: old print of Tosho-gu's pagoda.

masterpiece. Technically, it is a 12-column, two-story structure with hip-gable ends on right and left, and with cusped gables on four sides. This description, while accurate, is somewhat misleading, however. Even though its *keyaki*-wood columns are painted white to make it appear larger, the gate is quite small. Nearly every surface of the gate is adorned with delicate carvings of every sort – children at play, clouds, tree peonies, pines, bamboo, Japanese apricots, phoenixes, pheasants, cranes, wild ducks and other waterfowl, turtles, elephants, rabbits, a couple of furry tigers, Chinese lions, and the traditional symbols of regal power, dragons.

Building at Tosho-gu.

A large, white dragon (one of 92 in and around the shrine) is the main feature of the central beam in front of the second story of this fanciful structure, and two drawings of dragons appear on the ceiling of the porticos. The drawing nearer the entrance is known as *nobori-ryu* or ascending dragon, while the other is *kudari-ryu* or descending dragon.

Keep in mind that although it is designated a National Treasure and is considered an example of the heights of Japanese art, Yomei-mon's (and many of the other treasures at Nikko) nameless artisans were of Korean, not Japanese, origin. This is no small matter, given the sense of racial and cultural superiority that the Japanese tend to claim over Koreans.

What lies beyond this gate? Another gate, of course: **Kara-mon** (Chinese Gate), also a National Treasure. It is even smaller than the Yomei-mon (at about 3 by 2 metres overall) and is also laden with carvings – dragons (ascending and descending, and lounging around), apricots, bamboo, tree peonies, and more.

The ceiling has a carved figure of a fairy playing a harp, while on the ridge of the front gable is a bronze figure of a *tsutsuga*, which like quite a few other

BELOW: Tosho-gu's inner courtyard.

carvings and castings in the shrine precincts is not quite a real animal, but rather one created from hearsay and myth and mixed with a healthy (Korean, perhaps) imagination.

To help one get bearings, the Kara-mon is the last barrier to pass through before reaching the entrance to the *haiden* (oratory) and the *honden* (main hall), which is the place most visitors remember as they are requested to remove shoes. An official guidebook describes haiden and honden as the "chief edifices of the shrine". Chief they are, but interesting they are not – at least not to the casual visitor who, not knowing what to look for, tends to shuffle along with the crowd and then returns to the shoe lockers without a pause.

Unfortunately, many of the key elements inside are partially or entirely hidden from the view of this method. Confused (and no doubt somewhat bored) after their shuffle through the "chief edifices", most visitors exit, redon their shoes and spend the next 10 minutes or so looking for the famous **Nemuri-neko**, or carving of the Sleeping Cat. Some never find it at all and make their way back down the hillside feeling somewhat cheated. To make sure this doesn't happen to you, do not follow the logical path back toward the Yomei-mon. Instead, turn left (right if facing the haiden/honden complex) until you are back on the terrace between Yomei-mon and Kara-mon. Next, advance straight ahead (paying the small fee charged at a makeshift entrance to the Oku no In, or Inner Precincts) and into the open-sided, red-lacquered corridor that skirts the foot of the steep hillside, atop of which is the actual Tokugawa tomb. Nemuri-neko, a painted relief carving, is over the gateway.

This small and gray cat, well-enough executed and rather cute but otherwise unremarkable, is said to symbolise tranquillity. The fact that it is asleep is taken

Explaining Shinto's lack of ethical codes: "It is because the Japanese were truly moral in their practice that they require no theory of morals."
– MOTO-ORI NORINAGA
(1730-1801)

BELOW: storage casks of *sake* at a Nikko temple.

Continue west along the wide avenue for a few minutes to reach **Futarasan-jinja**, on the right side and away from Tosho-gu. Futarasan-jinja enshrines the three primary Shinto deities: Okuninushi no Mikoto, his consort Tagorihime no Mikoto, and their son Ajisukitakahikone no Mikoto. All three are revered for having helped to create and then make prosperous the Japanese islands.

Within the grounds is a large bronze lantern called **Bake-doro** (Goblin Lantern), which is said to once have taken on the shape of a goblin so frightening that a samurai attacked it one night, leaving "sword scratches" that are still visible to this day.

Beyond Tosho-gu

Further afield but still within the general area of Tosho-gu are several other places of interest. One is the **Hon-gu**, one of the oldest shrines in Nikko and established in 767 by the priest Shodo. The present buildings date back only to the end of the 17th century, when the shrine was rebuilt after being destroyed by fire. Just behind it is **Shihonryu-ji**, also founded by Shodo. In fact, it is not a Shinto shrine but rather a Buddhist temple. It also was destroyed by fire and the present three-story pagoda was erected in its place at the end of the 17th century. The pagoda and the image of the thousand-hand Kannon inside are the temple's main attractions.

Then there is **Rinno-ji**, a temple of the Tendai sect of Buddhism. Its significant claim is the fact that General Ulysses S. Grant, the 18th president of the United States and a hero of the American Civil War, stayed here during his eight-day sojourn to Japan and Nikko in 1879. It was one of Grant's few trips outside of North America. Actually, the temple has more than Grant-slept-here

Map on page 182

Amongst the world's religions, Shintoism is unique with a supreme being, the Sun Goddess or Amaterasu Omikami, that is female.

BELOW: the lake at Chuzenji.

Map on page 182

going for it. In its spirit hall are the tablets of its long line of abbots, all drawn from the imperial family. In another building, built in 1648 and still the largest in Nikko, are three quite amazing Buddhist statues, all measuring 8 metres (26 ft) in height and worked in gilded wood. The Bato Kannon, on the left, has the figure of a horse's head on its forehead and is the deity for animal protection.

In the forests and into the hills

The lush forests of Nikko are filled with ancient trees. The majority are *suji*, or Japanese cedar. When veiled in mist, one might think they have stood here since the beginning of time, or at the very least are part of a primeval virgin forest. They don't go back quite that far, but they are nevertheless very old, especially those trees in the Tosho-gu precincts proper and along the many kilometres of avenues and roads within and leading to Nikko. These cedars were planted as seedlings, one by one, from year to year, under the direction of a man named Matsudaira Masatsuna (1576–1648).

Matsudaira, so the story goes, was the daimyo of Kawagoe and one of the two persons honoured by edict of the shogun to supervise the construction of Tosho-gu. The extent of the man's personal wealth is not recorded nor how much of it was spent, in addition to the budget he was given by the Tokugawa shogun, in planting these trees.

However, it can be assumed that he wasn't very well off to begin with. When his turn to present a grand offering to the shrine came – as all the other daimyo were obliged to do – Matsudaira was broke. What could he do as an offering, he wondered. Around 1631, several years before the shrine itself was finished, he began to transplant cedar seedlings – plentiful in the surrounding mountains (which he owned) – into strategic positions around the shrine grounds and along the seemingly endless roads. It took him 20 years and an estimated 25,000 seedlings. Today, these trees are what in part define Nikko and its surroundings for travellers. The beneficence continues. The trees and the banks along the avenues are protected as Natural Treasures and Places of Historical Importance under Japanese law.

Thanks to the numbers of visitors who flock to Nikko and the region's fine scenery, the area abounds with other diversions. Unfortunately, getting around without a vehicle is a problem. If money permits, rent a car. (Not cheap.) If time permits, take a taxi (not bus) up the famed I-Ro-Ha switchback road to **Chuzenji-ko ⑫**, a large and quite picturesque lake due west of Nikko. Its heavily wooded shores are lined with hotels, inns, camping grounds, and other tourist wonders. If choosing not to stay overnight at the lake, try one of the several onsen on the picturesque Kinu-gawa, closer to Nikko itself.

Also in the area of the Kinu-gawa is **Nikko Edomura**, a theme park. The not-so-cheap entrance fee entitles one to stroll around the extensive grounds on streets that look like a movie set of the old Edo days. There is a "real" *ninja* show, a "poetry maze", and other attractions. It's great fun and a good way to spend a few hours to learn about the old days of pre-Meiji Japan. ❑

OPPOSITE: autumn colours in Nikko.
BELOW: fishing on Chuzenji-ko.

Map
on page
209

CENTRAL HONSHU

Central Honshu offers an industrialised Pacific coastline, lofty hot springs and skiing in the so-called Japan Alps, and a rugged and often isolated coast along the Sea of Japan

K nown for its flat, white *kishimen* noodles, its pickles known as *moriguchi-zuke*, and its confection called *uiro*, **Nagoya ❶** is better recognised as a centre of industry, producing construction materials and automobiles. Another of Nagoya's claims to industrial fame is the pinball game *pachinko*, adapted here from a Western game just after World War II. Most of Japan's millions of addictive pachinko machines are made in this region. Nagoya is located almost precisely in the centre of Japan along the old Tokaido highway and is a major hub for transportation to and from other cities, including Tokyo and Osaka. Japan's fourth-largest city with a little over 2 million people, Nagoya is primarily an industrial city with just a few sights for the traveller.

Nagoya was originally planned by the shogun Tokugawa Ieyasu to be a castle town; he built **Nagoya-jo (Nagoya Castle)** in 1612 for his ninth son, Yoshinao. But the town didn't quite develop into a powerful castle town. At any rate, Nagoya had to be redesigned and reconstructed after suffering extensive air-raid damage in 1945. The castle, rebuilt in 1959 and now functioning as a cultural and historical museum, is considered Nagoya's primary attraction. A museum displays treasures of the Tokugawa family.

BELOW: Nagoya
Castle in spring.

Nagoya's **Atsuta-jingu** is second only to the Ise-jingu, in Mie Prefecture, in its importance to the emperor of Japan and Shintoism. One of the imperial family's three sacred treasures, the Kusanagi sword (*kusanagi no tsurugi*), is kept here. (The other two sacred treasures, the jewel and mirror, are kept elsewhere at the Imperial Palace in Tokyo and at Ise, respectively.) All three treasures are said to have been given to the imperial family by the sun goddess Amaterasu Omikami. None are viewable by the public. Hundreds of ancient trees thrive amidst ancient artifacts, including the 600-year-old Nijugocho-bashi, a bridge made of 25 blocks of stone. The shrine's festival is in June.

Traditional Japanese carpentry tools.

There are museums all over Nagoya, ranging from the treasure-laden **Tokugawa Art Museum** (open Tuesday–Sunday, 10am–5pm; admission fee), displaying heirlooms of the Owari-Tokugawa family, to the **Aichi Bijutsukan (Fine Arts Museum)**, which often displays the works of Japan's up-and-coming artists. Visitors may participate in a quiet tea ceremony at the Tokugawa Art Museum, where once a year visitors may also view the exquisite but fragile scroll of the *Genji Monogatari*, or *Tale of Genji*.

Outside of Nagoya

North of Nagoya is **Inuyama**, site of Japan's oldest castle built in the mid-1400s. Standing in its original state above the Kiso-gawa, it has been owned by the same family since the 1600s. Near Inuyama is **Meiji-mura (Meiji Village;** open daily, 9.30am–5pm; admission fee), with 60 Meiji-era buildings collected from around Japan and reassembled here. Of special note is Frank Lloyd Wright's original Imperial Hotel, built in Tokyo and moved here when the new hotel was built. Every March, one of Japan's strangest festivals occurs not far

BELOW: *bochi* is popular with retired people, and making ornamentation for a new shrine.

Neighbourhood chat.

from Inuyama, at a little shrine – **Tagata-jingu** – dedicated to phalluses. A huge and anatomically-correct phallus is carried through the streets, and crowds of men and especially women try to touch it, hoping to enhance their fertility.

Further north of Nagoya, **Gifu** ❷ has a modern-apparel industry. But for Japanese tourists, Gifu is undoubtedly better-known for its 200-year history of cormorant fishing (*uaki*) on the three rivers – the Kiso, Ibi and Nagara – that cut through the city. In the 16th century, Oda Nobunaga legitimised the fishing of *ayu*, or trout, with cormorants. Later, shogun Tokugawa Ieyasu, who liked sashimi cut from ayu and often presented this delicacy at court, popularised the dish in Edo. Today, uaki is distinctly a tourist attraction with the collared birds doing their thing at night, illuminated by small fires suspended in iron baskets from the front of the boats.

The castle of Gifu commands an impressive view from the top of Kinka-zan (Golden Flower Mountain). It was built about seven centuries ago, has suffered numerous razings, and was rebuilt in 1956. A three-minute gondola ride to the foot of the mountain arrives at Gifu-koen (Gifu Park) and the Museum of History and the Museum of Insects. The latter contains various bugs, butterflies and spiders – some of which are uncomfortably large – from around the world.

Seto, a city just northeast of Nagoya, is thought to be the source of Japan's first glazed pottery in the 9th century.

Finally, no summary of the Nagoya region would be complete without mention of **Seki** ❸, a sword-forging village a bit east of Gifu and the site of the Battle of Sekigahara, waged in the early 17th century between the forces of Tokugawa Ieyasu and Toyotomi Hideyori. The battle was a significant turning point in Japanese history and a catalyst for a complete shift in the archipelago's

BELOW: harvesting of rice is by both machine and hand.

power structure. Although Tokugawa was outnumbered nearly two to one, his warriors slaughtered more than a third of the enemy troops to put Tokugawa in the shogun's throne, which he and his descendants held for the next 250-odd years. Today, only an unassuming stone marks the spot of Tokugawa's heroic triumph. In lieu of a memorial to him or an appropriate museum, Sekigahara offers an amusement park and ice-skating rink.

Takayama to the coast

The mountains beyond have much to offer in the way of natural beauty and outdoor activities. High in the mountains is **Takayama ❹**, luring travellers with *onsen* (hot springs), hikes, tennis courts and other vacation activities.

Originally established in the 1500s as a castle town for the Kanamori family, Takayama retains an old charm nurtured by its *ryokan* (traditional inns), breweries for sake, and craft shops. The Takayama area has long been noted for carpenters whose work was in high demand in Kyoto and Nara during their heydays as capital cities. **Takayama-jinya (Administrative House;** open daily, 8.30am–5pm) dates from the early 1600s; current buildings are early 19th-century reconstructions. Displays include a torture chamber.

In the centre of Takayama is Sanmachi Suji, with three streets lined by museums, traditional shops, sake breweries, and countless spots to eat. In the summer months it can be yet another tourist madhouse. Museums abound, but the not-to-miss museum is **Hida Minzoku-mura (Hida Folk Village;** open daily 8.30am–5pm; admission fee), an open-air assembly of traditional houses that was collected from around the Takayama region and reassembled here. Artisans demonstrate regional folk crafts. The town is especially famous within Japan for

Map on page 209

TIP

If Caucasian or black, expect to be stared at. People will point and openly talk about your physical attributes. When trying to talk with locals, know that the resulting giggles are not mocking, but are rather indicative of embarrassment or being uncomfortable.

BELOW: fishing for octopus along the eastern coast.

Map on page 209

two festivals: one in mid-April called Sanno *matsuri* (festival) with a procession of *yatai* (floats), and the Hachiman matsuri in October.

Matsumoto ❺ is popular in summer with Japanese heading off into the mountains on bikes and foot. In the 14th century it was the castle town of the Ogasawara clan. **Matsumoto-jo** is an excellent example of a Japanese castle with its original *donjon*, dating from late 1590s. Three turrets and six floors are punctuated with fine historical displays and a nice view at the top. Adjacent to the castle is **Nihon Minzoku Shiryokan (Japan Folklore Museum)**, with displays of regional artifacts and crafts, along with flora and fauna.

Venue of the 1998 Winter Olympics, **Nagano ❻** is a moderately sized city of half a million people and was established in the Kamakura Period as a temple town. That temple, Zenko-ji, dates from the 7th century and was the site for Ikko Sanzon, apparently the first Buddha image in Japan. Northeast of Nagano, in Obuse, is the **Hokusai-kan (Hokusai Museum**; open daily 9–4.30pm; admission fee), with a decent collection of Hokusai's *ukiyo-e*, or woodblock prints.

Because of the 1998 Olympics, Nagano now has a bullet train line direct from Tokyo, which means that post-Olympic crowds will probably be thicker.

Sea of Japan coast

On the coast of the Sea of Japan, **Kanazawa ❼** came under the rule of the Maeda clan in the 16th century, a stewardship that lasted nearly three centuries and which supported a vigorous artistic effort. Lacking military or industrial targets, Kanazawa was spared bombing during World War II. Today, samurai houses in the Nagamachi area line twisting streets. **Kenroku-en (Kenroku Garden)** is considered one of Japan's top gardens and has its heritage in an ancient Chinese garden from the Song dynasty. Feverishly crowded, the garden is not for the contemplative. Consider instead an excursion out onto **Noto-hanto ❽ (Noto Peninsula)**, which jabs out into the Sea of Japan like a crooked finger. The sedate eastern coast, encircling a bay, is moderately developed for tourism. The western coast, sculpted by the vigorous winds and currents of the Sea of Japan, is rocky and rustic. Noto's main town, **Wajima**, is noted for *Wajima-nuri*, a type of lacquerware. Wajima is also known for its morning market (*asa-ichi*), which can take on a tourist-focused mood at times but is still worth a visit. North along the coast is **Niigata ❾** in the centre of Japan's Yukiguni, or Snow Country, of which novelist Kawabata Yasunari wrote in his 1947 novel *Yukiguni*. Except as a transit point, there is little in Niigata for foreign travellers.

BELOW: fruit seller in Wajima.

Sado-jima

Two hours from Niigata by ferry, **Sado-jima ❿** was first an island of exile in the 13th century and later, during the Edo Period, a prison colony. Japan's fifth-largest (1,900 sq. km/850 sq. mile) island, Sado is mountainous and wonderfully accommodating in summer, but winters can be brutal. Sado is probably most famous for the Kodo Drummers, from a village near **Ogi**. In August is the Earth Celebration, three days of world music – from Africa to Japan to Europe – and dance. Workshops are also offered, but if planning to go, transportation and accommodation must be arranged well in advance. ❑

Central Honshu

0   50 km
0   50 miles

S E A

O F

J A P A N

P A C I F I C

O C E A N

THE NORTH

Most Japanese regard the northern extents of Tohoku and Hokkaido as the ends of the earth, however close they are

I might as well be going to the ends of the earth". That's how Basho, Japan's great 17th-century *haiku* poet, put it on the eve of his departure into the north in 1689. Back then, when Basho decided to prowl the back country, the roads were narrow and minimal, or nonexistent. Today, Sendai, Tohoku's predominant city and north-ward from Tokyo along the Pacific coast, is only two hours from Tokyo via *shinkansen*. Moreover, it is often mentioned as a new site for Japan's capital, should it be decided that Tokyo is just too big and too expensive and too congested.

Even the large island of Hokkaido, forcibly settled during the Meiji Restoration in the late 19th century, is but nine hours from Tokyo by train or two hours by plane. (In fact, the Tokyo–Sapporo air corridor is one of the world's busiest.)

The north has always been perceived as remote and strange, exist-ing outside the normal sphere of Japanese life. Even imagining that such a place as Hokkaido exists, for example, is a romantic effort, as it is so different from the rest of Japan, rather like Alaska is to Amer-ica. But perhaps this is not so much a matter of distance as of psy-chology – there is a seemingly limitless amount of open space and nature untouched by people. Both impressions are quite false.

Undoubtedly, the northern mountains have a lot of to do with per-ceptions of remoteness. There are mountains everywhere in Japan, but those in the north tend to be bigger, more imposing and, from late autumn to mid-spring, not especially accommodating.

Then, too, the people of the north bear some responsibility. Tohoku was originally settled by itinerant warlords and soldiers who con-structed castle fortresses to keep out potentially unfriendly neigh-bours, mostly from the south. These castle towns developed into insular communities with their own unique lifestyle, crafts, cottage industries, and language. The famous *Tohoku-ben*, still spoken by many people here, is actually a series of subdialects with numerous variations. For people from elsewhere in Japan, it is a foreign lan-guage requiring, literally, a dictionary.

It is perhaps no longer an easy matter to find ourselves – as Basho was able to do – alone in some idyllic spot. Yet it is possible, and for the adventurous at heart (for a little while anyway), losing oneself in the mysterious back-country of the north is bliss. ❏

PRECEDING PAGES: autumn leaves against an abandoned barn in Hokkaido; farm-land in southern Hokkaido.
LEFT: morning walk at hot spring in Shiretoko Peninsula.

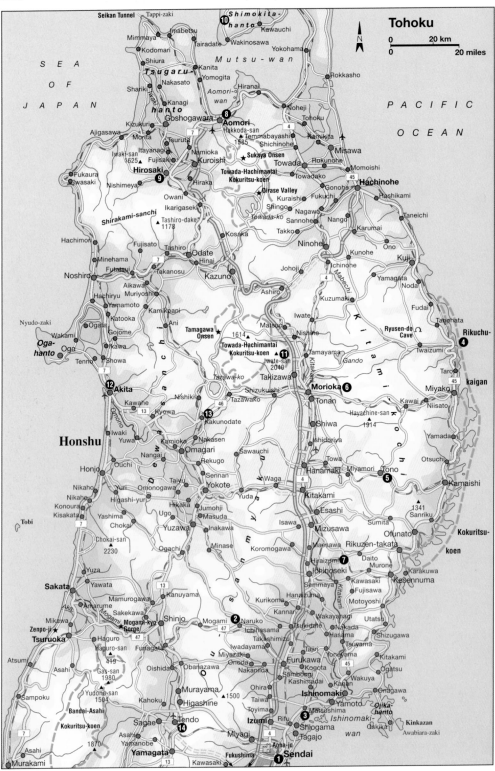

Tohoku

0   20 km

0   20 miles

N

S E A

O F

J A P A N

Seikan Tunnel   Tappi-zaki

Mimmaya
Kodomari   Imabetsu
Shiura   Tairadate
Nakasato
Shariki   Kanagi
Kizukuri   Goshogawara
Ajigasawa   Morita
Iwaki-san   Itayanagi
1625   Fujisaki
Fukaura
Iwasaki   Nishimeya

Hirosaki   ❾

Shirakami-sanchi

Hachimon
Minehama   Fujisato
Noshiro   Futatsui   Tashiro
Aikawa   Takanosu
Hachiryu   Muriyoshi
Yamamoto
Katooka   Kamikoani
Ogata   Gojome   Ani
Wakami   Ikawa
Oga-   Oga   Showa
hanto   Tenno

Nyudo-zaki

Akita   ⑫

Kawahe
13   Kyowa

Honshu   Iwaki
Yuwa
Kamioka   Nakasen
Honjo   Nangai   Rekugo
Nikaho   Ouchi
Nikaho   Yuri   Omonogawa
Konoura   Higashi-yuri
Kisakata   Yashima
7   Chokai
Ugo
Tobi   Yuzawa
Chokai-san   Inakawa
2230   Ogachi
Yuza   Minase
Sakata   Yawata
Amarume   Kanuyama
Mikawa   Sakekawa
Zenpo-ji   **Mogami-kyo**   Shinjo   Mogami
Tsuruoka   **Gorge**
Haguro   *47*
Atsumi   Haguro-san
Asahi   419   Funagata
Gas-san   Oishida   Obanazawa
1980
Yudono-san   Miyazaki
1504   Onoda
Sampoku   Murayama
Bandai-Asahi   Kahoku
Kokuritsu-koen   Higashine
Asahi   Sagae   ▲1500
7   **Tendo**   ⑭
Asahi   Yamanobe
1870   **Yamagata**
Murakami   Kawasaki
13

M u t s u -   w a n

Shimokita-   ❿
hanto
Kawauchi
Wakinosawa   Yokohama
Tairadate
Yomogita   Rokkasho
Hiranai
Noheji
Tohoku
Aomori   ❽   Kamikita
Hakkoda-san   Misawa
Temmabayashi   Shichinohe
1585   Sukaya Onsen   **Towada**   Rokunohe   Momoishi
Namioka   **Towada-Hachimantai**   Towadako   *45*   **Hachinohe**
Kuroishi   **Kokuritsu-koen**   Kuraishi   Gonohe   Hashikami
Hiraka   *Oirase Valley*   Fukuchi
Owani   Shingo   Nagawa   Taneichi
Ikarigaseki   *Towada-ko*   Sannohe   Nango
Tashiro-dake   Takko   Karumai
1178   Kosaka   Ono   Kuji
Tashiro   **Ninohe**   Kunohe   Yamagata
Odate   Johoji   Ichinohe   Noda
Hinai   Ashiro   Kuzumaki   Fudai
Kazuno   Iwate   Tanohata
Matsuo   Nishine   *Ryusen-do*   **Rikuchu-**
Tamagawa   1614   Tamayama   Cave   ❹
Onsen   **Towada-Hachimantai**   *Gando*   Iwaizumi
Kokuritsu-koen   Iwate-san
2040   Taro   *45*
Nishiki   *Tazawa-ko*   Takizawa   *kaigan*
46   **Morioka**   ❻   Miyako
Kakunodate   ⑬   Shizukuishi   Kawai   Niisato
Tazawako   *Kitakami*   Tonan
Hayachine-san   Yamada
Shiwa   ▲1914   Otsuchi
Sawauchi   Ishidoriya
Omagari   Waga   Towa   Miyamori   **Tono**   Kamaishi
Sennan   Yuda   Hanamaki   ⑤   *Kokuritsu-*
Yokote   ▲1341   *koen*
Jumohji   Kitakami   Sanriku
Masuda   Isawa   Esashi   Sumita
Koromogawa   Mizusawa   Ofunato
Maesawa   Rikuzen-takata
Hiraizumi   Daito
Ichinoseki   ❼   Murone   Karakuwa
Semmaya   Kawasaki   Kesennuma
Kurikoma   Hanaizuma   Fujisawa
Kannari   Wakayanagi   Motoyoshi
Naruko   ②   Ichihasama   Tsukidate   Utatsu
Mogami   *47*   Takashimizu   Nakada   Shizugawa
Iwadeyama   Hasama   Tsuyama
Tajiri   Yoneyama   Kitakami
Furukawa   Kogota   Ogatsu
Samboogi   Wakuya
Nakaniida   Kashimadai   Kanan   Onagawa
Ohira   *Oshika-*
Taiwa   *hanto*
Ishinomaki   Kinkazan
Toyama   Yamato   *Ishinomaki-*   Oshika-zaki
Matsushima   ③   *wan*   Awabiara-zaki
Izumi   Rifu   **Shiogama**
Miyagi   Tagajo
4   Aoba-jo   **Sendai**   ①
Fukushima

P A C I F I C

O C E A N

TOHOKU

Its dialect is as thick as the winter snows that blow in over the Sea of Japan from Siberia. Tohoku's hold on northern Honshu makes it seem another world to Japan's urban majority

Map on page 216

P erhaps as a way of explaining and coping with the difficult realities of weather and topography, the northern portion of Honshu known as Tohoku remains filled with myths – clever foxes who turn into beautiful women and lure unsuspecting men to their doom; green-headed river creatures who snatch small children venturing too close to the water; and devils and ghosts in great abundance.

By Japanese standards, the Tohoku region is sparsely populated, with 10 million people in an area just under 67,000 sq. km (26,000 sq. miles). This northern part of Honshu comprises six prefectures: Aomori, Akita, Iwate, Miyagi, Yamagata, and Fukushima. Its climate is comparable to New England in the United States, with the possible exception of the month of August when certain parts of southern Tohoku slyly pretend they are on the equator. (In fact, the city of Yamagata holds the record for the highest recorded temperature in Japan: 41°C or 104°F, in 1933.)

Long known for its natural beauty, rugged mountains, sometimes incomprehensible dialects, innumerable hot springs, and – it cannot be denied – its harsh winters, especially on the Sea of Japan side that gets the brunt of Siberian storms, Tohoku was once known as Michinoku (lit. interior or narrow road). The name was not as benign as it seems, for it implied someplace rather uncivilised and lacking in culture. In the old days, a barrier wall was constructed at Shirakawa, in southern Fukushima, to separate the civilised world of the south from the barbarians in the north. Although the name was eventually changed to the innocent *tohoku* (lit. northeast), the region's image of cultural immaturity lingers for many urban Japanese to the south.

There is a certain irony in this, since it is generally agreed that Tohoku is perhaps the last bastion of traditional Japanese culture. To a large degree, Tohoku has escaped the rapid modernisation that the rest of Japan has undergone since the end of World War II. In the north it is still possible to discover farms growing rice by methods used hundreds of years ago, tiny fishing villages nestled into cliffs overlooking unspoiled sea coasts, isolated hot-spring inns, and a people whose open friendliness is unstinting even as their dialect remains an exclusive mystery. No longer unknown, Tohoku is a place of spectacular beauty and a must-see for adventurous visitors.

BELOW: friendly smile while tending cultivated flowers.

Sendai

The largest city in Tohoku and on the eastern coast, **Sendai ❶** was originally called Sentaijo after the Thousand Buddha Statue Temple that once graced the top of Aoba-yama. The name was changed to Sendai, or Thousand Generations, by the Date clan during their reign of the area, possibly in the mistaken belief that they would reign supreme for that long.

Sendai is today a cosmopolitan city of approximately 910,000 people, the capital of Miyagi Prefecture, and the pre-eminent city of the entire Tohoku region. Sendai is the logical jumping-off point for exploring the rest of Tohoku. It is known as the Green City and the City of Trees, and visitors arriving on the *shinkansen* from treeless urban points south will understand why. From **Sendai-eki (Sendai Station)**, considered one of the most beautiful train stations in Japan, the main boulevards running east and west are all tree-lined.

Those wide, European-style avenues are a pleasure along which to stroll. If so inclined, the entire downtown area is small enough to cover in an hour or so of leisurely walking. From Sendai's tallest building, the brilliantly named **SS-30 Building** with its 30 floors, one can relax in numerous top-floor restaurants that offer an excellent view of mountains to the north and west, the Pacific Ocean to the east, and the city below. A 10-minute walk west up Aoba-dori from Sendai Station is **Ichiban-cho**, Sendai's main shopping arcade. Parts of it are covered in skylights and all of it is vehicle-free. Evenings suggest a walk a little further to Kokobuncho-dori, Sendai's main after-hours strip where there are the usual (and seemingly endless) Japanese-style bars, nightclubs, discos, karaoke boxes and other entertainment.

Just beneath the surface, the traditional ways of Tohoku remain in Sendai. The visitor can still watch artisans and craftsmen making knives, *tatami* flooring, and the famed *kayaki tansu* or chests in the traditional shops tucked into the shadows of much larger and more modern architecture.

BELOW: harvest before the first winter snow.

Map on page 216

Sendai didn't come into its own until Date Masamune, the great one-eyed warlord of the north, moved to his newly constructed castle on Aoba-yama. Both **Aoba-jo** (**Aoba Castle**) and the Date family collapsed during the Meiji era, but the walls of Aoba-jo remain. In addition, a small museum, souvenir shop, shrine, and statue of the great Masamune himself now occupy the grounds. Looking northward and down from the castle grounds, one can see the Hirose-gawa, unpolluted and thus unusual in Japan. Edible trout still swim downstream.

Zuihoden, the burial site of Date Masamune, sits atop Kyogamine-yama. There are several cemeteries along the way up, as well as a beautiful Rinzai Zen temple, **Zuiho-ji**. Above the temple are steps leading to the mausoleum at the very top, and nearby are the tombs of samurai who committed ritual suicide when Masamune died. There is also an exhibition room displaying pictures taken when the mausoleum was opened during restoration, necessitated by bomb attacks near the end of World War II.

Osaki Hachiman-jinja was originally built in 1100 and later moved to its present location by Date Masamune. Dedicated to the god of war or of archery, this shrine is one of Japan's national treasures. Walk up the 100 or so steps to the top – reportedly the count is never the same twice. Follow the stone-paved path lined with enormous cedar trees to the shrine, picturesquely set back in a small forest. It is done in Momoyama style with gold, black lacquer and bright colours.

There are several more modern attractions worth a look, especially in **Aobayama-koen** (**Green Hill Park**), including **Shiritsu Hakubutsukan** (**Sendai Municipal Museum**; open daily, 9am–5pm; admission fee) and a prefectural fine-art museum. The municipal museum is interesting architecturally, with an extensive and permanent exhibition of the area's history. There is also

BELOW: the drying of rice is a small-scale operation.

THE POETRY OF BASHO

Matsuo Basho, the pseudonym of Matsuo Munefusa (born 1644), is considered to be the greatest of Japan's *haiku* poets. Basho took the 17-syllable haiku form and enriched it with descriptive simplicity and contrast. Frequently used to describe Basho's poetry is *sabi* – the love of the old, faded, and unobtrusive. In 1679 Basho wrote his first verse:

*On a withered branch
A crow has alighted:
Nightfall in autumn.*

A samurai for a local feudal lord, Basho moved to the capital city of Edo (now Tokyo) after his lord's death. In 1684, Basho made the first of many journeys through the islands, to Tohoku and written of in *Oku no Hosomichi* (*The Narrow Road to the Deep North*), considered by many to be one of the most beautiful works in Japanese literature.

a children's exhibit where everything on display can be touched. The prefectural fine-art museum has a sculpture wing with an outdoor sculpture garden.

If with the time and the energy, consider the **Tohoku University Botanical Garden**, a place to cool off on a hot summer afternoon as well as to observe owls, bats, and the region's flora and fauna. The observatory here is a relatively good place for star and planet viewing if you don't mind waiting in line. Finally, there's Kotsu-koen, a "traffic park" for children complete with roads, red lights, busy intersections, and train tracks. Kids can cruise around in pedal-powered cars and get a taste for what real life is like on Japan's claustrophobic roads.

On the northern outskirts of Sendai, near Kitayama Station and a delightful place for a mountain stroll, are two Zen temples, **Rinno-ji** and **Shifuku-ji**. Both date from the 15th century and were destroyed then rebuilt many times over the years. They offer beautiful Zen-inspired gardens, as well as azaleas and irises in the spring, brilliant foliage in autumn, and dazzling winter scenes.

Captain of a tourist boat prepares to get underway on Matsushima Bay.

Matsushima

A short ride to the northwest of Sendai is **Naruko ❷**, Tohoku's most popular hot-spring *onsen*. Once a sacred site to honour the gods of the hot springs, Naruko is known for its medicinal waters (the treatment of nervous tension is a specialty here) and the production of wooden *kokeshi* dolls, with ball-shaped heads and limbless cylindrical bodies. Now produced in many regions, kokeshi originated in Tohoku as a winter industry.

BELOW: tourist cruise boat in Matsushima Bay.

Just north of Sendai is **Matsushima ❸**, considered by Japanese to be one of the three officially designated most-beautiful spots (*Nihon-sankei*) in Japan. (The others are on Miyazu Bay, north of Kyoto, and Miyajima, near Hiroshima.)

Be warned: such a banner guarantees crowds, tackiness and considerable noise, and Matsushima is just that. Still, the bay is filled with beautiful pine-covered islets of all shapes and sizes, and a fleet of cruise boats cruises the islands, sometimes in the form of ridiculous peacocks and other gimmicks. The poet Basho couldn't get enough of this place, nonetheless, declaring his arrival in Matsushima as the happiest moment of his life. While here, try the *sasa-kam-aboko* (molded fish paste) and maybe also the squid-on-a-stick.

Map on page 216

Northward along the coast

Continuing north along the coast, the fishing port of **Ishinomaki** is noted for seafood of all kinds. Try the *hoya* (sea squirt) in vinegar sauce. Ferries from Ishinomaki skirt around **Ojika-hanto** to **Kinkazan** (Gold Flower Mountain), a once-mysterious place of bamboo groves, dense forest, and roaming wild deer and monkeys.

At the northeast tip of Miyagi and on the coast is the city of **Kesennuma** and its variety of shark dishes. Beyond Kesennuma begins Iwate Prefecture's famed **Rikuchu-kaigan Kokuritsu-koen** ❹ (**Rikuchu-kaigan National Park**, commonly known as **Sanriku**), 200 km (125 miles) of fantastic coastline, fishing villages, and beautiful sandy beaches. Jodogahama (Paradise Beach) was named by a visiting priest long ago who assumed that this was as close to heaven-on-earth as he would ever get.

Midway up Sanriku and inland over the mountains is the town of **Tono** ❺, offering a perfectly preserved glimpse into feudal Japan. No modern trappings here. Farming is still done the old-fashioned way; note the *magariya* or traditional L-shaped farmhouses. The long side of the structure is for people, the

BELOW: morning walk, Matsushima.

Map
on page
216

*Temple in winter on
Haguro-san.*

short side for animals and ghosts. Do not go too near the rivers here – this is where the legendary *kappa* resides beneath the waters and waiting to pull people and horses under. (The traditional way to defeat a kappa, if encountered, is to bow in greeting, forcing the kappa to return the bow and thus drain the depression atop its head of the kappa's life-giving fluid, water.)

Just to the southeast and at the base of Iwate-san is **Morioka** ❻, Iwate's capital and self-proclaimed as famous for its competitions for eating *wanko soba*. Other than that, it's rather unremarkable. But further south is the town of **Hiraizumi** ❼, near Miyagi Prefecture. Hiraizumi's beautiful **Chuson-ji**, a temple dating from the 12th century, contains the Konjiki-do (Golden Pavilion), Japan's first National Treasure.

Aomori

Capital of Aomori Prefecture, the city of **Aomori** ❽ is a logical departure point for both Hokkaido and Towada-Hachimantai National Park to the south. **Hirosaki** ❾, an hour's ride southwest from Aomori, is an old castle town boasting the most elegant (some say most difficult) regional dialect in Tohoku, as well as what Japanese chauvinists claim are Japan's most beautiful women. It is also noted for retaining a bit of the old samurai-era ambience. To the southeast are the Hakkodo mountains, running down the middle of Aomori Prefecture to the river valley of Oirase. Before entering this spectacular valley of steep cliffs, churning rapids and waterfalls, spend a night at **Sukaya** onsen. The waters here are thought to be curative and the location is rustic and traditional.

North lies Aomori Prefecture and the **Shimokita-hanto** ❿ (**Shimokita Peninsula**). The world's northernmost community of wild monkeys can be found here, as well as the ominous **Osore-zan**, 870 metres (2,870 ft) high. With its bubbling, multicoloured mud pits and clinging sulfur clouds, Osore's translation of "dread" or "terror" seems apt.

Towada-Hachimantai Kokuritsu-koen (Towada-Hachimantai National Park) covers a vast area, touching the borders of three prefectures – Aomori, Akita and Iwate. The onsen at **Tamagawa**, on the Akita side of Hachimantai Plateau, has hot, acidic and slightly radioactive water, considered to be one of the best in the area. Excluding Hokkaido, this is Japan's last area of untamed wilderness with several volcanoes, including **Iwate-san** ⓫, 2,040 metres high (6,700 ft) and considered the Fuji-san of the north, bubbling mud pools, steam geysers, and scenic splendour. South of **Towada-ko**, Iwate-san is one of eight active volcanoes in the Tohoku region.

West from Hachimantai is Akita Prefecture, home of **Tazawa-ko** (reportedly Japan's deepest lake) and the spectacular **Oga-hanto**, home of the *namahage*, or the devils of the New Year. These horrible creatures burst into the local homes on 3 January each year and are not appeased until fed large quantities of *sake* and rice cakes. The city of **Akita** ⓬ is another city with nothing to distinguish it, save perhaps its winters. **Kakunodate** ⓭, however, is noted for having preserved several samurai houses and streets, some lined with luscious cherry trees.

South of Akita, the prefecture of **Yamagata** is rustic and traditional. The **Dewa San-zan** (Three Mountains of Dewa) are Yamagata's three holy mountains and where ascetic mountain priests called *yamabushi* still perform sacred rituals. They walk the trails dressed in checked jackets and baggy white pants and carrying conch shells. Join the other pilgrims and walk the 2,446 steps to the summit of **Haguro-san**. Afterwards, travel down the Mogami-gawa on a flat-bottomed boat while the boatman sings of the area's legends. Towards the inland highlands is **Tendo** ⓮, an onsen town famous for its craftsmen who make *shogi* chess pieces. Then follow any small road to its very end and old Japan. ❑

OPPOSITE: fishing boats, Matsushima.

HOKKAIDO

The northern island of Hokkaido holds a special place in the Japanese imagination, conjuring up images of wild lands and misty mountains amidst a romanticism of possibilities

Maps
on pages
226, 228

Hokkaido has been part of the Japanese nation only since it was settled in the 19th century as an example of Meiji Restoration development. Nowadays, Hokkaido is to many Japanese as Alaska is to Americans: the northern extents with a romantic sense of frontier, where summers are short and winters exceedingly cold, and where the people are just a little bit different for living there in the first place. Japan's northern island is where the temples and castles of the southern islands give way to mountains, forests and farms. One will find the residents here more direct and friendlier than their southern counterparts, and due to the Meiji-era Westernisation, quite sophisticated. Hokkaido is also home to Japan's last indigenous people, the Ainu, who are of Caucasian ancestry and with no genetic connection to today's Japanese. With a population of only 20,000, the Ainu are today a phantom culture with a forgotten language, looked upon by Japanese as a sightseeing curiosity and whose main occupation – besides fishing and farming – is dressing up and posing for photographs at tourist sites. A brutal statement, but unfortunately true.

Hokkaido has the feeling of remoteness, but this is mostly psychological. The Tokyo–Sapporo air corridor is one of the busiest in the world, and Hokkaido offers the standard overdeveloped and tacky tourist traps and loudspeaker-enhanced "scenic" places so common throughout Japan. But Hokkaido can also be high adventure in the rustic north, with some of Japan's most undeveloped areas. Its climate parallels Quebec and Finland, and in winter icebergs scrape its shores. In summer, hills and fields are riotous with wildflowers and tranquil with dairy cows.

OPPOSITE: sunrise over Kussharo-ko.
BELOW: Sapporo.

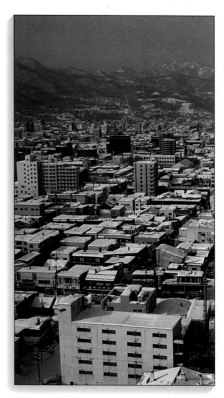

Sapporo

In southwest Hokkaido, **Sapporo ❶** is the island's capital and its largest city with 1.7 million people. It is an immensely livable city, especially by Japanese standards. Streets are laid out in a grid, making navigation easy and useful addresses a reality. Streets are also wider than most of those in Japan.

Downtown is anchored by **Odori-koen ❹ (Odori Park)**, running east and west through downtown and perhaps one of Japan's liveliest, most charming boulevards. In the first week of February, this broad avenue is the venue for Sapporo's world-famous Snow Festival. Snow statues and ice sculptures made by corporate, professional and amateur teams are decidedly complex and often quite large. In summer, beer gardens spring up on the grassy areas and people linger outdoors long into the night.

Amongst the Japanese, a must-see is **Tokei-dai ❽ (Clock Tower)**, an architecturally undistinguished structure built in the late 1870s and not really worth going out of one's way to see. Directly east of Odori-koen a couple of blocks is the **TV Tower** ◉, with a decent viewing platform 90 metres (295 ft) above the ground.

Just northwest of **Sapporo-eki** ◉ (**Sapporo Station**), itself a few blocks north of Odori-koen, is Hokkaido University. The university operates the nearby **Botanical Garden** ◉, which contains over 5,000 examples of Hokkaido's flora. Within its grounds is **Batchelor Kinenkan (Batchelor Memorial Museum**; open daily, 9am–4pm; admission fee), a museum with an excellent collection of Ainu artifacts and named after an Englishman who spent decades researching the Ainu of Japan. Rev. John Batchelor was a 19th-century minister who studied the indigenous people of both Hokkaido and Siberia. The collection of Ainu artifacts he left behind is probably the best in Japan.

To the east a couple of kilometres is the **Sapporo Brewery** ◉ and Beer Garden, built on the site of the original brewery. Sapporo was Japan's first beer brewery, dating from the mid-1870s.

Two blocks south of Odori-koen is **Tanuki-koji**, a vibrant strip of restaurants and shops. The market of Nijo serves every dining and household need for locals and purveys souvenirs in abundance for eager first-time visitors. Finally, a couple of more blocks south is **Susukino** ◉, Sapporo's nightlife and strip-joint district of "soaplands" (full-body massages lubricated by soap).

West of Sapporo is **Otaru** ②, once a fishing and trading centre and where many of the buildings are an eclectic blend of Western and 19th-century Japanese influences.

Otaru is gateway to the **Shakotan-hanto**, a peninsular microcosm of Hokkaido with its rugged coastlines, abundant campsites, ski areas, boating

BELOW: a small exhibit in Sapporo's snow festival.

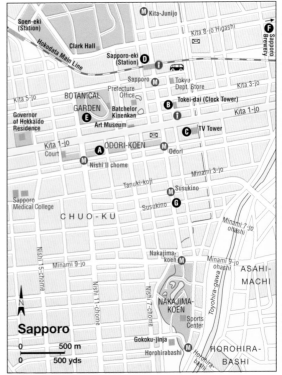

Sapporo

and fishing in the Sea of Japan, and glorious sunsets from the capes (*misaki*) of Shakotan and Kamui. This area's proximity to Sapporo makes sightseeing hectic at times, especially on holidays and weekends. But along the side roads and in quiet villages there is always an inn with a room, if not a view.

Maps
on pages
226, 228

To the south of Sapporo

The **Shikotsu-Toya Kokuritsu-koen (Shikotsu-Toya National Park)** is Hokkaido's most accessible national park and thus highly commercial and often crowded. Closest to Sapporo is **Shikotsu-ko ❸**, a huge caldera lake. Shikotsu Kohan, a fishing village, provides lodgings and tour boats of the lake, and there are numerous youth hostels and camping sites in the area. As in all of Hokkaido's national parks, youth hostels are where anyone – young or old – can get help in renting bikes, locating trails, or getting directions.

Toya-ko ❹, south of Shikotsu, is a round caldera lake with a large island smack in the centre. Tour boats visit its islands, where the view of **Yotei-zan**, at 1,893 metres (6,200 ft), to the north is best. Climbers can attack Yotei or three other peaks: Eniwa, Fuppushi and Tarumae. The latter, on the south shore of Shikotsu-ko and rising 1,040 metres (3,400 ft), is a volcano that still steams and fumes; it is probably the best climb. The route to Tarumae from Shikotsu-ko passes through the eerie beauty of Koke no Domon (Moss Gorge). The resort areas around Toya-ko are boisterous in summer, with fireworks during the August festival season. There are many *ryokan* in the area, with hot-spring baths (*onsen*) having lake views. The "must-see" here is **Showa Shin-zan**, a small volcano just south that emerged unannounced from the earth in 1944. **Usu-zan ❺**, Showa Shin-zan's parent volcano, stands nearby. A cable car

BELOW: smouldering Showa Shin-zan from the cable car on Usu-zan.

("ropeway" to the Japanese) runs from near Showa Shin-zan up Usu-zan; the view of Showa Shin-zan and the surrounding countryside is excellent. At the top of Usu-zan are the remains of trees destroyed when Usu-zan blew up in 1977, wreaking havoc on the resort. See it on film in the **Volcano Science Museum** (open daily, 9am–5pm; admission fee).

The best route from Toya-ko east to the tourist hot spring of **Noboribetsu ❻** is by bus through gorgeous Orofure Pass. Noboribetsu's notable sight and activity is at the Dai-Ichi Takimoto-kan Hotel, where 40 indoor, sex-segregated hot-spring baths, once of wood but now of marble, can hold 1,000 bathers simultaneously. There is nothing else like it, we think. (If you give the onsen a try, expect to be stared at. You are something foreign in the water.)

There are two festivals in August at Noboribetsu, recommended only if you love crowds. For a gourmet treat, in season ask for *kegani koramushi*, or small freshwater crabs. While here, tour the volcanic Jigoku-dani (Hell Gorge) and go up to the summit of Shihorei.

Hokkaido

Hakodate

At the southern tip of Hokkaido and just across the Tsugaru Strait from Aomori and Honshu's northern tip is **Hakodate ❼**. Known for its rather wicked weather, Hakodate also offers one of the most romantic views from atop **Hakodate-yama**. A cable car climbs to its 335-metre (1,100 ft) summit.

Hakodate is Hokkaido's historic city, with Japanese settlers arriving from the south as early as the 13th century. Russians followed in the mid-1700s. At the base of Hakodate-yama is **Motomachi**, a foreign enclave since the 1850s. A Russian Orthodox church and a Catholic church attest to the foreign background. In fact, Hakodate was one of three Japanese cities (including Yokohama and Nagasaki) opened to the West after Perry's opening of the country in the 1850s. Northeast of Motomachi is **Goryo-kaku**, a star-shaped fort (a typical Russian design) where loyalists of the collapsing Tokugawa shogunate lost the final battle against the Meiji imperial army in 1869. A commercially operated tower nearby offers good views of the fort and city.

Whereas Sapporo is a night city, Hakodate is at heart a morning city. Don't miss the fish market at dawn, when the squid fleet and the crab trappers return to port. Use the streetcar system, dating from 1913, to explore. For dinner, have Japan's freshest seafood. Crab and salmon are abundant and delicious; a unique salmon stew (*shake nabe*) called *sanpei-jiru* is truly remarkable. *Ika somen* – thinly sliced, noodle-like strips of raw squid – is the city's specialty.

West of the city is a Trappist convent, established in 1898 and today famous for its biscuits and sweets. South is Matsumae, Hokkaido's only castle town.

Kushiro and Akan National Park

To the east of Sapporo along the southern coast is the port city of **Kushiro ❽**, where ultramodern architecture contrasts with one of Japan's most congenial dockside scenes. Amongst the Japanese, Kushiro is noted mostly for the migrating cranes that put on elaborate and well-attended mating displays in the fields outside the city. Further east, Nemuro-hanto and the marshlands that stretch north from Kushiro along the eastern coastline are a recluse's paradise.

North of Kushiro in the centre of Hokkaido are the virgin forests, volcanoes, and caldera lakes that draw tens of thousands of visitors every year to 900-sq.-km (350 sq. mile) **Akan Kokuritsu-koen (Akan National Park)**, whose best staging point is Kushiro. Tour buses dominate this park, which makes a car or a bicycle a plus. Ainu are abundant in Akan National Park; they dance and sing on schedule when the tour buses arrive. The smiles evaporate when the tourists evaporate. Within the park, **Akan-ko ❾** is famous with the Japanese for *marimo* – odd, green algae balls also known as God's Fairies that will either delight or bore you. **Akan Kohan**, the main town, has 10 ryokan and the park has half a dozen youth hostels and plenty of campsites. Two volcanic peaks, Oakan-dake and Meakan-dake, tempt climbers; Meakan is the preferred jaunt, partly because an onsen awaits the weary climber. North of Akan Kohan, Bokke features bubbling, hot mud.

Map on page 228

The opening of Japan by the arrival of Perry not only forced Japan from its 250-year isolation, but it eventually resulted in the collapse of the shogun and the return of the imperial line to power.

BELOW: Ainu posing with tourists.

*Eggs cooked on a
steam vent on Io-san
for sale to tourists.*

BELOW: egg seller
near the steam
vents of Io-san.

The bus ride between Akan-ko and Mashu-ko to the northeast features wonderful views at **Sogakudai** overlooking Meakan and Oakan. Mashu-ko is a landmark and is called Devil's Lake by the Ainu. Its 200-metre-high (650 ft) cliffs towering over misty waters have often served as leaps of death for lovers.

Less touristy is **Kussharo-ko ⑩**, at 80 sq. km (30 sq. miles) the largest inland lake in Hokkaido and home to "Kusshi", Japan's very own "Nessie". Three congenial onsen surround Kussharo: Kawayu, Wakoto, and Sunayu, where hot sands provide a welcome novelty. **Io-san**, or Mount Sulfur, steams and reeks impressively and is worth a visit despite the commercialisation. **Bihoro**, a pass above Kussharo's west shore, has breathtaking vistas.

Daisetsuzan National Park

Wilder and colder than Akan and Shikotsu-Toya, **Daisetsuzan Kokuritsu-koen** (**Daisetsuzan National Park**) is the largest national park in Japan with 230,900 hectares (570,500 acres). Anchored directly in the centre of Hokkaido and to the west of Akan, the climate is nearly always cool, even in summer. This is a landscape of volcanic peaks and steep highlands, magnificent gorges, carpets of alpine wildflowers, and inevitable sightings of the park's rich wildlife, including deer, fox, bears and exotic birds. In the park, there are several good youth hostels and a series of campsites.

Start at **Sounkyo ⑪**, a tourist village near the gorges of Sounkyo (Gorges Reaching to the Clouds), with chiselled walls of volcanic rock punctuated by feathery waterfalls and more than 100 metres (300 ft) high. From Sounkyo, one of the park's two cable cars ends near the peak of Kuro, a jumping-off point for good hiking. The goal is Hokkaido's highest peak, **Asahi-dake ⑫**,

Map on page 228

2,290 metres (7,500 ft) high. Along the way, hikers come across vast tracts of creeping pine and virgin forests, timberline barrens, small lakes and side trails, volcanic vents, flower-covered hillsides, patches of year-round snow – and the inevitable pesky mosquitoes. Among the best festivals in Hokkaido are Sounkyo's Kyokoku Himatsuri, an authentic Ainu fire-festival in late June, and Sounkyo's Ice Festival in winter.

Shiretoko National Park

A beautiful, barely civilised finger of volcanic peninsula jutting into the Sea of Okhotsk, **Shiretoko-hanto ⓫ (Shiretoko Peninsula)** is nearly the end of the earth for the Japanese. A car or bike is necessary for exploring most of the 390-sq.-km (150 sq. miles) of **Shiretoko Kokuritsu-koen (Shiretoko National Park)**, and many places require backpacks and sleeping bags for overnight stays. This is also brown bear country, something to remember when hiking.

Starting from the fishing and onsen village of **Rausu**, a trip along the south coast is rugged and lonely but adequately relieved by the pleasures of scenic seaside *rotemburo* (outdoor bath). Seseki, for example, is a hot spring that steams on a rocky shore along the coast. There are no hotels in sight, no tourist shops, nor any place to eat.

The northern shore of the peninsula, starting from the mundane spa town of **Utoro**, offers more visitors' amenities. From Utoro, there are sightseeing boats and roads east. **Iwaobetsu** is a lovely and unspoiled onsen from which one can hike to the top of **Rausu-dake**, the peninsula's highest mountain at 1,660 metres (5,500 ft). From here, hikers can descend southward to Rausu or else turn eastward along a ridge of mountains toward 1,560-metre-high (5,100-ft) **Iwo-yama**,

Because of American agricultural experts brought to Hokkaido in the early 20th century, farms look rather similar to those in Iowa or Vermont. Likewise, Hokkaido's urban streets have a broad American look and are spacious by Japanese standards.

BELOW: farm with an American look.

Map on page 228

Buddhist tomb on the island of Rishiri.

OPPOSITE: waterfall at Tennin-kyo.
BELOW: early snow.

a steaming and active volcano. Just north of Iwo-yama and boasting a waterfall, hot spring, and a breathtaking view of mountain and ocean is **Kamuiwakka no Taki**, which for many travellers to Japan is the jewel of Shiretoko.

Along the northern coast

The best route away from the Shiretoko is west along the northern coast through the village of Shari and towards **Abashiri** ⓐ, with its interesting but quirky prison museum, pleasant walks along Tofutsu-ko, and the wildflower gardens. The **Abashiri Prison Museum** (open daily, 8am–6pm) features the preserved prison structures, including the minimalist cells barely adequate for this harsh climate. Japanese films about the *yakuza* often feature the notorious Abashiri prison. Also in Abashiri is a fine museum that displays the plants and animals of Shiretoko-hanto, along with excavated prehistoric artifacts. Best of all, Abashiri is at the beginning of Hokkaido's easiest long-distance bicycle trip, a trip along the island's northern coast with the Sea of Okhotsk that is popular with youths on summer holiday.

Wakkanai ⓑ lies at the northernmost tip of Hokkaido. In spring, the break-up of the ice pack to the north of Wakkanai is a mainstay of national television news. Wakkanai itself is undistinguished, although increasingly street and store signs in Russian suggest its popularity with Russians. In fact, the Russian island of Sakhalin is often visible to the north. Wakkanai is also a port for the export of older Japanese cars to Russia, where there is a thriving market for them, and it is the terminus for ferry service to some of the remote northern islands, including Rishiri and Rebun. Of course, in winter the ice pack can thwart travel by sea to these two small northwestern islands.

Rishiri and Rebun

The volcanic islands of **Rishiri** ⓰ and **Rebun** ⓱, part of the **Rishiri-Rebun-Sarobetsu Kokuritsu-koen** (**Rishiri-Rebun-Sarobetsu National Park**), are just west of Wakkanai, from where the ferry to the islands departs. Before boarding the ferry, visit the alpine wildflower reserve at **Sarobetsu**, a rainbow of colour as far as the eye can see, especially in July. (This is one of Hokkaido's real wonders worth investigating.) Rishiri and Rebun themselves offer delights for the biker, hiker, camper, and fisherman. It's possible to lodge at a *minshuku* (home-style inn) on either island and get up early in the morning with your host to go fishing in the Sea of Japan.

Hiking is excellent. Rishiri offers the best hiking with a climb up Rishiri-san, poking upwards to 1,720 metres (5,620 ft) above sea level, like Neptune's elbow. On Rebun, which is comparatively flat, hike from Sukotan-misaki to Momiwa, or bike from Kabuka to Funadomori to make the most of the rewarding coastline scenery. Joining a youth hostel group is good insurance against getting lost.

Accommodations on these northern islands are adventurous. There is a hotel, the Kitaguni Grand, but staying in a hostel (there are three on Rishiri and one on Rebun) or else a minshuku is a more down-to-earth choice and local experience. ❑

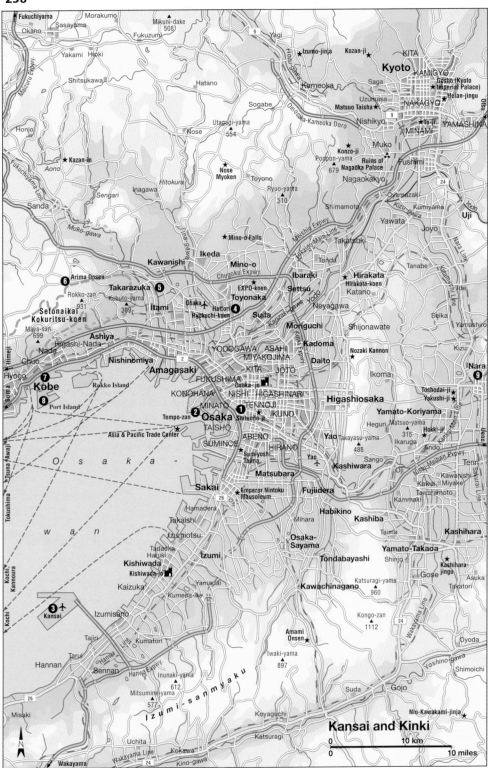

Kansai and Kinki

THE KANSAI REGION

*Unlike the Kanto to the north, the Kansai vibrates with more
entrepreneurial intensity and historical importance*

The old Tokaido (Eastern Sea Road) that connected the ancient capital at Kyoto with the seat of the feudal shogunate at Kamakura (and later, with Edo Tokyo) has all but disappeared. But it was along that much-travelled highway, at a point where it passed through the Hakone hills, that the Kamakura *bakufu* set up a heavily armed outpost in the 13th century to stifle threats by the western warlords and imperial loyalists. It is from this post that the regions to the west got their name: *Kansai,* or Western Barrier.

In the Kamakura days, virtually all lands west and south of those barriers – including the Nagoya and Gifu regions (covered in the Central Honshu chapter) – were considered to be in the Kansai. Later, around or just before the beginning of the Edo Period, the definition narrowed to include only the Kyoto, Nara, Osaka, and Kobe areas.

Naturally, persons native to the Kansai feel an intense rivalry with other parts of the country, particularly the Kanto region, home of Tokyo. Although much of the Kansai region is still agricultural, declaring that one is from Kansai doesn't evoke a backwater image. In fact, despite their snickers at the Osaka dialect and at the rather sophomoric sense of humour to be found in Kansai, those in Tokyo must yield to the renown and respect of the entrepreneurial skills of people from Osaka and Kobe. Indeed, the great commercial and industrial complexes of Osaka and Kobe are the centres of Japan's international commerce. Moreover, there is the unquestionable urban sophistication of ancient Kyoto, which, after all, was the nation's powerful premier city for well over 1,000 years.

Osaka is a street-smart city, a place where the successful person has read the signals and kept an eye out for both opportunities and problems. For what it's worth, Osaka is the centre of the *yakuza*, the organised crime activity in Japan. But it is also the base of Japan's most innovative electronics manufacturer, Matsushita, and is a leader – together with Nagoya in Chubu – in the development of robotic production techniques.

Whether the traveller chooses the hills of Kobe, the hustle of Osaka, the antiquities of Kyoto, or the sublime of Nara, the Kansai region probably offers more to the first-time visitor than does that megalopolis 500 km (300 miles) to the north, Tokyo. ❏

PRECEDING PAGES: Kyoto's Kiyomizu-dera in winter; Osaka Castle.

OSAKA AND KOBE

*Tokyo may be where the bureaucrat and banker confer, but Osaka
is where the entrepreneur and marketer huddle, making it Japan's
centre of commerce with a gritty straightforwardness*

Map
on page
238

Kansai shakes and hustles. You can see it in the restless crowds on the
streets and packed in the subways. Osaka especially is an entrepreneurial
city where lost time equates to lost opportunities and lost profits. This
merchants' entrepôt thrives, as it has for centuries, on the manipulation of the
soroban (abacus), which many here claim has a language all its own and that in
Japan only Osakans understand.

Some Japanese look askance at **Osaka ❶**, as if it belonged to another somewhat unrelated part of the hemisphere. Its humour is different and a bit more rollicking than Tokyo. Greetings are to the point: *Mokarimakka?* Making much
money? Even the language and intonation have a distinctly gritty, home-cooked
flavour, raising eyebrows of disdain in sophisticated and bureaucratic Tokyo.
Osaka is known for the character of its people: straightforward, business-savvy
jay-walkers who know how to eat well. While sophisticated Kyotoites are said
to spend their money on clothes, Osakans prefer to dispose of their hard-earned
yen on culinary exploits.

Osaka goes by all sorts of nicknames – so many that they would put even an
enthusiastic civic promoter to sleep. Among them are the City of Water, for its
numerous rivers and one-time canals, and City of a
Thousand Bridges, for the nearly 1,000 *bashi* that
span the waterways. But all the waterways and
bridges have only served one purpose: moving goods
and material in and out of Osaka, Japan's commercial entrepôt to the world.

Osaka's business connection is documented as far
back as the 4th century, when Emperor Nintoku made
Naniwa (Osaka) his capital. His business acumen was
considerable for a politician; for example, he astutely
decided to rebate all taxes to local businesses for three
years after he was informed of an impending recession. His ploy worked rather well and the Osaka business ethic was conceived, as was its unique language
of the merchants, *akinai kotoba*.

The city's stellar port and river connection to the
capital in Kyoto played a central role in its economic
and cultural development. Merchants from around the
country – and from China and Korea – flooded the
city. Osaka grew in strength and economic power, cul-
minating with the shogunate of legendary Toyotomi
Hideyoshi (1536–98), who chose Osaka as his seat of
government, built himself a fine castle, and then
turned the city into Japan's foremost commercial and
industrial centre.

For the next 270 years, Osaka was the "kitchen of
Japan" with raw materials pouring in and high-qual-
ity finished products flowing out. Kyoto and fledg-

OPPOSITE: Kirin
Plaza Building, in
Osaka's Dotonbori.
BELOW: bar reading
material.

TIP

Domestic flights to
Osaka arrive at the
older airport near
downtown, while
international flights
use the newer Kansai
International Airport, in
Osaka Bay.

ling Edo (present-day Tokyo) were consumers, Osaka the provider. When the capital and commercial centre moved to Tokyo, Osaka was – and remains – where the coin-of-the-realm is minted. And even though the aerial bombings of World War II nearly destroyed Osaka (unlike nearby Kyoto, spared the wrath of American air raids for its cultural, historic and religious landmarks), the city quickly returned to its commercial prominence and hustle.

Tokyo, of course, is Japan's economic and political engine, but Osaka remains an industrial, money-making dynamo with a gross national product greater than that of Canada. While Tokyo looks toward New York and London, Osaka casts its gaze towards the Asian mainland. Centuries of commerce and entrepreneurialism has given Osakans an ingenuity, enthusiasm and friendliness that outshines those up in Tokyo.

Contemporary Osaka

Osaka has an extensive, user-friendly subway and circular train line that makes exploring the city painless. Flanking Chuo-ku (Central District) are two sides of the Osakan coin: one half centres on Umeda, in Kita-ku (North District), the northern area around Osaka Station, while the other side is Minami-ku (South District), the southern part of downtown in and around Namba Station. While only 10 minutes apart by subway, they are worlds apart in mind and manner. Umeda is Osaka's newer face where most of the city's skyscrapers, offices, hotels and shopping centres are sprouting. Minami, the unpretentious side of the city, is claimed to be the real Osaka. Most Osakans will say that Umeda is where one works, but Minami is where the Osakan heart beats. It's also where the say-what-you-mean *Osaka-ben* (Osaka dialect) is spoken with pride.

BELOW: Osaka
shopping centre.

Since most trains (except the *shinkansen*, or bullet train) arrive at the **Osaka-eki Ⓐ** (**Osaka Station**) complex in Umeda, it is from here that a tour of the city might start. At Osaka Station, three train lines (JR, Hankyu and Hanshin lines) meet with Osaka's three main north–south subway lines. Like most train stations in Japan, Osaka Station offers an underground shopping mall, perhaps one of the largest underground malls in the world. Meandering corridors connect station exits and entrances with department stores, hotels, hundreds of shops and boutiques, and uncountable places to eat. The main areas of the shopping mall cover over 3 hectares (7.4 acres). San-Ban-Gai, located directly under the Hankyu Umeda part of the station, features another collection of shops and restaurants and is notable for the creative use of water and lights.

From the Shin (New) Hankyu Hotel, cross under the railway lines west to the twin towers of the futuristic **Umeda Sky Building**, where the 41st-floor observation deck (open daily, 10am–10.30pm; admission fee) offers panoramic views of the city; in the basement is a 1960s retro-style restaurant food court.

Back up on the street from the station complex is **Midosuji**, Osaka's main north–south boulevard. South from Umeda is **Nakano-shima Ⓑ** (**Nakano Island**), one of the most valuable pieces of real estate in the city. This narrow island between the canals of Dojima-gawa and Tosabori-gawa is the centre of city government and home to many major Osaka companies. A footpath runs most of the way around Nakano-shima; sightseeing boats to tour the canals can be picked up nearby.

From Midosuji, follow the path on Nakano-shima east along the river, passing in front of Osaka city hall, library, and the quaint, red-brick public hall. Across from the public hall is the superb **Toyo Togei-kan Ⓒ** (**Museum of**

Maps on pages 238, 243

Osaka has made some cultural contributions through the centuries as well, such as the poet Matsuo Basho (1644–94). The puppetry of bunraku, with its large, two-thirds of life-size puppets, was another Osaka contribution.

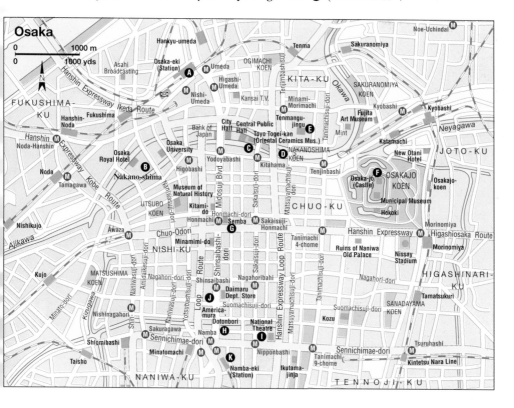

Oriental Ceramics; open Tuesday–Sunday, 9.30am–5pm; admission fee), housing the famous Ataka collection of Chinese and Korean porcelain, one of the best such collections in the world and with over 1,000 pieces. East of the museum is **Nakanoshima-koen** ❿ (**Nakanoshima Park**), with a rose garden and willow-draped paths.

The hard-to-miss Osaka Castle rising to the east is reached by following the footpath to the eastern end of Nakano-shima, then up the spiral ramp onto Ten-jin-bashi. Walk north across the bridge, then right at the police box. A short jaunt ends at the entrance of **Sakuranomiya-koen** (Cherry Garden). A few blocks north of this point sits funky **Tenmangu-jingu** ❺, dedicated to the god of learning. Sakuranomiya-koen has extensive trails lined with cherry trees. If lucky enough to be here during the second week in April, you'll get a good look at Japan's national flower, the cherry blossom, in full bloom. In the evenings, uncountable numbers of Osakans will be at their merriest – and most uninhibited – while drinking and singing under the trees at lively *hanami* (flower-viewing) parties.

Follow the footpath about a kilometre along the river past the Osaka mint, then take the foot bridge (Kawasaki-bashi) over the river to the castle straight ahead. Up and then down through an underpass and up onto an overpass eventually leads to it. (Yes, indeed, one might also have taken a taxi from Nakano-shima.)

Osaka-jo ❻ (**Osaka Castle**) is the most visited site in the city. (*See picture on pages 236–37.*) The magnificent castle on the hill is an ode to everything that was great in the past and even of future possibilities. Unfortunately for the romantic and historian, it is not the original castle, but rather a replica. The main *donjon*, towering above the expansive gardens and stone walls, is a 1931

Gambling spawned the name "yakuza". In an old card game, points came from the last digit of the hand's total. A hand of 20 (the sum of 8, 9 and 3 and the worst possible), has a score of zero. The hand 8-9-3 is pronounced ya-ku-sa, used to suggest the thugs' uselessness.

BELOW: *yakuza member sharing his fine tattoos.*

YAKUZA

Yakuza origins date to the 1600s, when the unemployed samurai sometimes dressed in odd clothing and carrying longswords terrorised people for leisure. Later, men called *bakuto* were hired by the shogun to gamble with labourers paid by the government so as to reclaim some of the substantial wages. The bakuto introduced *yubitsume* (finger-cutting), an act of apology to the boss, and tattooing.

Osaka is home to the Yamaguchi-gumi, founded in the 1920s and the largest of a dozen or so conglomerate gangs in Japan. Overall, police estimate over 150,000 yakuza members in 2,000 gangs affiliated with the conglomerate groups.

The yakuza have established alliances with Chinese Triads, Mafia in the U.S. and Italy, drug cartels, and others. Legitimate businesses mask their criminal activities; it is estimated that yakuza have funnelled well over US$10 billion into legitimate investments in the U.S. and Europe.

concrete replica of the original that was built by Toyotomi Hideyoshi in 1585. With the conscripted help of all the feudal lords of the nation and the labour of tens of thousands, the massive structure was completed in just three years. It was destroyed 30 years later by Tokugawa Ieyasa and then again rebuilt. Much of the original grounds, moats and walls still stand. Extensive restoration work to the castle building, which houses an impressive multi-story museum, was completed in 1997. The view from the top floor is impressive.

Adjacent to the castle is the **Osaka Business Park**, worth a visit to see what the future of Osaka may be like. Planners aim to make this one of Osaka's main centres. Already it sports a slew of state-of-the-art skyscrapers, theatres, shopping centres, restaurants, and the New Otani Hotel.

South of Nakano-shima, head south on Midosuji under the *ginkgo* trees. Japan's thriving pharmaceutical industry started in Osaka with the import of Chinese herbal remedies, and most of Japan's drug companies still have their headquarters here along Doshomachi, just off Midosuji. Tucked away in a corner sits the pharmaceutical shrine of Sukuna-Hikona. It's a tiny little place that blossoms in importance entirely out of proportion to its size once a year in November, when the Shinno Matsuri is held. The festival memorialises the discovery that ground tiger bones, among other things, combated malaria.

South on Midosuji is the district of Honmachi, where Midosuji and Honmachi boulevards cross. Just north of the crossing is **Semba G**, the apparel wholesale area of Osaka. Most large wholesalers have outgrown their Semba origins, but some 800 small wholesalers still operate in the Semba Centre Building, a two-story structure entirely under a 930-metre-long (3,000-ft) expanse of elevated highway. Many of Osaka's most venerated businesses got their start in

Map on page 243

BELOW: Nakano-shima.

Late at night Japan's urban areas are often punctuated by the shriek of racing motorcycles with no mufflers, driven by bosozuku ("speed tribes"), who are renegade youth intent on disrupting the norms of society.

Semba, and some Japanese say that there is no one as astute in business as a Semba-trained businessman manipulating a soroban faster than a calculator.

Follow Midosuji south until the next major crossing, Nagahori. The first landmark to look for is the **Sony Tower**, at the mouth of Osaka's premier covered-shopping street, Shinsaibashi-suji, which extends south toward Namba Station. Here are ancient little shops sitting in apparent ignorance of the outrageously fancy boutique plazas towering on either side. The Shinsaibashi Daimaru, flagship of a prestigious chain of department stores, is worth a few minutes if for nothing else than to admire its lovely art-deco interior. (Seek out the elevators.)

South on Shinsaibashi is one of the most fascinating stretches in Osaka. In the **Dotonbori** ❶ amusement quarter, neon lights illuminate giant moving crabs, shrimp and octopuses that adorn the façades of neighbourhood seafood restaurants. For Japanese tourists, it's *de rigueur* to stop and pose with *kuidaore*, a mechanical drum-beating clown more famous locally than Ronald McDonald and Colonel Sanders combined (and both of them are quite famous in Japan).

At the Dotonbori Canal, Shinsaibashi ends and Ebisusuji begins. Here, Shin Takamatsu's *son et lumière* **Kirin Plaza Building**, architecturally akin to something out of the film *Blade Runner*, stands on the north bank of the canal. Venture about halfway across the **Ebisu-bashi**, a bridge across the canal, and squeeze in along the stone railing. Then sit tight for one of the best nonstop people-watching parades in the country.

There is more to Dotonbori than just the passing crowds, however. For hundreds of years, this was the theatrical heart of Japan with six *kabuki* theatres, five *bunraku* playhouses, and a myriad of other halls where the great storytellers and comics of Osaka performed. Today, most of the old theatres have been replaced

BELOW: canal along Dotonbori.

by cinemas, among which the elegant old **Shochiku-za** is an architectural link to the golden age of black-and-white films. The venerable **Naka-za**, with its kabuki and *geisha* dances, and the vaudevillian Kado-za are still active, but they are the last of the legitimate theatres left in Dotonbori. Several years ago, the Bunraku Puppet Theatre moved from its old Asahi-za home to the **National Theatre ❶**, a few blocks to the east. Performances are held only at certain times of the year.

Just south of Naka-za, the alley named Hozenji Yokocho is lined with scores of traditional Osaka eating and drinking establishments. (Some can be quite expensive, so confirm prices before ordering.) Continue down the alley to **Hozen-ji**, one of the most visited and venerated temples in Osaka. Local businessmen come to pray for good business, young couples to ask for happy futures, and older people to pray for good health. A very serviceable temple.

For a glimpse of a more modern Japan, stroll through **America-mura ❷** (**America Village**) tucked into the narrow streets on the west side of Midosuji. This potpourri of Americana done Japanese-style is where stylish youth are out en masse to see and be seen. The area is filled with used-clothing boutiques and make-shift flea markets, where the right pair of old, smelly Nike shoes can demand hundreds of dollars and where vintage Levis can fetch thousands of dollars. There are numerous restaurants and bars modelled after everything from outlaw biker haunts to woodsy, honky-tonk cowboy saloons.

South is the wide boulevard of Sennichimae-dori. Cross it and walk east a block to Printemps (pronounced *plantam*) department store. Turn right and enter the Sennichimae shopping arcade, a typical blue-collar area of *pachinko* parlours, movie theatres and cheap restaurants. The arcade leads to one of

Map on page 243

BELOW: a pinball game, *pachinko* is a serious and noisy pastime for men.

Osaka's most famous wholesale areas, Doguyasuji, an entire market devoted to kitchen and restaurant supplies. As is the case in most Japanese cities, certain streets and neighbourhoods in Osaka are noted for a particular commodity: Matchamachi, or Toy Town; Nipponbashi, or Den-Den Town, for computers and electric appliances; Tachibana-dori for furniture; Hakimonodonya-gai for Japanese-style footwear and umbrellas; and Itachibori for tools.

From Doguyasuji, it's just two blocks to **Namba-eki ❻ (Namba Station)**, where there is nothing too remarkable save the vast underground shopping arcade of Namba City and Rainbow Town. Three main subway lines connect at Namba Station, also the terminus for both the Kintetsu and Nankai railways serving Nara, Wakayama and points south. Namba is also one of the best connecting points from downtown Osaka to the Kansai International Airport. Both JR West and Nankai railroads and frequent buses serve the airport from here.

In the far west of Osaka along **Osaka-wan (Osaka Bay)**, **Tempo-zan Harbour Village ❷** makes an excellent place to explore for a half day. The highlight of this waterfront development is the excellent and enormous **Kaiyukan Aquarium** (open daily, 10am–8pm; admission fee), where visitors can get a close-up glimpse of giant whale sharks and immense spider crabs. Other attractions nearby include the **Suntory Museum** (open daily, 10am–8pm; admission fee) with galleries and an Imax cinema. At 112 metres (368 ft) high and difficult to miss, the world's largest Ferris wheel looms nearby.

Seemingly afloat in Osaka Bay, **Kansai International Airport ❸** opened in the late 1990s as an alternative to Tokyo's overextended Narita. On an artificial island and away from developed areas, the airport allows flights 24 hours daily, whereas Narita is closed late at night.

Kansai International Airport in Osaka Bay.

BELOW: Kaiyukan Aquarium.

For those without time to explore the age-old traditional architecture in the Japanese countryside, consider a trip to **Hattori Ryokuchi-koen ➍**, north of central Osaka and near the old international airport. Here is an open-air museum of old Japanese-style farmhouses, displaying nine different styles of *minka* farmhouses with thatched roofs and thoughtfully restored as an attractive indoor/outdoor museum.

Maps on pages 238, 243

Beyond Osaka and Kobe

Theatre lovers and the culturally adventurous might want to make the trek (about 30 minutes from Osaka's Umeda station or Kobe's Sannomiya station) out to **Takarazuka ➎**, where high-stepping women have been staging flashy musical extravaganzas for nearly 90 years. Back in 1910, Takarazuka was a small town at the end of the then newly opened Hankyu rail line. In order to attract passengers, the train company built a hot-spring resort and put together an all-female performing company. There are 400 performers divided into four casts, two performing simultaneously here and in the Takarazuka Theatre in Tokyo, while the other two troupes rehearse.

To the west, scalding (*onsen*) hot springs await weary hikers north of scenic, 930-metre-high (3,000-ft) **Rokko-zan** in the town of **Arima ➏**. Reached by bus and cable car from Rokko Station, this ancient spa boasts all the usual hot-springs amenities plus is the home of nationally recognised basket-makers.

One bargain in town is the public Arima Onsen Kaikan, where for a few hundred yen one can bathe in the same curative waters offered at the much costlier inns. Arima's waters are said to sooth all human ailments except love – an irony since the town has done much to nurture that particular affliction.

The female actors of the Takarazuka play the male parts. Lead performers are well-known and have a devoted following of female fans who throng to Tokyo's Takarazuka Theatre, across from the Imperial Hotel.

BELOW: Tempo-zan Harbour Village.

Kobe

The Chinese *kanji* characters for Kobe translate as "god's door". But **Kobe ❼**, 30 km (20 miles) east of Osaka, is more like a doorsill – a long and narrow ledge squeezed between the coastal mountains and Osaka Bay. Although lacking in fantastic attractions for travellers – and so is usually overlooked by travellers – Kobe is one of the most livable and attractive cities in Japan, perched on hills overlooking a harbour.

In 1995, Kobe was jolted by the horrific Great Hanshin Earthquake that killed over 6,000 people in the Kobe area. Entire neighbourhoods, especially in the western sections of the city, were flattened when Japanese-style homes – wooden post-and-beam frames with heavy tiled roofs – collapsed and burned in the resulting fires. Buildings and elevated roads, mostly of contemporary concrete construction, spectacularly collapsed. Transportation routes were severely damaged, including Kobe's container port facilities, which are on land-fill.

The earthquake wreaked havoc beyond anyone's belief and the government's inept emergency response was equally astounding. Dire predictions that Kobe would take several years to rebuild proved true; it was not until the summer of 1998 that the last of the tens of thousands of displaced residents were finally able to resettle into homes after four years in temporary housing.

Today, for the most part, Kobe has returned to normal. Yes, damage from the earthquake can still be seen in some empty blocks and boarded buildings, but the trains are running, the port is busy, and shops, restaurants and hotels are open.

Those arriving in Kobe by shinkansen will disembark at **Shin Kobe-eki (New Kobe Station**; regular trains from Osaka and Kyoto stop at Sannomiya-eki). A few blocks to the west and still on high ground, **Kitano-cho** is where rich for-

The Korean War in the early 1950s pulled Japan from economic depression. UN forces used Japan's ports, including Kobe, as staging areas and Japanese suppliers provided most of the goods and services.

BELOW: Kobe's port facilities.

Map on page 238

eign traders once staked out impressive residences at the turn of the 20th century, their growing influence freeing them from the foreign ghetto originally allocated near the wharves. Presenting a fanciful potpourri of European and American architectural styles, several of these *ijinkan* – foreign residences now sharing the hill with trendy boutiques and restaurants – are open to the public. Westerners tend to find the interiors unexceptional (and full of cheap souvenirs for domestic tourists), but standouts include the impeccably restored Kazamidori and the Choueke House, which offer an intimate glimpse into the life-style of long-time foreign residents.

While in the neighbourhood, try to locate the Muslim mosque, Jewish synagogue, and the Catholic, Baptist and Russian Orthodox churches, all within a few blocks of one another in a unique assemblage for an Asian city this size.

The cardinal point on the Kobe compass is **Sannomiya**, where **Sannomiya-eki (Sannomiya Station)** is embraced by this popular shopping and entertainment district. Extending west from Sannomiya, parallel shopping arcades extend to Motomachi-eki (Motomachi Station) and beyond. The arcade directly beneath the overhead tracks is the remnant of a black-market that surfaced amid the post-World War II rubble and today is a bonus for bargain-hunters seeking second-hand or imitation goods.

South of Motomachi Station and just west of the elegant Daimaru department store look for the dragon gate announcing **Nankinmachi**, Kobe's two-block-long Chinatown. While not of the calibre of Chinatowns elsewhere in the world, this small but vibrant enclave surpasses in its aura of foreignness anything that can be seen in the historic ports of Yokohama and Nagasaki.

From Chinatown, it's a short walk south to **Meriken Hatoba** and the water-

BELOW: shipping on the Inland Sea.

Map on page 238

front. The park was named for the American consulate that once stood nearby. The surrounding redeveloped wharf frontage is the site of an informative and strikingly designed maritime museum. A visit here should also include a ride to the top of adjacent Port Tower and the 45-minute harbour cruise.

Offshore is the hard-to-ignore **Port Island ❽**, also its Japanese name. In a feat of near science fiction and biblical dimensions, Kobe has "recycled" its surplus mountains to build up from the sea floor two of the world's largest artificial islands. This massive undertaking was to confirm Kobe as a prime trading port – it has sea links with 150 countries – and its position as a world leader in the handling of containerised cargo.

The *Portliner* monorail from Sannomiya Station provides a convenient elevated loop ride around Port Island. Here – and on neighbouring **Rokko Island** (hard-hit by the earthquake) and also reachable by a monorail from JR Sumiyoshi Station – visitors can get a first-hand look at the future of container vessels. Moreover, the centre of the island has been zoned to accommodate a hotel, sports and convention facilities, plus an amusement park and sea-view apartments for 20,000 residents. Port Island is also where the jet-boat shuttle from **Kobe City Air Terminal** (KCAT) departs for the 30-minute ride to the Kansai International Airport.

Port Island, incidentally, offers a good vantage point from which to gaze back at Kobe, especially at night when it becomes a flickering tiara augmented by two insignia on the mountainside. One symbol is an anchor and the other a pair of interlocking fans that represent the unification of Hyogo Prefecture and Kobe. It was due to the fan-shaped perfection of the harbours of these villages that the trading port flourished as early as AD 700.

OPPOSITE: damage from 1995 Kobe earthquake.
BELOW: "Fish Dance", a sculpture in Kobe.

For an intriguing look at the cultural side of foreign trade, drop in at the nearby **Kobe Municipal Museum** (open Tuesday–Sunday, 10am–5pm; admission fee), housed in a former bank with Doric columns. This small, admirable museum focuses on Japan's early encounters with the West and features a rare collection of *namban* ("southern barbarian") art, works inspired by contacts with the first Portuguese and Spanish traders who arrived here during the 16th and 17th centuries.

Finally, down the coast from Sannomiya at the southern end of Kobe is one of the largest beaches to be found in western Japan, **Suma**, where there is Aqualife Park with a large aquarium and a dolphin show. From the vantage point of Suma's beach, the Akashi Kaikyo Ohashi, claimed to be the world's longest suspension bridge, can be seen connecting Japan's main island of Honshu to Shikoku via the large island of Awaji.

Kobe and Osaka are at the eastern end of **Seto Naikai**, or the **Inland Sea**. This protected 9,500-sq.-km (3,700-sq.-mile) body of water is encircled by western Honshu, Shikoku and Kyushu. Numerous ferries from all major cities on the Inland Sea offer an interesting and relaxing alternative to travelling in the area. One can take a ferry from Honshu, for example, to Shikoku or Kyushu, then continue one's journey on the train. ❑

Earthquakes

Japan is highly prone to earthquakes. There are minor shakes recorded on seismological instruments almost every day, and bigger ones that startle people from their sleep, rattle dishes, and knock objects off shelves occur several times a year. From time to time over the centuries, a major quake has hit the Tokyo area, causing heavy damage and leading to huge loss of life.

The reason for the earthquakes is that the Japanese archipelago is at a place where three moving segments of the earth's crust – the Pacific Plate, the Philippine Plate, and the Eurasian Plate – come into violent contact. (This explains Japan's volcanic activity and many hot springs.)

The Philippine Plate is the prime culprit, sliding in under central Honshu in a northeast direction at about 3 centimetres a year. The movement, in turn, puts stress on the primary fault that affects Tokyo and other earthquake-prone regions. Add to this a nest of faults spread widely under the islands, sometimes as deep as 100 km (60 miles).

In Tokyo, the danger from earthquakes is made worse because much of the city is on unconsolidated alluvial soil and on land-fill. This is a very poor foundation, which makes buildings tremble and oscillate more than they would on solid ground. Much of the waterfront damage during the 1995 Kobe earthquake was because of land-fill liquification. Much of the remaining damage was due to fire from burst gas mains.

A major tremor whiplashes the Tokyo area every 60 or 70 years on the average, and the last one, the Great Kanto Earthquake – a 7.9 magnitude jolt on the Richter scale – took place in 1923. It's about that time again.

In the 1923 earthquake, most of the central part of the city was levelled and totally destroyed by fire and over 100,000 people were killed. Close to Ryogoku Station is where 40,000 people were incinerated to death when a fire tornado swept across an open area where they had sought safety.

When it does happen, what will it be like? Some experts say that Tokyo is now much safer than it was in 1923. Buildings, bridges, and elevated highways are reinforced and built according to the latest techniques. In addition, much of the city is made to be fire-proof. There are also shelters and elaborate plans to provide help should the worst happen. But the 1995 Kobe earthquake has shattered just about every one of those assurances. In Kobe, earthquake-proof structures collapsed like jelly. Rescue and relief plans proved unworkable, and government response, both on the local and national levels, was inept and embarrassingly inadequate. Nearly 6,000 people died.

Is Japan – and the world's largest metropolitan area, Tokyo – prepared? Given the experience of the 1995 Kobe quake, the preparations and assumptions for a Tokyo-area earthquake have had to be reassessed.

Tokyo is the world's most-populated city, with extensive underground networks of subways and gas lines, and above ground, glass-covered buildings and flimsily constructed residences. Tens of thousands of people will probably die in a Kobe-strength quake. Many experts, Japanese and foreign, doubt that government plans are sufficient. ❑

KIMONOS FOR ALL SEASONS AND STYLES

Adopted from ancient Chinese court attire, the Japanese kimono today is mostly a ceremonial dress of exquisite textures and appeal.

Western dress is the norm amongst today's Japanese, and few wear traditional attire except on special occasions such as weddings or festivals. But when a busy street of suited businessmen and trendy schoolgirls is punctuated by the colours and elegance of a *kimono,* Japan momentarily reverts to another time and place.

Contrary to expectations, the kimono did not originate in Japan. Like many things "distinctly" Japanese, the kimono has its roots in China – the Chinese court. During the Nara Period (710–784), the Japanese imperial court adopted the Chinese-style *p'ao,* a long, kimono-like attire brilliant with colours and embellishment; kimono styles used by Japanese women during this time were similar to the p'ao garments of women in Tang-dynasty China. Indeed, the Heian-era court dress worn by Japan's emperor and empress today during special occasions displays Chinese characteristics unchanged since the 12th century.

Of course, as did most things adopted by the Japanese over the centuries, the kimono underwent changes that eventually made it distinctly Japanese. During the Muromachi Period (1338–1573), for example, women introduced the *obi,* a narrow sash, and adapted the kimono sleeves to fit Japanese climate and styles.

△ **OBI ACCESSORIES**
The *obi* – often ornate and made of embroidered silk – today is about 25 cm (10 in) wide and 3.7 m (12 ft) long.

▽ **SHICHI-GO-SAN**
In November, shrines are filled with girls of 3 and 7 and boys of 5 wearing kimono, often rented.

▽ **KIMONO**
The evolution of the kimono adopted Chinese styles while taking on distinctly Japanese lines, whether for ceremony (as with these kimono), theatre, or fashion.

▽ **HEAVY GATHERINGS**
Although said to be comfortable, elaborate kimono can also be "heavy" to wear, but feminine to see.

◁ DIFFERENCES
While the basic kimono design is consistent, regional and ceremonial differences abound.

△ TYING THE KNOT
The traditional marriage of Shintoism involves complicated kimono for both man and woman.

▽ EVOLVING DESIGNS
While conservative kimono are common, Japan's youth often demand something a little more spunky.

◁ YUKATA
Sumo wrestlers wearing *yukata*, a summer kimono of cotton with stencil-dyed patterns.

▷ RITUAL
Three-year-old girls at shrine for blessing.

THE OBI: SIMPLE AND EXQUISITE

Once a simple and narrow sash introduced by Muromachi-Period women, the *obi* has evolved into one of the most beautiful – and complicated – aspects of the *kimono* today.

The obi's need came about when the Japanese made changes to the adopted Chinese-court *p'ao*. A short-sleeved form of kimono (*kosode*) began to be worn as an outer garment, constrained by the obi. Later, the obi took on increased importance when women of the feudal estates wore an elaborate and exquisite outer kimono called *uchikake*. As centuries passed, only married women wore the kosode, while unmarried women wore the long-sleeved *furisode*.

The wider and more embellished silk obi seen today developed in the early 1700s during the Edo Period. This obi can be tied in a number of ways and may be embellished with *netsuke*, beautifully carved images used to cinch cords and fasten the details of the woman's obi.

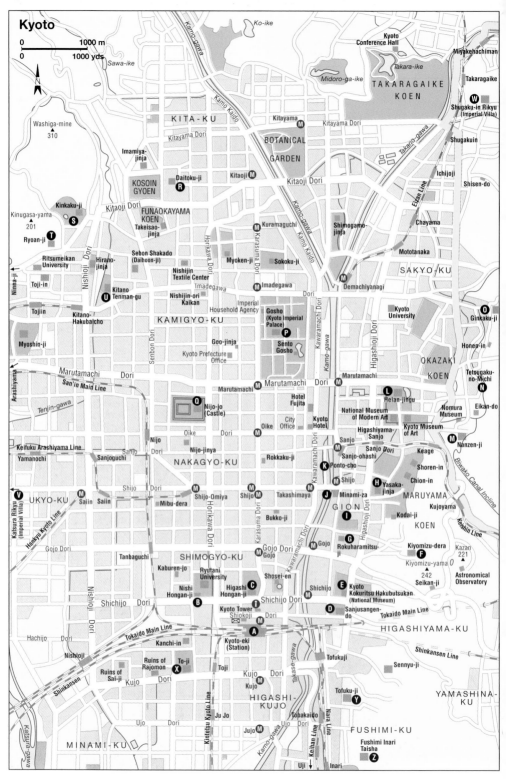

Kyoto

0 — 1000 m
0 — 1000 yds

Ko-ike

Sawa-ike

Kamo-gawa

Kyoto Conference Hall

Miyakehachiman

Midoro-ga-ike

Takara-ike

TAKARAGAIKE KOEN

Takaragaike

KITA-KU

Kitayama

W
Shugaku-in Rikyu (Imperial Villa)

Washiga-mine 310

Kitayama Dori

Kitayama Dori

Takano-gawa

Shugakuin

Imamiya-jinja

Kitayama Dori

M

Kitayama Dori

Ichijoji

Eikan Line

Shisen-do

Kinugasa-yama 201

Kinkaku-ji

Daitoku-ji

KOSOIN GYOEN

R

Kitaoji

Kitaoji Dori

M

Kitaoji Dori

Chayama

Ryoan-ji

T

S

FUNAOKAYAMA KOEN

Takeisao-jinja

Kitaoji Dori

Kuramaguchi

M

Shimogamo-jinja

Mototanaka

SAKYO-KU

Ritsumeikan University

Hirano-jinja

Sebon Shakado (Daihoon-ji)

Myoken-ji

Sokoku-ji

M

Ninna-ji

Toji-in

Nishijin Textile Center

Imadegawa

M

Imadegawa

Demachiyanagi

Kyoto University

Tojiin

Kitano-Hakubalcho

Nishijin-ori Kaikan

Imadegawa Dori

U

Kitano Tenman-gu

Imperial Household Agency

Gosho (Kyoto Imperial Palace)

Ginkaku-ji

Myoshin-ji

KAMIGYO-KU

Goo-jinja

P

Honen-in

O

Kyoto Prefecture Office

Sento Gosho

Tetsugaku-no-Michi

N

Arashiyama

Marutamachi Dori

San'in Main Line

Marutamachi Dori

Marutamachi Dori

Marutamachi

OKAZAKI KOEN

Tenjin-gawa

Hotel Fujita

Heian-jingu

Nomura Museum

Eikan-do

Keifuku Arashiyama Line

Nijo-jo (Castle)

Q

Oike Dori

City Office

Kyoto Hotel

National Museum of Modern Art

L

Yamanochi

Sanjoguchi

Nijo

Nijo-jinja

Oike Dori

M

Higashiyama-Sanjo

Kyoto Museum of Art

M

Nanzen-ji

Sanjo Dori

Sanjo

M

Nanzen-ji

Biwako Canal Incline

UKYO-KU

Saiin

M

Saiin

NAKAGYO-KU

Rokkaku-ji

Ponto-cho

K

Sanjo-ohashi

Keage

Shoren-in

Katsura Rikyu (Imperial Villa)

V

Hankyu Kyoto Line

Mibu-dera

Shijo-Omiya

Shijo

M

Shijo Dori

Shijo

M

Takashimaya

Shijo

H

Yasaka-jinja

Chion-in

MARUYAMA

Keage Line

Horikawa Dori

Bukko-ji

J

Minami-za

GION

I

Kodai-ji

KOEN

Kujoyama

SHIMOGYO-KU

Tanbaguchi

Kaburen-jo

Ryutani University

Shosei-en

Gojo Dori

M

Gojo

Rokuharamitsu-ji

G

Kiyomizu-dera

Kazan 221

Gojo Dori

M

Gojo

Higashiyama Dori

Kiyomizu-yama 0

F

242

Astronomical Observatory

Nishioji Dori

Nishi Hongan-ji

B

Higashi Hongan-ji

C

Shichijo

M

Shichijo

E

Kyoto Kokuritsu Hakubutsukan (National Museum)

Seikan-ji

Shichijo Dori

Shichijo Dori

Shichijo Dori

Kyoto Tower

f

Shiokoji Dori

D

Sanjusangen-do

HIGASHIYAMA-KU

Hachijo

Kanchi-in

A

Kyoto-eki (Station)

Tokaido Main Line

Tokaido Main Line

Shinkansen Line

Nishioji

Ruins of Rajomon

To-ji

X

Toji

Kujo Dori

Tofukuji

Sennyu-ji

Ruins of Sai-ji

Kujo Dori

Kujo

Kujo

Takase-gawa

YAMASHINA-KU

Shinkansen

HIGASHI-KUJO

Tofuku-ji

Y

Ujo Dori

Ju Jo

Tobakaido

Nara Line

Katsura-gawa

MINAMI-KU

Jujo

M

Ujo Dori

Uji

Inari

FUSHIMI-KU

Kamo-gawa

Kintetsu Kyoto Line

Keihan Line

Fushimi Inari Taisha

Z

Around Kyoto Station

Most people first encounter Kyoto from inside the gargantuan **Kyoto-eki** Ⓐ (**Kyoto Station**), less than three hours from Tokyo by *shinkansen*. Construction of this futuristic 16-story building, completed in 1997, created one of the hottest controversies in Kyoto's 1200-year history. Preservationists, environmentalists, and much of the city's population were opposed to its construction, especially for the sheer size of the complex, its obstruction of the mountain skyline, and its modern-glass structure lacking semblance to traditional architecture.

Exiting the station, the horrific sight of Any City, Japan, greets the visitor. The station area, and tragically much of central Kyoto, displays the characterless, cluttered sprawl of all Japanese cities. But fortunately, amid all of the ugly, thoughtless creations that increasingly plague the city are a vast treasure of sights behind fading imperial walls, down narrow lanes, and amidst the surrounding hills. This paradoxical element of Kyoto's physical evolution is, for many, a part of its appeal.

Directly north of Kyoto Station are two notable temples, Nishi (West) Hongan-ji and Higashi (East) Hongan-ji. As was the case with many of Kyoto's historical treasures, Japan's great unifier, Toyotomi Hideyoshi (1536–98), was responsible for establishing **Nishi Hongan-ji** Ⓑ. In 1591, Toyotomi brought the Jodo-shinshu Buddhist sect to the temple's current location. Its Chinese influences are many and historians sometimes consider it the best example of Buddhist architecture still around. The *hondo*, or main hall, was rebuilt in 1760 after fire destroyed it. The founder's hall – *daishido* – contains a self-carved effigy of the sect's founder. Cremated after his death, his ashes were mixed with lacquer and then applied to the effigy. The study hall (*shoin*) contains a

With some 40 universities, Kyoto is the educational centre of western Japan. A decline in the student numbers, however, has been spurned on by a lack of campus expansion funds; unable to afford more land in the city, many campuses are moving to rural areas.

BELOW: Kyoto's main train station obscures the city's horizon.

number of rooms named for their decorations: Wild Geese Chamber, Sparrow Chamber, and Chrysanthemum Chamber.

To the east, **Higashi Hongan-ji ●** was established in 1603 when the first Tokugawa shogun, wary of the Jodo-shinshu monks' power at nearby Nishi Hongan-ji, attempted to thwart their influence by establishing an offshoot of the sect. Only the main hall and founder's hall are open to the public. The present buildings were erected in 1895 after fire destroyed the predecessors. When these current structures were being built, female devotees cut and donated their hair, which was woven into 50 ropes used during construction; some of the ropes are on display between the main temple buildings.

Eastern Kyoto

Just east of Kyoto Station and across the Kamo-gawa, **Sanjusangen-do ●** (**Sanjusangen Hall**, also called Rengeo-in) was last rebuilt in 1266. The temple houses 33 (*sanju-san*) alcoves nestled between 33 pillars under a 60-metre-long (200-ft) roof. Inside is a 1,000-handed Kannon, the *bodhisattva* of mercy and compassion, and her 1,000 disciples. Each of their faces are different; Japanese look for the face that resembles their own – or that of a relative – to whom to make an offering. A famed archery festival, first started in 1606, takes place at the temple on 15 January.

On the opposite side of Shichijo-dori to the north is the **Kyoto Kokuritsu Hakubutsukan ●** (**Kyoto National Museum**; open Tuesday–Sunday, 9am–4.30pm; admission fee), founded in 1897 and exhibiting artifacts of history, art and crafts. Several other temples are east of the museum. Up the Kiyomizu-zaka, a slope on the east side of Higashioji-dori, is **Kiyomizu-dera ●**.

The record-holder for the archery competition at Sanjusangen-do shot 13,000 arrows during a 24-hour period in the late 1600s; just over 8,000 of the arrows hit the target.

BELOW: the hall at Sanjusangen-do.

(*See photo on pages 234-35.*) The temple's main hall (hondo) sits perched out over the mountain side on massive wooden pilings. The veranda, or *butai* (dancing stage), juts out over the valley floor overlooking the city below. A popular Japanese proverb equates taking any big chance in life to jumping off the elevated stage at Kiyomizu. Founded in 788, Kiyomizu-dera predates Kyoto and is dedicated to the 11-faced Kannon. The two 3.6-metre-tall (12-ft) deva kings (*nio*) guarding the front gate speak the whole of Buddhist wisdom: the right one has lips pursed in the first letter of the Sanskrit alphabet, *a*, while the one on the left mouths *om*, the last letter. Behind the main hall with its dancing stage is Jishu, one of the most popular Shinto shrines in the country, and where the god of love and good marriage resides. (Most Buddhist temples in Japan also house some sort of Shinto shrine.) Don't trip over the blind stones (*mekura-ishi*) or the people walking between them with their eyes closed. The belief is that if one can negotiate the 20 metres (60 ft) between the stones with their eyes closed, silently repeating the name of their loved one, love and marriage are assured.

Steps lead down from Kiyomizu's main hall to **Otowa-no-taki**, a waterfall where visitors sip water from a spring said to have many health benefits, if not sheer divine power for the true believer. A short walk leads up the other side of the valley to a small pagoda with a view encompassing the entire hillside.

From Kiyomizu, return down the slope and follow down a flight of stone steps to Sannen-zaka, a street meaning "three-year slope". It is said that any pilgrim who trips or stumbles along this slope will have three years of bad luck. Today, the cobbled lane is less superstitiously known as Teapot Lane for all of the pottery shops lining its path. Continue to the charming Ninen-zaka, or "two-year slope". The restaurants near here are good for *soba* or *udon* noodles.

Map on page 256

Temple signs are generally explicit.

BELOW: tour group from the country.

Back across Higashioji-dori sits **Rokuharamitsu-ji** 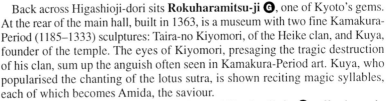, one of Kyoto's gems. At the rear of the main hall, built in 1363, is a museum with two fine Kamakura-Period (1185–1333) sculptures: Taira-no Kiyomori, of the Heike clan, and Kuya, founder of the temple. The eyes of Kiyomori, presaging the tragic destruction of his clan, sum up the anguish often seen in Kamakura-Period art. Kuya, who popularised the chanting of the lotus sutra, is shown reciting magic syllables, each of which becomes Amida, the saviour.

North are the brilliant-orange buildings of **Yasaka-jinja** ⑭, affectionately called Gion-san after the adjoining Gion pleasure quarter. One of the tallest granite *torii* in Japan at 9 metres (30 ft) in height marks the portal to the shrine. From the shrine's back gate, one enters adjoining Maruyama-koen. The park is known for its beautiful garden and magnificent cherry blossoms in early April. Two interesting temples sit just beyond: **Chion-in** and **Shoren-in**.

East of the Kamo-gawa in central Kyoto, **Gion** ❶ is Kyoto's famous pleasure-quarter or *geisha* district, today an uncanny blend of traditional and grotesque modern architecture. In Kyoto, geisha are known as *maiko* and *geiko*, not geisha. The word *geisha* in old Kyoto referred to male entertainers dressed as women; in Tokyo and Osaka, however, it came to mean women. Maiko debut at about 16 years old and wear distinctive long trailing *obi*. At about 21, they may advance to the ranks of geiko, with their highly-ornate kimono.

Along Gion's narrow streets, one will rarely see geiko, but there's a good chance to catch sight of a maiko hurrying to entertain a guest. The tea houses in the quarter are in the style of Kyoto's old *machiya* town houses, but with added delicate touches such as the orange-pink plastered walls (*ichirikijaya*). The best place to see the houses is along the alleyways that splinter off Hamani-koji,

BELOW: a *maiko* in kimono, Gion.

JAPAN'S LOLITA COMPLEX

You see both groups on the rush-hour trains: tired blue-suited middle-aged men reading newspapers with baseball scores on one page and adverts for sex clubs on the other, and chattering groups of high-school girls wearing sailor uniforms, white socks, and an assortment of electronic toys. It's not unusual for the men to cast an eye at the girls, who are in increasing numbers catering to the men's fantasy. In Japanese it's called *enjo kosai*, or paid dating, usually translating as the oldest profession.

Japanese men seem obsessed with high-school girls. Animated TV programs, adult comic books, weekly tabloid magazines, and sports newspapers — all display ads for cute girls in school uniforms and photos of "AV girls", or porn actresses. Television advertising directed towards men often features school girls.

A couple of years ago, the Tokyo government issued a report that said one-fourth of high-school girls in Tokyo had called a telephone-dating club at least once. In every major city, public telephone booths are covered with stickers advertising teenage dates. Today, however, it is tougher for enjo kosai. Police have cracked down on telephone dating clubs, which had started recruiting junior high-school girls.

Map on page 256

south of Shijo-dori. Just north of here is Gion Shimbashi, another well-preserved neighbourhood of old wooden buildings. At the intersection of Shijo-dori and the Kamo-gawa, **Minami-za** ❶, built in the early 1600s, is the oldest theatre in Japan and is still used for *kabuki* performances.

For the height of imperial drama, try a *noh* play, which developed in Kyoto in the 14th century. Rooted in *sarugaku*, or ballad operas, the lyrical and melodramatic form became known as *sarugaku no noh*, later shortened to noh. A classical presentation includes five plays with several humourous interludes called *kyogen*. Most presentations today show only two plays and two interludes. Noh greatly departs from Western ideas of drama by abandoning realism in favour of symbolism. Three performers, all men, enact the play on a bare stage with a painted pine-tree backdrop. Musicians and chorus sit openly on the stage.

Noh developed in Kyoto as one of Japan's original art forms, along with kabuki and *bunraku* (puppet theatre). Kabuki (*ka-bu-ki*, or singing-dancing-performing) was the last purely Japanese art form to develop, developing during the Edo Period as a commoner's entertainment. Originating from dancing shows of women, which the shogun declared immoral and forbidden to women, kabuki turned to men as performers. It has more variety and greater dynamic force than noh and appeals to a wider audience.

Other areas for traditional nightlife include traffic-free **Ponto-cho** ❸ along the west bank of Kamo-gawa and just across from Gion. The narrow street is lined with interesting bars, restaurants and *tayu* (top-ranked courtesan) houses. Kawaramachi is another busy shopping, eating and entertainment neighbourhood, also located beyond the Kamo's west bank. An excellent spot to dine in summer are the restaurants along Kamo-gawa, between Shijo and Sanjo streets.

The many hostess-staffed "snack" bars in Gion are a pricey diversion in which an hour or two can easily cost US$500.

BELOW: a *maiko* making her way down a Kyoto alley.

Cross over Sanjo-dori and continue north to **Okazaki-koen**. This park holds museums, halls, a library and zoo. An arching 24-metre-high (80 ft) *torii* leads from Okazaki-koen to the vermilion-coloured gate of **Heian-jingu** , more of an architectural study than a Shinto centre. The shrine, dedicated to Kyoto's first and last emperors, is a replica of the original Imperial Palace built in 794 and last destroyed by fire in 1227.

The shrine was erected in 1895 to commemorate Kyoto's 1,100th anniversary and displays architecture of the Heian Period, when Chinese influence was at its zenith. Shinto shrines took on Buddhist temple features during this period, when the plain wooden structures were first painted.

Passing through the shrine's massive gate, it's hard to imagine that the shrine is but a two-thirds scale version of the original palace. The expansive, white-pebble courtyard leads the eye to the Daigoku-den, or main hall, where government business was conducted. The Blue Dragon and White Tiger pagodas dominate the view to the east and west. To the left of the main hall is the entrance to the garden, designed in the spirit of the Heian Period for the pleasures of walking and boating. Mirror ponds, dragon stepping-stones, and a Chinese-style bridge are some of the beguiling features.

From Heian-jingu, walk east a bit to **Nanzen-ji** , which was originally the residence of 26-year-old Emperor Kameyama (1249–1305) after his abdication in 1274. Impressed by the powers of *zazen* (seated meditation), he deeded part of his palace to the establishment of the temple in 1290.

Nanzen-ji sits nestled in a pine grove at the foot of Daimonji-yama and is part of the Rinzai school of Zen Buddhism, Zen's largest and best-known school. It's also one of Kyoto's most important Zen temples. The complex consists of the

BELOW: Heian-jingu.

main temple and 12 sub-temples, of which only four are regularly open to the public. Nanzen-ji provides an example of the Zen's belief in the relationship between all things. The pine grove influences the architecture, art influences the garden, and taken together they all influence the observer. The temple reflects the Chinese style (*kara-yo*) that arrived in Japan along with Zen. This style, evolving through the Ashikaga Period (1338–1573), achieved a near-perfect balance between the lordly Chinese style and the lightness of the native Japanese style. Exploring the two buildings of the abbots' quarters – Daiho-jo and Shoho-jo – reveals how garden architecture and landscape painting interrelate. The quarters are full of famous paintings, like *Tiger in the Bamboo Grove*, and the surrounding gardens are renowned as some of the best in Japan. Here, the gardens are for sitting and contemplation, not strolling.

From Nanzen-ji, follow **Tetsugaku no Michi** , or the Philosopher's Walk, north past the Nomura Museum, Eikan-do temple, and the intriguing hillside temple of Honen-in. The walk, named for the strolling path of Japanese philosopher Nishida Kitaro (1870–1945), snakes about 2 km along the bank of a narrow canal to Ginkaku-ji. The quiet path – save for the crowds of tourists at times – is noted for its spring cherry blossoms and fall foliage. Along the path are interesting homes, shops, tea rooms, and small restaurants – try a bowl of Kyoto's famous tofu and vegetable stew (*kyo-yudofu*).

The walk ends at the **Silver Pavilion**, or **Ginkaku-ji** . The Ashikaga-era shogun who erected it in 1489 died before its completion and contrarily it remains sans silver. However, its exquisite pavilion and Zen garden are not disappointing. The first floor of the pavilion was a residence and displays the Japanese *shinden* style. The second floor served as the alter room and shows a

Map on page 256

Ginkaku-ji.

BELOW: purification at Heian-jingu.

Chinese Buddhist style. The mound of white stones (Kogetsudai) in the garden was designed to reflect moonlight onto the garden. The quaint tea room in the northeastern section of the pavilion is touted as the oldest in Japan.

Central Kyoto

Due west on the other side of the Kamo-gawa, the **Gosho** ❿ (**Kyoto Imperial Palace**) remains the emperor's residence in Kyoto and thus under the control of the Imperial Household Agency, which dictates every nuance and moment of the imperial family's life. Originally built as a second palace for the emperor, the Kyoto Imperial Palace was used as a primary residence from 1331 until 1868, when Tokyo became the new residence with the fall of the shogunate and with the Meiji restoration of the imperial system. The palace has gone through many restorations over the centuries; the current buildings and structures were built in the mid-1800s. Shishinden (Enthronement Hall), standing with its sweeping cedar roof before a silent stone courtyard, is an impressive emblem of imperial rule. It was constructed in the shinden style, where all buildings are connected by covered walkways or galleries. The court town that once surrounded the hall is now **Kyoto Gyoen**, the public Kyoto Imperial Park.

From the palace, a few blocks west is **Nishijin**, the weaver's quarter. The **Nishijin Textile Centre** has excellent displays of working looms and woven goods. Here, try on a kimono. After browsing the centre, walk through the narrow side streets – the ancient crafts of weaving and dying are still practiced in the old wooden buildings.

South is **Nijo-jo** ❾, a castle begun in 1569 by the warlord Oda Nobunaga and finished by Tokugawa Ieyasu, ally to Oda Nobunaga, to demonstrate his mili-

BELOW: *sayanora* to guests at a *ryokan*, or traditional inn.

Map on page 256

tary dominance over the city. In 1867, it served as the seat of government from where Emperor Meiji abolished the shogunate. Rectangular in dimensions, the castle's magnificent stone walls and gorgeous gold-leafed audience halls reflect the power of the Edo-Period shoguns. The linking corridors of the castle's Nino-maru Palace feature "nightingale" (creaking) floors to warn of intruders. The garden is a grand example of a lord's strolling garden.

Just south of the castle is **Nijo Jinya**, originally the home of a wealthy merchant and later used as an inn by visiting *daimyo*. The old manor house is full of trap doors, secret passageways, and hidden rooms – the stuff from which samurai and ninja dramas are made.

To the northwest and west

To the north and west of the city centre, skirting the foothills, are three renowned Zen temples that should not be missed. Established as a small monastery in 1315, the present buildings of **Daitoku-ji ®** were built after 1468 when one of the several fires in its history burned down the temple. It is the holy of holies, where Zen married art. The great Zen calligrapher Ikkyu (d. 1481), painter Soga Dasoku (d. 1483), and founders of the tea ceremony Murata Juko (d. 1502) and Sen-no Rikyu (d. 1591) all came from Daitoku-ji.

The great warlord Oda Nobunaga is buried here. Although a brutal warrior, Nobunaga was fundamental to the 16th-century unification of Japan and was a leading patron of the arts.

Some eight of Daitoku-ji's 22 subsidiary temples are open to the public. The three best-known are Daisen, Zuiho and Koto. In Daisen-in is Kyoto's second most famous – maybe the best – Zen garden. Unlike the abstractions of other

BELOW: covered shopping arcade, and one of Kyoto's strolling gardens.

gardens, the Daisen garden more closely resembles the ink-wash paintings of Zen art. Look for the mountains, rivers and islands in the water, which appears to flow under the veranda.

The Daitoku complex has been criticised for its commercialism, but it is still worth the visit. This is also one of the best places to sample authentic Zen temple food, just like the monks eat. The Izusen, in the Daiiji-in sub-temple, offers traditional high-protein, low-calorie vegetarian meals of wheat gluten and tofu served in a delightful garden setting. The meal is delivered in red-lacquer begging bowls, which are nestled into each other when finished.

Original structure of Kinkaku-ji in the early 1900s. It was destroyed by arson in 1950.

Walk west along Kitaoji-dori past Funaokayama-koen to the best-known temple in Kyoto, if not all Japan: **Kinkaku-ji ❺**, or the **Golden Pavilion**. It's a replica built in 1955 of a 15th-century structure and last recovered in gold-leaf in 1987. Each of the pavilion's three stories reflect a different architectural style. The first floor is of the palace style, the second floor of the samurai-house style, while the third floor reveals the Zen-temple style. The large pond in front of the pavilion and surrounding grounds make it a perfect setting.

The original temple was burned down in 1950 by a man who entered the Buddhist priesthood after being seduced by the pavilion's beauty. Thinking that his sense of aesthetics might approach perfection if he burned down the very object that had enchanted him in the first place, he did exactly that. The author and right-wing nationalist Mishima Yukio fictionalised the burning episode in his 1956 book, *Kinkakuji*.

Further west, visit **Ryoan-ji ❼**, or Temple of the Peaceful Dragon, early in the day before the peace is shattered by the bus-loads of tourists and students. Here is the most famous Zen rock garden (*karesansui*, or dry landscape) in the

BELOW: Kinkaku-ji.

Map on page 256

world and one of Kyoto's main tourist attractions. The 16th-century garden is an abstract of an ink-wash painting executed in rock and stone. No one knows the exact meaning of its 15 rocks (one is always out of sight) and raked gravel, but speculations abound. Take a seat on the veranda and let the mind empty (that is if you can arrive before the crowds, or else wait until they leave). The barren area of the raked stones and the contours of the rocks convey a sense of infinite space said to lift the mind into a Zen state.

A little past Ryoan-ji to the west, **Ninna-ji**'s formidable gate with its fierce-looking *nio* guardians is one of the best in Japan. Returning east, **Myoshin-ji** was founded in 1337 on the old site of an imperial villa. Cast in 698, Japan's oldest bell hangs here. Tenth-century **Kitano Tenman-gu** is one of Kyoto's most earthy shrines and hosts a popular antique market on the 25th of each month. Its restrained wooden architecture enshrines Sugawara Michizane, a 9th-century scholar and statesman. Small wood votives, or *ema* – with a picture of a horse on one side and a wish or prayer (most for success in school exams) written on the other side – hang in the courtyard. The shrine also celebrates the first calligraphy of the year, when school children offer their writings to the shrine. The present shrine structure was built in 1607. Tenman-gu is known for its splendid plum trees that bloom in the snows of February, and for the geisha that serve tea under the flowering trees.

Out in the western hills, **Arashiyama** was once the playground of Heian aristocrats. Today it is punctuated by temples. Cross over the Hozu-gawa on picturesque Togetsu Bridge to the shop-lined promenade along the river. Just beyond sits **Jikishian**, a refuge temple for women escaping messy relationships; women have written assorted tales in some 2,000 books of reminiscences.

TIP

Had enough of temples? This may put a spring back in your step and a wry smile on your face. West of Myoshin-ji is a funky diversion: Toei Eiga-mura, or Toei Movieland, a working studio specialising in samurai TV dramas and open to tourists.

BELOW: figuring out life at Ryoan-ji.

One of Japan's most famous strolling gardens lies inside **Katsura Rikyu** (**Katsura Imperial Villa**), due west of Kyoto Station on the west side of Katsura-gawa. Its garden features a number of splendid tea houses overlooking a large central pond. Katsura, with its severe refinement, has exercised more influence on contemporary architecture than perhaps any other building in Japan. (Visitors require advance permission from the Imperial Household Agency.)

To the northeast

In the northern foothills, the **Shugaku-in Rikyu** ⓦ (**Shugaku-in Imperial Villa**) was built in 1659 as an emperor's retreat. The imperial villa at Shugaku-in seems pure fantasy compared to Katsura Imperial Villa. It consists of three large, separate gardens and villas. In Rakushiken (Middle Villa) stands a cedar door with carp painted on both sides. It's said that the carp would escape each night to swim in the villa's pond. Not until golden nets were painted over them, in the 18th century, did they stay put. (Shugaku-in requires permission from the Imperial Household Agency before visiting.)

Hiei-zan, an 850-metre-high (2,800-ft) mountain northeast of Shugaku-in Imperial Villa, has long held historic and religious importance to Kyoto. Here, **Enryaku-ji** was founded to protect the new capitol from evil northeast spirits. Apparently this exalted mission gave the temple's monks an inflated sense of importance. Over the decades, they became aggressive friars of the martial arts and swept into Kyoto on destructive raids. Their not-so-monastic rumbles were quenched by warlord Oda Nobunaga, who destroyed the temple in 1571. Today, there are three pagodas and 100 sub-temples, some offering accommodations and making Hiei-zan one of the area's most accessible hiking areas.

TIP

Both Japanese and foreign visitors need special permission to visit one of the imperial villas. Bring your passport to the Imperial Household Agency office at the Kyoto Imperial Palace early on the day you wish to visit.

BELOW: garden at Katsura Rikyu.

South of Kyoto Station

Just south of Kyoto Station, **To-ji** ⊗ boasts one of the nation's enduring post-card images: the five-story Goju-no-to pagoda. Rebuilt in 1644, it stands at 55 metres (180 ft) as Japan's tallest pagoda. The temple itself was established in 796 and today draws large crowds to its flea markets. Built next to the old city's south gate, To-ji became Japan's main Buddhist temple. Its main hall (*kondo*) reflects Buddhist traditions from India, China, and Japan.

To the east up against the hills, **Tofuku-ji** ⊗ rests as one of the best places for autumn foliage. It contains Japan's oldest and perhaps most important Zen-style gate, from the 15th century. Yet its 25 subsidiary temples are rarely visited and the grounds are usually quiet. Walk through the abbot's quarters (*hojo*) to the platform over the ravine looking down on Tsuten Bridge – it's one of the most delightful views in Kyoto. During the last week of November, don't miss the festival of old brushes and pens. Writers and painters bring their used pens and brushes to be cast into a sacred fire. A few block south of Tofuku-ji is where tunnel-like paths of hundreds of bright-red torii tempt walkers. Actually, there are over 10,000 torii covering the paths of **Fushimi Inari Taisha** ⊗ – the fox shrine founded in the 9th century in honour of the fox that farmers believe is the messenger of the harvest god. Walk the full 4-km (2½-mile) course.

About 10 km (6 miles) south of Fushimi Inari Taisha, on the way to Nara and in the town of **Uji**, is famous **Byodo-in**, depicted on the back of the 10-yen coin (and replicated on Oahu, in Hawaii). Built as a retreat villa for a powerful aristocrat of the Heian Period, it was converted to a temple by his son. Most of the temple was razed during war in the 1300s. One structure, Phoenix Hall, survived the destruction.

Map on page 256

BELOW: *torii* of Fushimi Inari Taisha, and Amida, Buddha of Paradise at Byodo-in.

Map on page 256

Festivals of Kyoto

Japanese, especially in Kyoto, define their year with festivals, rituals, and ceremonies. The years pass infused with a natural rhythm; the 1,200th recorded cycle of the four seasons of a year passed in Kyoto in 1994.

January: At the stroke of midnight, people dressed in their finest kimono head for the nearest temple or shrine to pay their New Year's respects.

February: The last day of lunar winter falls during the first week with the celebration of *setsubun*. At Yasaka-jinja, butterfly-like maiko dancers swing to the lilting twang of ancient lutes (*biwa*). Throwing symbols of luck – red *azuki* beans – into the crowed, they chant, "Out with demons, in with good fortune".

March: Camellias fall like the heads of samurai worriers, which years ago didn't make samurai very happy. But for the tea masters, falling camellia symbolised spring. The best place to see falling camellias is at Seiryo-ji.

April: Spring arrives with geisha dancing under the blossoming cherry trees. Kyoto has a multitude of blossom-viewing (*hanami*) parties, the most famous being Daigo-ji. Nothing contemplative about hanami, it should be noted.

May: Spring is in full bloom. Azaleas, peaches and rhododendrons blossom, and temples air their sacred treasures in the fresh breeze. Jingo-ji displays its art collection, normally hidden from public view, in its Insect-Drying Festival.

June: The summer rains (*tsuyu*) blanket Kyoto from mid-June through mid-July, when rain falls constantly in a heavy drizzle. Kifune-jinja, dedicated to the god of water, celebrates the season in a vibrant water festival.

July: With the end of tsuyu comes the heat of summer and Tanabata. According to legend, two stars that are lovers cross the Milky Way to meet once a year on Tanabata. The biggest Tanabata festival is at Kitano Tenman-gu.

The biggest festival in Kyoto is the Gion Matsuri, dating from the 10th century. On 17 July, floats decorated in elaborate Chinese and European tapestries parade through town with hundreds of participants in traditional costume.

August: This is the month of Obon, when the spirits of the dead revisit the world of the living to be entertained for a few days before returning to the other side. Lamps and fires are lit by families to guide their departed relatives along their way. Around Kiyomizu-dera, once the site of an immense burial ground, thousands of paper lanterns are strung by the gravestones and the grounds are open all night to visitors. On 16 August at 8pm on the five mountains around the city, *gozan okuribi* sends the spirits of the dead back to the other world with spectacular mountainside bonfires in the shape of immense Chinese characters.

September: This is the neutral month of Zen. Mid September is the time for moon-viewing, with numerous events across town. Osawa Pond, behind Daikaku-ji, has been known since Heian times as one of Japan's three great moon-viewing sites. Massive crowds.

October: This is the month of dress-up and strange happenings. The Bull Festival at Koryu-ji is known as one of the "Weird Festivals" of Kyoto. Jidai Matsuri (Festival of the Ages) climaxes the Weird Festivals and apexes October's round of fancy dress. Some 2,000 participants lead a parade through town representing famous people in Japanese history, dressed in their traditional styles.

November: People travel out of the city to see the fall foliage. North of town, the small village of Ohara with its hillside villages is spectacular, as is the Arashiyama and Sagano areas in the west.

December: Face-showing (*kaomise*) is Kyoto's gala kabuki performance at Minami-za, when the actors reveal their real faces. Senbon Shaka-do celebrates the day of Buddha's enlightenment with a radish-boiling ceremony, where the radishes are inscribed with magic Sanskrit letters. And in December, temples and shrines all over town begin cleaning in preparation for the New Year. ❑

*On the last day of December, the old year departs at exactly midnight with 108 strikes on temple bells (*joya no kane*) all across town. It takes 17 monks at Chion-in to ring Japan's largest bell.*

Young boy in ancient costume during the jidai matsuri.

OPPOSITE: contrasts in Ponto-cho.

NARA

Japan's capital in the 8th century, Nara later escaped the civil wars that shook the country. A repository of ancient treasures, it embodies Chinese, Korean, and even Middle Eastern styles

Maps on pages 238, 278

The ancient site of **Nara** belongs to an era before Zen gardens and tea ceremony, before Japan became Japan. Buddhist thought from India and arts from as far as Greece and Turkey flowed east along the Silk Road and Nara was the last stop. Preserved here long after extinction in their home countries are the finest examples of Tang-dynasty architecture from China, early Korean religious sculpture, and treasures from Iran.

Japan had its capital at Nara from AD 710 to 784, after which the government moved to Kyoto and the Nara area lost political importance. This was Nara's great blessing. As a result, it avoided the wars that destroyed other ancient capitals of China, Korea, and Japan.

Nara Buddhism represented an early exuberant form of Buddhist thought, rich in symbolism. Everywhere in Nara are *mandala*, the diagrams or arrangements representing cosmic truth. Represented at the centre is the essence of the main god. Expanding outward in circles or squares are other gods exerting their powers to help the centre. Mandalas can be represented in the arrangement of statues on an altar to the layout of temple buildings. Every placement and gesture has meaning. For example, two guardian figures flank the gates to large temples. One has his mouth open, the other closed. These symbolise the sounds *a* and *om*, the first and last letters of the Sanskrit alphabet. Being first and last, they encompass all and hence have magical power to protect against evil.

Hand gestures, clothing and implements are significant. Most ornate are the *mandorla*, or halos, in which can be seen the intercultural impact of the Silk Road. The halos originated in Indian Buddhism and travelled east to Japan and west to Europe, where they were adopted by Christianity. The flames in the halos signify divine light.

Statues with great power were hidden from the public and became the so-called secret Buddhas, shown only on rare occasions. For instance, the Kuze Kannon of Horyu-ji was hidden from the public for a thousand years before seeing the light of day in the late 19th century. Many statues are still only shown in the spring or fall or on religious holidays.

Many Nara masterpieces owe their beauty to the technique of dry lacquer, in which the contours of the figure are molded out of a paste of lacquer applied over a central core. The use of a soft plastic material, rather than carving, allows for great subtlety of expression. While the origins of using lacquer are rather obscure, the technique of lacquer in its most basic form is found throughout Asia, including China, Korea, Thailand, and Burma.

LEFT: lanterns at Kasuga Taisha. **BELOW:** a fortune for success.

Old Nara

Old Nara, much larger than the city today, followed the traditional model of Chinese imperial cities: a sacred square with streets radiating from the central palace in a grid pattern. During the centuries of neglect after 784, the palaces of Nara disappeared, but the temples and shrines on the northeastern edge of the city survived. This corner of the city is now a public park, **Nara-koen (Nara Park)**. Tame deer, sacred to the shrine of Kasuga Taisha, are its symbol.

A temple to the east of **Nara-eki** **(Nara Station)** is **Kofuku-ji B**, on the western side of Nara-koen. The patrons of Kofuku-ji were the Fujiwara clan, who gained power in the mid-7th century and succeeded in dominating the government for the next 500 years. Even after the capital moved to Kyoto, the Fujiwara continued to support Kofuku-ji as the family temple. Kofuku-ji is known for its two pagodas. The five-story pagoda, built in 1426, is a copy of an original dating from 730 and is the second-tallest pagoda in Japan; the three-story pagoda dates from 1114.

The attached **Kokuhokan (Treasure House;** open Tuesday–Sunday, 9am–5pm; admission fee) – a dreary, concrete building – offers the best introduction to Japanese sculpture available. Most famous is the set of guardians (734) with sweet, child-like faces molded out of dry lacquer. Of these, the six-armed Ashura is one of the best-loved statues in Japan. In addition, the museum displays a cast bronze head of Yakushi Nyorai, practically Egyptian in its abstract simplicity, and massive heads of temple guardians originally from statues that must have been 15 to 20 metres (50 to 65 ft) high. (Nara developed in an age before Japan became the land of the miniature. The buildings and statues aimed to exceed even the grandeur of Imperial China.)

Scent of chrysanthemums, And in Nara All the ancient Buddhas.

– BASHO
17TH CENTURY

BELOW: tame deer at Nara-koen.

Northwest

The best place to begin here is **Hannya-ji**, the Temple of Wisdom. Surrounded by a garden of wildflowers, it has great charm. In the garden is a Kamakura-era gate with elegant upturned gables and a 13-story Heian-era stone pagoda. The temple houses a Kamakura statue of Monju, the god of wisdom. Monju rides on his sacred lion, carrying in his hand the sword to cut through ignorance. About 2 km (1¼ miles) from Nara-koen, it was the centre of the ancient city. Of the palace nothing survives but a large field with circular clipped hedges showing where the pillars used to stand. Just east of the palace field is **Hokke-ji**, a nunnery known for its 8th-century statue of Kannon. The statue is of unpainted wood and with features said to be copied from the face of Empress Komyo and surrounded by a halo of sprouting lotus leaves.

North of Hokke-ji are imperial tomb mounds surrounded by moats, and beyond them to the northwest is **Akishino-dera**, patron temple of the arts. The original temple was founded in 775, but the present hall dates from the Kamakura Period. Inside is Gigeiten, god of the arts and a favourite of Nara cognoscente. The head is original Nara, with the delicacy of expression typical of dry lacquer. The body, a recreation from the Kamakura Period, has the S-curve of Chinese sculpture.

Southwest

The southwestern temples are a major destination for travellers. The first temple from Nara-koen is **Toshodai-ji**, founded by the Chinese monk Ganjin in 751. The roof of the *kondo* (main hall) is the finest surviving example of Tang-dynasty architecture. Note the inward curving fish tails on the roof, unique to Nara. **Yakushi-ji** is a 10-minute walk due south from Toshodai-ji. All of the

Map on page 278

The statue of Kannon at Hokke-ji is one of the secret Buddhas, on view only from 30 March to 7 April, 6 to 8 June, and 25 October to 8 November each year.

BELOW: entrance to traditional tea shop.

DIALECTICAL ROOTS

Japanese ranks ninth worldwide in the number of speakers. Since the mid-20th century following World War II, no nation other than Japan has used Japanese as a language.

The origins of Japanese are not known with any certainty. A strong hypothesis connects Japanese to Korean, with the introduction through Kyushu over 2,000 years ago of a language of southern Korea, along with the cultivation of rice.

Dialects abound in this archipelago punctuated by mountain peaks and deep valleys, not to mention the islands themselves. Some dialects – those of Kyushu and Tohoku come to mind – are nearly unintelligible to most Japanese. Even the differences between Tokyo and Osaka (known for its earthier language) are pronounced. *Kyotsu-go*, or "common language" and based on the Tokyo/Kanto dialect, linguistically unifies the islands.

original buildings have been destroyed by fires except the eastern pagoda, originally built in 698 and rebuilt 718. This is constructed of a harmonious arrangement of three roofs, with smaller roofs underneath creating the illusion of six stories. Unfortunately, the complex as a whole lacks the Nara charm due to modern reconstructions of the western pagoda (1981) and the main hall (1976). The main hall houses an original triad (considerably restored) of Yakushi flanked by Nikko, Light of the Sun, and Gakko, Light of the Moon.

The goal of most travellers in this area is **Horyu-ji**, which boasts the oldest wooden buildings in the world. Horyu-ji was founded in 607 by Prince Shotoku, the pivotal figure who established Chinese culture in Japan. The temple is something of a time capsule preserving hundreds of art works from the 7th and 8th centuries. Horyu-ji is divided into two wings. Most visitors start from the western cloister. The main gate, dating from 1438, leads to an avenue lined by earthen walls characteristic of Horyu-ji. Note the wood-grain patterns created by pressing the walls with boards, thought to make the walls earthquake resistant. At the end of the avenue is **Chu-mon** (Middle Gate). The pillars of the gate (dating from 607, rebuilt circa 670) are famous for their entasis (outward curvature), a feature of Greek architecture that travelled to Japan via the Silk Road.

Inside the western cloister are the pagoda and kondo (main hall), circa 670. The kondo houses a rare group of bronzes dating from 620 in Wei style. They are distinguished by elongated faces, the "archaic smile," and the abstract, almost art-deco lines of the falling drapery and the flames of the mandorla. In the centre is the Shaka Triad (Sakyamuni, the historical Buddha, with attendants). To the right is Yakushi and to the left is Amida, the Buddha of Paradise. Guardians, standing on demons, are Japan's oldest "Four Heavenly Kings."

BELOW: procession of Buddha images in Nara.

Map on page 278

One of the pleasures of Horyu-ji is the walk out through the cloister, an old example of a Chinese form that influenced temples and palaces throughout eastern Asia. Outside the cloister, walk east to the two concrete buildings of the museum, **Daihozod-en** (**Great Treasure House**). These buildings are even uglier than the museum of Kofuku-ji, but the treasures inside are important. Among the displays in the museum: the Kudara Kannon from Korea, the portable shrine of Lady Tachibana, and the Hyakuman pagodas, which contain strips of paper printed with short prayers. Published in 764 in an edition of one million, they are the world's oldest printed material.

From the museum there is a walk bordered by temples and earthen walls to the eastern cloister. In the centre is an octagonal building of Chinese inspiration, surmounted by a flaming jewel and known as the **Yumedono**, Hall of Dreams. Built around 740, it commemorates a dream of Prince Shotoku in which an angel appeared to him while he was copying the sutras. The Yumedono contains a secret Buddha, the Kuze Kannon, that is only on view in the spring and fall.

Behind the eastern cloister is **Chugu-ji**, a nunnery housing a wooden statue of Miroku, god of the future and the supreme statue of Nara. Possibly of Korean workmanship, it dates from the early 7th century. With one leg hanging down in the posture known as "princely ease", Miroku sits with his head tilted slightly and a hand raised to his cheek in a thinking gesture. Although Miroku is enshrined in a drab concrete building, this is an ideal place to stop, rest, and meditate for a while.

Slightly removed from the Horyu-ji complex are the two temples of **Hokki-ji** and **Horin-ji**, around 1 km (1,100 yards) north of Chugu-ji. Hokki-ji contains a three-story pagoda built in 706. Horin-ji was rebuilt only in 1975.

BELOW: roof lines of Taima-dera.

Map on page 278

South Yamato and Asuka

Taima-dera and **Shakko-ji** are known for their thousands of varieties of peonies. Taima-dera contains two Nara-Period pagodas and a "secret" mandala painting (an Edo-Period copy is on view). On 14 May each year parishioners don masks of the Buddhas and parade through the grounds in a unique display of walking sculpture.

Asuka, the capital before Nara from 552 to 645, was the first city to have avenues on the Chinese grid pattern and large Buddhist temples. It was here that Prince Shotoku introduced Chinese law and philosophy. And it was here that the poems of the *Manyoshu*, Japan's first anthology of poetry, were written. Today, there is only a village of farmhouses and rice paddies, but the ruins conjure up a scent of the past. In Asuka, two burial mounds open to the public contain Japan's only known tomb murals. Excavated in 1972, they are displayed in a modern building often crowded with visitors. More evocative is the inner chamber of a 7th-century tumulus. The earthen covering has disappeared, leaving 75-ton boulders exposed. **Tachibana-dera** stands at the site of Prince Shotoku's birthplace. Most of the temple's buildings date from the Edo Period, but the pleasant country surroundings exude something of old Asuka. Most important of the area's temples is **Asuka-dera**, enshrining the Great Buddha of Asuka, a bronze image of Shaka and Japan's oldest large-scale Buddhist statue.

Northern hills

The northern and eastern hills are convenient for relaxing afternoon drives out of Nara, notably the Nara Okuyama road, starting from behind Todai-ji. The jewel of the northern hills is **Joruri-ji**, one of the few surviving Heian temples. Joruri-ji, establish in 1179, is a miniature Buddhist paradise. In the centre is a pond symbolising the lake of heaven. To the right is the Western Paradise and the temple of Nine Amida. During the year, the rays of the sun sweep across the temple lighting each Buddha image in turn. In a direct line across the pond is a pagoda with a statue of Yakushi, lord of the Eastern Paradise. About one kilometre's walk into the hills are the **Tono-o Sekibutsu**, stone carvings dating from the Kamakura Period. Buddhas cut into the rock – in an abstract, even crude style, and covered with lichens – are called *magaibutsu* and have a magical aura about them. The hills of Nara contain hundreds of such carvings.

Eastern mountains

Soon after leaving Sakurai, at the southeastern end of the Yamato Plain, the road begins to climb into verdant hills. The first stop is **Hase-dera**, known for its peony festival in the last week of April. A covered stairway of 399 steps hung with lanterns leads up to the main hall, which enshrines Japan's largest wooden statue, an eleven-headed Kannon carved in 1538. A half hour's drive to the east leads to the village of Ono. Turn south on the winding road along the Muro-gawa. Across the river is the **Miroku Magaibutsu** cut into the cliff face. This is the largest hillside carving in Japan, dating from 1207. ❑

OPPOSITE: bundled ceremonial rice stalks at Ise Shrine. **BELOW:** trees in spring blossom.

The Shrines of Ise

While not part of the Kansai district, Ise and its shrines, east from Nara and Kyoto, perhaps best exemplify the nature and purpose of the Japanese Shinto belief. An excursion to Ise can be enlightening, but know beforehand that visitors are not allowed into the shrines' compounds under any circumstances.

No one can say exactly how long the two main shrines of what are collectively called the Grand Shrines of Ise have existed. Historical evidence suggests that **Naiku**, or the Inner Shrine, has been in place since around the 4th century, and **Geku**, or the Outer Shrine, since the late 5th century.

At Ise, the venerable cypress-wood (*hinoki*) shrine buildings stand today in perfect condition – almost new and mocking the ravages of time. The secret of the fine condition of these most sacred of Shinto shrines is *sengu*, or shrine removal, performed at Ise every 20 years over the past 13 centuries, the latest and 61st sengu taking place in 1993. Sengu consists of the razing of the two main buildings of both shrines, along with 14 smaller auxiliary structures. In the sengu, before the existing structures are destroyed, new shrine buildings of identical scale and materials are erected on adjacent foundations set aside for that purpose. Then Japan's largest and most important festival, Jingu Shikinen Sengu, begins as the deities of the respective shrines are invited to pass from the old into the new structures. Later, the old structures are torn down and sections of the timbers sent to Shinto shrines throughout Japan.

Why this work? First, the 20-year period can be viewed as a transition point. In human life, it is a line of demarcation between generations. Thus, sengu perpetuates an appreciation and an awareness of the cultural and religious significance of the shrines from age to age. Two decades is also perhaps the most logical period in terms of passing on from generation to generation the technological expertise needed for the reconstruction.

Geku is dedicated to Toyouke no Omikami, the goddess of agriculture. The grounds of Geku cover about 90 hectares (220 acres). A thatched gateway stands at the outermost of the three formidable fences, which is as far as anyone except imperial personages, envoys and shrine officials get to Shoden, the main hall. The clean, simple lines of the building are the very essence of Japanese architecture, showing nary a trace of the often bolder Chinese and Korean influences that dominate shrines elsewhere in Japan.

Naiku is a few kilometres from Geku. Here, as in the Outer Shrine, the object of attention is enclosed in a series of fences and can be viewed only from the front of a thatched-roof gate in the outermost fence. Here, too, the view is limited (and, again, no photos permitted) but worthwhile.

Naiku is said to contain the *yata no kagami* (sacred mirror), which, along with a sword and a jewel, constitute the Three Sacred Treasures of the Japanese imperial throne. Mythology says that the mirror was handed by Amaterasu Omikami to her grandson when he descended from heaven to reign on earth. She gave him the gift of rice agriculture and a blessing for Japan. ❏

THE SOUTH

Southern Japan includes western Honshu and two main islands, Kyushu and Shikoku, along with Okinawa

H ere we should mention that "south" is a bit of a misnomer, as the Japanese will refer to this area as western Japan. Still, this part of the Japanese archipelago extends south*ward*. Chugoku, Shikoku and Kyushu are exceedingly different yet have one element in common: Seto Naikai, or the Inland Sea. All three regions also face the open ocean, and as a result, each area has widely varying climate and local qualities. In fact, beyond geography and the fact they are all in Japan, these regions sometimes bear little or no resemblance to each other.

That section of Honshu from, say, Himeji down the coast along the Inland Sea to Hiroshima is markedly different from the Sea of Japan side. Likewise, Shikoku, though the smallest of Japan's four main islands, could as well be in a different hemisphere from the one occupied by the islands of Okinawa. As for Kyushu – well, there are those who believe that this large island, particularly the southern part, is a nation unto itself and who cite the long tradition of fierce independence stemming from the Satsuma clans, not to mention Kyushu's thick dialect, as proof.

Even in the most populous and industrial cities of Kyushu, or even in large and well-developed cities like Honshu's Okayama and Hiroshima, the pace is mellow, if not downright placid, compared with Tokyo and Osaka. Not all is idyllic down this way, however. The southern parts lie in the path of seasonal typhoons and thus are regularly given good soakings by torrential rains riding up from the Philippines and Taiwan. Moreover, there are more active volcanoes on Kyushu than on any other Japanese island. Among the notable are Sakura-jima, near Kagoshima, Aso-san (with the world's largest-diameter caldera), and Unzen-dake, which violently blew up in 1991.

Volcanoes have given the archipelago an unlimited variety of ceramic-quality clays, along with natural chemicals for glazes. Kyushu and parts of Chugoku are noted for their hearty pottery, an art with a considerable amount of Korean influence.

Shikoku, Chugoku and Kyushu are large enough to keep travellers occupied for quite some time. Smaller gems await even further south, however. Like pearls upon the ocean, islands drip away from Kyushu's southern tip and stretch down to within 200 km (125 miles) of Taiwan. This string of islands, Nansai-shoto, is over 1,200 km (750 miles) in length. Best-known by foreigners is Okinawa for its historical importance in World War II and also for its cultural uniqueness. There are numerous other islands, each significantly distinct from its neighbours and worthy of exploration. ❏

PRECEDING PAGES: Sakura-jima volcano, near Kyushu's Kagoshima; cherry trees in blossom at Himeji Castle.
LEFT: an island amongst bigger islands of the Seto Naikai, or Inland Sea.

Oki-shoto ↑

SEA

OF

JAPAN

Shimane Sakaimi
Kashima ⑫ Matsue
Izumo Taisha Hirata Shinji-ko Yas
Hino-misaki ★ Hikawa ⑨ Higashiizumo
Taisha Shinji Hirose
Kuryo ⑪ ⑩ Izumo Haku
Kisuku Daito
Taki Sada Kakoya Yoshida Nita Yokota
Oda H Tonbara 54 126
Nima Ochi 1126 Takano I
Yonutsu Go Takano O
Gotsu Kawamoto Akagie K
Daiwa Funa Kuchiwa Saijo
Hamada Iwami Mizuho Sakugi Shobara Tojo
Kanagi U Sakugi Soryo Jins
Misumi Yasaka Asahi Takamiya Miyoshi Mirasaki Yuki
Geinoku Oasa Midori Sanwa Kisa Sanwa
Masuda Mito C Toyohira Yoshida Mukaihara Toyosaka Kozan
1346 Kake Yachiya Daiwa Fuchu
Susa Tamagawa Hikimi Tsutsuga Togeuchi Koda Kui Shinich
Nichihara Yoshiwa Yuki 54 Fukutomi Kochi Mitsugi
Ai Abe Tsuwano Higashihiroshima Hongo Mihara Onomich
Tsuno Yuya Nagato Hagi ⑨ Fukue Itsukaichi Kaita ⑥ Hiroshima 2 Unnoshim Inno ⑤
Hohuku Heki Misuni Asahi Kawakami Saeki Hatsukaichi Kumano Akitsu Yasuura Setoda
Hibiki- Shuho Mito Kano Miwa Otake ⑦ Kure Osaki-Kami Kamijiri Omi
nada Toyota Mine Tokuji Mikawa Eta Ondo Yukita Miyakuno Oshim
Toyoura Yamaguchi Shuto Aki Kintai Kurahashi Namikata Onishi Kokurits
Kikugawa Kusunoki Ogori Hofu Tokuyama Kuga Bridge Gei Imabari ⑳
Sanyo Ajisu Aio Kumage Yu Kurahashi Kikuma Hiuch
⑧ Onoda Ube Shinnanyo 2 Yanai Obatake Kua Nakajima Hojo Tamagara Niiha
Shimonoseki Kitakyushu Kudamatsu Hikari Hirao Oshima Tashibana Uwa Yashiro Gogo Dogo Saijo
Kanda Otsu Kasado Naga Kaminoseki Onsen Tanbara 11
Kusu Setonaikai Kokuritsu- koen Himeshima Hime Iwai Ya Heigun Iyo- Komatsu
Yukuhashi Himeshima Iwai Matsuyama ㉑
Tsuiki Shiida nada Kunimi Kawauchi
Tagawa Kakaji Masaki 1981 Hongawa
Soeda Buzen Nakatsu Kunisaki- Futami Shigenobu
Taihei hanto Kunisaki Iyo Tobe 33 Omogo
Yabakei Honyabakei Usa Musashi Nagahama Nakayama Kuma Ikegawa Gohe
Yamakuni Innai Ajimu Yamaga Aki Uchiko Hirota Mikawa Yanadani Agawa
Hoshuyama Kusu Kitsuki Ikata Honai Ozu Oda 1562 Niyodo Sakawa
Kyushu Hita Hiji Kawabe Niyodo
Amagase Kusu Beppu- Misaki Seto Yawatahama Hijikawa Higashitsuno
Oyama Kokonoe Beppu wan Sada- Mikame Shirokawa Susaki
Nakatsue Ogumi Yufuin Hasama Oita misaki Uwa Hiyoshi Nakatosa
Kamitsue Shonai Akahama Yoshida Hiromi Towa Taisho
Kokuritsu-koen Naoiri Notsuharu Ashizuri- Uwajima ㉓ Matsuno Nishitosa Kubokaw
Aso-Kuju Inukai Usuki Hiburi Tsushima ㉔ Saga
Ubuyama Ono Tsukumi Nippo- Uchiumi 56 Ogata
Aso Kuju Asaji Mie Kamiura Nishiumi Misho Nakamura
Ozu Ichinomiya Taketa Saiki Johen Sukumo
Choyo Aso-san Ogi Yayoi Yonouzu Uwakai- Mihara
57 1592 Ume Naokawa kaigan Otsuki
Hakusui 1753 Kamae Sukamo- wan
Seiwa Soyo Kitaura Tosa-shimizu
Yahe Takachiho Kitegawa Kokuritsu-koen Kokuritsu-koen Okino ㉕ Ashizuri-misaki

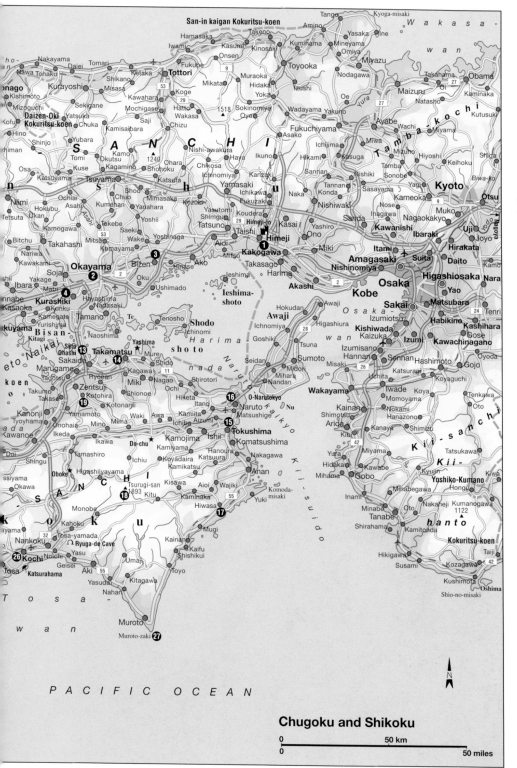

Chugoku and Shikoku

San-in kaigan Kokuritsu-koen

Wakasa-wan

Tango · Kyoga-misaki
Amino · Ine
Takeno · Yasaka · Mineyama · Omiya · Miyazu
Hamasaka · Kasumi · Kinosaki · Kumihama · Nodagawa · Takahama · Obama
Iwami · Kinosaki · Toyooka · Maizuru · Kaminaka
Fukube · Onsen · Muraoka · Hidaka · Izushi · Oe · Natasho · Kutsuki
Nakayama · Daiei · Tomari · Tottori · Mikata · Yoka · Wadayama · Yakuno · Ayabe · Wachi · Shiga
Nawa · Tohaku · Shikano · Koge · Sokinomiya · Oya · Fukuchiyama · Mizuno · Hiyoshi · Keihoku

SANCHI · Shohoku · Kozuki · Yamasaki · Ichikawa · Kouder a · Sanda · Kawanishi · Ibaraki · Uji · Joyo
Shu · Kyoto · Otsu

Okayama · Bizen · Hinase · Ako · Takasago · Akashi · Kobe · Osaka · Sakai · Matsubara · Tenri

Kurashiki · Tamano · Shodo · Harima-shoto · Awaji · Osaka-wan · Izumi · Kawachinagano

Takamatsu · Naruto · Tokushima · Wakayama · Kii-sanchi

SHIKOKU · Tsurugi-san 1893 · Kochi · Muroto · Muroto-zaki

Kochi · Katsurahama

Tosa-wan

PACIFIC OCEAN

0   50 km
0   50 miles

CHUGOKU

*While we might consider this portion of Honshu and
the adjacent island of Shikoku as southern Japan, the Japanese
call the area western Japan. In fact, it's southwest*

Map
on pages
290–1

ost travellers would look at a map of Japan's main island of Honshu
and consider Chugoku to be the southern part. The Japanese, however,
consider it to be the western part. In fact, of course, it is southwest.
Compass directions aside, the Chugoku region spreads over the bottom third of
Honshu, bounded by **Seto Naikai** (Inland Sea) to the south and the Sea of Japan
to the north. Not many foreign travellers get to Chugoku other than to its main
cities of Okayama and Hiroshima. The region includes the prefectures of
Okayama, Hiroshima, Yamaguchi, Shimane and Tottori, and it offers some
splendid views of rustic Japan, especially along the Sea of Japan coast.

Seto Naikai, or the Inland Sea of Seto, is a 9,500-sq.-km (3,700-sq.-mile)
body of water surrounded by Kyushu, Shikoku, and the western extent of Honshu. Over 1,000 small islands pepper the sea. Osaka, Kobe, and Hiroshima are
all on the sea's coast. Although often industrialised these days, the sea still
retains some exquisite vistas, enough for the area to have been designated
Japan's first national park in 1934.

Himeji

At the upper end of Chugoku, the industrial city of
Himeji ❶ is dominated by the marvellous snow-
white castle that seems to hover above the town. Variously called the White Egret or Heron castle,
Himeji-jo (Himeji Castle; open daily, 9am–6pm;
admission fee) is a 15-minute stroll from the
shinkansen station along a road lined with modern
sculptures. Resting resplendent on the banks of the
Senba-gawa, the castle of Himeji is the largest and
most elegant of the dozen existing medieval castles in
Japan. Although the city was extensively bombed during World War II, the castle emerged unscathed and
has been maintained in pristine condition.

The site occupied by the castle has been fortified
since 1333, and an actual castle was built here in
1580 by Toyotomi Hideyoshi. In 1681, Ikeda Terumasa, Tokugawa Ieyasu's son-in-law, rebuilt and
expanded the castle to its present form. Castles in
this period served both as military strongholds and
as administrative centres. Terumasa's design, with
financial help from the shogunate, elegantly merged
martial necessity and artistic form on a scale previously unknown in Japan.

The castle's construction was a Herculean task
requiring 400 tons of wood, 75,000 tiles weighing a
total of 3,000 tons, and a huge number of large stones.
These stones weren't easy to come by and tales of
their procurement live on in the ramparts. Ancient

LEFT: tending to
cherry trees.
BELOW: Himeji-jo.

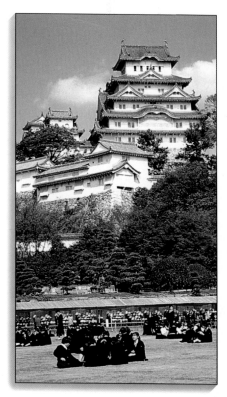

A Japanese castle in its original state such as Himeji-jo is rare, as most were either burned to the ground during feudal wars or in World War II.

stone coffins mined from nearby tombs can be seen in one part of the precinct. The contribution of a millstone, from a woman living in the town below the castle, is still remembered today.

The castle was never tested in battle, but walking up past the succession of defensive lines – three concentric moats surrounding high, curved ramparts punctuated by gates and watch towers with arrow slits and gun ports – it seems an impregnable bastion. Roads within the castle grounds twist and turn, the better to confuse hostile forces if the outer defenses were breached, and the uppermost floors of the castle contain hidden places where troops could continue to shoot at the enemy until the bitter end. (*See picture on pages 286–87.*)

Himeji-jo is a hillock (as distinct from a mountain or flatland) castle atop a 45-metre-high (150-ft) hill. There are spectacular views from the main *donjon*, which rises 30 metres (100 ft) from the castle grounds. *Shachihoko*, huge ornamental fish that were strategically placed on the roof as charms to ward off fire, can be seen close up from the top floor. (Some now support lightning rods.)

The **Hyogo-kenritsu Rekishi Hakubutsukan (Hyogo Prefecture History Museum**; open Tuesday–Sunday, 10am–5pm; admission fee) nearby to the north contains displays about Japanese castles, including the most magnificent of all, Himeji.

Okayama

BELOW: banners representing carp on Boys' Day, and the architecture of Kurashiki.

The rapidly growing city of **Okayama ❷** has once again asserted itself as the region's most dynamic metropolis. For this reason it often finds itself playing host to visiting foreigners, mostly on business and not for sightseeing. Okayama's most notable attraction, the **Koraku-en (Koraku Garden)**, was

originally laid out in 1686 for the warlord Ikeda. This garden is generally regarded as one of the three or four most beautiful gardens in Japan. Located on an island in the Asahi-gawa across from **Okayama-jo** (Okayama or Crow Castle because of its black exterior), Koraku-en is unusual for its large grassy areas and the cultivation of such crops as rice and wheat. Tea is also grown and harvested here and tea houses are scattered throughout the fine strolling garden.

Other sights in Okayama include the **Orient Museum** (open Tuesday–Sunday, 9am–5pm; admission fee), with exhibits tracing the impact of Near Eastern civilisation on Japan; the **Okayama Prefectural Museum of Art** (open Tuesday–Sunday, 9am–4.30pm; admission fee); and the **Yumeji Art Museum** (open Tuesday–Sunday, 9am–5.30pm), with works by Yumeji Takehisa.

Bizen ❸, about 45 minutes by train east along the coast from Okayama, is famous for its unglazed, coarse pottery that is frequently enhanced by kiln "accidents", such as a stray leaf or a bit of straw sticking to the side of a pot that leaves an interesting pattern after firing. There are more than 100 kilns in Imbe, the 700-year-old pottery-making section of Bizen, along with several museums including the Bizen Togei Bijutsukan (Ceramics Museum) and Fujiwara Kei Kinenkan gallery.

Kurashiki

West of Okayama, **Kurashiki ❹** is a textile-producing city containing the pearl of Japanese tourist attractions: an arts district that brings world-class Japanese and international art and traditional crafts together in an exquisite setting. Thirteen and a half hectares of 300-year-old rice warehouses, Meiji-era factories, and the homes of *samurai* and wealthy merchant families have been elegantly pre-

Map on pages 290–1

BELOW: canal through Kurashiki.

served and converted into museums, craft shops, and art galleries. Kurashiki is for walkers, with most of the attractions within a block or two of the central canal. The streets and alleys bordering on this central canal look much as they did during the town's cultural and economic zenith in the 18th century. Automobiles are not allowed to disturb the ambiance of its preserved quarter.

The tourist centre here provides maps, information, and a cheerful place to rest weary feet. Better still, Kurashiki is patrolled by Sato Yasuzo, a charming and mildly off-beat retired English teacher whose main pleasure in life is befriending foreign tourists ("It is my serendipity to meet you here today") and showing them the hidden corners of his home town. Sato is a fount of information and able to point out the dolphin sculptures placed on roofs as a talisman against fire, obscure shops selling traditional wedding accoutrements, off-duty *geisha*, locations where major documentaries and period films were shot, and a score of other fascinating minutiae. He expects no recompense for his informal guided tours and probably does more to promote this part of Japan than any single member of the national tourism organisation.

During the Edo Period, Kurashiki was a central collection and storage site for the shogun's taxes and tribute – paid in rice – from communities throughout western Honshu, Seto Naikai, and Shikoku. Numerous stone rice warehouses (*kura*) are clustered around willow-lined canals, thus giving the town its name. Their striking designs employ dark-black tiles deeply set in bright-white mortar, capped by roofs of black tile. Stone bridges, arched so that barges piled high with sacks of rice from the hinterland could pass below them, span the waterways. Kurashiki's preservation was largely the work of Ohara Magosaburo, the wealthy scion of Kurashiki's leading family. The Ohara family's tex-

BELOW: pearl farms.

tile mills were the primary source of employment in Kurashiki during the Meiji period, by which time rice levies had been replaced by cash taxes and thus making the city's huge rice warehouses redundant.

Ohara Magosaburo built the nation's first museum of Western art in 1930, the **Ohara Museum of Art** (open Tuesday–Sunday, 9am–5pm; admission fee), and stocked it with works by El Greco, Monet, Matisse, Renoir, Gauguin, and Picasso. The neo-classical building remains the city's centrepiece, although new galleries have proliferated around it over the years. The restored kura next to the main gallery are likely to be of more interest to visitors already familiar with European art as they contain Japanese folk art and a fine collection of ancient Chinese art. Semi-separate rooms are devoted to the works of the great *mingei* (Japanese folk art) potters such as Hamada Shoji, Kawai Kanjiro and Tomimoto Kenkichi.

Many of Kurashiki's warehouses-turned-art-houses are devoted to preserving and revitalising mingei. Among the most interesting is the **Japanese Folk Toy Museum** (open daily, 8am–5pm; admission fee). The first floor is packed with traditional Japanese toys, dolls and kites, while a collection of toys from around the world can be seen on the second floor. The adjacent toy store is as interesting as the museum. Next door, the **Kurashiki Mingei-kan (Museum of Folk Craft**; open daily, 9am–5pm; admission fee) displays about 4,000 simple, hand-made objects that are or were used in everyday life. The building that houses this museum, parenthetically, is itself of historical interest, as it was remodelled from four two-story wooden rice granaries.

Visitors can learn about the daily life of one of Kurashiki's leading families at the **Ohashi House** (open Tuesday–Sunday, 9am–5pm; admission fee), con-

Map on pages 290–1

BELOW: red-carpet tour bus.

structed in 1796 for a merchant family. Of samurai status, the house is much larger than typical merchant houses of that time. Note the unusual roof tiles. Ivy Square, an arts complex created out of the red-brick textile factories that brought about the Ohara family its fortune, houses the Kurabo Memorial Hall, with displays on the textile industry as well as scores of shops and restaurants.

Leaving the canal area, weary travellers might stop for a drink at the Kurashiki Kokusai Hotel, designed by Kurashiki native Shizutaro Urabe, before heading for the city's more distant attractions. These include the **Seto Ohashi Memorial Museum of Bridges** (the building is shaped like an arched *taiko* bridge), and **Washu-zan**, a hill with tremendous views of the great bridge itself, Seto Ohashi, as well as the Inland Sea, Seto Naikai. There is also Kurashiki's former city hall, designed by Japan's most famous architect, Tange Kenzo, and which was transformed in 1983 into the municipal art museum.

A nondescript city at the northern centre of the Inland Sea, **Onomichi ❺** was an important commercial port 800 years ago. Wealthy merchants flocked to the city during the Edo Period, building 81 temples on the steep slopes overlooking the sea to celebrate their prosperity. With the coming of the railroad in the late 19th century, however, commerce literally passed the city by. Because of its relative lack of importance, American bombers also passed by Onomichi, and when the shinkansen route was mapped, Onomichi was passed over again, a station being placed in the up-and-coming Fukuyama instead. As a result of its slide into relative obscurity, the city has unselfconsciously retained much of its pre-Meiji heritage. Some 25 of the old temples remain, the most interesting being the 1,100-year-old **Senko-ji**, best reached via the tram. From here, walk down the hill towards town taking in as many temples as you can stand.

The Seto Ohashi Memorial Museum of Bridges in Kurashiki.

BELOW: Genbaku Domu, Hiroshima.

Maps
on pages
290–1, 300

Hiroshima

One moment – 8.15am, 6 August 1945 – irrevocably changed world history. An atomic flash signaled the instant destruction of **Hiroshima** ❻, the eventual loss of over 200,000 lives, and forever linked the city's name with nuclear holocaust. The immediate and lasting impact on Hiroshima gives concrete reality to the horrors of atomic and nuclear war. Unlike Nagasaki, the second city to have received such an attack but which doesn't dwell much on past history, there seem to be reminders of Hiroshima's atomic bombing around virtually every corner in the city.

Amazingly, Hiroshima's people quickly rebuilt a vibrant city from the ashes, making it larger and more prosperous than the old one and leaving a few carefully chosen scars to memorialise its abiding atomic legacy. A shining example of the city's metamorphosis is the Mazda automobile factory, where the humans appear to play second fiddle to the computers and robots that put entire cars together in a matter of hours, on a single production line that snakes remorselessly around the factory floor.

Industrial Promotion Hall before the atomic bombing.

Hiroshima was chosen for the first atomic-bomb attack because of its military importance. The city was one of Japan's most vital military depots and industrial areas (not mentioned in the atomic bomb museum's exhibit). But Hiroshima's military significance predates World War II by several hundred years. Troops were staged here in preparation for the invasion of Korea in 1582. A castle incorporating the latest construction and defensive techniques was built here seven years later by the Mori clan. It rested on pilings driven into reclaimed swampland, and the outer moats were built above the level of the surrounding land so that their walls could be breached, flooding the plain where siege troops would likely mass. The castle was an important bastion of the Tokugawa shogun's forces, a western outpost facing the often hostile Choshu and Satsuma clans. In the 19th century, **Hiroshima-jo** ❹ **(Hiroshima Castle)** was occupied by the emperor during the occupation of Manchuria. The castle also served as an important Japanese Army headquarters during World War II and was completely destroyed by the atomic bomb. Reconstructed in 1958, the castle contains an excellent museum, which is appropriately devoted to castles.

BELOW: Genbaku Domu through the Cenotaph.

A few blocks east of the castle, **Shukkei-en** ❸ **(Shukkei Garden)** was built on the banks of the Kyobashi-gawa in 1620 in emulation of a famous Chinese lake. Early spring to the garden brings cherry blossoms, while azaleas bloom a little later, and multicolored carp inhabit the garden's central pond throughout the year.

The **Heiwa Kinen-koen** ❸ **(Peace Memorial Park)**, southwest of the castle and wedged between the rivers of Motoyasu and Ota, is adjacent to the **Genbaku Domu** ❹ **(Atomic Dome)**, which marks ground zero of Hiroshima's atomic explosion. At its maximum intensity, the temperature approached that on the sun's surface and almost everything within sight was vaporised instantly. The famous building with the carefully maintained skeletal dome once housed the Industrial Promotion Hall and was one of the few surviving vertical structures. Today the park has a serene air; men old enough to remember the explosion sit meditatively on benches, the sonorous tones of the Peace Bell echo through the trees, and the solemnity is varied only by the exuberance of children who dash about with clipboards in hand for their school projects and then stand silent in prayer before the many shrines.

Mushroom cloud over Hiroshima about an hour after the atomic blast.

Tange Kenzo designed the heart of the park complex, which comprises the **Peace Memorial Museum** Ⓔ (open daily, 9am–5.30pm; admission fee), Peace Memorial Hall, the Cenotaph, and Peace Flame. The museum contains graphic portrayals of the bombing. Although the museum is filled with powerful images of terrible suffering, it certainly is not the hall of horrors one might expect. Still, a visit to the museum is an emotional experience for most, even though the exhibit has been accused of failing to place the bombing in historical perspective, mostly a result of right-wing nationalist opposition. The museum's context is that the bomb fell on Hiroshima, figuratively as well as literally, out of the blue. There is little suggestion of Japan's brutal conquest of Asia, and nowhere is there the least sign that any other nation or race might have suffered comparable wartime tragedies.

The **Cenotaph**'s inverted U-shape reflects the design of the thatched-roof houses of Japanese antiquity. It contains a stone chest with the names of the victims of the atomic bombing and bears an inscription, "Sleep in peace: the error will not be repeated". The **Peace Flame** and Atomic Dome can be seen through it. The statue of the children killed by the bombing is dedicated to Sasaki Sadako, who died of leukemia caused by radiation when she was just 12 years old. She believed that if she could fold 1,000 paper cranes – a symbol of happiness and longevity for Japanese – she would be cured. Despite the rigors of

BLACK RAIN

It was like a white magnesium flash... We first thought to escape to the parade grounds, but we couldn't because there was a huge sheet of fire in front of us... Hiroshima was completely enveloped in flames. We felt terribly hot and could not breathe well at all. After a while, a whirlpool of fire approached us from the south. It was like a big tornado of fire spreading over the full width of the street. Whenever the fire touched, wherever the fire touched, it burned... The whirlpool of fire that was covering the entire street approached us... After a while, it began to rain. The fire and the smoke made us so thirsty... As it began to rain, people opened their mouths and turned their faces towards the sky and try to drink the rain... It was a black rain with big drops.

Takakura Akiko
300 m (1,000 ft) from ground zero

her illness, she managed to complete folding 1,000 cranes. As she had not gotten better, she started on a second thousand. She had reached some 1,500 when she finally died in 1955, 10 years after the atomic bomb exploded. Her spirited actions inspired an outpouring of national feeling and her classmates completed the second thousand paper cranes. Today, school children from all over the country bring paper cranes by the tens of thousands to lay around Sadako's memorial, a tribute that is simultaneously heart-rending, beautiful, and a terrible condemnation of militarism.

Many visitors ring the Peace Bell before crossing the Motoyasu-gawa to the dome. Colourful rowboats can be rented by the hour near the **Heiwa Ohashi** (**Peace Bridge**), offering a more cheerful perspective on Hiroshima. Sightseeing cruises depart from the nearby pier.

Half an hour away and northwest of central Hiroshima, **Mitaki-ji** is set in a lush forest with three waterfalls. Buddhas adorn the hillsides, and a fierce, lifesize baby-killing devil statue of wood hangs out on the temple's porch. A friendly dog often welcomes visitors to the tea house, which is decorated with a colourful collection of masks and kites. The walk from the central train station to the temple grounds passes a grouping of graves belonging to many unknown atomic-bomb victims.

Miyajima

Though it is formally called **Itsuku-shima** (Strict Island), this major Hiroshima-area tourist attraction is better known as **Miyajima ❼**, the Island of Shrines. To find the spirit and splendour of Miyajima, one of the country's holiest sites, visitors must wade through the litter and droppings of thousands of tourists and

Maps
on pages
290–1, 300

TIP

The best way to see Hiroshima is from a street car. As other Japanese cities tore up their streetcar tracks after World War II, their cars were sent to Hiroshima; the city has acquired an eclectic collection of tram cars, many dating back to the 1940s.

BELOW: famous *torii* of Miyajima.

A Shinto shrine always has a torii, *or pi-shaped gate, in front of it. Torii come in various colours and designs, but the function is always the same: dividing the shrine's sacred grounds from secular areas beyond.*

herds of tame deer. Most of the island is covered with uninhabited virgin forest. A good way to see it is from the 1.6-km-long (1 mile) cable car that runs over Momijidani-koen to the top of Misen.

The large crimson *torii* (shrine gate), rising out of the sea in front of the **Itsukushima-jinga**, is probably the most familiar Japanese cultural icon and representative of Shintoism. But this torii, which is plastered on nearly every travel poster and guide book that has anything to do with Japan, hasn't suffered from the overexposure. It is especially breathtaking at sunset, even when the tide is out and one is able to filter the noise from fellow admirers.

The current gate was built in 1874, but a similar torii has lured visitors for seven centuries. The island's spiritual roots are much older, however. The first shrine, honouring Amaterasu's three daughters – goddesses of the sea – was built in the 6th century. To maintain the island's "purity", births and deaths have been prohibited on Miyajima from the earliest times.

The entire island of Miyajima was dedicated as a sanctuary by Taira no Kiyomori, who ordered the Itsukushima-jinga completely rebuilt in 1168. Kiyomori and his clan prospered, eventually attaining a brief rule over Japan that ended tumultuously in 1185.

Itsukushima-jinga itself rests on stilts and seems to float like a giant ship when the tide comes in. Costumes and masks used in the *bugaku*-dance festival (first week of January) and the *noh* plays, performed in mid-April, are on display in the Asazaya (morning prayer room), which is reached via a vermilion-coloured bridge. Next to Itsuku-shima, one of the oldest noh theatres in Japan, built in 1568, also seems to float a few inches above the sea. A nearby building contains hundreds of government-designated National Treasures and Important Cultural Objects, including illuminated sutras made by the Taira clan in the 1160s.

BELOW: during *shichi-go-san* on 15 November, boys 5 years old and girls 3 and 7 years of age go to shrines to receive blessings.

A five-story pagoda, built in 1407, and the hall of **Senjokaku (A Thousand Mats)** are at the top of a hill behind Itsukushima-jinga. Senjokaku, built in 1587, is the great warlord Toyotomi Hideyoshi's contribution to Miyajima.

Shimonoseki

At the western limit of Honshu, **Shimonoseki** ❸ is the gateway to Kyushu and to Korea as well, with shinkansen (bullet train) service to Hakata Station in Fukuoka and daily overnight ferries to Pusan, South Korea. There isn't much reason to linger here, but one of the largest aquariums in Asia, the **Shimonoseki Suizokukan**, and the shrine of Akamon may be of interest to those waiting for a boat to Korea.

Shimonoseki has long been an important port over many centuries, although its importance today is less so. The area was also the site of some of Japan's most important sea battles. History and literature students will recall that the final scenes of *Tale of the Heike* were set here. It is where the exiled empress dowager hurled herself and the infant emperor into the swirling tides. Several spots in the area claim to be the actual location, but, in fact, any would do, as the cliffs are high and the waters do swirl frighteningly as the Sea of Japan meets Seto Naikai.

Honshu's northern coast

From Shimonoseki, the coastal road loops back around east along the northern coast of Honshu and the Sea of Japan. Samurai footsteps echo through the narrow streets in the heart of **Hagi** ❾, and indeed the whole town resounds to the beat of historical events that have shaped Japan as it is today. If there is one reason to journey to this part of the coast, it is here in Hagi – a place that is as picturesque as it is fascinating.

Many of the statesmen who played significant parts in the Meiji Restoration came from here, Korean potters brought their art and flourished in Hagi, and it is the site of some of the earliest steps taken in glass-making.

Start where Hagi itself started, at the castle site at the foot of **Shizuki-san**. Built on the orders of Terumoto Mori in 1604, who then presided over the area that is now Yamaguchi Prefecture, the castle stood until 1874 when it was pulled down to express allegiance to the new Meiji government, which had returned the emperor to power. Parts of the walls and the former dungeon remain today, and there's a Japanese teahouse in the adjacent gardens.

From here, head to the Asa Mori clan residence, the largest of the surviving samurai houses that arose in Hagi beyond the castle walls. The streets of the castle town, or Jokamachi, were divided into three sections: one for lower-ranking samurai, a second for rich politicians, and the third for merchants. Wandering its lanes – particularly Edoya, Iseya and Kikuya – every turn reveals another pocket of days gone by. The son of a doctor and one of the Meiji Restoration's dynamos, Kido Takayoshi, grew up in a house on Edoya. Another prominent Restoration figure, Takasugi Shinsaku, lived on Kikuya and was cured of smallpox by Dr Aoki Shusuke, another inhabitant of Edoya. All their residences are

Map on pages 290–1

TIP

Although noted for its historical and artistic qualities, remember that, like Kyoto, Hagi is also a modern city with the clutter and commercialism of any other city.

BELOW: local train outside of Hagi.

Map on pages 290–1

on view to the public. After the Meiji Restoration, a number of *natsu mikan* (orange or tangerine) trees were planted in Hagi, mainly to provide some relief to the unemployed samurai. Many trees dot the Horiuchi (inner moat) district, and in May and June the scent of the blossoms is almost intoxicating.

Hagi's other great influence on Japan is its pottery, ranked the second-most beautiful in the country after that of Kyoto. At first glance it can appear deceptively simple and rustic, but closer examination reveals subdued colours and classical features, especially in the glazing that is exceptionally clear and vivid. *Hagi-yaki* (Hagi pottery) came to Japan in the wake of the warlord Hideyoshi Toyotomi's invasion of Korea in the 16th century, when two Korean potters were brought with the returning armies to practice their craft. Today there are some 100 kilns scattered about the city. Many feature small exhibition rooms and some will let visitors take a turn at the wheel. Traditional tea ware is fired for about 30 hours in a wood-burning kiln (*nobori-gama*) at temperatures of around 1250°C (2,300°F).

Lesser known is Hagi's glass, introduced around 1860 as the Edo Period drew to a close and using European techniques. After a century-long hiatus, the old techniques are now being used again to make Hagi glass.

Eastward along the coast

Further on along the coast, **Shimane** and its modest peninsula consists of three ancient districts: Izumo, Iwami, and the islands of Oki-shoto. It is one of the longest inhabited areas of Japan and offers special insights into the cultural heritage of the nation. **Izumo** ❿ covers the eastern part of the prefecture and is known as the mythical province where the history of Japan began. Several shrines, temples and ancient buildings can be seen around the prefecture, including the **Taisha** ⓫, the oldest Shinto shrine in the country. Dedicated to the spirit god of marriage, it is paid particular heed by couples and even more by those wishing to become a couple.

Shinji-ko sits at the eastern end of the prefecture. The lake's 45-km-long (30 miles) coastline offers beautiful sights throughout the year, and sunset over the lake is one of the finest evening scenes in Japan. At the eastern end of the lake sits **Matsue-jo**. Often called Plover Castle because of its shape, the castle was built in 1611 by Yoshiharu Horio, a samurai general. It is the only remaining castle in the Izumo area and very little has been done to modernise it, so the feeling inside is truly authentic. Across the castle moat to the north lies Shiominawate, an area where ranking samurai once lived.

Matsue ⓬ was also the home of a renowned writer and observer of Japan, Lafcadio Hearn (1850–1904). Greek-born Hearn was raised in America and came to Japan in 1891 as a *Harper's* magazine reporter. In his many years in Japan, he wrote numerous works, including *Kwaidan: Stories and Studies of Strange Things*; *Shadowings, Japan: An Attempt at Interpretation*; *Bushido: The Soul of Japan*; and *A Daughter of the Samurai*. They all make for good reading today although written over a century ago; his observations carry well over time. In Matsue is the ancient shrine of **Kamosu**. Its unique architectural style, *taisha-zukuri*, is the oldest architectural style in Japan.

The islands of **Oki-shoto** sit between 40 and 80 km (50 miles) off Shimane-hanto. The old province surrounds some 180 islands and islets in the Sea of Japan. The islands, once a dumping grounds for convicts, sit inside the Daisen-Oki National Park. A unique sight in the islands are the bullfights, sans matador. Two bulls just lock horns and push away. Bullfighting was originally devised in the 1200s to entertain Emperor Go-Daigo while he was in exile. Temples, shrines, rugged coasts, and great fishing mark this area off the beaten path. ❑

Lafcadio Hearn lived in Matsue for about two years.

OPPOSITE: concrete barriers, being cast here, are used to prevent coastal erosion.

SHIKOKU

Until 1988, the only way to reach Japan's fourth-largest island was by air or water. It's an island of rugged land and open exposure to Pacific typhoons, and its people are fiercely independent

Map on pages 290–1

The least-developed and rarely visited of Japan's four main islands, Shikoku's attractions (and drawbacks) are attendant on its relative isolation. The island can provide a more "Japanese" experience than either Honshu or Kyushu. Its people are less familiar with foreigners and its ambiance has been less influenced by the homogenising aspects of modern culture. It is also more diffused. Places likely to be of interest to travellers are relatively far apart and more difficult to get to than on more widely travelled pathways.

Shikoku's separate identity is not as isolated as before. The smallest of Japan's main islands, it was the last to be linked by bridge with Honshu, the largest and most populated of Japan's islands. In 1988 the completion of the **Seto Ohashi** ⓭ gave Shikoku a ground transportation link to the rest of Japan. The bridge carries both automobiles and trains from Honshu, near Kurashiki, to Sakaide on Shikoku. (*See picture on page 45.*)

The Seto Ohashi is actually a series of six bridges using five small islands as stepping-stones across **Seto Naikai** (**Inland Sea**). At 12.3 km (7.6 miles) in length, it is one of the longer double-deck bridges in the world, carrying four lanes of automobiles above dual rail tracks. First suggested by a prefectural assemblyman in 1889, officials were finally persuaded of its logic in the late 1960s. Construction was set to begin in 1973 but was postponed in the aftermath of the first oil shock of the 1970s. Construction finally began in 1978 and after nearly 10 years of work and expenditures exceeding some US$1 billion, the first cars and trains finally rolled across in 1988. The extremely high tolls, around US$50, have left the bridge under-used. Still, it is a popular attraction for Japanese tourists, but unless a bridge engineer or civil engineer, just use it to get to Shikoku or else take one of the ferries from Osaka or Kobe.

The most numerous and distinctive visitors to Shikoku today – arriving by plane as often as not – are *ohenrosan* – devout Buddhist pilgrims making the rounds of the 88 holy temples and shrines established on Shikoku by the priest Kobo Daishi some 1,200 years ago. In the feudal period, it was common for white-robed pilgrims carrying staffs to complete the circuit on foot, a feat requiring more than two months. Today's similarly adorned pilgrims usually make the rounds in two weeks or less via air-conditioned buses.

Shikoku is split into northern and southern sections by steep, rugged mountains. The relatively dry northern part, facing the Seto Naikai, is more industrialised. The south is wilder, warmer, and wetter. The weather is most favourable in early spring and at the beginning of the fall.

PRECEDING PAGES: planting *igusa* for *tatami* mats. **LEFT:** Cape Ashizuri. **BELOW:** 88-temple pilgrim enroute.

Hotel key drop.

Takamatsu

The capital of Kagawa Prefecture, **Takamatsu** ⑭ is the main railway terminal and ferry port in eastern Shikoku. **Ritsurin-koen (Ritsurin Park)** contains one of the finest traditional gardens in Japan with 54 hectares (133 acres) of ponds, hills, pine forests, and a botanical garden. One of the garden's best rewards is a cup of tea at the beautiful Kikugetsutei tea house. The **Sanuki Mingeikan (Folk Art Museum)**, near the entrance of the park, displays comprehensive collections of crafts from Shikoku and throughout Japan. The local woodcrafts are particularly valued. However, the region's most popular craft (not on display here) are the distinctive *sanuki-udon* noodles, presented daily at thousands of *udon* restaurants throughout the area.

About 20 minutes and a few kilometres east by train from the centre of Takamatsu is **Yashima**. It was one of the seemingly countless battlefields of the Gempei War (1180–85) between the Minamoto and Taira clans. The architectural embodiments of Shikoku's past – an open-air *kabuki* theatre, a vine suspension bridge, thatch-roofed farmhouses, and a variety of other traditional buildings – have been collected and preserved in **Shikoku-mura (Shikoku Village)**. This tiny part of Shikoku island was itself once an island; now a narrow strip connects it to the mainland. It juts out into Seto Naikai and provides extensive views, particularly from Yashima's lofty temple on the hill.

Eastern Shikoku

BELOW: Seto Naikai, or the Inland Sea, near Takamatsu.

Tokushima Prefecture faces Osaka Bay and the Pacific Ocean along the western end of Shikoku. In ancient times, Tokushima was known as Awa no Kuni – Millet Country. Today, most of the prefecture's traditional arts still use the Chi-

Map
on pages
290–1

nese characters for millet country. The Awa Odori – the summer "crazy dance" festival – is held in mid-August and is perhaps the most humourous of Japanese festivals, with residents and tourists joining in processional dances and contests for the "biggest fool of all". Another home-grown entertainment are puppet shows featuring giant puppets accompanied by *samisen* and performed by farmers between growing seasons.

The garden of the old castle of **Tokushima** ⓕ is set against the backdrop of forest-covered Shiro-yama. The garden consists of a traditional landscaped area with a fountain. Over a quarter of the 88 Kobo Daishi temples are in the immediate vicinity of Tokushima. The city has several old, fire-resistant *godown* (warehouses) used by merchants to store their goods in earlier times. The godown line both sides of the once-prosperous and busy main highway through the centre of Tokushima.

About 20 km (12 miles) to the north, **Naruto** ⓖ faces the **Naruto-kaikyo** (**Naruto Straits**), where the **O-Narutokyo (Great Naruto Bridge)** connects Tokushima with Awaji-shima and is one of the longer suspension bridges in Asia. The attraction to travellers is not the bridge, however, but rather the countless whirlpools, some as large as 20 metres (60 ft) in diameter, that swirl in the 1,300-metre-wide (4,200-ft) Naruto Straits flowing beneath the bridge. The whirlpools are largest in the spring and autumn, when tides reach a speed of 20 kilometres an hour (12 mph). Sightseeing boats chug right up to the whirlpools during peak tourism season.

The 100-km-long (60-mile) coastline of Tokushima Prefecture holds some of the best beaches in Japan. Along the centre of the coast, **Komoda-misaki (Cape Komoda)** stretches out into the Pacific. The peninsula is noted for its luxuriant

BELOW: canal through a rural Shikoku village.

Families are often three generations.

subtropical flora. The offshore reefs, washed by the warm Japan Current, are the site of some of the best surf-fishing in Japan. The area is also noted as an egg-laying location for giant loggerhead turtles. In **Hiwasa** 🕧 to the south is a sea turtle museum. Also in Hiwasa is **Yakuo-ji**, a temple known to ward off evil. Men and women in their *yakudoshi* (unlucky years) visit here to ask for divine help by placing a one-yen coin on each step as they climb up to the temple.

Tsurugi-san 🕘 (1,893 metres/6,200 ft) dominates the interior of eastern Shikoku and is one of the main peaks of Shikoku. In contrast to its name – meaning "sword" – the crest of the mountain slopes gently. A lift brings visitors up to near the summit, followed by a 40-minute hike to the peak. A lodging house, skiing area, and old shrines make Tsurugi a major recreation area.

South of Tsurugi-san, the gorge of **Konose** lies deep in the mountains at the source of the Naka-gawa. It is a site of magnificent natural beauty, and in autumn, red and yellow foliage covers the surrounding mountains.

To the west of Tsurugi-san is the gorge at **Oboke**, formed by the upper reaches of the Yoshino-gawa. The site is noted for towering cliffs and giant rocks polished like marble from the cascading waters. Spring and autumn are the best times to visit the gorge, which is naturally filled with bus-loads of tourists.

The valley along Yoshino-gawa, north of Tsurugi-san and running due west from Tokushima, holds most of the area's main attractions. The valley is full of ancient temples, shrines, museums, and cultural sites. Too, the area is peppered with *ai yashiki* (indigo-dyeing plants); *awa*-style indigo dyeing has flourished as the main industry of Tokushima for centuries.

About 30 km (20 miles) up the Yoshino-gawa from Tokushima is **Do-chu** (**Earthen Pillars**). The strangely shaped pillars were formed over millions of

BELOW: vegetable drying while waiting out a political campaign.

years as the result of soil erosion. Nearby are the historic streets of Udatsu and the Awagami traditional paper factory. The entire valley is served by the JR Yoshinogawa rail line from Tokushima.

Southwest of Takamatsu, **Kotohira** is home to one of the most famous and popular shrines in Japan, **Kotohira-gu** (also called Konpira-san). Dedicated to Okuninushi no Mikoto, the guardian of seafarers, the shrine has lured sailors and fishermen seeking propitious sailing since the shrine's inception in the 11th century. In recent years, their numbers have been swelled by the 4 million Japanese and foreign tourists arriving each year. The main shrine is at the end of a long, steep path lined with stone lanterns. A trip to the top of the 785 stairs and back takes at least an hour.

The **Kanamaru-za**, restored to its original early 19th-century condition, is the oldest existing *kabuki* theatre in Japan. Its stage, resonating with the fading echoes of thousands of performances, is exciting to visit even when empty. In the third week of April, the nation's best kabuki actors bring it alive. The revolving section is turned by strong men pushing the 150-year-old mechanism under the stage, and the audience is seated on cushions on *tatami*.

Western Shikoku

Facing Seto Naikai along Shikoku's northeastern shore, Ehime Prefecture was described as early as AD 712 in the *Kojiki*, Japan's first chronicle of historical events and legends. Ehime has many cultural properties, historical places, hot springs, and festivals.

Several castles dot the Ehime landscape. In **Imabari** ❷⓿ is **Imabari-jo**. It is a rare coastal castle built in 1604 by Takatora Todo. The massive walls and

Map on pages 290–1

BELOW: harvesting cultivated pearls.

moats, filled by water from the sea, let its masters fight attacks by land or sea.

Ancient temples and shrines are another attraction of Ehime Prefecture. **Oya-mazumi-jinja**, on **Omi-shima**, has been worshiped since ancient times as the central shrine of all village shrines in Japan. It is a shrine to the gods of the sea and of soldiers; many old camphor trees give the shrine a solemn atmosphere. **Ishite-ji**, the 51st temple on Shikoku's 88-temple pilgrimage, was built by the decree of Emperor Shomu in 728. It was restored by the great priest Kobo in the early 9th century. Its treasure hall holds some 300 important historical articles.

Matsuyama-jo, which stands in the middle of the city of **Matsuyama** ㉑ and with a slightly incongruous baseball park and athletic stadium at its base, has had a checkered history. It was completed in 1603, burnt down but was rebuilt on a slightly smaller scale in 1642, struck by lightning and razed to the ground in 1784, and then not fully rebuilt until 1854. The present-day edifice is a result of restoration work completed in 1986, so it's not exactly an original, but the cable car ride up to it is fun and this is a good place to get your bearings.

Away to the west near **Dogo-koen** stands the **Dogo Onsen Honkan**. People in Matsuyama have been coming to Dogo for more than a century, taking off their shoes at the entrance to the rambling three-story castle affair topped with a white heron and leaving their clothes and cares behind as they wallow in the glory of the alkaline hot spas. In fact, history shows that they've been doing so for as long as 3,000 years – the Dogo Onsen is reckoned to be the oldest in Japan. It was first mentioned in Japan's oldest historical record, the *Kojiki*, and in the *Manyoshu*, the country's first anthology started in the 5th century.

One can get a basic soak in **Kamin-yu** (Water of the Gods) for a few hundred yen, but that would be like going to a Michelin-star restaurant and merely nib-

TIP

Remember that in the Japanese *onsen* or hot spring no clothes are worn (though a small handtowel offers modesty), and one should thoroughly wash and rinse before entering the water, used only for soaking.

BELOW: ship in the Inland Sea.

Map
on pages
290–1

bling on the breadsticks. Pay the full price and head up Dogo's precipitous stairways to **Tamano-yu** (Water of the Spirits). Language is not a problem as smiling ladies point the way to a private tatami room where you can leave clothes in a locker, don a *yukata*, and head for the bath itself.

Males and females go their separate ways at this point, but as in all onsen, soap and thoroughly rinse off first, sitting on a little wooden stool and dousing your body from a wooden bucket. Then – bliss is the only word for it – it's time to lower yourself inch by inch into the waters (hot but not scalding) and let the body gradually adjust. It's a tingling cleanliness that washes over you, that penetrates beneath the skin, and that drowsily wafts over the mind. After 10 or 20 minutes, heave yourself out, dry off, and climb back up to the tatami room. The maid will pull out your sitting pillows and serve tea and marzipan balls. The balcony looks out over tiled roofs and trees, and laughter and the contented buzz of conversation drifts over from adjoining rooms.

Japanese poets and novelists have long sung of the joys of this onsen, but as the drum booms gently from the *shinrokaku* room on the third floor to mark the passing hours, time and the other vagaries scarcely seem relevant any more.

One of Ehime's more interesting historical sites is the kabuki theatre in **Uchiko ㉒**. This full-scale kabuki theatre was built in 1916 in the Irimoya-zukuri style and with a tiled roof, a typical Japanese housing style of the 1800s. Its restoration in 1985 preserved the old-style drum tower on the top floor, a rotating stage, an elevated passageway, and box seats.

Uwajima-jo was built in 1595 by Takatora Todo. The castle's three-storied tower stands atop an 80-metre (260-ft) hill overlooking the city of **Uwajima ㉓**, noted throughout Japan for bull-fights. Curious libertines drawn to Uwajima by tales of **Taga-jinja** (and its sex museum) should be aware that many of the more tantalising exhibits within this shrine are locked away in glass cases and there is little interpretation in English, although, of course, most of the items on display – from lurid photos to well-proportioned fertility sculptures – are self-explanatory to most adults. Children might require some expert clarifying explanation, however.

To the south in **Tsushima ㉔** is a strolling garden, **Nanrakuen-koen**, covering more than 15 hectares (37 acres) and the largest on Shikoku. Developed in 1985, the garden has four theme areas: mountains, villages, towns, and the sea. Some 30,000 irises, which bloom in early May, cover most of the gardens. Near Nanrakuen-koen is a gorge, **Nametoko**, carved out by the Shimanto-gawa, which is reported to be the last clear river in Japan. The gorge runs through Ashizuri-Uwakai National Park.

Ehime Prefecture is also noted for its many and varied festivals covering a number of subjects. The Ikazaki Kite Festival in May, for example, displays Ehime's 300-year history of kite-making. The Saijo Festival in October features 80 movable shrines. The Niihama Drum Festival in October includes a competition between 33 massive drums, or *taiko*. Other festivals include bull fights, samba (yes) competitions, a deer-mask dance, and the Matsuyama Spring Festival in April.

Japan's countless hot springs are indicative of the islands' continuing volcanism.

BELOW: fishing boat leaving Uwajima.

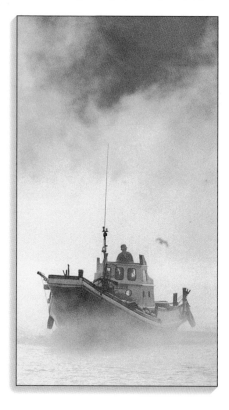

Map on pages 290–1

Southern Shikoku

Two large capes frame Kochi prefecture. On the far western side of Kochi lies **Ashizuri-misaki** ㉕. This cape is noted for towering marble cliffs and Japan's first underwater park. In early spring, camellia cover the cape in a dazzling red carpet of blossoms.

The prefecture of Kochi broadly encircles the wide **Tosa-wan** (**Tosa Bay**), with its capital of **Kochi** ㉖ facing the south on a flat plain. Kochi is best known for the role its leading families played in forging the alliance between the Satsuma and Choshu clans and the ensuing imperial Meiji Restoration of 1868. Its most renowned citizen from this period is Sakamoto Ryoma. Sakamoto – from a half-merchant, half-samurai family – left the class system and set up a trading company in Nagasaki.

While there, he helped establish a network of anti-Tokugawa samurai but was assassinated in Kyoto in 1867 – just a year before the overthrow of the shogun and restoration of the emperor to legitimate rule. He is remembered in the museum at **Kochi-jo** (**Kochi Castle**), an elegant castle built in the 17th century and rebuilt in the 18th. A market is held every Sunday on the road leading to the Ote gate of Kochi-jo. The market is popular with local residents, with as many as 700 small stands selling vegetables, antiques, plants, and just about everything else imaginable. The market runs for about a kilometre along both sides of the road. A statue of Sakamoto Ryoma graces the beach at **Katsurahama**, more famous as one of the few locations in Japan where dog-fighting is legal. This beautiful beach is a popular spot for admiring the moon. Katsurahama-koen is nearby, and there are many places of interest such as a shell museum, dog-fighting centre, and aquarium.

OPPOSITE: harvest of *mikan* on a steep coastal hill. **BELOW:** aqua-farming is heavily practiced.

Ryuga-do, a limestone cave 25 km (15 miles) east of Kochi and gradually molded over a period of 50 million years, boasts a mysterious natural beauty that supposedly enthralls everyone who visits. About 4 km (2½ miles) of Ryuga-do, one of Japan's largest caves, is open to the public. The scenic skyline road to the top of the mountain where the cave is buried offers the better vista of the Pacific Ocean.

A few kilometres west of Kochi, in **Ino**, is a fabulous paper museum. Ino has a long history of paper-making, and Kochi paper is famous throughout Japan. (For a place to be viable in Japan's domestic tourism industry, it must be "famous" for something, for anything.) In the museum, visitors can try their hand at paper-making in addition to observing the paper-making process. Near Kochi sits the Nishijima Fruit Farm. Its 11 huge hothouses, each measuring 70 metres (230 ft) in length and 45 metres (150 ft) in width, cover the spacious grounds. The temperature within each hothouse is maintained at 25°C (77°F). Sample the delicious Kochi melons here year-round.

On the far eastern side of Kochi from Ashizuri-misaki, **Muroto-zaki** ㉗ points out southward into the Pacific Ocean. The cape is warm year-round and at its tip the towering waves of the Pacific have eroded the rocks and reefs into strange shapes. The area is also noted for its connection with the venerable Kobo Daishi, founder of the Shingon sect of Buddhism. ❑

UNDERCURRENTS OF LIFE AND RITUAL

At the core of Japanese life is the ancient, animist belief of Shintoism, which informs daily life in basic ways, enriched by introduced Buddhism.

An outsider may perceive a certain fog enveloping the Japanese beliefs in gods and afterlife and in the metaphysical concerns of life. Buddhism and Shintoism coexist, and on occasion appear to meld together. Unlike believers in a monotheistic system, Japanese are more willing to accept a world that has a lot of gray areas with few absolutes, in which compromise and tolerance of thought is essential. It is not uncommon to find Shinto shrines and Buddhist temples sharing the same sacred grounds, each tending to specific needs but complementing one another as a whole.

Shintoism doesn't exist as doctrine, but rather as an integral undercurrent to one's daily life. Shinto is Japan's indigenous religion, but the term Shinto did not appear in any Japanese literature until the 6th century, and in fact the label came into existence only as a way to distinguish it from Buddhism, introduced from mainland Asia. Nor were there visual images of Shinto deities – *kami* – until the imagery of Buddhism established itself in the archipelago. Over the centuries, Daoism and Confucianism also influenced Shinto.

Ancient Shinto was polytheistic, maybe even pantheistic, and people believed kami existed not only in nature, but also in abstract ideas such as creation, growth, and human judgment.

△ **GIFTS TO THE GODS**
Offerings at a small shrine in Okinawa. Some of the most sacred sites are simple and lack grand structures.

△ **GOOD HARVEST WISH**
As in ancient times, prayers and imagery of good rice harvests often punctuate festivals in Japan.

▷ **COEXISTING WITH BUDDHISM**
Buddhist priests, such as these Zen priests at a Kyoto temple, have no qualms in sharing the metaphysical with Shinto priests.

A LIFE OF SHINTO BLESSINGS

Traditions of Shinto (and of Buddhism, too) are the traditions of Japan itself. They pepper the daily lives of the Japanese, who perform them as routines of life when the urge or need arises.

The small votives *(ema)* above are hung at shrines to seek good luck in exams or other secular rituals. Infants are brought to the shrine 30 to 100 days after birth to initiate the child as a new believer. On 15 November of every year, Japan is embellished with children in kimono for *shichi-go-san* (seven-five-three). Girls three and seven years old and boys five years old visit the shrine to thank the *kami* for their life so far and to pray for health. In January, 20-year-olds return to the shrine marking their becoming adults. When they are married, it is usually a Shinto ceremony (although a separate Western-style ceremony is increasingly common. Death, however, usually is of Buddhist ritual and family remembrance.

△ **MORNING PRAYERS**
Shinto priests at morning prayers. The sacred image is often kept from view, seen only by the head priest.

△ **QUICK PRAYER**
There are no weekly holy days. Rather, the Japanese attend a shrine or temple when the need arises.

▽ **VANISHING POINT**
Torii – dividing the secular world from Shinto shrines – make an unusual tunnel at Fushimi Inari, Kyoto.

◁ **SHRINE IMAGERY**
The rope, white paper, and other symbols announce a sacred site as of Shinto importance.

▷ **SADO**
Tea ceremonies – symbolic of Japanese ways – are mostly Zen Buddhist influenced.

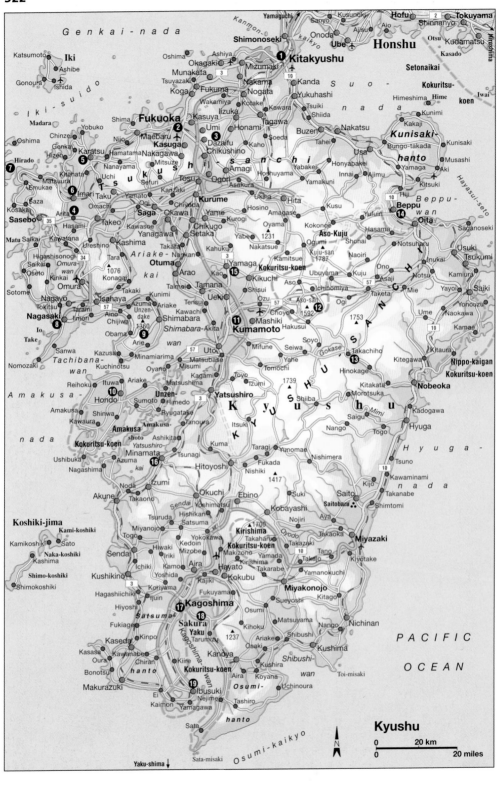

Kyushu

KYUSHU

Map
on page
322

*An erupting volcano next to a large city, Kagoshima,
and the history of a port city, Nagasaki, are unique to Kyushu, as
are some of Japan's most independently minded leaders*

Kyushu is far to the south and, it seems at times, almost forgotten by the rest of Japan. But Kyushu has always been in the vanguard of development and change. Kyushu is where the Yamato tribe – and thus the Japanese people – first took root in what was to become their homeland. It was Kyushu that withstood the onslaught of the Mongols from the mainland. It is also from where the Japanese first struck out on foreign conquest – the invasion of Korea in 1594 – and where ancient Chinese and Korean culture entered the archipelago as foundations for Japanese art and philosophy. In later years, it was one of a few places where Westerners had a foothold in the xenophobic islands.

Any traveller coming from the north usually enters Kyushu at **Kitakyushu ❶**, considered by some as a city in search of a soul – it is an amalgamation of five cities (Moji, Kokura, Yawata, Tobata and Wakamatsu) with a combined population of over a million. The civic marriage was arranged by Tokyo bureaucrats in 1963, but it has yet to be consummated by a blending of culture or politics. It is a lacklustre city with little of interest for travellers. Kitakyushu is linked to Shimonoseki on Honshu by a bridge across the Kanmon Strait. Immense steel mills (now an endangered species) and factories were built here to take advantage of the region's rich coal deposits.

Fukuoka

Northern Kyushu has a long history of overseas influence. In the 13th century it was targeted by foreign invaders, but other "imports" have been of a more peaceful nature. **Fukuoka ❷** is reportedly where both tea and Buddhism were introduced to Japan, and Korean captives brought back here were responsible for starting up a sizeable pottery industry. Today, with a population of 1.2 million, Fukuoka competes with Kitakyushu as the largest city on Kyushu.

The city remains an important hub in regional trade and commerce, but while shopping and hotel complexes such as the glistening Canal City dominate the skyline, Fukuoka still retains a lot of charm at ground level. Canals crisscross the central urban area and in the evenings and on weekends small stalls selling snacks and alcohol are set up on the paths beside the water, each an oasis of relaxation and merriment for the hordes of harried *sararimen* ("salarymen") wending their way home from work.

Fukuoka's history has not always been benign. During the Nara and Heian periods, the area was the principal Japanese port for trade with China and Korea, but in 1274 a reconnaissance force of some 30,000 Mongols landed near Fukuoka after annihilating garrisons on the islands of Tsushima and Iki, just to the

PRECEDING PAGES:
Kagoshima and
Sakura-jima.
BELOW: unhappy
three-year-old at
temple blessing.

north of Kyushu in the Korea Strait. The invaders enjoyed similar success on Kyushu, but the death of their commander, along with serious storms that threatened their ships, forced them to retreat. Seven years later, in 1281, Kublai Khan dispatched another Mongol expeditionary force of 150,000 troops, the largest amphibious assault recorded in history prior to World War II. Backed by a ferocious armoury of catapults and cannons, the Mongols gradually wore down the fanatical Japanese resistance, but when they were on the brink of victory after 53 days of fighting, a terrific typhoon – *kami-kaze* (lit. divine wind) – sent most of the invading fleet to the bottom of the sea. Remnants of the defensive wall built to repel the Mongols can be still be seen on the outskirts of Fukuoka, although nowadays they are rather unimpressive.

Relics of Fukuoka's most famous visitors are preserved 2 km (1¼ miles) northeast of Hakata Station at the **Genko Kinekan (Mongol Invasion Memorial Hall)**, along with a statue of Nichiren, who was among the mystics taking credit for the fortuitous kamikaze storm that sank the Mongol fleet.

Modern Fukuoka traces its roots to 1601, when a castle was built on the west side of the **Naka-gawa** in what is today Ohori Park and the town that grew up around the castle took the same name of Fukuoka. Only the castle's walls survive nowadays, but they provide an excellent view over the city. Hakata, a town for merchants who enjoyed a less important status than the ruling samurai, was built on the other side of the river. Hakata-ku has been a ward within Fukuoka since 1889, but the name remains – **Hakata-eki (Hakata Station)**, the southern terminus of the *shinkansen* line; Hakata clay dolls; and the popular Hakata Yamagasa festival are all named after the merchant city.

In its role as the cross-roads between Japan and China, Fukuoka was the

Hakata Yamagasa takes place in the first half of July; seven enormous floats are displayed around the city for a fortnight. On the 15th, groups of brawny men race the floats, which each weigh a ton, through the streets in a hilarious tumult of noise, excitement and general frenzy.

BELOW: modern building, and retired man at the park.

place where Zen Buddhism first touched the archipelago's shores. Located northwest of Hakata Station near Mikasa-gawa, **Shofuku-ji** is the oldest Zen temple in Japan, founded in 1195 by Eisai after years of study in China. Sadly, much of the temple suffered bomb damage during World War II and the current complex is only a fraction of its former self. Eisai is also credited with bringing the first tea seeds into the country; tea shrubs here are said to be descendants.

Map on page 322

The **Sumiyoshi-jinja**, the oldest extant Shinto shrine on Kyushu, was built in 1623. South of Shofuku-ji and due west of the train station, it sits atop a hill that provides an excellent city view. **Shiritsu Rekishu Shiryokan** (near Tenjin Station) is a decent museum dedicated to Fukuoka's history.

All in all, Fukuoka today is still very much open to outside influence and sees itself as the cultural crossroads of this part of Asia. The downtown **ACROS Centre**, easily recognisable for its imaginative stepped-garden exterior, stages international opera, ballet, symphony orchestras, and popular musical extravaganzas, as well as more traditional Japanese performances.

Two other significant structures overlook life in the city. A mammoth seaside stadium, **Hawks Town**, whose retractable dome is the first of its kind in Japan, is home to the local baseball team as well as a hotel and shopping mall. And a little further along the coast above Momochi-koen stands the 234-metre-high (768-ft) **Fukuoka Tower** (open daily, 9.30am–9pm; admission fee), with two observation towers that provide stunning views over the surrounding area.

Other points of interest in Fukuoka include **Fukuoka-shi Bijutsukan**, an art museum housing a collection of Japanese art, and **Ohori-koen (Ohori Park)**, a pleasant park harbouring the remains of **Fukuoka-jo (Fukuoka Castle)** and reconstructions of its turret and gates.

BELOW: bridge at Ohori Park.

Forty minutes from Fukuoka and inland to the southeast, **Dazaifu ❸** is home to **Tenman-gu**, a shrine built in 1591 to commemorate the poet-scholar Sugawara Michizane, who died in AD 903 after being unjustly exiled from the court in Kyoto. Successive mishaps befell Kyoto, supposedly because of Sugawara's banishment. As a result, he gradually came to be acknowledged as Tenman, a deity of culture and scholars.

Much of the pottery and ceramics found in western Honshu and Kyushu is defined by both an elegance and a rustic simplicity.

Nowadays, students of all ages tramp over the bright-orange shrine's arched bridge to beseech his help in passing school examinations, which can make or break careers and lives in Japan. Sections of defensive walls built after the first Mongol invasion can still be seen on the road to Dazaifu.

Ceramic cities

When Ri Simpei, an ordinary Korean potter, first chanced upon *kaolin* clay – the essential ingredient for producing fine porcelain – in **Arita ❹**, 50 km (30 miles) west of Fukuoka around the turn of the 17th century, he probably had little notion of the ramifications of his discovery.

Nearly 400 years later, Arita and its neighbours **Karatsu ❺** and **Imari ❻** are the hub of a thriving pottery industry. The delicate craftsmanship and brightly coloured glazes that are the hallmarks of pottery from this region are prized all over Japan, and further afield, too. Simpei and the other potters who were brought over from Korea as prisoners of the Nabeshima *daimyo* were kept under close guard so their trade secrets did not slip out.

BELOW: *sumo* lessons for kids; Fukuoka is host to an annual sumo tournament.

To understand something about those times, the **Nabeshima Hanyo-koen** at Okawachiyama (a short bus ride from Imari) portrays the sort of techniques and living conditions that Simpei and his fellow workers lived in. Several of the

potters' graves, including Simpei's, are located here, too. There are plenty of working potteries in the area as well, but **Kyushu Toji Bunkakan** (**Kyushu Ceramic Museum**) in Arita is the best place to view the full range of Kyushu pottery. Imaizumi Imaemon and Sakaida Kakiemon are celebrated workshops with galleries and shops open to the public.

Karatsu is also highly regarded for its stoneware. Several galleries and workshops, including the Nakazato Taroemon and the Ryuta kilns, are open to visitors. The Hikiyama Tenijo museum exhibits 19th-century Karatsu *kun-chi* festival floats, which are paraded through the town every November.

For a breath of fresh ocean air, take a stroll or hire a bike to explore the pine groves of **Niji-no-Matsubara**, which stretch 5 km (3 miles) along the beach found at Matsuragate.

Hirado

Continuing west from Imari another 40 km (25 miles), the focus shifts to Japan's early Christians. The first foreign settlement in Japan was established by Dutch traders on **Hirado-shima** ❼ (**Hirado Island**) in 1550, although the one-time island is now connected to the mainland by a bridge.

The Francis Xavier Memorial Chapel consecrates the saint's visit to Hirado after he was expelled from Kagoshima in southern Kyushu. European activity here ended when the Dutch were forced to move to Dejima, in Nagasaki Harbour, in 1641. But secretive Christians maintained a version of the faith here for centuries afterwards, often with the threat of imprisonment and death. This bit of historical lore has provided the basis for a thriving domestic tourist industry here, with "real" icons for sale.

Map on page 322

Shoes are never worn in the house or school but are kept near the entrance.

BELOW: Kyushu farms are small and family-owned.

Nagasaki

Like Hiroshima, **Nagasaki** ❽ is a name automatically associated with the atomic bomb that brought World War II to a tumultuous climax. It is particularly ironic that this most terrible manifestation of Western technology (although Japan was developing its own bomb) should have been detonated in a city that was one of the first to open up to the outside world and where foreign inventions and ways were once eagerly adopted.

The path was not always smooth, of course, and many early Christian converts were brutally executed and foreign residents were expelled from time to time. But Nagasaki was one of the first Japanese cities to take a serious interest in Western medicine. It was here, too, that the first railway and modern shipyard in Japan were established.

Now home to more than half a million people, Nagasaki clings to steep hills wrapped around a very active deep-water harbour, competing with Kobe for designation as Japan's San Francisco. Like San Francisco, it has a lively Chinatown and a continuing spirit of receptiveness to novel ideas. One of the most interesting cities in Japan, travellers on a restricted time budget should allow for two days or more to explore Nagasaki and its surroundings.

Nagasaki's harbour has played a prominent role in Japan's relations with the outside world. Dutch traders initiated the first sustained European presence here, on an island in the harbour that also acted as a conduit for most of the early Christian missionaries. The port at Nagasaki was established in 1571 to serve Portuguese traders. A decade later, Omura Sumitada, a local daimyo who had grown rich on trade with the foreigners, turned over partial administration of the port to the Jesuit missionaries who followed in the merchants' wake.

BELOW: an old man and his rising sun.

A generation later, fearing that the Christians and their converts would subvert his authority, the shogun Toyotomi Hideyoshi banned Christianity. He ordered six Spanish priests and 20 Japanese Christians, including two teenage boys, to be rounded up in Kyoto and Osaka. They were brought to Nagasaki and crucified in 1597 as a warning to Japan's largest Christian community. A memorial constructed in 1962 and museum (open daily, 9am–5pm; admission fee) stands in **Nishizaka-koen** (**Nishizaka Park**) on the spot of the crucifixions, near **Nagasaki-eki Ⓐ** (**Nagasaki Station**) at the north end of downtown.

Christianity was utterly and viciously suppressed following the Christian-led Shimbara Rebellion of 40,000 peasants south of Nagasaki in 1637. As a result, Japan's sole officially sanctioned contact with Europeans for the next two centuries was through a settlement on **Dejima Ⓑ**, in Nagasaki Harbour and south of the present-day Nagasaki Station. The artificial island – now part of the mainland – was built for Portuguese traders but it was occupied by the Dutch after the Portuguese were banished in 1638. Its occupants were confined to a small, walled area and contact with Japanese was limited to a small circle of officials, traders, prostitutes, and in the later years, scholars.

As no other Europeans were permitted in Japan until 1854, whatever news of European technology and culture that filtered into Japan came through this settlement. The **Shiryokan** (**Dejima Museum**; open Tuesday–Sunday, 9am–5pm; free) near the site preserves relics of the settlement.

Like the Dutch, Nagasaki's Chinese, mostly from Fujian along China's southern coast, were officially confined to a walled ghetto but restrictions on their movements were not as strictly enforced. The Chinese in Nagasaki left the only pure Chinese architecture to be found in Japan, along with one of the three Chi-

Maps on pages 322, 329

TIP

Like Fukuoka, also on Kyushu, Nagasaki is thought by many foreigners to be one of Japan's most pleasant large cities.

BELOW: pool smiles.

natowns remaining in Japan. (The others are in Yokohama and Kobe.) The narrow and winding streets of **Shinchimachi** are filled with Chinese restaurants catering to tourists, as there are very few Chinese remaining in Nagasaki.

Two popular "Chinese" dishes in Japan, *saraudon* and *champpon*, were invented in Shinchimachi. Like most of the foreign food served in Japan, they bear only a passing resemblance to the original but they are still quite palatable. On the subject of food, the other "foreign" delicacy that survives in Nagasaki is the *kasutera* or sponge cake that is supposedly baked to an old Portuguese recipe and sold (in exquisitely wrapped packages) in bakeries around town.

The Chinese community was granted permission to build its own temples. Teramachi (Temple Town) contains two of the oldest Chinese temples in Japan, as well as numerous Japanese Buddhist temples and graveyards. **Kofuku-ji ☉**, founded in 1620, was built on the edge of the original Chinatown in the northeast part of town. The Chinese quarters burned down in 1698; the current Shinchimachi occupies land designated for Chinese merchants following the fire. Centrally located, **Sofuku-ji ☉** is a bright, elaborate Ming-style temple and is in better condition than most Ming-era temples in China. A Zen priest from Fujian built Sofuku-ji in 1629. Shaka and 18 disciples inhabit the main hall. The Masodo (Hall of the Bodhisattva) contains an image of the goddess of the seas, flanked by fierce guardians reputed to have thousand-mile vision.

Within walking distance of the temples, the **Nakashima-gawa (Nakashima River)** is bridged by a picturesque range of bridges. The best known and most photographed is **Megane-bashi ☉**, whose English translation of Spectacles Bridge becomes apparent when there is enough water in the river to ensure a good reflection. The original bridge was the oldest stone arch bridge in Japan,

Fugu, or blowfish, is the local speciality and is reputed to be especially good in winter. If prepared incorrectly, deadly toxins in the fugu can poison the diner.

BELOW: Sofuku-ji.

built in 1634 by a priest from Kofuku-ji. However, a flood in 1962 destroyed it and the present structure is a carbon-copy restoration.

True to its traditional receptiveness to new ideas, Nagasaki embarked on an aggressive modernisation campaign in the latter part of the 19th century. Thomas Glover, a Scotsman, was one of the first and most significant of the European traders who arrived soon after Commodore Matthew Perry's Black Ships reopened the country. Glover helped Nagasaki achieve many Japanese firsts: the first railroad, the first mint, and the first printing press with movable type were all built in Nagasaki as a result of his efforts. He was also very active in supporting the rebels who defeated the shogun's forces – mainly through a profitable line in gun-running – and re-established the emperor's rule in 1868 in the Meiji Restoration. There is considerable controversy over whether Glover's marriage to a *geisha* did, as many guidebooks assert, inspire Puccini's opera *Madame Butterfly*. Glover also built the first Western-style mansion in Japan.

At the southern end of the city, **Glover-en** ❻ (**Glover Gardens**; open daily, 8.30am–5pm; admission fee) contains this house, built in 1863, and several other early Meiji-era, Western-style houses – elegant mixtures of Japanese and European architecture plus the inevitable statues of Puccini and his tragic Japanese heroine. It's amusing to wander around the grounds today, which now have covered escalators complete with recorded announcements and full complements of vending machines, and speculate that these are technological innovations of which Glover himself would have approved.

If your trip does not coincide with the annual Okunchi Festival in early October, when Chinese-style dragon dances and parades are held in the vicinity of Suwa-jinja, a trip to the **Kunchi Shiryokan** (**Kunchi Museum**) near Glover

BELOW: Glover House, Nagasaki.

WHAT KIND OF ARMY?

A rticle 9 of the postwar constitution, set up by the Americans, states that Japan is prohibited from possessing or having the potential of an external military force. In place of a military is the *Jieitai*, or Self-Defence Forces (SDF). Established in 1954, the SDF is a highly sophisticated military entity and one of the strongest armies in the world with nearly 300,000 troops, a situation that increasingly concerns Japan's neighbours. However, ships and planes in the SDF have limited operating range, and officially the SDF's responsibility extends 1,600 kms (1,000 miles) from Japan's shores.

With memories of Japan's aggression, Japan's military role today is a continuing and delicate debate, often igniting right-wing nationalists and conservatives.

In 1992, a law authorised sending troops overseas in limited numbers and intended for non-combatant U.N. peace-keeping operations, such as in Cambodia.

Garden will at least give a visitor some idea of the floats and costumes involved.

Nearby in the same neighbourhood is **Oura Tenshu-do (Oura Catholic Church)**, said to be the oldest Gothic-style structure in Japan. Completed in 1865, it is dedicated to the 26 Christian martyrs who were crucified in the 16th century and has some very fine examples of stained glass.

If construction of Glover's mansion marked the beginning of an era of infatuation with European institutions in Japan, the detonation of a plutonium bomb over Nagasaki 82 years later marked its realignment.

The bombs dropped on Hiroshima and Nagasaki.

A simple stone obelisk stands at the epicentre ("hypocentre" in Japan) of the atomic blast that devastated much of Nagasaki on the morning of 9 August 1945. The plutonium bomb, which was nearly twice as powerful as the uranium bomb dropped earlier over Hiroshima, landed about 3 km (2 miles) off course over **Urakami**, a Christian village just to the north of downtown. (The Mitsubishi Heavy Industry shipyard, on the west side of the port and the first modern shipbuilding facility in Japan, was the intended target; the pilot's vision was hampered by poor visibility.)

Urakami Roman Catholic Church, the largest Christian church in Japan, stood a few hundred metres from the epicentre; it was rebuilt in 1958. Headless statues of saints scorched in the blast remain as mute witnesses to the tragedy. A similarly poignant memorial is the small hut used by Dr Takashi Nagai, who struggled to treat bomb victims as best he could until he himself succumbed to radiation sickness in 1951.

BELOW: Peace Statue and cranes.

The **Atomic Bomb Museum** Ⓖ (open daily, 9am–6pm; admission fee) at the International Culture Hall contains photos, relics, and poignant details of the blast and its 150,000 victims. Simple objects – a melted bottle, the charred

Map on page 329

remains of a kimono – as well as photos of victims provide stark evidence of the bomb's destructive powers.

As important as its displays are, the museum (like the more elaborate one in Hiroshima) fails to provide historical context or background to the bombing. Nothing is said about the reasons for the war, much less that Japan was the aggressor, and there is no comparison with other mass killings of civilians committed by Japan in China and Korea. (The Japanese killed more civilians in Nanjing than were killed by both of the atomic bombs; nevertheless, Japanese text books call the Rape of Nanjing a "minor incident".)

Heiwa-koen (**Peace Park**) is dominated by the Peace Statue – a man with right hand pointing to the sky (signaling the threat from the atomic bomb) and left hand extended (symbolising world peace). The Peace Fountain, on the south side of the park, was built in remembrance of the bomb victims who died crying for water. Heiwa-koen was built on the site of a former jail, whose occupants and warders were all killed in the blast.

On the other side of the harbour, the cable car climbing the 332-metre (1,089 ft) peak of **Inasa-yama** ❶ provides fantastic vistas of the harbour and surrounding hills, especially at night. Further south is the Mitsubishi shipyard, intended target for the atomic bomb.

An hour out of Nagasaki stands **Huis Ten Bosch**, one of the most graceful theme parks in Japan with many replicas of Dutch buildings and windmills, canals, tulips and clogs galore. Theme park is perhaps an understatement, as Huis Ten Bosch has been carefully constructed on environmentally friendly lines and stands as a modern-day testimony of the area's close links with the Dutch. Built at a cost of US$2 billion when the country's banks were awash

BELOW: fisherman, and some girls sharing a laugh.

with money, there is something particularly Japanese about the place in the way that the replicas are built to look precisely like the originals, even to the point of making the Amsterdam canal houses lean out at an angle over the water. Once through the pricey gate most attractions are free, and it's as much fun to watch the Japanese tourists dressing up in traditional Dutch clothing for photos and even getting married at the Royal Palace. There are five very expensive hotels.

Shimbara Peninsula

The most scenic route between Nagasaki and Kumamoto takes travellers through Shimbara Peninsula and the Amakusa Islands on a combination of buses and ferries. Down the peninsula, roughly midway between Nagasaki and Kumamoto, is **Unzen-dake ❾**, whose *jigoku* (hell) pits of boiling mud and coloured mineral waters are less dramatic but less commercialised than those in Beppu, on the east coast of Kyushu. In the 17th century, Christians who refused to renounce their faith were thrown into these jigoku. Later, Unzen was popular with colonial officials in Shanghai during the glory days of the British Empire. The town is named after the 1,360-metre-high (4,460 ft) volcano Unzen-dake, on the peninsula and in **Unzen-Amakusa Kokuritsu-koen (Unzen-Amakusa National Park)**. Unzen erupted in 1991, causing considerable death and damage.

Shimabara-jo (Shimabara Castle), destroyed in a 1637 Christian rebellion, was reconstructed in 1964. The castle houses a museum displaying the *fumi-e* Christian images, which suspected believers were forced to walk upon.

Amakusa-shoto (Amakusa Islands), about 70 islands in all, lie between Unzen and Kumamoto. The Kirishitankan in **Hondo ❿** is a museum containing relics of the Amakusa Christians.

BELOW: highway in southern Kyushu.

Kumamoto

Although it isn't a popular tourist destination, **Kumamoto ⓫** is an interesting and dynamic provincial capital. This city of half a million people is best known for its 17th-century castle, 350-year-old **Suizenji-koen (Suizenji Park)**, and – believe it or not – its horse-meat *sashimi*. Eager to retain its vitality in the 21st century, Kumamoto also boasts the most successful technical research park (adjacent to the airport) in Japan. Kumamoto Prefecture has a sister-state relationship with the American state of Montana, due more to the power and influence of the former American ambassador to Japan, Mike Mansfield, a Montanan, than to any similarity between the two places. The Texas swing music on one of the newer street cars might be explained by Kumamoto's sister-city relationship with San Antonio, Texas.

Kumamoto-jo (Kumamoto Castle) was built in 1607 by Kato Kiyomasa. Unfortunately, the castle's 49 towers were made of wood and most were incinerated in an 1877 siege. The restored *donjon*, housing a museum as well as original turrets, moats and stone palisades, evoke the grandeur of what was one of Japan's most impressive castles.

Honmyo-ji, a Nichiren temple housing Kato's tomb, can be seen from the castle's towers. A cup of tea can be enjoyed in the basement of the **Kumamoto Traditional Crafts Centre** (open Tuesday–Sunday, 9am–5pm; admission fee) across the street from the castle. The first floor features a colourful collection of toys, tools, jewellery, and ceramics produced by Kumamoto craftsmen. The museum is part of the prefecture's efforts to sustain traditional crafts, largely abandoned after World War II. Most of the items are on sale in the museum. Suizenji-koen, designed in 1632 and south of the modern city, contains landscaped models of Mount Fuji.

Aso-Kuju Kokuritsu-koen (Aso-Kuju National Park), an hour's drive east from Kumamoto, contains the world's largest volcanic crater, an active volcano, and a volcano museum. Actually comprised of five craters, **Aso-san** ⑫ (1,592 metres/5,223 ft) erupts every two or three years but in a passive way. The drive from Kumamoto leads past Aspecta, which some say is largest outdoor theatre in the world. (Spend enough time in Japan and one recognises the Japanese love of world's-something superlatives, whether true or not.)

East of Kumamoto and on the other side of Aso, the shrine at **Takachiho** ⑬ is where the *iwato kagura*, a sacred dance, is performed for tourists every night. **Takachiho-kyo (Takachiho Gorge)**, featuring 80-metre (260-ft) cliffs, is another one of the many spots where the sun goddess Amaterasu is said to have emerged from her cave to create the islands and people of the archipelago. A cave near the shrine at Iwato is touted as the very one.

If seeking to go to hell and then come back, head for **Beppu** ⑭ on the northeastern coast of Kyushu. The resort town is famous – and thus highly commercialised – for its jigoku, or variously coloured ponds of water and mud that steam and boil, as well as its hot springs. A popular destination for Japanese tourists, Beppu is gaudy and rather tacky and a far cry from the serene ele-

Map
on page
322

Throughout history, the leaders and people of southern Kyushu have been known for their independence if not spunky feistiness.

BELOW: Aso's main caldera.

Blood Pond Hell.

gance of Japanese travel posters. Besides the hype, there are other hells, more than can be experienced in a lifetime, including: Blood Pond Hell, a vermilion-coloured boiling pond; Sea Hell, a boiling mud pond 120 metres (400 ft) deep; and Mountain Hell, a mud pond in the hills complete with statues of gorillas. All these are far too hot for bathing, but in the many *onsen* inns, comfortable hot-sand and hot-mud baths are available.

The Usuki Sekibutsu, a collection of more than 60 stone Buddhas, is all that remains of the **Mangetsu-ji**, once an important temple. The stone images are some of the most exquisite and mysterious Buddhist images in Japan.

The recently restored Edo-style **Yachiyo-za**, in **Yamaga** ⑮ and 50 minutes by bus from Kumamoto, is one of 10 *kabuki* theatres in Japan and well worth a visit. Built in 1910, it is a mixture of traditional Japanese construction and imported innovations, including a revolving stage and concealed trap doors. Patrons sat on tatami, warming themselves with a *hibachi* in winter. Around the corner, a lantern museum displays hundreds of handmade lantern head-dresses worn by young women in the local annual festival.

The bay near **Minamata** ⑯, in the southern part of Kumamoto Prefecture, is a monument to the excesses of industry, the results of laissez-faire government controls, and to sheer ignorance, greed and disregard for ethical conduct in general. The reason: a severely debilitating and often fatal ailment known as Mina-mata disease (in Japanese, *itai-itai byoki*, or hurt-hurt disease).

The affliction was traced to shellfish and other products taken from its waters, into which local industries had been discharging mercury and other heavy-metal wastes for decades. Legislation hurriedly passed by the Diet soon after the disease's discovery in the 1970s now constitutes the basis of Japan's still-weak pollution-control laws. Nevertheless, litigation regarding the responsibility for the mercury dumping was dragged out until the mid-1990s, with no entity ever admitting responsibility. Minamata Bay itself is being reclaimed and turned into an ecological park.

BELOW: empty *sake* bottles being stacked at a Kyushu brewery.

Kagoshima

This prefecture in the far south of Kyushu consists of two peninsulas, Satsuma and Osumi, that encircle **Kagoshima-wan** (**Kagoshima Bay**) and also a chain of islands stretching south towards Okinawa. A distinct, rapid-fire dialect is spoken here – and in much of Kyushu – and the speech of older people, lacking the homogenising influences of national television and radio, is almost incomprehensible to other Japanese. **Kagoshima** ⑰, on the interior side of Satsuma-hanto and the southernmost metropolis in Kyushu, is situated on large Kagoshima Bay. It is famous for being Japan's most unintentionally polluted city.

The pollution comes from **Sakura-jima** ⑱ (Cherry Island), the very active volcano east across the bay and rising 1,120 metres (3,670 ft) directly above the water. (*See pictures on pages 284-85 and 320–21.*) The mountain has erupted more than 5,000 times since 1955, sending clouds of ash and often large boulders raining down on Kagoshima. (Umbrellas are used as much for ash as for rain.) More than half a million people live within 10 km (6 miles) of Sakura-

Map on page 322

jima's crater. No other major city is as precariously positioned; Naples, Kagoshima's sister city, is twice as far from Vesuvius. Sakura-jima itself can be reached via a short ferry ride from Kagoshima or by road around the periphery of the bay. As the name indicates, it was once an island but an eruption in 1914 spilled some 3 billion tons of lava down its southeast flank and joined the island to the peninsula. There are dramatic views from the **Yogan Tenbodai** on the southeast side of Sakura-jima. Extra-large *daikon* (Japanese radishes) grow in the rich volcanic soil, along with kumquats, summer oranges, and other fruits.

Aside from the gritty ash and sometimes polluted air of Kagoshima, the city itself is delightful and retains much of the spirit of the once-powerful Satsuma clans, from whom the area takes its name. The Satsumas were ruled by the Shimazu daimyo, among the most dynamic of the Japanese hereditary rulers, for seven centuries. The Shimazu's distance from Edo Tokyo bred a fierce independence here in southern Kyushu. The Shimazu were open to new ideas from abroad. They welcomed Francis Xavier to Kagoshima, the first Japanese city he visited, in 1549. Returning from Japan's ill-fated invasion of the Korean peninsula in the early 17th century, the Shimazu brought captive Korean potters to Kagoshima, who then developed *satsuma* ware.

Despite their receptiveness to outsiders, the Satsuma clans opposed the Edo shogunate's capitulation to European demands that Japan open its ports to trade. Demonstrating resistance to the shogun's edicts, Shimazu retainers killed an Englishman near Edo in 1862. The British retaliated the following year by sending a squadron of ships to bombard Kagoshima. To the British sailors' surprise, the lords of Satsuma reacted favourably to this demonstration of modern naval power. They welcomed Her Majesty's officers to the still-smoking

BELOW: dusk falls on Sakura-jima.

Map on page 322

city and purchased some of their ships, which later were incorporated into the Japanese navy. In 1866, the Satsuma clan joined with the rival Choshu clan in a successful military coup against the shogun, which restored imperial rule with the Meiji Restoration in 1868. (Close relations between the Japanese and British navies lasted until the 1920s, and Satsuma clansmen dominated Japan's navy until World War II.)

Satsuma-ware and the more rustic Kuro-Satsuma pottery can be purchased in **Naeshirogawa**, a village that was settled by Korean potters in the 1600s. In addition to pottery, Kagoshima is known for *kiriko* cut-glass. Local artisans were compelled to cease kiriko production under the terms of peace imposed on the region in 1877. They resumed kiriko production in 1985 following a hiatus of nearly a century.

Iso-koen, containing a garden laid out in 1661, provides excellent views of Sakura-jima. Just outside the park, the **Shokoshuseikan (History Museum)** houses one of the first Western-style factories in Japan. It contains exhibits on the factory and the Shimazu family, whose mansion has also been preserved.

The cemetery of Nanshu holds the remains of Saigo Takamori (1827–77), who led the forces that defeated the shogun. Saigo later perished after leading the 1877 rebellion against the Meiji regime he had created. Saigo made his last stand at the hill called Shiroyama. With defeat inevitable, he had a loyal follower decapitate him. Saigo was buried at Jyokomyo-ji.

Ibusuki ⓳ is a spa town southwest of Kagoshima with hot-sand baths near **Kaimon-dake**, a 900-metre-high (3,000-ft) volcano looking much like Fuji.

Japan's ambitious space program, if small by American, Chinese, French and Russian standards, operates a launch pad at **Uchinoura**, on Osumi-hanto to the east of Kagoshima. Most launches, however, are now made from Tanega-shima, an island south of Kagoshima and near another island, Yaku-shima.

Yaku-shima

A circular island 1,000 km (600 miles) south of Tokyo and 135 km (80 miles) from Kagoshima, **Yaku-shima** is a naturalist's fantasy, declared a United Nations World Heritage Site in 1993 for its flora. There is the rare Yaku-shima rhododendron, but more fetching are the *Yaku-sugi*, Japanese cedar trees that are over 1,000 years old. (Youthful cedar trees here that are less than 1,000 years old are *ko-sugi*.)

Existing at 700 to 1,500 metres on the slopes of some of Yaku-shima's 40 peaks that are higher than 1,000 metres (600 ft), the cedar trees are like elderly sages amidst the dense foliage. The largest of the cedars is also said to be the largest in the world: a circumference of 43 metres (141 ft) at its roots; a trunk circumference of 16.4 metres (54 ft); and a height of 25 metres (80 ft). The Japanese also claim that it is the oldest in the world at 7,200 years; however, there is some dispute about the age amongst global experts, though an age of at least 1,500 years is certain.

Waterfalls and lush hiking trails lace this ancient volcanic island that is nearly 30 kms (20 miles) in diameter. Two small towns with accommodation are home to most of the island's 14,000 people. ❑

OPPOSITE: waterfall on the island of Yaku-shima.
BELOW: taking the sands at Ibusuki.

OKINAWA

*Once an independent kingdom called Ryukyu,
Okinawa is a world of its own. Bloodied by World War II, tropical
Okinawa is today Japan's domestic resort escape*

Map on page 346

E
xtending for 1,200 km (600 miles) southwest from Kyushu, the 70-plus islands of the Ryukyus, or **Nansei-shoto**, stretch across the ocean to within 200 km (125 miles) of Taiwan. For centuries, the Okinawans minded their own business and accommodated themselves to outsiders. But during the age of imperialism in the late 19th century, their independence fell prey to the ambitions of powerful neighbours.

Ryukyu is the Japanese pronunciation of the Chinese name Liugiu, which is what the Ming-dynasty Chinese called the islands. Taken over by Japan, which then long ignored the islands like a faraway province, Okinawa was the final beachhead for a planned Allied invasion of the Japanese archipelago in World War II. The battle for Okinawa was bloody for both sides and for the Okinawan civilians. Placed under American control by the U.N. following the end of World War II, the islands reverted back to Japanese sovereignty in 1972. Now, all islands north of the main island of Okinawa are part of Kyushu, and the main island and islands to the south are in Okinawa Prefecture.

Okinawa sits in a subtropical belt, blessed with average temperatures of around 23°C (73°F). A short rainy season blankets the area in heavy rains during May and June. Enjoyable are spring and autumn, typhoons in September and October notwithstanding.

There are exquisite white-sand beaches, azure waters, and some unusual flora and fauna. Okinawa is, along with Guam, Japan's backyard resort escape. But Okinawa has the highest unemployment rate in Japan and an average annual income half that of Tokyo's average. Yet, its gentle, friendly people give no hint of Tokyo-envy nor of the incredible suffering that Okinawans have known through times of war – and even during times of peace. Okinawans are proud of their heritage and will often remind travellers that they are not Japanese. A fine and relaxing manner in which to gauge the differences between Okinawa and the rest of Japan is a visit to a local pub. No disco or ubiquitous *karaoke* that is *de rigueur* at big-city clubs elsewhere in Japan. Rather, listen to the frequently plaintive sounds of the *sanshin*, the three-stringed, snakeskin-covered Okinawan banjo known elsewhere as the *samisen*. Traditional Okinawan dance and theatre differ considerably from their Japanese counterparts.

Okinawans are quite proud of their exquisite textiles, which are typically hand-woven from linen and silk and feature beautiful designs created with painted-on dyes. The designs traditionally differed by area, and the *bingata* stencil-dyed fabric, originally made exclusively for aristocrats, is the most highly prized of the fabrics.

PRECEDING PAGES: protective *shisa*.
OPPOSITE: Naha.
BELOW: Okinawan beach resort.

Naha

The centre of Okinawa's tourism is the city of **Naha ❶**, and Naha's centre of tourist activity is Kokusai-dori (International Road), which is a jangle of typical Japanese urban architecture – cluttered and without aesthetic appeal – and crowds of walkers and swarms of vehicles. Indeed, Kokusai-dori is nearly indistinguishable from any other urban centre in Japan. Yet only a short distance away are typically Okinawan neighbourhoods. **Naminou-gu**, a small Confucian shrine, and the **Gokoku-ji**, a temple that was once considered a national religious centre, are along the waterfront not far from the central post office and just north of an old pleasure quarter that retains its fair share of bars, cabarets, and steak houses.

Okinawan crafts are a delight. Active since 1617, the **Tsuboya** pottery-making district, off Himeyuri-dori and southeast of Kokusai-dori, houses two dozen kilns that make everything from the *kara-kara* flasks once carried by country gentlemen to the fearsome *shisa* figures that guard dwellings. A central pottery outlet sells items from all the kilns.

Tsuboya's pottery history began in the early 1600s when a Korean potter was forced to settle here after being taken prisoner during Hideyoshi's invasion of the Korean peninsula during the late 1500s. Pottery produced in Tsuboya bears strong 17th-century Korean characteristics, as is also the case in Kyushu.

Naha is the perfect spot for initial experiments with Okinawan cuisine. Now familiar with the *sashimi, unagi, yakisoba,* and other delicacies of central Japan, travellers might be ready to plunge into *mimiga* (sliced pig ears with vinegar), *ashite-bichi* (stewed pig legs), *rafutei* (pork simmered in *miso*, sugar, rice wine and soy sauce), *goya champuru* (stir-fried meat and bitter melon), or one of the

Shisa *images are placed atop buildings for protection from evil demons.*

BELOW: Naha Port.

many kinds of local *somen* noodles. *Awamori*, the local distilled rice brew that is served with ice and water, packs a wallop that puts anything else to shame. Some bottles – large and small – of awamori come with a coiled *habu* – a type of poisonous snake – in the bottom for increased male virility.

Map on page 346

Shuri

The first castle on **Shuri**, due west of downtown on a lofty hill overlooking Naha and the vast oceans beyond, was established in 1237. Under the second Sho dynasty, established in 1469 by King Sho En, Shuri became a mighty palace and temple complex. Shuri remained the political and cultural centre of the Ryukyus until 1879, when the last Okinawan king, Sho Tai, was forced to abdicate by the Meiji government in Tokyo.

During the 82-day battle of Okinawa in 1945, when the Japanese army chose Okinawa as the definitive last stand against the Allies before an anticipated invasion of the main Japanese islands, **Shuri-jo (Shuri Castle)** was the headquarters of the Japanese forces. It was destroyed during the fighting. Prewar accounts describe a marvel on a par in architectural and artistic interest with Kyoto, Nara, and Nikko. Much of the castle's stonework has been rebuilt in the past decade.

Nearby, **Ryutan-koen** is an expansive park barely able to absorb the hordes of tour buses or the clusters of on-going group photographs posing with classically attired Okinawan women in front of **Shuri no Mon**, the traditional gate to the castle grounds. The **Tama-udon**, minutes from the gate, contains the bodies of Sho En and other members of his family. A so-so prefectural museum nearby offers displays on Okinawan history and culture.

BELOW: tourists at Shuri, and a main gate to Shuri-jo.

South of Naha

Southern Okinawa is noted for caves. The most famous caves are the tunnel labyrinths at **Romogusuku**, near the Naha airport and the last headquarters of the Imperial Navy. The military commanders refused to surrender as the Allies pounded the island's south with naval bombardments; over 4,000 Japanese men committed suicide. Reminders and memorials of the bloodiest battle of the Pacific war that cost the lives of 13,000 Americans, 110,000 Japanese, and 140,000 Okinawan civilians (one-eighth of the population) are numerous throughout the south of the island.

The islands of Okinawa were under American control from 1945 until 1972, when they were returned to Japan. Today, most of the U.S. military's presence in Japan is on Okinawa.

The coastal highway south past the international airport leads to **Itoman ②**, claimed to be the home of some of the most fearless sailors in the world. Itoman's mid-August tug-of-war with intertwined "male" and "female" ropes draws crowds from afar. Several heavily promoted and developed caverns pepper the southern coastline, including **Hakugin-do**, a cavern with a shrine dedicated to the guardian deity of Itoman.

Famous is the story of **Himeyuri no To (Lily of the Valley Tower)**, a deep pit where a group of high school girls and their teachers committed suicide – rather than endure the possibility of capture by Americans – after singing their school song. **Mabuniga-oka**, on a promontory overlooking the ocean, is the site of the last resistance of the Japanese army.

Gyokusen-do ③ is said to be East Asia's largest cave. Only about one-fifth of it is open to the public; unfortunately, in this part visitors have broken off most of the stalactites and stalagmites, and the cave's floor has been pockmarked by wayward footprints. Near the entrance to the caves is the **Habu-koen (Snake Park)**, where there are displays of fights between mongooses and habu snakes, whose venom is strong enough to fell a horse.

A 5-km (3-mile) ferry ride from **Chinen ④** on Okinawa's southeast coast brings visitors to small and flat **Kudaka-jima**, the so-called island of the gods. This is where the great ancestress of the Ryukyuan people, Amamikiyo, is said to have descended from heaven and bestowed on them the five grains.

Covered with sugar cane and *fukugi* trees, Kudaka-jima, which has a resident population of about 300 people, is usually somnolent. But in mid-November every 12th year, the five-day Izaiho Festival is held, in which local women between the ages of 30 and 41 serve collectively as *noro*, or priestesses, to perform rites and communicate with the gods.

Central and northern Okinawa

The central portions of Okinawa are largely occupied by controversial U.S. military bases, most important of which is the air base at **Kadena ⑤**, about a quarter of the way up this skinny island's west coast. In the 1990s, Okinawans vocally sent the message that they wanted some of their land returned; much of the bases' land is atop leased private land, which the central Japanese government has mandated. Some of the American military presence is slowly being shifted away from Okinawa.

Outside Kadena, offerings are sleazy and garish, but there are good beaches in the area. The ruins of the castle at **Nakagusuku** ➏, built in the 15th century, are the largest in Okinawa. The Nakamura home in Nakagusuku offers an inspection of how an 18th-century gentry family lived.

Jutting out from the west coast about two-thirds of the way to the northern tip of Okinawa, **Motobu-hanto** ➐ (**Motobu Peninsula**) was the site of an ocean exposition in the 1970s. Most of the tourist-focused offerings are on the exposition's former site, Exposition Memorial Park, including several exhibitions about Okinawan culture and the ocean. The restored ruins of **Nakijin-jo** (**Nakijin Castle**), on the peninsula's northern tip, are a fine place to watch a sunset. (*See picture on page 349.*) Offshore, tiny **Ie-jima** is where a famous American war correspondent, Ernie Pile, was killed in World War II.

A visit to the far north of Okinawa, or *yanbaru*, will reward the adventurous with rugged hills, beaches, and secluded fishing villages, along with some of the friendliest people anywhere. In the village of **Kijoka** ➑, one can watch the various steps required to produce the plantain-fibre textile *bashofu*. The view at **Hedo-misaki** ➒, the cape at the northern tip of the island, is stunning. But don't go wandering off in the bush in yanbaru, as this is habu – the deadly poisonous snake found in Okinawa – country.

One of the Ryukyu's sacred islands is **Iheya-jima** ➓, to the northeast of Okinawa. According to Okinawan legend, King Jimmu Tenno began his conquest of Japan from here. Moreover, a huge cave on the island, referred to as the "Hiding Place", is said to be the very cave where the sun goddess Amaterasu hid herself until the other deities could coax her out of the cave and thereby restoring light to the world. Priestesses governed over that island until sometime during the 19th century.

American influence over Okinawa.

BELOW: waters designed for scuba diving and pictures.

Map on page 346

Outer islands

The best bet for experiencing the Ryukyuan way of life is to visit the outer islands, or *saki-shima*, reached by ferry or air from Naha. **Kerama**, only 35 km (20 miles) west of Naha, is an excellent scuba-diving haunt embellished with numerous sea snakes among its gorgeous coral reefs. **Kume-jima**, three hours by ferry from Naha's main harbour, has preserved several fine traditional homes in Nakazato and elsewhere.

Further afield is the Miyako group of eight islands. **Miyako-jima**, the main island, is an hour by air or 10 hours by boat from Naha. At its port of Hiraya are the *o-honoyama* (tax stones). After the *samurai* of Satsuma (now Kagoshima) on Kyushu invaded the Ryukyu kingdom in 1609, it became in everything but name a tributary to that fief's lord, even though the country also continued to pay tribute to the Ming dynasty in China. At the time, all children on Miyako-jima were paraded once a year before the *ninto-zeiseki*. Those taller than the stone had to pay the tax or else were shipped off to work as forced labour. So burdensome were the taxes that on some of the remote islands islanders resorted to killing the weak and old because there was not enough food. This system was abolished in 1918. Miyako-jima earned a place in Japanese school books when five local fishermen spotted the Czarist fleet steaming towards Japan during the Russo-Japanese War (1904–05). The timely warning allowed the Imperial Navy, under Admiral Togo Shigenori, to surprise and annihilate the Russians in the Battle of Tsushima Straits. Nearby **Irabu**, an island that can be reached by boat from Hiraya, offers attractive scenery and fine diving.

The island group of **Yaeyama-shoto**, best reached by air (the ferry from Naha only puts in about once a week), was long relatively isolated from the rest of the Ryukyus. It will appeal to those interested in folklore or the outdoor life. The main island of **Ishigaki-jima** was for years embroiled in an ongoing controversy regarding whether an offshore airport would be built near Shiraho, one of the largest and most unique coral reefs in this part of the Pacific. Finally, in the mid-1990s after over a decade of dispute, it was decided that the airport would not be built near the reefs, an unusual environmental victory in Japan where the will of development typically runs rampant. The municipal museum near the harbour has a collection of local artifacts and folk crafts. Kabira is an idyllic lagoon-like area with small islands and sandy beaches.

A short ferry or hovercraft ride from Ishigaki takes travellers to **Taketomi**, a flat island famed throughout Japan for the star-shaped sand at Kondoi. The island is beautiful and peaceful.

A ferry also goes to the large island of **Iriomote**, which is no doubt the most unusual and unique island in the Japanese archipelago – a touch of New Guinea in Japan. Except for the towns of Ohara in the southeast and Funaura in the north, the island is mostly tropical rain forest. Thankfully, development on the island has been limited to only one resort, although others have been proposed. Iriomote is noted for several unique flora and fauna, especially the Iriomote cat, a wild feline that is found nowhere else, as is the case with a large moth over 30 cm (1 ft) in diameter. ❏

OPPOSITE: Nakijin Castle. **BELOW:** resort on Miyako.

...AND THE LOCAL TIME AT YOUR DESTINATION IS 1

S | M | O | O | T | H |

A.D.

Your specially tailored
Royal Orchid Holidays begin
the moment you board
when you fly with THAI,
official carrier to
Amazing Thailand.

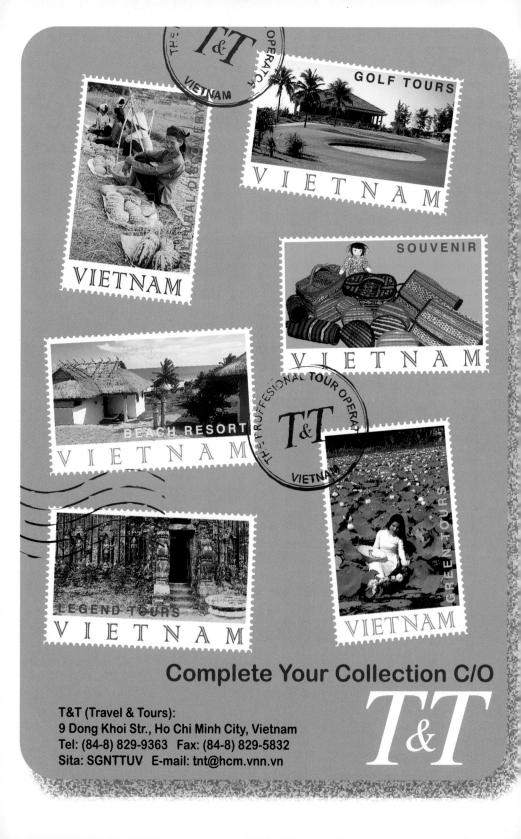

Complete Your Collection C/O

T&T

CONTENTS

Getting Acquainted

The Place

Japan is made up of four main islands – Honshu, Hokkaido, Kyushu and Shikoku – and several thousand smaller ones that stretch nearly 3,000 km (1,900 miles) in the temperate and sub-tropical zones, between 20° and 45° latitude. The total land area is 377,435 sq. km (145,728 sq. miles), 85 percent of which is mountainous. The country is divided into four different climatic and cultural zones by mountain ranges: the Japan Sea and Pacific Ocean on the northeast half, and the Japan Sea and Inland Sea on the southwest half. The famed Mount Fuji, seen on clear days from many places in and around Tokyo, is the country's highest mountain at 3,776 metres (12,388 ft). The population of Japan is about 130 million.

Climate

"Japan has four seasons" is a phrase you will hear often, though it is still not clear why the Japanese feel that it is a feature unique to their country. The climate in Tokyo can be a bit of everything, and in recent years, the manifestation of the "four seasons" has not been all that clear, but generally in spring most of Japan is pleasant until May. In June begins the rainy season which should last about a month, but often longer. The summers are hot and sticky through to September. The typhoons usually come through in August and September. Fall begins in late September and lasts through mid-November and is cool and pleasant.

The winter lasts from mid-November to the end of February or beginning of March.

The People

Population density: 326 persons per square kilometre
Life expectancy at birth: 76 for males; 82 for females

Life expectancy has been steadily rising for the last three decades, and the "greying" of Japan is becoming a major social concern. In 1985, only 10.3 percent of the population was 65 or older; in the year 2020 it is expected to reach 25 percent.

Retirement age for salaried employees, stable at 55 during most of the post-war era, is now gradually being raised to 60 by many major companies. Private and national pension plans are provided, covering 99 percent of the country's working population. However, the economic downturn in Japan during the 1990s, which lasted into the 21st century, has restructured the "life-time" employment expectation of workers. Moreover, the cost of providing pensions is expected to create considerable economic problems as the population ages.

Government

Form: Parliamentary Democracy
Head of State: Emperor Akihito (born December 23, 1933, took office January 7, 1989)

While the emperor's actual power is less than that of, say, the queen of England, his social, cultural and political influence is much stronger than intended by the allied powers who, during the occupation of Japan following World War II, "guided" the drafting of Japan's present constitution.

Although Article 1 of that document states the the "Emperor shall be the symbol of the State," and that he derives his position from the will of the people, the exact powers of the emperor are not specifically defined. Still, he has no control or influence over national or international policy of the Japanese government, and his public speeches are carefully scripted by the Imperial Household Agency, which administers the imperial family.

Prime Minister: (President of majority party in Lower House, currently – and since 1955 except 1993–1996 – the Liberal Democratic Party (LDP).

Education

Japan's public education system is tax-funded (although many private schools exists). Compulsory for all children are 6 years junior high school (enrolment 100 percent); high school (3 years) is elective (enrolment over 90 percent nationwide, nearly 100 percent in urban areas); higher education at college/university (4 years) or trade schools is also elective (over 30 percent of all high school graduates go on to higher educational studies).

The school year begins in April; vacations include about 40 days in summer and around 10 days each for spring and New Years.

The three-year high school program is compressed to two in many of the best high schools to allow students to prepare for college entrance exams.

There are about 95 national, 34 public and 31 private 4-year universities/colleges in Japan. The quasi-national radio/TV network NHK runs the University of the Air that combines radio and TV and correspondence.

Literacy: 99 percent
Juku: These "after-school schools" – cram schools is more appropriate – are estimated to number about 200,000, earn ¥500 billion annually and attract as many as 1.5 million elementary and 2 million high school students. In the main, they focus on preparing students for entrance exams.

Customs and Culture

At work and in most formal situations, the Japanese may seem a very reticent and reserved people, lacking in spontaneity or personality. There are books and theories explaining this behaviour, but it only provides one side of the picture. Japanese (especially men) can become extremely raucous when drinking and often let out their real opinions and feelings after a few drinks. The next morning in the office, all is forgotten. Intentionally.

On the crowded trains you will find yourself being pushed and bumped around. You do not need to be polite here; just push along with everyone else. It is often said that "the Japanese are only polite with their shoes off," which means that they are polite and courteous with people they know well and would be indoors with (where shoes are almost always removed).

The Japanese distinguish between inside and outside the home. Inside the entrance to all homes (and some restaurants) is an area for removing shoes. You then step up into the living area, wearing slippers or in your stockinged feet. (Slippers are never worn on *tatami* mats, however, only socks and bare feet.) Taking shoes off keeps the house clean, besides being more relaxing, and it also increases the amount of usable space, since you can sit on the floor without worrying about getting dirty. The toilet, however, is one area of the house that is considered "dirty," so separate slippers are provided there.

The custom of bowing has, in many cases, become somewhat a conditioned reflex. Foreigners, in general, are not expected to bow, and this is especially evident if a Japanese person first reaches out to shake hands.

As to punctuality and keeping appointments, the Japanese have a reputation for not being very punctual. At several of the famous "meeting places" (in Tokyo, in front of Ginza's Sony Building or at the Hachiko entrance to Shibuya Station, as examples) you can observe people waiting, often for an hour or more, for someone.

After several apologies and explanations, everything is usually forgotten and forgiven.

The way the Japanese usually speak and express themselves gives a very good picture of their culture. Direct statements of fact are most often avoided as this implies that the speaker has a superior knowledge, and this is considered impolite. Therefore, much "beating around the bush" is done which often leads to misunderstandings and seems like a waste of time to foreigners, but this must be taken into consideration when dealing with the Japanese.

In Japanese, the Japanese are expert and adept at reading between the lines and interpreting deft nuances of words and tone.

In any case, whatever happens, foreigners are usually forgiven for any breach of etiquette, so there's no need to spend time worrying about what is right and wrong. Japanese behaviour in general is situational, and the Japanese themselves often do not know the right thing to do in any given situation. "It all depends on the situation," remarks the smart alec, but it's often fun for everyone involved when one of "us" makes a slip. Sometimes it actually does help to break the ice and put everyone in a more relaxed mood.

Gaijin: Foreign Objects in a Strange Land

One of the first words of Japanese the foreigner visitor is likely to learn, after the usual pleasantries, is *gaijin*. It is interpreted as both "foreigner" and "alien", but it is often the latter term, in every sense of the word, that best describes Japanese attitudes towards non-Japanese. Literally translated, gaijin means "outside person".

According to Japanese census bureau statistics, roughly 1 percent of the population, or over one million people, is of non-Japanese descent. While many are of Chinese or Korean ancestry, in the popular mainstream imagination, "foreigner" means Westerner or European.

There exists something of a belief that Westerners are unique beings. In the countryside, and even in cities, this takes the form of children shouting "Gaijin, gaijin!" or people openly staring and talking about you. Yet being a Westerner in Japan means both being admired and ignored. If foreigners are, to a large extent, free from the rules of polite Japanese society and given much latitude for their lack of understanding, they are also kept at a distance and expected to behave in a certain way. If they try to close that distance by bridging the language or culture gap, they may suddenly find they are treated quite differently. Japanese may gasp with amazement when a foreigner speaks a few words of rudimentary Japanese and shower effusive praise for learning what they believe is the world's most difficult language. Flattery can quickly sound condescending, however, when the foreigner masters the language only to find that it can be more difficult to communicate. For by learning to speak Japanese, the foreigner has crossed an invisible barrier and enters Japanese society. But, because they are foreign, they can never truly be a part of it.

You will be an object of a certain amount of attention and inspection. There's nothing to be done about it.

Planning the Trip

Getting There

The most practical way of entering Japan is by air and through one of its several international airports. **New Tokyo International Airport (Narita Airport)**, 60 km (37 mi) from Tokyo city centre, is the busiest and one of the two main gateways to Japan. (Narita is also a major transit airport; consider a stopover if flying from elsewhere in Asia to Europe or North America.) Flights on China Airlines are served by **Haneda Airport**, Tokyo's domestic airport located between Tokyo and Yokohama. Osaka's 24-hour, offshore **Kansai International Airport**, the other main gateway, serves routes plying the Americas, Europe and Asia. **Nagoya Airport** connects flights to and from various points in the Pacific and the Americas. Three airports on Kyushu – **Fukuoka, Kumamoto** and **Kagoshima** – serve those from cities in Europe, Korea and mainland Asia. Three major domestic airlines maintain air routes throughout Japan: Japan Air Lines (JAL), All Nippon Airways (ANA) and Japan Air Systems (JAS).

There is an airport tax for all passengers departing on international flights.

Entry Regulations

VISAS AND PASSPORTS

A proper visa is necessary for foreigners living in Japan and engaged in business or study. Passengers with confirmed departure reservations can obtain a stopover pass for up to 72 hours.

Visitors from the following countries are not required to obtain a visa prior to arrival in Japan, provided they do not intend to stay for more than 90 days nor receive remuneration in Japan: Argentina, Belgium, Canada, Chile, Colombia, Costa Rica, Cyprus, Denmark, Finland, Greece, Holland, Iceland, Israel, Italy, Luxembourg, Malaysia, Norway, Portugal, Singapore, Spain, Sweden, Turkey, United States.

Visitors from the following countries may reside in Japan for up to 6 months providing they are not earning an income: Austria, Germany, Ireland, Liechtenstein, Mexico, Switzerland and the U.K.

EXTENSION OF STAY

Foreigners wishing to extend their stay in Japan must report, in person, to the Immigration Bureau within two weeks before their visa expiration. Present your passport, a statement with the reasons why you want an extension of stay, and documents certifying the reasons. The fee is ¥4,000.

Foreigners living in Japan must obtain a re-entry permit from the Immigration Bureau if they leave Japan and plan to return. Present, in person, your passport and certificate of alien registration (held by foreign residents in Japan) along with the appropriate re-entry form to the Immigration Office. Fees are charged for both single and multiple re-entry permits.

Those wishing to transfer visas to new passports must report to the Immigration Bureau in Tokyo. Present both old and new passports and certificate of alien registration.

Immigration Information. Tel: (03) 3213-8523 or 3213-8527. Open Monday–Friday 9.30am–noon, 1–4pm. Answers to questions regarding immigration rules, regulations and restrictions. Languages: English, Chinese, Korean, Spanish, Portuguese, and Thai.

Tokyo Regional Immigration Bureau, 1st Otemachi Common Government Office 2nd Floor, 1-3-1 Otemachi, Chiyoda-ku, Tokyo. Tel: (03) 3213-8523–8527. Open 9am–noon, 1–4pm. Closed on Saturday and Sunday.

Shibuya Immigration Office, 1-3-5 Jinnan, Shibuya-ku (just beyond "In the Room" dept. Store). Tel: (03) 5458-0370 or (03) 3286-5241. Open Monday–Friday 9am–noon, 1–5pm.

Hakozaki Immigration Branch Office, Tokyo City Air Terminal, 42-1 Nihombashihakozaki, Chuo-ku. Tel: (03) 3664-3046. Open 9am–noon, 1–5pm. Closed on Saturday and Sunday. (Near the Royal Park Hotel.)

Yokohama Regional Immigration Bureau. Tel: (045) 681-6801.

Osaka Immigration Information. Tel: (06) 774-3409. Visa/Immigration Information in Osaka. Language: English, Chinese, Portuguese, Spanish. Open Monday–Friday 9.30am–noon, 1pm–4.30pm.

Automated Immigration Info. Tel: (03) 3213-8141. Usage: with a touch-tone phone, enter 1 for Japanese, 2 for English. Dial the code number for the information you want (about 800 available). The code list is available at immigration/ward offices.

ALIEN REGISTRATION

Foreigners planning to stay in Japan for more than three months are required to register at the ward office in their residing area. The application must be made in person within 90 days. The applicant must have his/her passport containing the proper visa and two photographs (3 cm x 4 cm).

If the alien registration card is lost or defaced, report to the ward office within 14 days. Take your passport and two new photographs and you will be issued a new one.

For visitors under 16 years of age, applications may be made by a parent or legal guardian by producing the applicant's passport. No photograph is necessary.

Ward office hours are from 8.45am–5pm. Monday through Friday, and 8.45am–12.30pm on Saturdays.

Tokyo Metropolitan Government, Tokyo Daisan Chosha, 3-5-1 Marunouchi, Chiyoda-ku, Tokyo. Tel:

(03) 3211-4433. English service is available on Monday and Thursday from 1–4pm.

Information regarding alien status and visas presented above is general and subject to change. For further information contact your appropriate embassy, consulate or the Japan Immigration Bureau.

Customs

Japan strictly bans the import and use of narcotic drugs, firearms and ammunition. If caught in possession of any of these, the offender will not face the death penalty, but can expect no leniency. Many a foreigner is still sitting in a Japanese prison, long forgotten by everyone but himself.

You can bring in any currency, personal ornaments and other valuables into Japan, but there is an official limit of ¥5 million that can be taken out.

You are also allowed to bring with you into Japan, free of tax, three 760 ml (25 fl oz) bottles of spirits, 400 cigarettes and 100 cigars or 500 g of tobacco, and 2 fl oz (50 g) of perfume.

Pornography?

Magazines and videos showing any pubic hair are technically forbidden in Japan. This issue of films and magazines displaying pubic hair is a curious one. Photographs in *Playboy* magazine, for example, are literally sanded to obliterate pubic hair, but maybe only every other photo.

Yet at convenience stores like 7-Eleven, teenage boys can buy magazines with very explicit photographs or *manga* illustrations. Likewise, films sometimes will have fuzzy spots or electronic mosaics floating over offending parts. Other films are shown untouched. For most Westerners, whether bringing in offending material or not, Japanese offerings are more brusque and offensive.

Health

In general, levels of hygiene are very high, and it is very unlikely that you will become ill as a result of eating or drinking something. The tap water, though heavily chlorinated, is potable. Most food is of a high standard. However, because the Japanese place so much emphasis on presentation and how food looks, there is wide use of chemical fertilisers in Japan, and therefore it is not recommended to eat the peels of fruits and some vegetables.

Toilets: Apart from major hotels and some train stations, most toilets in Japan are of the Asian squatting type, which takes some getting used to, but are supposed to be the most hygienic (no part of your body actually touches them) and physiologically best. In Tokyo and other major cities, they are slowly being replaced with Western-style toilets in many establishments. By law, every coffee shop and restaurant etc. must have its own toilet, or access to one in the same building. Toilets in train stations and other large places are often dirty and smelly.

Electricity

The power supply is 100 volts AC. Eastern cities in Japan, including Tokyo, run on 50 cycles, while those in the west such as Kyoto, Osaka and Nagoya, use 60 cycles.

Currency

The unit of currency is the yen (indicated as ¥), and the coins are ¥1, ¥5, ¥10, ¥50, ¥100 and ¥500. Bills are ¥1,000, ¥5,000 and ¥10,000. Japanese stores, services, and merchants are legally forbidden to accept foreign currencies. You can buy yen at foreign exchange banks and other authorised money changers on presentation of your passport. At the international airports at Narita and Osaka, the banks are open 24 hours. Traveller's cheques are useful only at banks and major hotels. Elsewhere, they are virtually worthless. Many banks in the large cities will issue international Traveller's cheques.

Major credit cards, such as American Express, Diners Club, MasterCard and Visa, are accepted at establishments in and around Tokyo and Osaka/Kyoto, and there is no surcharge for their use. Unfortunately, acceptance is sporadic. Even at establishments displaying acceptance of Visa or MasterCard, for example, it is often quite difficult for a merchant to get approval for a credit card issued by a non-Japanese bank. If they refuse your card, don't get testy. Carry lots of cash instead, just in case.

BANKS

Despite the wide use of computers and on-line systems, Japanese banks are often slow and inefficient in many fields. Especially when transferring money in or out of the country, you can expect the process to take a long time and to be costly. Also, small neighbourhood branches are often not able to process any international transactions. In order to send money out of the country, or cash foreign cheques, you will find it much easier to go to a major branch, where someone *may* be able to speak English and usually understand what you want to do. (An exception is Citibank, which has aggressively shaken up the way banks in Japan do business. If you are a Citibank customer elsewhere, your chances in Japan are much, much better.)

Banks are open Monday to Friday between 9am and 3pm for normal banking. Cash dispensers (ATMS) are few and far between, located usually only at bank branches and with restricted hours; most only "speak" Japanese, too. Moreover, most cash dispensers can't be used for cash advances on cards not issued by a Japanese bank. Even if there is a logo for Visa or MasterCard, it's for a Japanese bank-issued card only. In short, don't plan on cash advances from an ATM – you'll be caught short.

Special Facilities

DISABLED

In general, Japan is not user-friendly for the disabled. Doors, elevators, toilets and just about everything else have not been designed for wheelchairs, nor are there any regulations regarding access for the disabled. It is a struggle for the disabled to get around Japan, but it can be done. (Traditionally, the handicapped have kept a low profile, as they are sometimes considered an embarrassment for the family.)

Forget about using a wheelchair in train or subway stations, much less trains, during rush hour, 7–9am and 5–7pm. The crowds are just too thick, and too rude.

To arrange assistance – in advance – at **Tokyo Station**, call the JR English InfoLine at (03) 3423-0111. They will make arrangements at Tokyo Station for you.

It is possible to reserve a special seat for wheelchairs on the *shinkansen*, or bullet train. Reservations can be made from one month to two days before departure. You must also reserve ahead to use the elevators for the shinkansen platforms.

In many stations, staff will help with escalators and elevators, although a wait of half an hour to an hour may be involved.

For general information about travel or help in Japan, call in Tokyo the **Tell-Tokyo English Lifeline**, Tel: (03) 3968-4099.

Useful Addresses

TOURIST OFFICES

Tourists may write or contact any of the following offices of the Japan National Travel Organisation for assistance:

JNTO Overseas Offices

Australia: Level 33, The Chifley Tower, 2 Chifley Square, Sydney, NSW 2000. Tel: (02) 9232-4522, fax: (02) 9232-1494.
Canada: 165 University Ave, Toronto, Ont. M5H 3B8. Tel: (416) 366-7140, fax: (416) 366-4530.

Public Holidays

1 January: *Ganjitsu* (New Year's Day)
15 January: *Seijin no Hi* (Coming-of-Age Day)
11 February: *Kenkoku Kinen no Hi* (National Foundation Day)
21 March: *Shumbun no Hi* (Vernal Equinox Day)
29 April: *Midori no Hi* (Greenery Day)
3 May: *Kempo Kinembi* (Constitution Memorial Day)
4 May: *Kokumin no Kyujitsu* (bank holiday)
5 May: *Kodomo no Hi* (Children's Day)
15 September: *Keiro no Hi* (Respect-for-the-Aged Day)
23 September: *Shubun no Hi* (Autumnal Equinox Day)
10 October: *Taiiku no Hi* (Sports Day)
3 November: *Bunka no Hi* (Culture Day)
23 November: *Kinro Kansha no Hi* (Labour Thanksgiving Day)
23 December: *Tenno Tanjobi* (Emperor's Birthday)
25 December: *Kokumin no Kyujitsu* (bank holiday)

If a holiday falls upon Sunday, the following Monday will be a "substitute holiday".

France: 4-8, rue Sainte-Anne, 75001 Paris. Tel: (01) 42-96-20-29, fax: (01) 40-20-92-79.
Germany: Kaiserstrasse 11, 60311 Frankfurt/M. Tel: (069) 20353, fax: (069) 284281, e-mail: info@jntofra.rhein-main.com
Hong Kong: Suite 3704-05, 37/F, Dorset House, Taikoo place, Quarry Bay. Tel: 2968-5688, fax: 2968-1722.
Switzerland: 13 rue de Berne, 1201 Geneva. Tel: (022) 731-81-40, fax: (022) 738-13-14.
United Kingdom: Heathcoat House, 20 Savile Row, London W1X 1AE. Tel: (0171) 734-9638, fax: (0171) 734-4290, e-mail: jntolon@dircon.co.uk

United States
New York: One Rockefeller Plaza, Suite 1250, New York, NY 10111. Tel: (212) 757-5640, fax: (212) 307-6754, e-mail: jntonyc@interport.net.
Chicago: 401 North Michigan Ave., Suite 770, Chicago, IL 60611. Tel: (312) 222-0874, fax: (312) 222-0876, e-mail: jntochi@aol.com
San Francisco: 360 Post St, Suite 601, San Francisco, CA 94108. Tel: (415) 989-7140, fax: (415) 398-5461, e-mail: sfjnto@aol.com
Los Angeles: 624 South Grand Ave, Suite 1611, Los Angeles, CA 90017. Tel: (213) 623-1952, fax: (213) 623-6301, e-mail: hideki.tomioka@sit.com

Domestic Offices of JNTO

If you have a message or questions, send e-mail to: jnto@jnto.go.jp. It may take some time until you get the answer.

Tourist Information Centres:
Tokyo, Tokyo International Forum, 3-5-1 Marunouchi, Chiyoda-ku, Tokyo 100. (Located between Yurakucho and Tokyo stations.) Tel: (03) 3201-3331. Open from 9am–5pm on weekdays, 9am–noon Saturday, closed Sundays and national holidays.
Narita TIC, Airport Terminal Bldg, Narita, Chiba Pref. 282. tel: (0475) 32-8711 or (0476) 34-6251.
Kyoto Office (TIC): 1st fl., Kyoto Tower Bldg, Higashi-Shiokojicho, Shimogyo-ku, Kyoto 600. Tel: (075) 371-5649. Open from 9am–5pm weekdays, 9am–noon Saturday, closed on Sunday and national holidays.

Japan Travel-Phone is a nationwide toll-free service offering travel-related information and language assistance. If within Tokyo or Kyoto, call the respective TIC offices. You will be connected to an English-speaking travel officer. Note that they will *not* book reservations, but simply offer information. Weekdays 9am–5pm, Saturday, 9am–noon. Numbers are toll-free:
Tokyo: (0120) 44-4800, (0088) 22-4800, or (03) 3201-3331 (toll).

Eastern Japan: (0088) 22-2800 or (0120) 222-800.
Western Japan: (0088) 22-4800 or (0120) 444-800.

The **Teletourist Service** offers recorded information in English on events currently taking place that might be of interest to travellers. Tel: (03) 3201-2911.

TRAVEL AGENCIES
The following agencies, listed by the JNTO, offer travel services for foreign travellers:
Japan Travel Bureau (JTB), Int'l Travel Division, 5-5-2 Kiba, Koto-ku, Tokyo 135. Tel: (03) 5620-9411, Fax: 5620-9502. Internet (English): web2.jtb.co.jp/eng/index.html
Kinki Nippon Tourist Co., Kanda-Matsunaga-cho, Chiyoda-ku, Tokyo 101. Tel: (03) 3255-6535, Fax: 3251-1113. Internet (English): www.knt.co.jp/kokusai/top.htm www.kintetsu.com/index.html
Nippon Travel Agency, Shimbashi Ekimae Bldg., 2-20-15 Shimbashi, Minato-ku, Tokyo 105. Tel: (03) 3572-8716, Fax: 3574-9610. Internet (English): www.nta.co.jp /nippon/kokusai2.htm
JTB Traveland, Kotsukosha Ikebukuro Bldg., 1-13-6 Higashi-Ikebukuro, Toshima-ku, Tokyo 170. Tel: (03) 3983-9444, Fax: 3983-5148.
Japan Gray Line, Pelican Bldg., 3-3-3 Nishi-Shimbashi, Minato-ku, Tokyo 105. Tel: (03) 3433-4831, Fax: 3433-4807.
Toppan Travel Service, Towa-Hamamatsucho Bldg. 7F, 2-6-2 Hamamatsucho, Minato-ku, Tokyo 104. Tel: (03) 5403-2500, Fax: 5403-2504.
Okinawa Tourist Service, 1-2-3 Matsuo, Naha, Okinawa 900. Tel: (098) 862-1111, Fax: 861-7965.

EMBASSIES AND CONSULATES
Australia, 2-1-14 Mita, Minato-ku. Tel: (03) 5232-4111, Fax: 5232-4114.
Austria, 1-1-20 Moto Azabu, Minato-ku. Tel: (03) 3451-8281.
Belgium, 5-4 Nibancho, Chiyoda-ku. Tel: (03) 3262-0191.

Canada, 7-3-38 Akasaka, Minato-ku. Tel: (03) 3408-2101, Fax: 3479-5320.
China, 3-4-33 Moto Azabu, Minato-ku. Tel: (03) 3403-3380.
Denmark, 29-6 Sarugakucho, Shibuya-ku. Tel: (03) 3496-3001.
Finland, 3-5-39 Minami Azabu, Minato-ku. Tel: (03) 3442-2231.
France, 4-11-44 Minami Azabu, Minato-ku. Tel: (03) 5420-8800.
Germany, 4-5-10 Minami Azabu, Minato-ku. Tel: (03) 3473-0151.
Indonesia, 5-2-9 Higashi Gotanda, Shinagawa-ku. Tel: (03) 3441-4201.
Ireland, No. 25 Kowa Bldg, 8-7 Sanbancho, Chiyoda-ku. Tel: (03) 3263-0695.
Israel, 3 Nibancho, Chiyoda-ku. Tel: (03) 3264-0911.
Korea, 1-2-5 Minami Azabu, Minato-ku. Tel: (03) 3452-7611.
Malaysia, 20-16 Nanpeidaicho, Shibuya-ku. Tel: (03) 3476-3840.
Netherlands, 3-6 Shibakoen, Minato-ku. Tel: (03) 5401-0411.
New Zealand, 20-40 Kamiyamacho, Shibuya-ku. Tel: (03) 3467-2271.
Norway, 5-12-2 Minami Azabu, Minato-ku. Tel: (03) 3440-2611.

Peak Travel Seasons

There are three periods of the year when the Japanese travel and holiday *en masse*. You would be wise not to make any travel plans during these periods:
● **New Year's**: from around 25 December to 4 January
● **Golden Week**: from 29 April to 5 May
● **Obon**: a week centring around 15 August

Philippines, 11-24 Nanpeidaicho, Shibuya-ku. Tel: (03) 3496-2731.
Singapore, 5-12-3 Roppongi, Minato-ku. Tel: (03) 3586-9111.
Sweden, 1-3-10 Roppongi, Minato-ku. Tel: (03) 5562-5050.
Switzerland, 5-9-12 Minami Azabu, Minato-ku. Tel: (03) 3473-0121.
United Kingdom, 1 Ichibancho, Chiyoda-ku. Tel: (03) 5211-1100, Fax: 5275-0346.

United States, 1-10-5 Akasaka, Minato-ku. Tel: (03) 3224-5000, Fax: 3505-1862.
Vietnam, 50-11 Motoyoyogicho, Shibuya-ku. Tel: (03) 3466-3311.

AIRLINE OFFICES
Air Canada, New Akasaka Bldg, 6th Floor, 3-2-3 Akasaka, Minato-ku. Tel: (03) 3586-3891.
Air France, Shin Aoyama Bldg, Nishi-kan, 15th Floor, 1-1-1 Minami Aoyama, Minato-ku. Tel: (03) 3475-1511.
Air New Zealand, Shin Kokusai Bldg, 3-4-1 Marunouchi, Chiyoda-ku. Tel: (03) 3287-1641.
Alitalia, Tokyo Club Bldg, 3-2-6 Kasumigaseki, Minato-ku. Tel: (03) 3580-2242.
ANA, Yammer Tokyo Bldg, 2-1-1 Yaesu, Chuo-ku. Tel: International (03) 5489-1212. Domestic (03) 5489-8800.
American Airlines, Kokusai Bldg, 3-1-1 Marunouchi, Chiyoda-ku. Tel: (03) 3248-2011.
British Airways, 1-16-4 Toranomon, Minato-ku. Tel: (03) 3593-8811.
Canadian Airlines, Hibiya Park Bldg, 1-8-1 Yurakucho, Chiyoda-ku. Tel: (03) 3281-7426.
Cathay Pacific Airways, Toho Twin Towers Bldg, 1-5-2 Yurakucho, Chiyoda-ku. Tel: (03) 3504-1531.
China Airlines, Matsuoka Bldg, 5-22-10 Shimbashi, Minato-ku. Tel: (03) 3436-1661.
Continental Airlines, Sanno Grand Bldg, 5th Floor, 2-14-2 Nagatacho, Chiyoda-ku. Tel: (03) 3508-6411.
Delta Airlines, Kokusai Bldg. #254, 3-1-1 Marunouchi, Chiyoda-ku. Tel: (03) 5275-7000.
Iberia Airlines, 3-1-13 Shibakoen, Minato-ku. Tel: (03) 3578-3555.
Japan Air Lines, Daini Tekko Bldg, 1-8-2 Marunouchi, Chiyoda-ku. Tel: Tokyo (03) 5489-1111.
KLM Royal Dutch Airlines, Yurakucho Denki Bldg, 1-7-1 Yurakucho, Chiyoda-ku. Tel: (03) 3216-0771.
Korean Air, Shin Kokusai Bldg, 3-4-1 Marunouchi, Chiyoda-ku. Tel: (03) 5443-3311.
Lufthansa Airlines, 3-1-13 Shibakoen, Minato-ku. Tel: (03) 3578-6777.

Malaysian Airlines, Hankyu Kotsusha Bldg, 3-3-9 Shimbashi, Minato-ku. Tel: (03) 3503-5961.

Northwest Airlines, 1-1 Uchisaiwaicho, Chiyoda-ku. Tel: (03) 3533-6000 (Imperial Hotel).

Qantas Airways, Urban Toranomon Bldg, 4th Floor, 1-16-4 Toranomon, Minato-ku. Tel: (03) 3593-7000.

SAS, Toho Twin Tower Bldg, 1-5-2 Yurakucho, Chiyoda-ku. Tel: (03) 3503-8101.

Singapore Airlines, Yurakucho Bldg, 1-10-1 Yurakucho, Chiyoda-ku. Tel: (03) 3213-3431.

Swissair, Hibiya Park Bldg, 1-8-1 Yurakucho, Chiyoda-ku. Tel: (03) 3212-1011.

Thai Airways, Asahi Seimei Hibiya Bldg, 1-5-1 Yurakucho, Chiyoda-ku. Tel: (03) 3503-3311.

United Airlines, Kokusai Bldg, 3-1-1 Marunouchi, Chiyoda-ku. Tel: (03) 3817-4411.

Virgin Atlantic Airways, Alliance Bldg, 4th Floor, 5-2-1 Minami Aoyama, Minato-ku. Tel: (03) 3499-8811.

FOREIGN BANKS

Bank of America, 1-12-32 Akasaka, Minato-ku. Tel: (03) 3587-3111.

Bank of Korea, Hibiya Park Bldg, 1-8-1 Yurakucho, Chiyoda-ku. Tel: (03) 3213-6961.

Barclays Bank, 2-2-2 Otemachi, Chiyoda-ku. Tel: (03) 5255-0011.

Chase Manhattan Bank, 1-2-1 Marunouchi, Chiyoda-ku. Tel: (03) 3287-4000.

Citibank, Chiyoda-ku. Tel: (0120) 223-773 (toll-free).

Commerzbank A.G., Nippon Press Centre Bldg, 2-2-1 Uchisaiwaicho, Chiyoda-ku. Tel: (03) 3502-4371.

Commonwealth Bank of Australia, 1-1-3 Marunouchi, Chiyoda-ku. Tel: (03) 3213-7311.

Credit Lyonnais, Hibiya Park Bldg, 1-8-1 Yurakucho, Chiyoda-ku. Tel: (03) 3217-1111.

Credit Suisse, 1-11-30 Akasaka, Minato-ku. Tel: (03) 3589-3636.

Standard Chartered Bank, 3-2-3 Marunouchi, Chiyoda-ku. Tel: (03) 3213-6541.

Union Bank of Switzerland, Yurakucho Bldg, 1-10-1 Yurakucho, Chiyoda-ku. Tel: (03) 3214-7471.

CREDIT CARDS

American Express, Toranomon Mitsui Bldg, 3-8-1 Kasumigaseki, Chiyoda-ku. Tel: (03) 3504-3348.
 Cardmember services: (0120) 020-222 (toll-free)
 Lost/stolen card: (0120) 376-100 (toll-free)

Diners Club, Senshu Bldg, 1-13-7 Shibuya, Shibuya-ku. Tel: (03) 3499-1311.

MasterCard. Tel: (03) 5350-8051.

Visa. Tel: (0031) 65-3624 (toll-free).

COURIER SERVICES

DHL, 1-37-8 Higashi Shinagawa, Shinagawa-ku, Tokyo. Tel: (03) 5479-2580, Fax: 5479-5844.

Federal Express, Kyodo Bldg, 1st Floor, 16 Ichibancho, Chiyoda-ku, Tokyo. Tel: (0120) 003-200 (toll-free), Fax: 5275-7712.

OCS (Overseas Courier Service), 2-9 Shibaura, Minato-ku, Tokyo. Tel: (03) 5476-8111.

United Parcel (UPS)/Yamato: 15-10 Kobuna-cho, Nihombashi, Chuo-ku, Tokyo. Tel: (03) 3639-5441, Fax: 3639-5477.

GUIDES AND ESCORTS

Japan Guide Association, Shin Kokusai Building 9F, 3-4-1 Marunouchi, Chiyoda-ku, Tokyo. Tel: (03) 3213-2706, Fax: 3213-2707.

Japan Federation of Licensed Guides, 2-1-10 Kamitakada, Nakamo-ku, Tokyo. Tel: (03) 3319-1665, Fax: 3319-1960.

TRANSLATORS AND INTERPRETERS

Most languages are covered for translation or interpretation by the following companies, or check with a hotel business centre. Rates are not cheap.

ILC, Urban Point Sugamo Building 4F, 1-24-12 Sugamo, Toshima-ku, Tokyo. Tel: (03) 5395-5561, Fax: 5395-5566.

Adecco Japan, 45 Kowa Building 4F, 1-15-9 Minami Aoyama, Minato-ku, Tokyo. Tel: (03) 3470-9300, Fax: 3470-9334.

ORGANISATIONS

America-Japan Society, Marunouchi Bldg, 3rd Floor, 2-4-1 Marunouchi, Chiyoda-ku. Tel: (03) 3201-0780.

American Centre, ABC Kaikan, 2-6-3 Shibakoen, Minato-ku. Tel: (03) 3436-0901.

American Chamber of Commerce, Bridgestone Toranomon Bldg, 3-25-2 Toranomon, Minato-ku. Tel: (03) 3433-5381.

Asia Centre of Japan, 8-10-32 Akasaka, Minato-ku. Tel: (03) 3402-6111.

British Council, 1-2 Kagurazaka, Shinjuku-ku. Tel: (03) 3235-8031.

Foreign Correspondents' Club, Yurakucho Denki Bldg, 20th Floor, 1-7-1 Yurakucho, Chiyoda-ku. Tel: (03) 3211-3161.

Institute Franco-Japonais, 15 Funagawaracho, Ichigaya, Shinjuku-ku. Tel: (03) 5261-3930.

Italian Institute of Culture, 2-1-30 Kudan Minami, Chiyoda-ku. Tel: (03) 3264-6011.

Tokyo German Culture Centre, 7-5-56 Akasaka, Minato-ku. Tel: (03) 3583-7280.

JETRO (Japan External Trade Organisation), 2-2-5 Toranomon, Minato-ku. Tel: (03) 3582-5511.

www.airport.jp

Two good Internet sites for learning everything there is to know about Japan's two main international airports include info on everything from baggage-storage locations in the terminals to flight schedules to handicapped access. It's too bad that the orderliness of the site for Narita can't be shifted to the airport itself, a mess.

Narita Airport:
www.narita-airport.or.jp/ airport-e/index-e.html

Kansai International Airport:
www.kansai-airport.or.jp/ index-e.html

Practical Tips

SECURITY AND CRIME

About 13 million crimes are reported a year, about one-eighth the number reported in the United States in the same year. Murders and violent assaults each average about 1.5 per 100,000 population. Although the crime rate has risen by 20 percent in Japan over the past decade, its growth is far lower, and the arrest/conviction rate remarkably higher, than in other industrialised nations.

EMERGENCY NUMBERS

Police (crime and accidents): 110
Fire and ambulance: 119
Police info in English: (03) 3501-0110
Emergency calls can be made from any phone without using coins or prepaid telephone cards.

Japan Hotline, information and help about everything, in English, 10am–4pm weekdays. Tel: (03) 3586-0110.

For **hospital information**, call (03) 5285-8181 in Tokyo (English, Chinese, Korean, Thai and Spanish spoken).

MEDICAL SERVICES

Try to remember that you are in Japan and must be prepared to adapt to the Japanese system. Although some doctors may speak English, the receptionist and nursing staff will not, so it is advisable to bring along a Japanese friend or someone else who can speak both languages. Most hospitals and clinics do not have appointment systems (national health service, you know), so you have to be prepared to wait your

turn, however frustrating that may be. Here is a list of hospitals and clinics in Tokyo where you would have no problem in being understood or treated. They all have different hours and systems.

Hospital Hotline (English): in Tokyo, Tel: (03) 3212-2323.
Tell-Tokyo English Lifeline: in Tokyo, Tel: (03) 3968-4099.

Prescriptions: Pharmacies do not dispense prescription drugs. Prescriptions (in Japanese only) must be taken to a doctor or hospital for filling. Call one of the two above numbers for assistance.

Hospitals in Tokyo

International Catholic Hospital (Seibo Byoin), 2-5-1 Nakaochiai, Shinjuku-ku. Tel: (03) 3951-1111. Open Monday–Saturday 8–11am. Closed Sunday and 3rd Saturday.
Red Cross Medical Centre (Nisseki), 4-1-22 Hiroo, Shibuya-ku. Tel: (03) 3400-1311. Open Monday–Friday 8.30–11am; Saturday 8.30–10.30am. Closed Sunday.

Most Western-style, over-the-counter medicines are hard to find in Japan, and when they are available, prices are high. Pharmacists can help you with Japanese or Chinese remedies. Best to bring your own favourite cold and allergy medicines with you. But note that many popular brands, like Sudafed, contain small amounts of amphetamine-like drugs and are illegal in Japan.

St Luke's International Hospital (Seiroka Byoin), 10-1 Akashicho, Chuo-ku. Tel: (03) 3541-5151. Open Monday–Saturday 8.30–11am. Closed Sunday.
International Clinic, 1-5-9 Azabudai, Minato-ku. Tel: (03) 3582-2646. Open Monday–Friday 9am–noon, 2.30–5pm; Saturday 9am–noon. Closed Sunday.

Tokyo Adventist Hospital (Tokyo Eisei Byoin), 3-17-3 Amanuma, Suginami-ku. Tel: (03) 3392-6151. Open Monday-Saturday, 8.30am-11.
Toho Fujin Women's Clinic, 5-3-10 Kiba, Koto-ku. Tel: (03) 3630-0303. Open Monday–Saturday 1–5pm. Closed Sunday.

If possible, carry as little luggage as possible when travelling in Japan. Trains and stations, especially, are not designed for travellers with more than a small overnight bag. If you think you can make all your Tokyo train and subway connections while hauling several large bags, positively, absolutely forget it. The train/subway map looks neat and tidy. But station connections are serious hikes with no carts or porters available, and seemingly endless stairs.

Hotels, of course, will usually store luggage for guests heading off on adventures.

International Airports. For security reasons, bombs in particular, the international airports have no coin lockers. There are checkrooms, however, at international airports. While staff may not speak English, forms are bilingual and the staff will know why you're standing there.
ABC Skypartners: between the South Wing and the Central Building. ¥400 or ¥800/day per bag, with no time limit for storage. 7am–10pm.
GPA (Green Port Agency): South Wing, 1F and 4F. ¥400/day per bag, 30 day limit. 7am–10pm.

Train and subway stations. Most train and subway stations have coin lockers of varying sizes for ¥200 to ¥500 per day, depending on station and size of the locker. Time limit is 3 days. After that, contents are removed. You'll have no problem finding them; Japanese use them as a habit and convenience.

Checkrooms for large bags are located at several main JR stations. Luggage can be stored for up to two

Loss of Belongs

Fortunately, Japanese are quite honest about turning in found items. If you've lost a wallet packed with cash or a camera, or simply an overnight bag with dirty socks, chances are it's safe.

JR trains: Items left on trains will usually be kept for a couple of days at the nearest station. After that, they are taken to one of the major stations to be stored for five more days. Inquiries can be made in Japanese to lost-and-found centres at Tokyo Station (03) 3231-1880, or Ueno Station (03) 3841-8069. In English, inquiries can be made with the JR East Infoline (03) 3423-0111 from 10am to 6pm weekdays.

Subways: Things left on Tokyo's Eidan trains are stored for three or four days at the station nearest to where the item was found, then taken to a lost-and-found centre.

In Japanese, Tel. (03) 3834-5577, 9.30am–7pm weekdays, 9.30am–4pm Saturday. On the Toei trains, or on Tokyo city-operated buses, inquire about lost property at terminals the same day, or call the lost-and-found centre, in Japanese, at (03) 3815-7229, from 9am–6pm weekdays.

Taxis: All taxi companies in Tokyo report unclaimed items to a single centre, the Tokyo Taxi Kindaika Centre. Tel. (03) 3648-0300, in Japanese.

Police: At last resort, contact the police. The Tokyo Metropolitan Police Department maintains an immense – a *very* immense – lost-and-found centre, with everything from forgotten umbrellas (zillions of them) to bags full of cash. Tel. (03) 3814-4151, 8.30am–5.15pm weekdays. English sometimes, Japanese mostly.

office is Japan's largest holder of personal savings. Postal service and delivery is highly efficient and fast, but expensive for both international and domestic post.

Local post offices are open Monday–Friday, 9am–5pm; some are open Saturday mornings. Larger central post offices are open Monday–Friday, 9am–7pm, and Saturday, 9am–noon. For late owls, there's a 24-hour window at the **Tokyo Central Post Office**, on the Marunouchi side of Tokyo Station. For 24-hour, 365-day international mail services, there's a special **Tokyo International Post Office** (*kokusai yubin kyoku*), also near Tokyo Station and for foreign mail only, 2-3-3 Otemachi, Chiyoda-ku.

International express mail: Larger post offices offer EMS services; for some reason, the isolated post office outside of the major cities of Tokyo and Osaka may require that an account be opened, though it's just a formality. If language is proving to be a problem in getting a package sent via EMS, this could be the reason.

International parcel post: foreign parcel post cannot exceed 20 kg per package to any international destination. For heavier packages or those that exceed certain size or content restrictions (which vary by country), a commercial courier service must be used.

Postal information (English) in Tokyo: (03) 3241-4877.

weeks, ¥400/day per bag for the first five days, ¥800/day per bag for each additional day.
Tokyo Station, outside Yaesu south exit, 8.30am–6pm.
Ueno Station, in front of central exit, 8am–8pm.
Shin Osaka Station, outside the central exit, 5am–10pm.
Kyoto Station, Karasuma central exit and Hachijo central exit, 8am–8pm.

that they tend to close the store only twice or three times a month, which varies with each store.
Restaurants are open for lunch from 11.30am to 2pm and for dinner from 5 to 9 or 10pm. **Major companies** and **offices** are open from 9am to 5pm Monday to Friday. Some are also open on Saturday mornings. Most **small shops** open between 9 and 11am and close between 6 and 8pm.

Business Hours

Officially, business is done on a 9am to 5pm basis, but this is in theory only. The Japanese will often do overtime till 8 or 9pm. In general, **government** offices are open from 8.30 or 9am to 4 or 5pm Monday to Friday, and from 9am to noon on the 1st and 3rd Saturday of the month. **Main post offices** are open 9am to 7pm Monday to Friday, 9am to 5pm on Saturday, and 9am to noon on Sunday and holidays. **Branch post offices** are open 9am to 5pm Monday to Friday. **Department stores** are open daily from 10am to 7.30 or 8pm, except

Tipping

No tipping remains the rule in Japan, except for unusual or exceptional services. Porters at large stations and airports charge a flat rate of around ¥300 per piece of luggage. Taxi drivers don't expect any tips, nor do hotel staff.

Postal Services

There are nearly 30,000 post offices in Japan, and in a small country like this, that means they are nearly ubiquitous. In addition to postal services, post offices offer savings services; in fact, the post

Telecoms

Japan's country code: 81
Domestic area codes:
Fukuoka: 092
Hiroshima: 082
Kagoshima: 099
Kyoto: 075
Nagasaki: 0958
Nagoya: 052
Naha: 098
Osaka: 06
Sapporo: 011
Sendai: 022
Tokyo: 03
Yokohama: 045

To use the public telephones, which come in a variety of colours and abilities, just insert a ¥10 coin and dial the number desired. ¥10 for three minutes. Yellow and green phones accept ¥100 coins, which make them more convenient for long-distance calls, but no change is returned for unused portions.

Most common are the green phones, all taking prepaid telephone cards and some taking only prepaid cards, no coins. Telephone cards can be obtained at any Nippon Telegraph and Telephone (NTT) office, KDD office, many stores, or through special vending machines near phones.

Domestic calls, expensive over 60 km distant, are cheaper at night and on weekends and holidays by as much as 40 percent.

NTT Information, domestic telephone directory information, in English. 9am–5pm weekdays.
Tokyo: Tel: (03) 5295-1010
Narita: Tel: (0476) 28-1010
Yokohama: Tel: (045) 322-1010
Hiroshima: Tel: (082) 262-1010
City Source, free English telephone directory from NTT. Tel: (03) 5256-3141, fax: (03) 5256-3148. Osaka, Tel: (06) 571-7866, fax: (06) 571-4185.
Japan Hotline (NTT/KDD), broad-based, hard-to-find phone numbers. Tel: (03) 3586-0110. Monday–Friday, 10am–4pm.

TOLL-FREE NUMBERS
Domestic telephone numbers that begin with "0120" or "0088" are toll-free, or "free-dial", calls.

INTERNATIONAL
Foreign companies such as AT&T and call-back companies have been revolutionising international phone service in Japan. Western-style hotels, of course, usually offer the standard IDD capabilities. Elsewhere, the situation is changing so quickly that it's best to ask around for the current conditions.

International calls can be made only from specially-marked – in English and Japanese – green telephones; look for an IDD sticker on the phone or booth. Increasingly, dark-gray card phones are appearing in hotels, public places, and at airports. They have analog and digital computer connections, with small screens displaying operating instructions in both Japanese and English.

To make a **person-to-person**, **collect**, or **credit-card** call from anywhere in Japan through KDD, the dominant international telecom company, simply dial 0051.

KDD Information, international telephone information, in English: 0057 (toll free).

TELEPHONE CARDS
The Japanese love prepaid cards, and telephone cards – not coins – are the primary form of payment for public telephones. These cards come in a number of different denominations and are for sale just about everywhere, including from vending machines. Companies and groups have customised cards printed for promotion and gifts. Collecting telephone cards is a big thing in Japan.

There are actually two types of prepaid cards available: NTT (domestic) and KDD (international). The cards are slightly different sizes and can only be used in the appropriate phone.
Note: touts on the street, usually illegal immigrants overstaying their visas, will try to hustle cards at large discounts. These are definitely counterfeit and may not work in phones. This is a persistent problem around Ueno Park and Ueno Station.

TELEGRAMS
Domestic: 115
Overseas: (03) 3344-5151
Central Post Office
Domestic: (03) 3284-9539 (Japanese)
International: (03) 3284-9540 (Japanese)
For telegram inquiries, call: Tokyo, (03) 3346-2521; Yokohama, (045) 671-4347.

INTERNET AND E-MAIL
If carrying a laptop or PDA and you already have an ISP in your home country, check to see if they have a local phone number in Japan to make a connection; many do. Telephone costs are high everywhere in Japan, and thus surfing the internet comes at a price if making a toll call.

For those who must have their own connection in Japan while travelling, **Global OnLine** offers a modified account that costs approximately ¥500 per month for 5 hours, with additional per-minute costs after 5 hours. Local access numbers throughout Japan. In English, Tel: (03) 5334-1720, Fax: 5334-1711. E-mail: sales@gol.com.

An account may be set up from anywhere using their Web site: http://home.gol.com/index_e.html.

Newspapers

Readers of English are blessed with four English-language daily newspapers published by Japanese media: *The Japan Times, Mainichi Daily News, Asahi Evening News*, and *The Daily Yomiuri*.

Travellers should read one or more for their coverage of local news, features, and events, and for the advertisements that can yield deals. Monday's edition of *The Japan Times* is the place to find help-wanted ads, half of them for English teachers (and a few for French or German) and the rest for everyone else. Papers can be purchased at most newsstand kiosks on the street and in train and subway stations. Also found frequently at kiosks is the *International Herald-Tribune* and *The Asian Wall Street Journal*. Other foreign newspapers can be found at most hotels and at the larger bookstores.

Getting Around

FROM NARITA AIRPORT

A taxi to downtown Tokyo from Narita costs between ¥20,000 and ¥30,000, depending on destination and traffic. Most people prefer either the bus or train, a tenth of the price of a taxi. Either way, it's 2–3 hours by road.

Bus: A regular limousine bus service runs between Narita and TCAT (Tokyo City Air Terminal) in downtown Tokyo, to Tokyo and Shinjuku Stations, and to most major hotels in Tokyo. Tickets (around ¥3,000) are bought at the airport after clearing immigration and customs. There are several routes depending on destination. Buses are boarded outside the terminal at the curb, and will accept any amount of luggage at no extra charge. The buses leave every 20 minutes or so, taking two to three hours to arrive at the hotel. There are also buses to Yokohama and Haneda, the domestic airport.

Trains: There are two train alternatives into Tokyo: the Keisei Skyliner and the JR Narita Express. Both are twice as fast as by taxi or bus, but not as convenient, as once at a station, you'll have to make arrangements for transport around the city. (While the city's subway system is all-encompassing, if carrying more than one small bag, or unless of considerable stamina, forget getting around or getting to the hotel by train or subway, especially during the humid and hot months of summer. You've been warned...)

In terms of connections, the Narita Express is more convenient, stopping at JR Stations in Chiba, Tokyo (Station), Shinjuku, Ikebukuro, Yokohama and Ofuna. The Skyliner stops just at Ueno Station and nearby Nippori. Both take about the same time to reach Tokyo – an hour – and both have no restrictions on luggage. (Be warned, however, that carrying luggage through train and subway stations in Japan, especially in Tokyo, is a feat of considerable effort with long hikes and Fuji-like climbs. If carrying more than one piece of luggage, and if not taking the limousine bus directly to a hotel, consider a baggage delivery service at the airport, which delivers the next day.)

The Narita Express costs about ¥3,000 for regular class and tickets must be bought in advance. The Skyliner costs around ¥2,000 and tickets can be bought in advance or at the Station for the next train.

The Skyliner is far more comfortable than the Narita Express (unless travelling in first class, which is a delight). Narita Express's regular seats are small with almost no leg room: usually you sit facing another seat, knee to knee, in groups of four. When travelling with families, the Japanese prefer this style. But for the arriving traveller trying to shake jet lag, or exhausted from last-minute sightseeing before leaving Japan, this arrangement leaves a lot to be desired, especially for the price and especially when the train is overcrowded. (JR permits standing passengers when trains are full, making them even fuller.)

The Keisei Skyliner, on the other hand, is never overbooked or crowded, and the seats are quite comfortable with lots of leg room. Considering the difference in price, the Skyliner is far and away the better deal, both in price and in comfort. If one isn't carrying a lot of luggage, a connection can be made at Ueno Station to JR trains or the subway. Or there's the taxi.

Domestic air connections: If making a domestic air connection, you must take the taxi, bus or train into Tokyo and make the connection at Haneda Airport. No domestic flights are made out of Narita. The limousine bus will take you directly from Narita to Haneda, as will a very expensive taxi.

Baggage delivery: Most residents of Japan take advantage of Japan's fast and reliable delivery network. After clearing immigration and customs, take your luggage to the ABC counter in the main terminal (there are several). Often a line indicates the counter. For about ¥1,500 per bag, ABC will deliver the bag by the following day wherever you are. If carrying more than a couple of bags, seriously consider this alternative.

FROM HANEDA AIRPORT

If you are coming into Haneda Airport, then a taxi to the town centre will cost about ¥5,000 to ¥6,000 and takes about 30–40 minutes. Provided your luggage is light, you can take the Monorail to Hamamatsucho Station on the JR Yamanote Line. The trip takes about 17 minutes.

FROM KANSAI AIRPORT

The Kansai International Airport (KIX) has replaced Osaka Airport (Itami) as the international air terminus for the Kansai region. It was also intended to relieve the overcrowding at Narita Airport, which has restricted operating hours. However, some domestic flights still fly from Itami, possibly necessitating an inconvenient connection from international to domestic flights. The second largest and the first 24-hour-operation airport in Japan, Kansai International Airport, opened in 1994. It is located southeast Osaka Bay, 5 km off the coast and about 60 km from JR Shin-Osaka Station for *shinkansen* (bullet train) connections. KIX, constructed on an artificial island in Osaka Bay and one of the world's most expensive – ¥2,600 departure tax – is architecturally impressive and extremely functional. All international and domestic connections at KIX are made at the same terminal in a matter of minutes. (Note: Make sure to confirm that domestic flight connections are from KIX and not Itami-Osaka Airport.) Despite being on an island, getting to and from KIX is relatively easy: two railways, two expressways, some 10 limousine bus lines, and four high-speed ferries connect the island to every point in the Kansai.

For travel information, the **Kansai Tourist Information Centre** is located in the arrival lobby (1st Fl.) and is open daily from 9am to 9pm. For handling currency exchange, there are 10 banks at the airport, with one or more open from 6am to 11pm. Japan Rail Passes can be exchanged either at the JR West Information Counter in the International Arrivals Lobby (1st Fl, open daily, 8am to 9pm), at the TIS-Travel Service Centre (open daily, 10am to 6pm), or at the green-coloured Midori-no-madoguchi Reservations Ticket Office (open daily, 5.30am to 12 midnight) of JR Kansai Airport Station.

To/From Osaka

Train: JR (Japan Railway) Haruka Express, with reserved seating, runs between KIX and Osaka's Tennoji Station (29 min) and Shin Osaka Station (45 min), where you catch the *shinkansen*, or bullet train. The JR Kuko-Kaisoku connects KIX with Osaka's Tennoji Station (45 min) and Namba Station's Osaka City Air Terminal (O-CAT), which offers express baggage check-in (60 min). **JR train information:** Tel: (0724) 56-6242.

Nankai Railroad also connects KIX with Osaka's Namba Station. Three trains make the run. For Nankai train information tel: (0724) 56-6203.

Bus: There are a number of deluxe buses between KIX and various Osaka hotels and rail stations. These take about an hour, on a good day, and are a bit cheaper than the train. For bus information call Keihan Bus Co. tel: (07240) 55-2500.

Ferry: Two high-speed ferries connect KIX with Osaka's Tenpozan port (40 min). For ferry information tel: (06) 575-1321.

To/From Kyoto

Train: JR Haruka Express, reserved seats, connects Kyoto Station with KIX (75 min). For JR train information tel: (075) 351-4004.

Bus: A Keihan bus leaves from Uji, south of Kyoto, for KIX and takes about 2 hours. For bus Keihan bus information call tel: (0724) 55-2500.

To/From Nara

Bus: A bus runs from KIX to Nara JR Station (95 min). For bus information call Keihan Bus Co. tel: 0724-55-2500.

To/From Kobe

Bus: Connect by bus from KIX to Kobe's Sannomiya Station (90 min). For bus information call Keihan Bus Co. Tel: (0724) 55-2500.

Ferry: The Kobe Jet Shuttle is the best and fastest way to get to

Taxis

Taxis are the most comfortable way of getting around, but also the most expensive. The basic fare in Tokyo is ¥650 for the flag drop. A short trip can easily run ¥3,000 to ¥5,000. Once again, no tipping is expected or required. Taxis are readily available on almost every street corner, major hotel and railway station. A red light in the front window is illuminated if the taxi is available.

● *Don't touch the door when getting in or out of a taxi.* The doors on taxis are operated by the driver with a remote lever. Get out, walk away and forget the door. Try opening or closing the door and you'll get a scowl from the driver.

● Most taxi drivers speak only Japanese, so it can be helpful to have your destination written in Japanese.

● Don't be surprised if an available taxi ignores you late at night; the driver is looking for a *sarariman* – and a nice, tidy fare – on his way back to the suburbs.

or from Kobe. The Jet Shuttle runs between KIX and the Kobe City Air Terminal (K-CAT) on Port Island (30 min), where free bus service is provided to Kobe's Sannomiya Station. For Jet Shuttle information tel: (078) 306-2411.

To/From Southern Islands

Ferries: Two high-speed ferries connect KIX with Awaji and Shikoku islands: To Tsuna and Sumoto on Awaji Island (40 min), for information tel: (0799) 24-3333. To Tokushima on Shikoku Island (82 min), for information tel: (06) 575-2101.

FROM FUKUOKA

20 minutes from Fukuoka/Hakata and linked by regular bus services. Domestic flights connect to most cities (Tokyo 1 hour 40 minutes and Osaka 1 hour). International flights connect to Australia, China, Guam, Honolulu, Indonesia, Korea, Malaysia, New Zealand, Philippines, Singapore, Taiwan, and Thailand.

FROM HIROSHIMA

40 minutes from town and linked by regular bus services. Domestic flights connect to most cities (Tokyo 1 hour 20 minutes and Osaka 45 minutes). International flights connect to China, Hong Kong, Korea, and Singapore.

FROM NAGASAKI

One hour or more from town and linked by regular bus services. Domestic flights connect to most cities (Tokyo 2 hours and Osaka 1 hour). International flights connect to China and Korea.

FROM OKINAWA

15 minutes from Naha and linked by regular bus services. Domestic flights connect to most cities (Tokyo 3 hours and Osaka 2 hour). International flights connect to Guam, Hong Kong, Korea, and Taiwan.

FROM SAPPORO

30 minutes from town and linked by regular bus services. Domestic flights connect to most cities (Tokyo

2 hours and Osaka 3 hours). International flights connect to Australia, Guam, Hong Kong, Honolulu, and Korea.

FROM SENDAI

25 minutes from town and linked by regular bus services. Domestic flights connect to most cities (Tokyo 45 minutes and Osaka 1 hour 30 minutes). International flights connect to China, Guam, Hong Kong, Honolulu, Korea, and Singapore.

Goodwill Guides

Goodwill Guides are volunteers who assist overseas visitors. All volunteers are registered with the JNTO. With over 40,000 members, the guides are affiliated with 74 groups throughout Japan, and guides are available in over two dozen regions to offer local information or guide you on walking tours.

Tokyo: (03) 3201-3331
Yokohama: (03) 3201-3331
Kyoto: (075) 861-0540 and (075) 371-5649
Osaka: (06) 635-3143
Nara: (0745) 74-6800 and (0742) 45-5920
Nikko: (0288) 54-2027
Sendai: (022) 275-3796
Himeji: (0792) 72-3605
Kurashiki: (086) 424-7774
Fukuoka: (092) 725-9100
Kagoshima: (099) 224-3451

Public Transport

RAIL

JR Train Information, in English, information only, no reservations, 10am–6pm weekdays. Tel: (03) 3423-0111.

Japan has one of the most efficient and extensive rail networks in the world. Rail service is provided by **Japan Railways (JR)** and several regional private lines. The trains on important routes run every few minutes. Trains – such as JR's

shinkansen, sometimes called the bullet train and which travels at speeds of up to 275 kph (170 mph) – offer alternatives to air and long-distance bus travel. Between Tokyo and Kyoto, travel times are the same for both air and shinkansen. The train, however, is from city centre to city centre; air, from airport to airport.

The **subway** systems in Japan are clean, safe, and convenient. Subways are faster than congested road transportation. However, Japanese trains are notorious for being crowded, especially during morning and evening rush hours. Trains and subways are sometimes packed to more than three times their specified capacity (and during holiday periods the bullet train is packed to standing room only), though it actually feels like more.

All subway stations post a timetable. Regular service is Monday through Saturday. The Sunday and holiday schedule has slightly fewer runs. Trains run until around after midnight, so be sure to check the time of the last train. All subway and train stations have a route map with fares for each stop near the ticket machines. However, it is not always in English. Your present location is indicated with a red mark.

The fares are regulated on a station-to-station basis, so if you cannot determine the fare required, just purchase the cheapest ticket available. You can pay the difference, if needed, at the exit gate upon arrival at your destination. The ticket machine will dispense the ticket and give the correct change.

A child's ticket is half fare. Most ticket machines accept coins only, although some will take ¥1,000 notes or prepaid cards. There is usually a machine that gives change or sells prepaid cards nearby.

Transportation cost savings can be made by buying a **teiki** (train pass), valid for one, three or six months. Major subway and train stations issue passes. Another way to save on train fares is to buy a **kaisuken**, a series of 11 tickets

between two destinations for the price of 10. Lastly, one-day tickets good on either subway lines or JR trains are available.

Station arrivals are announced in Japanese inside the trains but are often difficult to understand. There is usually a map of the stops on the line and connecting lines above the train doors. The names of the stations are usually written in both Japanese and English.

Timetables and subway maps in Japanese can be obtained at most stations. Subway maps in English are available in various English-language publications and at some major train and subway stations.

DISCOUNT TICKETS

In the major cities, there are special tickets that allow unlimited travel for one day. If doing a lot of sightseeing, the savings are considerable. Can be purchased at ticket windows and sometimes at special ticket machines, often marked in English.

Tokyo

Tokyo Free Kippu: One-day pass for JR trains, Toei trains, Toei buses, and TRTA (Eidan) subways. All may be used as often as possible (except JR express trains). Approx. ¥1,500.

Tokunai Free Kippu: Unlimited-use, one-day pass in Tokyo for use only on JR trains (except JR express trains) running within the 23 wards of Tokyo. Approx. ¥800.

Toei Economy Pass: Unlimited-use, one-day pass for Toei trains, buses and subways within Tokyo on any day within a 6-month period. Approx. ¥700.

TRTA (Eidan) Subways: Unlimited-use, one-day open ticket for all TRTA (Eidan) subways. You can take all TRTA (Eidan) subways. Approximately ¥700.

Kyoto

Unlimited-use, one-day bus and subway ticket that can be used on all city buses and subways in the Kyoto area. Approx. ¥1,200; 2-days, ¥2,000.

Osaka

Unlimited-use, one-day pass for buses and subway. Approx. ¥900.

JR TRAIN DISCOUNTS

If you've not purchased a Japan Rail Pass or don't qualify, JR offers a number of special fare discounts. Amongst them:

Discount round-trip: a 20-percent discount to destinations more than 600 km one-way.

Shuyuken tickets: excursion tickets with a savings of around 20 percent for direct travel between a starting point and a designated area in which unlimited travel can be made. Valid on all JR trains and bus lines.

Package tours: discount lodging as well as discounted rail and bus travel. Packages may be purchased at JR Travel Centres, at the Green Window (*midori no madoguchi*) or leading travel agents.

Orange Card: a prepaid card with discounts for travel on JR trains. Cards come in several denominations and are used to buy JR tickets from vending machines for distances less than 100 km.

Full Moon Green Pass: senior-citizen discount for couples.

Available for a husband and wife whose total age is over 88 years. Good for a Green Car (first-class) and B-type sleeping car berth on any JR line except the JR bus line. Extra charges for other services. Prices start at ¥80,000 for 5 days.

Seishun 18 Kippu: a coupon good for five days' travel, each section used for one day's unlimited train travel. Good for ordinary JR trains, rapid JR trains, and the JR ferryboat between Miyajimaguchi and Miyajima Island. Passengers may get on and off as many times as wanted at any JR station and at the JR ferry terminal within the same date. Price is approx. ¥12,000 yen both for adults and children. It may be shared by several people, provided they travel together and do not split the coupon.

Private Transport

Driving in Japan is a headache and on the whole not enjoyable. Roads are narrow and crowded, signs confusing, and rental cars and petrol are expensive. Expressway tolls are very costly, as are bridge tolls. If at all possible, consider flying or, better, taking the train.

Japan Rail Pass

Japan's rail services are unsurpassed in the world. Frightfully efficient, they go nearly everywhere, even to the remotest neck of the woods. Foreign travellers intending to travel in Japan should consider the Japan Rail Pass.

The pass allows for virtually unlimited travel on the national JR network, including the *shinkansen*, or bullet trains. Passes cannot be purchased within Japan – they must be purchased outside of Japan – and you must be travelling in Japan under the visa entry status of "temporary visitor".

Once in Japan, the pass must initially be validated at a JR Travel Centre (which are everywhere in Japan). Once it

is validated, reservations can be made at any so-called Green Window (*midori no madoguchi*) at major stations.

While trains are not especially cheap in Japan (long-distance fares equal air fares), the pass is a great deal. A 7-day pass costs around ¥30,000 – less than the round-trip fare from Narita Airport to Kyoto via Tokyo.

	regular	first-class
7-day:	¥30,000	¥40,000
14-day:	¥50,000	¥65,000
21-day:	¥60,000	¥80,000

Prices are approximate.

Children aged 6 to 11 travel at half of the above prices.

Where to Stay

Hotels

There are hotels everywhere, but unfortunately few of them are up to international standards. Those that are reflect it in their price. However, convenience is a very dear commodity here, so often you are paying for the location more than the service or luxury. Below is a brief listing of major hotels in alphabetical order. Please note that the rankings are according to prices of single or twin rooms. In most hotels and all *ryokan*, you are provided with a *yukata* robe, toothbrush, razor, shower cap, etc.

Many hotels offer only twin beds, which are the most popular arrangement in Japan. Smoking rooms may have a thick stench of stale smoke.

Finally, hotel rooms are quite compact. Even a ¥20,000 room in a deluxe hotel can be snug. So-called business hotels, generally found in the moderate and budget categories (and a few in the expensive category), have rooms that are not just snug, but cramped. Expect submarine-style spaciousness.

Western-style hotels offer rooms whose rates may vary from ¥8,000 to ¥30,000. There are hotels which also provide Japanese-style guest rooms and landscaped gardens. Others have restaurants serving Continental food as well as local *sukiyaki*, *sushi*, *tempura*.

Ryokan (Japanese-style inns) exude an atmosphere of traditional Japanese living. They charge an average of ¥9,000 per person, depending on the type of bath facilities offered.

There are about 80,000 *ryokan* in Japan, of which 2,000 are members of the Japan Ryokan Association (JRA), who ensure that a high standard of service is maintained. Guests sleep in rooms covered with *tatami* (straw) mats, on *futon*. The baths are communal, though there are usually separate baths for men and women. Morning and evening meals are served in the guest's room.

Minshuku are bed-and-breakfast lodgings without the frills (toiletries and *yukata* gowns etc). Rates are from ¥5,000 up. The Japan National Tourist Organisation (JNTO) lists some 230 minshuku for overseas visitors.

Japanese Inn Group offers the foreign traveller recommendations and bookings for traditional Japanese inns, usually with traditional *tatami* floors, *futon* bedding, *yukata*, and *furo*, the Japanese-style bath. The Japanese Inn Group consists of about 90 reasonable *ryokan*, hotels, *minshuku* (family-run accommodation) and pensions located throughout Japan. Most of member facilities are small, family-run Japanese-style accommodations with home-town atmosphere and affordable rates (per person between ¥4,000-6,000), with meals extra.
Head office: c/o Sawanoya Ryokan, 2-3-11 Yanaka, Taito-ku, Tokyo 110. Tel: (03) 3822-2251, Fax: (03) 3822-2252.
Kyoto office: c/o Hiraiwa Ryokan, 314 Hayao-ho, Kaminokuchi-agaru, Ninomiya-cho-dori, Shimogyo-ku, Kyoto 600. Tel: (075) 351-6748, Fax: (075) 351-6969.

Japan Minshuku Centre Booking office, B1, Tokyo Kotsu Kaikan Bldg, 2-10-1, Yurakucho, Tokyo. Tel: (03) 3216-6556 (English spoken). 10am–6pm, Monday–Saturday. Average fee: ¥6,000–¥13,000 per person with 2 meals. Reservation by phone is basically not accepted. Reservation for high tourist season (July–August, April 29–May 5, December 25–January 4, weekends) can only be accepted for more than 2 persons per room.

Tokyo

Expensive
Akasaka Prince Hotel, 1-2 Kioicho, Chiyoda-ku. Tel: (03) 3234-1111. One of the Prince chain. Very modern and efficient, and great views from every room.
Akasaka Tokyu Hotel, 2-14-3 Nagatacho, Chiyoda-ku. Tel: (03) 3580-2311. One of the most conveniently located hotels in Akasaka; it is just minutes away from all the action.
ANA Hotel Tokyo, 1-12-33 Akasaka, Minato-ku. Tel: (03) 3505-1111. An exquisite hotel in the heart of Ark Hills, a popular office and shopping complex. Down the hill from Roppongi. Convenient for business and fun.
Capitol Tokyu Hotel, 2-10-3 Nagatacho, Chiyoda-ku. Tel: (03) 3581-4511. Formerly the Tokyo Hilton. A very comfortable and relaxing setting, blending Japanese and Western design. Excellent restaurants and pool (summer only).
Century Hyatt Tokyo, 2-7-2 Nishi Shinjuku, Shinjuku-ku. Tel: (03) 3349-0111. One of the buildings amidst all the skyscrapers of Shinjuku. Japanese-style Hyatt service and accommodation. Health facilities and disco.
Crowne Plaza Metropolitan, 1-6-1 Nishi-Ikebukuro, Toshima-ku. Tel: (03) 3980-1111. Three minutes from Ikebukuro Station's west exit, Ikebukuro's finest hotel.
Hotel Okura, 2-10-4 Toranomon, Minato-ku. Tel: (03) 3582-0111. Officially rated the 2nd-best hotel in the world. Health facilities, excellent restaurants and executive salon.
Hotel New Otani, 4-1 Kioicho, Chiyoda-ku. Tel: (03) 3265-1111. The largest hotel in Asia. Health facilities, a 400-year-old Japanese garden, and very good location.
Imperial Hotel, 1-1-1 Uchisaiwaicho, Chiyoda-ku. Tel: (03) 3504-1111. First built in 1890, with a new tower completed in 1983. Pool, shopping arcade, several excellent restaurants. Convenient to government offices and Ginza.
Keio Plaza Hotel, 2-2-1 Nishi Shinjuku, Shinjuku-ku. Tel: (03) 3344-0111. A 45-story skyscraper on the west side of Shinjuku. Near the Tokyo Metropolitan Government Office towers. Health facilities and executive salon.
Miyako Hotel, 1-1-50 Shiroganedai, Minato-ku. Tel: (03) 3447-3111. Affiliated with the famous Miyako Hotel in Kyoto. Health facilities and quiet, though not too convenient.
New Takanawa Prince Hotel, 3-13-1 Takanawa, Minato-ku. Tel: (03) 3442-1111. Addition to the Takanawa Prince. All of the rooms have private balconies. Pool (summer only).
Roppongi Prince Hotel, 3-2-7 Roppongi, Minato-ku. Tel: (03) 3587-1111. A few minutes from Roppongi Station. Outdoor heated pool.
Palace Hotel, 1-1-1 Marunouchi, Chiyoda-ku. Tel: (03) 3211-5211. Old but quiet and peaceful surroundings overlooking the Imperial Palace moats and gardens.
Royal Park Hotel, 2-1-1 Nihombashi, Kakigaracho, Chuo-ku. Tel: (03) 3667-1111. Next door to the Tokyo City Air Terminal. Indoor swimming pool, fitness club, Japanese garden and executive floors. Convenient to many different locations.
Takanawa Prince Hotel, 3-13-1 Takanawa, Minato-ku. Tel: (03) 3447-1111. Convenient to Shinagawa and the southwest part of Tokyo. Traditional Japanese garden. Pool (summer only).
Tokyo Hilton International, 6-6-2 Nishi Shinjuku, Shinjuku-ku. Tel: (03) 3344-5111. Completed in 1984 and follows in the tradition of the former Hilton. Health facilities and executive salon.
Tokyo Prince Hotel, 3-3-1 Shibakoen, Minato-ku. Tel: (03) 3432-1111. Another of the Prince chain. Located next to Zojo-ji temple. Pleasant outdoor garden restaurant, which is very popular in summer. Pool (summer only).

Moderate
Asakusa View Hotel, 3-17-1 Nishiasakusa, Taito-ku. Tel: (03) 3842-2111. Good location for

sightseeing and shopping in downtown Asakusa. There is always something happening in the area.
Diamond Hotel, 25 Ichibancho, Chiyoda-ku. Tel: (03) 3263-2211. Just a few minutes from Hanzomon Station. Nice quiet area.

Tokyo Hotel Rates

Japan's rates for hotels and traditional inns are very high. They are also seasonal and increase with each person in the room. The pricing here is just a guide for Tokyo rooms:

- Expensive: US$350 +
- Moderate: US$200–350
- Economical: US$50–200

Fairmont Hotel, 2-1-17 Kudan Minami, Chiyoda-ku. Tel: (03) 3262-1151. Old British style. About six minutes from Kudanshita Station, right in front of the Imperial Palace moat.
Ginza Dai-Ichi Hotel, 8-13-1 Ginza, Chuo-ku. Tel: (03) 3542-5311. Conveniently located, less than five minutes from Shimbashi Station.
Ginza Nikko Hotel, 8-4-21 Ginza, Chuo-ku. Tel: (03) 3571-4911. About four minutes from Shimbashi Station.
Ginza Tokyu Hotel, 5-15-9 Ginza, Chuo-ku. Tel: (03) 3541-2411. Reasonably priced hotel located close to the Kabuki-za Theatre in Ginza.
Haneda Tokyu Hotel, 2-8-6 Haneda Kuko, Ota-ku. Tel: (03) 3747-0311. Right next to Haneda Airport. Shuttle service between the hotel and the airport.
Hillport Hotel, 23-19 Sakuragaokacho, Shibuya-ku. Tel: (03) 3462-5171. A three-minute walk from Shibuya Station. Excellent access to restaurants, department stores and theatres.
Hilltop Hotel, 1-1 Surugadai, Kanda, Chiyoda-ku. Tel: (03) 3293-2311. Five minutes from Ochanomizu Station. An and very pleasant hotel. This is an old favourite of writers and artists. Excellent food and service.

Hotel Atamiso, 4-14-3 Ginza, Chuo-ku. Tel: (03) 3541-3621. Convenient to the Kabuki-za (*Kabuki* Theatre) and to all Ginza shopping. Two minutes from Higashi Ginza on the Hibiya line. Formerly a *ryokan*, it opened as a Western-style hotel in 1984.
Hotel Grand Palace, 1-1-1 Iidabashi, Chiyoda-ku. Tel: (03) 3264-1111. Downtown location. Ten minutes by car to Tokyo Station and Tokyo City Terminal.
Hotel Ibis, 7-14-4 Roppongi, Minato-ku. Tel: (03) 3403-4411. Trendy decor with 200 rooms located where a lot of the action can be found.
Hotel New Kanda, 2-10 Kanda, Awajicho, Chiyoda-ku. Tel: (03) 3258-3911. Quiet and yet only a 5-minute walk to noisy Akihabara electronic quarter.
Hotel Park Side, 2-11-18 Ueno, Taito-ku. Tel: (03) 3836-5711. Overlooking Ueno Park. Very delightful atmosphere. Easy access to public transport.
Mitsui Urban Hotel, 8-6-15 Ginza, Chuo-ku. Tel: (03) 3572-4131. Great location.
President Hotel, 2-2-3 Minami Aoyama, Minato-ku. Tel: (03) 3497-0111. Located near the Crown Prince's residence and the Roppongi and Aoyama areas.
Shiba Park Hotel, 1-5-10 Shibakoen, Minato-ku. Tel: (03) 3433-4141. Quiet and cozy, away from all the noise and bustle.
Shibuya Tokyu Inn, 1-24-10 Shibuya, Shibuya-ku. Tel: (03) 3498-0109. Good location.
Shimbashi Dai-Ichi Hotel, 1-2-6 Shimbashi, Minato-ku. Tel: (03) 3501-4411. Very central location. Convenient for business, shopping and sightseeing.
Shinagawa Prince Hotel, 4-10-30 Takanawa, Minato-ku. Tel: (03) 3440-1111. Good year-round sports facilities.
Shinjuku Prince Hotel, 1-30-1 Kabukicho, Shinjuku-ku. Tel: (03) 3205-1111. Right in the heart of exciting Shinjuku.
Sunshine City Prince Hotel, 3-1-5 Higashi-Ikebukuro, Toshima-ku. Tel: (03) 3988-1111. A modern hotel

located in the Sunshine City complex.
Washington Hotel, 3-2-9 Nishi Shinjuku, Shinjuku-ku. Tel: (03) 3343-3111. Very modern, very reasonable and very convenient, though the rooms are rather small.
Yaesu Fujiya Hotel, 2-9-1 Yaesu, Chuo-ku. Tel: (03) 3273-2111. One minute from Tokyo Station.

Budget
Taisho Central Hotel, 1-27-7 Takadanobaba, Shinjuku-ku. Tel: (03) 3232-0101. Just one minute from Takadanobaba Station on the JR Yamanote Line.
Dai-ichi Inn Ikebukuro, 1-42-8 Higashi Ikebukuro, Toshima-ku. Tel: (03) 3986-1221. Good for shopping and business.
Hotel Sunroute Ikebukuro, 1-39-4 Higashi-Ikebukuro, Toshima-ku. Tel: (03) 3980-1911. Convenient location. Minutes away from Ikebukuro Station on the JR Yamanote line.
Ryogoku River Hotel, 2-13-8 Ryogoku, Sumida-ku. Tel: (03) 3634-1711. One-minute from Ryogoku Station. Good for *sumo* watching if a tournament is on.
Tourist Hotel, 3-18-11 Higashi Ueno, Taito-ku. Tel: (03) 3831-0237. Minutes away from Ueno Station.

The North

TOKOHU
Sendai (022)
Dai-Ichi Tokyo Hotel Sendai, 2-3-18 Chuo. Tel: 262-1355, fax: 265-2890.
Sendai Hotel, 1-10-25 Chuo, Aoba-Ku. Tel: 225-5171, fax: 268-9325.
Hotel Sendai Plaza, 2-20-1 Honcho, Aoba-Ku. Tel: 262-7111, fax: 262-8169.
Sendai Tokyu Hotel, 9-25 Ichibancho 2-chome, Aoba-Ku. Tel: 262-2411.
Hotel Zuiho, 26-1 Akiu-cho, Yumoto. Tel:397-1111, fax: 397-1131.

Aomori (0177)
Hotel Aomori, 1-1-23 Tsutsumi-Machi. Tel: 75-4141.

Aomori Grand Hotel, 1-1-23 Shin-machi. Tel: 23-1011, fax: 34-0505.
Hotel Sunroute Aomori, 1-9-10 Shinmachi. Tel: 0176-75-2321, fax: 0176-75-2329.

Lake Towada (0176)
Towada Prince Hotel, Okawatai, Towadako, Kosaka-machi. Tel: 75-3111, fax: 75-3110.

Yamagata (0236)
Hotel Castle, 2-7 Toka Machi 4-chome. Tel: 31-3311, fax: 31-3373.
Onuma Hotel, 2-1-10 Kojirakawa-machi. Tel: 32-1111.
Hotel Yamagata, 1-1 Saiwai-cho. Tel: 42-2111, fax: 42-2119.
Yamagata Grand Hotel, 1-7-42 Honcho. Tel: 41-2611, fax: 41-2621.
Yamagata Tokyu Inn, 1-10-1 Kasumi cho. Tel: 33-0109.

Morioka (0196)
Morioka Grand Hotel, 1-10 Atagoshita. Tel: 25-2111, fax: 22-4804.
Morioka Terminal Hotel, 1-44 Morioka Ekimaedori. Tel: 25-1211.
Hotel Rich Morioka, Morioka ekimae-dori. Tel: 25-2611, fax: 25-2673.
Hotel Royal Morioka, 1-11-11 Saien. Tel: 53-1331, fax: 53-3330.
Star Hotel Morioka, 2-7-16 Chuodori. Tel: 52-3730.

HOKKAIDO
Sapporo (011)
Hotel Alpha Sapporo, S1, W5, Chuo-Ku. Tel: 221-2333, fax: 221-0819.
ANA **Hotel Sapporo**, 2-9 Kita-Sanjo-Nishi 1-chome. Tel: 221-4411, fax: 222-7624.
Keio Plaza Hotel Sapporo, 7-2 Nishi Kita 5 Chuou. Tel: 271-0111, fax: 221-5450.
Hotel New Otani Sapporo, 1-1 Nishi 2-W, Chuo-Ku. Tel: 222-1111, fax: 222-1111.
Sapporo Grand Hotel, 4-2 Nishi, Kita-1, Chuo-Ku. Tel: 261-3311, fax: 222-5164.
Sapporo Park Hotel, 3-1-1 Nishi, Minami-10, Chuo-Ku. Tel: 511-3131, fax: 511-3451.
Sapporo Prince Hotel, Nishi 11-

chome, Minami 2-jo. Tel: 241-1111, fax: 231-5994.
Sapporo Renaissance, 1-1 Toyohira 4-Jo 1-chome. Tel: 821-1111, fax: 842-6191.
Sapporo Royal Hotel, Higashi 1, Minami 7, Chuo-Ku. Tel: 511-2121, fax: 511-2133.
Sapporo Tokyu Hotel, Nishi 4-chome, Kita 4-Jo, Chuo-Ku. Tel: 231-5611.

Hakodate (0138)
Hakodate Harborview Hotel, 14-10 Wakamatsu-cho. Tel: 22-0111, fax: 23-0154.
Hakodate Kokusai Hotel, 5-10 Otemachi. Tel: 23-8751, fax: 23-0239.
Hotel Hakodate Royal, 16-9 Omoricho. Tel: 26-8181, fax: 27-4397.
Hotel Ocean, 19-13 Ohtemachi. Tel: 23-2200.
Hotel Rich Hakodate, 16-18 Matsukaze-cho. Tel: 26-2561.

Kushiro City (0154)
Kushiro Pacific Hotel, 2-6 Sakaecho. Tel: 24-8811, fax: 23-9192.
Hotel Sun Route Kushiro, 13-26 Kurogane. Tel: 24-2171, fax: 24-2180.

Kansai
Ise (0596)
Asakichi (Ryokan). Tel: 22-4101, fax: 22-4102.
Ise City Hotel & Annex. Tel: 22-5100, fax: 22-5101.
Ise City Hotel. Tel: 28-2111, fax: 28-1058.
Ise International Hotel. Tel: 23-0102, fax: 23-0109.
Todaya (Ryokan). Tel: 28-4855, fax: 28-2025.

Ise-Shima Nat'l Park (0599)
Shima Kanko Hotel. Tel: 43-1211, fax: 43-3538.
Thalassa Shima. Tel: 32-1111, fax: 32-1109.
Toba Hotel International. Tel: 25-3121, fax: 25-3129.
Toba Kowaki-en. Tel: 25-3261, fax: 25-3260.

Kobe (078)
Gaufres Ritz. Tel: 303-5555, fax: 303-5560.
Kobe Bay Sheraton Hotel & Towers. Tel: 857-7000, fax: 857-7001.
Kobe Meriken Park Oriental Hotel. Tel: 325-8111, fax: 332-3900.
New Otani Kobe Harborland. Tel: 360-1111, fax: 360-7799.
Okura. Tel: 333-0111, fax: 333-6673.
Portopia Hotel. Tel: 302-1111, fax: 302-6877.
Seishin Oriental Hotel. Tel: 992-8111, fax: 992-8108.
Shinkobe Oriental Hotel. Tel: 291-1121, fax: 291-1154.

Kyoto (075)
Alpha Kyoto. Tel: 241-2000, fax: 211-0533.
ANA **Hotel Kyoto**. Tel: 231-1155, fax: 231-5333.
Fujita Hotel Kyoto. Tel: 222-1511, fax: 256-4561.
Hiiragiya (Ryokan). Tel: 221-1136, fax: 221-1139.
Holiday Inn Kyoto. Tel: 721-3131, fax: 781-6178.
Kyoto Brighton Hotel. Tel: 441-4411, fax: 431-2360.
Kyoto Century Hotel. Tel: 351-0111, fax: 343-3721.
Kyoto Grand Hotel. Tel: 341-2311, fax: 341-3073.
Kyoto Hotel. Tel: 211-5111, fax: 221-7770.
Kyoto Royal Hotel. Tel: 223-1234, fax: 223-1702.
Kyoto Takaragaike Prince Hotel. Tel: 712-1111, fax: 712-7677.
Kyoto Tokyu Hotel. Tel: 341-2411, fax: 593-6520.
Miyako Hotel. Tel: 771-7111, fax: 751-2490.
New Hankyu Kyoto. Tel: 343-5300, fax: 343-5324.
Nikko Princess. Tel: 342-2111, fax: 342-2295.
Tawaraya. Tel: 211-5566, fax: 211-2204.

Nagoya (052)
Castle Plaza. Tel: 582-2121, fax: 582-8666.
Century Hyatt. Tel: 571-0111, fax: 569-1717.
International Hotel Nagoya. Tel: 961-3111, fax: 962-5937.

Nagoya Castle. Tel: 521-2121, fax: 531-3313.
Nagoya Dai-Ichi Hotel. Tel: 581-4411, fax: 581-4427.
Nagoya Hilton. Tel: 212-1111, fax: 212-1225.
Nagoya Kanko Hotel. Tel: 231-7711, fax: 231-7719.
Nagoya Miyako Hotel. Tel: 571-3211, fax: 571-3242.
Nagoya Tokyu Hotel. Tel: 251-2411, fax: 251-2422.

Nara (0742)
Fujita Nara. Tel: 23-8111.
Kasuga Hotel. Tel: 22-4031.
Kikusuiro (Ryokan). Tel: 23-2001.
Nara Hotel & Annex. Tel: 26-3300, fax: 23-5252.
Nara International Hotel. Tel: 26-6001, fax: 23-1552.
Pacific Nara. Tel: 27-5808
Shikitei (Ryokan). Tel: 22-5531, fax: 26-3289.

Osaka (06)
ANA Hotel Osaka. Tel: 347-1112, fax: 348-9208.
Grandvia Osaka. Tel: 344-1235, fax: 344-1130.
Hankyu International. Tel: 377-2100, fax: 377-3628.
Holiday Inn Nankai Osaka. Tel: 213-8281, fax: 213-8640.
Hyatt Regency Osaka (near INTEX). Tel: 612-1234, fax: 614-7800.
Imperial Hotel Osaka. Tel: 881-1111, fax: 881-4111.
Mitsui Urban Hotel Osaka Bay Tower. Tel: 577-1111, fax: 576-5155.
Miyako Osaka Hotel. Tel: 773-1111, fax: 773-3322.
Nankai South Tower Hotel. Tel: 646-1111, fax: 648-0331.
New Hankyu & Annex. Tel: 372-6600, fax: 374-6885.
New Otani. Tel: 941-1111, fax: 941-9769.
Nikko Osaka. Tel: 244-1111, fax: 245-2432.
Osaka Dai-Ichi Hotel. Tel: 341-4411, fax: 341-4930.
Osaka Grand Hotel. Tel: 202-1212, fax: 227-5054.
Osaka Hilton. Tel: 347-7111, fax: 347-7001.
Osaka Tokyu Hotel. Tel: 373-2411, fax: 376-0343.

Osaka Toyo Hotel. Tel: 372-8181, fax: 372-8101.
Plaza. Tel: 453-1111, fax: 454-0169.
Royal Hotel. Tel: 448-1121, fax: 448-4414.
Westin Osaka. Tel: 440-1111, fax: 440-1100.

Near Kansai Int'l Airport (0724)
Holiday Inn KIA. Tel: 69-1112, fax: 69-5660.
Hyatt Regency Osaka (near INTEX). Tel: 612-1234, fax: 614-7800.
Kansai Airport. Tel: 55-1111, fax: 55-1154.
Rihiga Royal Hotel Sakai. Tel: 24-1121, fax: 24-1120.

The South
CHUGOKU
Okayama (086)
Granvia Okayam, 1-5 Ekimotomachi. Tel: 234-7000, fax: 234-7099.
Hotel New Okayama, 1-1-25 Ekimaecho. Tel: 223-8211, fax: 223-1172.
Okayama Castle Hotel, 7-1 Saiwaicho. Tel: 233-3111.
Okayama Grand Hotel, 2-10 Funabashicho. Tel: 233-7777, fax: 225-1692.
Okayama Kokusai Hotel, 4-1-16 Kadota Honmachi. Tel: 273-7311, fax: 271-0292.
Okayama Plaza Hotel, 2-3-12 Hama. Tel: 272-1201.
Okayama Royal Hotel, 2-4 Ezucho. Tel: 254-1155, fax: 254-0777.
Okayama Tokyu Hotel, 3-2-18 Daiku. Tel: 233-2411, fax: 223-8763.

Himeji (0792)
Himeji Castle Hotel. Tel: 84-3311, fax: 84-3729.
Hotel Himeji Plaza, 158 Toyosawacho. Tel: 81-9000.
Hotel Sunroute Himeji, 195-9 Ekimae-cho. Tel: 85-0811, fax: 84-1025.

Kurashiki (086)
Hotel Kurashiki, 1-1-1 Acchi. Tel: 422-0730, fax: 422-0990.
Kurashiki Ivy Square, 7-2 Honcho. Tel: 422-0011.
Kurashiki Kokusai Hotel, 1-1-44

Chuo. Tel: 422-5141, fax: 422-5192.
Mizushima Kokusai Hotel, 4-20 Mizushima-Aobacho. Tel: 444-4321, fax: 444-4320.

Hiroshima (082)
ANA Hotel Hiroshima, 7-20, Naka-machi, Naka-Ku. Tel: 241-1111, fax: 241-9123.
Granvia Hiroshima, 1-5, Matsubaracho, Minami-Ku. Tel: 262-1111, fax: 262-4050.
Hiroshima City Hotel, 1-4, Kyobashi-cho, Minami-Ku. Tel: 263-5111, fax: 262-2403.
Mitsui Garden Hotel, 9-12, Naka-machi, Naka-Ku. Tel: 240-1131, fax: 242-3001.
Rihga Royal Hotel, 4-4, Kami-hatchobori, Naka-Ku. Tel: 502-1121, fax: 228-5415.

Hagi (0838)
Hagi Grand Hotel, 25 Furuhagicho. Tel: 25-1211, fax: 25-4422.

SHIKOKU
Takamatsu (0878)
Keio Plaza Hotel Takamatsu, 11-5 Chuocho. Tel: 34-5511, fax: 34-0800.
Okura Hotel Takamatsu, 1-9-5 Joto. Tel: 21-2222
Rihga Hotel Zest Takamatsu, 9-1 Furujin-machi. Tel: 22-3555, fax: 22-7516.
Takamatsu Grand Hotel, 5-10 Kotobuki-Cho 1-chome. Tel: 51-5757, fax: 21-9422.
Takamasu Kokusai Hotel, 2191-1 Kiacho. Tel: 31-1511, fax: 61-0293.

Matsuyama (0899)
ANA Hotel Matsuyama, 3-2-1 Ichiban-cho. Tel: 33-5511, fax: 21-6053.
Hotel Nisshin, 8-11-2 Sanbancho. Tel: 46-3111.
Hotel Okudogo, 267 Suemachi. Tel: 77-1111, fax: 77-5331.

Kochi (0888)
Dai-Ichi Kochi Hotel, 2-2-12 Kitahon-machi. Tel: 83-1441, fax: 84-3692.
Kochi Washington Hotel, 1-8-25 Outesuuji. Tel: 23-6111.
Hotel Sunroute, 1-1-28 Kita Moto-cho. Tel: 23-1311, fax: 23-1383.

KYUSHU

Fukuoka (092)

ANA Hotel Hakata, 3-3-3 Hakata-Ekimae. Tel: 471-7111, fax: 472-7707.

Central Hotel Fukuoka, 4-1-2 Watanabedori, Chuo-Ku. Tel: 712-1212, fax: 761-8980.

Dai-Ichi Tokyo Hotel Fukuoka, 5-2-18 Nakasu. Tel: 281-3311, fax: 281-3948.

Hakata Miyako Hotel, 2-1-1 Hakata-eki Higashi. Tel: 441-3111, fax: 481-1306.

Hakata Park Hotel, Hakata Ekimae 4-chome, Hakata-Ku. Tel: 451-1151, fax: 441-5614.

Hakata Tokyu Hotel, 1-16 Tenjin 1-chome, Chuo-Ku. Tel: 781-7111.

New Otani Hakata, 1-1-2 Watanabe-Dori, Chuo-Ku. Tel: 714-1111, fax: 715-5658.

Nishitetsu Grand Hotel, 6-60 Daimyo, Chuou-Ku. Tel: 771-7171, fax: 751-8224.

Hotel Station Plaza, 2-1-1 Hakata Ekimae, Hakata-Ku. Tel: 431-1211, fax: 431-8015.

Nagasaki (0958)

Hotel Majestic, 2-28 Minami-Yamate-machi. Tel: 27-7777, fax: 27-6112.

Nagasaki Grand Hotel, 5-3 Manzai-machi. Tel: 23-1234, fax: 22-1793.

Nagasaki Tokyu Hotel, 1-18 Minami-Yamate-cho. Tel: 25-1501.

Nagasaki Washington Hotel, 1 Shinchimachi 9-chome. Tel: 28-1211, fax: 25-8023.

Unzen-Amakusa National Park

Kyushu Hotel, 320 Unzen, Obama-machi. Tel: 73-3234, fax: 73-3733.

Unzen Kanko Hotel, 320 Unzen, Obamacho. Tel: 73-3263, fax: 73-3419.

Kumamoto (096)

Hotel Hokke Club, 20-1 Tori-cho. Tel: 322-5001.

Kumamoto Hotel Castle, 4-2 Joto-machi. Tel: 326-3311, fax: 326-3324.

Kumamoto Station Hotel, 1-3-6 Nihongi. Tel: 325-2001.

New Sky Hotel, 2 Higashi Amidaji Cho. Tel: 354-2111, fax: 354-8973.

Hotel Sunroute Kumamoto, 1-7-18 Shimotori. Tel: 322-2211, fax: 322-6987.

Aso National Park

Aso Kanko Hotel, Yunotani, Choyo-mura. Tel: 767-0311, fax: 767-1889.

Kagoshima (0992)

Kagoshima Hayashida Hotel, 12-22 Higashi-Sengokucho. Tel: 24-4111, fax: 24-4553.

Kagoshima Hokke Club, 3-22 Yamanokuchicho. Tel: 26-0011.

Kagoshima Sun Royal Hotel, 1-8-10 Yojiro. Tel: 53-2020, fax: 55-0186.

Kagoshima Tokyu Hotel, 22-1 Kamoike-Shinmachi. Tel: 57-2411.

Shiroyama Kanko Hotel, 41-1 Shinshoincho. Tel: 24-2211, fax: 24-2222.

OKINAWA

Naha (098)

Naha Tokyu Hotel, 1002 Ame-Ku. Tel: 868-2151, fax: 868-7895.

Okinawa Fuji Hotel, 1-6-1 Nishi. Tel: 868-1118, fax: 868-2189.

Okinawa Grand Castle Hotel, 1-132-1 Yamakawa-cho. Tel: 886-5454, fax: 887-0070.

Okinawa Harbor View Hotel, 2-46 Izumizaki. Tel: 853-2111, fax: 834-6043.

Okinawa Miyako Hotel, 40 Matsukawa. Tel: 887-1111.

Okinawa Oceanview Hotel, 1-5 Kume 2-chome. Tel: 853-2112, fax: 862-6112.

Hotel Seibu Orion, 1-2-21 Asato. Tel: 866-5533, fax: 862-9039.

Where to Eat

The Basics

Japan is an eater's paradise, and the eclectic diversity of possibilities would fill a separate Insight Guide. For a broad-brush survey of Japanese cuisine, see the *Cuisine* chapter on pages 133-37. But since you've come so far, be bold and try anything that you come across, and stay away from the fast-food joints, increasingly ubiquitous in Japan.

We have chosen to include restaurants only from the Tokyo region. This is done in part to keep this guide from being distracted from the culinary feast that awaits any traveller, and because, to be perfectly honest, the economic situation in Japan in the late 1990s and into this new century left the restaurant scene in bit of a turmoil, relatively speaking, of course. There are many, many restaurants in Japan – alleys are lined with them – but many places opened up during the heady bubble economy, supported in large part by businessmen with expense accounts often devoted to food and entertainment. Not that tourists would necessarily go to some of these places, but even the lowliest of businessman and eatery found themselves mutually benefitting from the overheated economy.

Now that the economy has deflated, any listing of restaurants covering the entire country would become hopelessly outdated as restaurants closed, changed names or management, or moved to less expensive locations.

We hope that Japan's economy settles down before the next edition of this guide, because there's fine food in Kyoto, Osaka, Naha...

What to Eat

The list below is roughly divided into sections. Please note that unless otherwise stated, the relative cost is for dinner and does not include drinks. However, most restaurants in Tokyo, regardless of their dinner prices, have special lunch menus with prices beginning at around ¥1,000. The closing times stated are, in most cases, for last orders and not the time the restaurant actually closes.

Also note that both times and prices are subject to considerable change as restaurants adjust to new economic realities.

In general, don't expect to escape from most decent restaurants for less than ¥5,000 per person, excluding drinks. On the average, a night on the upscale side of town can run ¥10,000 to ¥15,000. Stick to fast-food and street stands, and to convenience stores, to stay on the cheap side.

Japanese

08 (Maru Hachi), Shopping Caminito 1st Floor, 1-3-1 Higashi, Shibuya-ku. Tel: (03) 3409-8369. Open 5pm–12.30am. Closed Sunday and holidays. From ¥5,000.
Daigo (Shojin), 2-4-2 Atago, Minato-ku. Tel: (03) 3431-0811. Lunch noon–3pm; dinner 5–9pm. Closed Thursday. From ¥13,000.
Hidano Takayama, 1-20-16 Jinnan, Shibuya-ku. Tel: (03) 3463-5959. Open daily: lunch 11.30am–2.30pm; dinner 5–11pm. From ¥3,000.
Kocho, Shin Yurakucho Bldg, 1-12 Yurakucho, Chiyoda-ku. Tel: (03) 3214-4741. Lunch 11am–2pm; dinner 5–9.30pm. Closed Sunday and holiday. From ¥40,000. Reservation required.
Kogetsu, 5-50-10 Jingumae, Shibuya-ku. Tel: (03) 3407-3033. Open 6–11pm. Closed Sunday and holidays. From ¥13,000.
Miyagawa Honten, 1-4-6 Tsukiji, Chuo-ku. Tel: (03) 3541-1293. Lunch 11.30am–2pm; dinner 5–8.30pm. Closed Saturday. From ¥1,500. They specialize in eel.

Ryorijaya Hashimoto, 4-4-11 Roppongi, Minato-ku. Tel: (03) 3408-8388. Dinner 5.30–10pm. Closed Sunday and holidays. Dinner from ¥4,000.
Shin Hinomoto, Yurakucho Denki Birumae (below the Shinkansen), 2-4-4 Yurakucho, Chiyoda-ku. Tel: (03) 3214-8021. Noisy, friendly atmosphere, very reasonable prices.
Hyakunincho, Shinjuku-ku. Tel: (03) 3361-1991. Open daily 5pm–1am. Excellent country-style dishes and wooden slabs to bang to call the waiter. Next to Shin Okubo Station (JR). From ¥2,000.
Tengu. A famous chain of cheap food and good drinking spots. Just look for the black and red picture of the long nosed goblin, or just ask for the nearest Tengu.
Ukai Toriyama, 3426 Minami-Asakawacho, Hachioji-shi. Tel: (0426) 61-0739. Open daily 11am–9.30pm (last orders at 8pm). This restaurant is like a small village completely surrounded by tree-covered mountains. There are twelve dining rooms in separate traditional wooden houses, each with a charcoal robata grill. From ¥4,000.
Yagurajaya, 3-8-15 Roppongi, Minato-ku. Tel: (03) 3405-7261. Open Monday–Friday 5pm–1am; Saturday, Sunday and holidays 5pm–5am. Space for groups of all sizes, decor changes with the seasons, and colorful waitresses do the serving. From ¥3,000.
Yamamura, 2-7-18 Nihombashi, Chuo-ku. Tel: (03) 3271-5345. Lunch 11am–2pm; dinner 5–9.30pm. Closed Sunday and holidays. Dinner from ¥6,000.

Sushi

Thin slices of only the choicest parts of the freshest fish, served on a bed of specially-prepared vinegared rice, with a dab of wasabi (green horse radish) in between.
Fukusuke, 2BF., Toshiba Bldg, 5-2-1, Ginza, Chuo-ku, Tokyo. Tel: (03) 3573-0471. Open Monday–Saturday 11am–10pm; Sunday and holidays noon–9pm.

Fukuzushi, 5-7-8 Roppongi, Minato-ku. Tel: (03) 3402-4116. Weekdays 5.30–11pm; holidays 5–10pm. Closed Sunday. Some say this is the best.
Hamato, 787 Bldg, 2nd Floor, 7-14-18 Roppongi, Minato-ku. Tel: (03) 3479-2143. Midnight–10pm. Closed Sunday and holidays.This shop specializes in fugu (blowfish).
Ichikan, 10-5 Daikanyamacho, Shibuya-ku. Tel: (03) 3461-2002. Lunch 11am–2pm; dinner 5–11pm.
Iseto, 4-2 Kagurazaka, Shinjuku-ku. Tel: (03) 3260-6363. Dinner 5–8.30pm. Closed Sunday and holidays.
Ki-Zushi, 2-7-13 Ningyocho, Chuo-ku. Tel: (03) 3666-1682. Lunch 11.45am–2.30pm; dinner 4.30–8pm. Closed Sunday.
Kiyota, 6-3-15 Ginza, Chuo-ku. Tel: (03) 3572-4854. Open 11.30am–9pm. Closed Sunday and holidays. Reservations required.
Shimbashi Tsuruhachi, New Shimbashi Bldg, 2nd Floor, 2-16-1 Shimbashi, Minato-ku. Tel: (03) 3591-1551. Lunch noon–2pm; dinner 5–10pm. Closed Sunday and holidays.
Sushi Sei, Kanai Bldg, 1st Floor, 8-2-13 Ginza, Chuo-ku. Tel: (03) 3572-4770. Lunch noon–1.30pm; dinner 5–10.40pm. Closed Sunday.
Tamazushi, 2BF., Ginza Core Bldg, 5-8-20, Ginza, Chuo-ku, Tokyo. Tel: (03) 3573-0057. Open daily 11am–10pm.
Tsukiji Fish Market, Tsukiji Station on the Ginza line. Try to go early in the morning and you'll get the freshest fish at one of the many sushi shops in the area.

Sukiyaki, et cetera

Sukiyaki is thinly-sliced beef, sauteed for just a few seconds in a hot pan in front of you. A broth is added, and the beef is lightly simmered. Vegetables are added after the beef is cooked. Shabu-shabu is prepared in a similar way, but the broth is different. For sukiyaki, the broth is soy-based, thick and slightly sweet, while for shabu-shabu the broth is a clear stock, only lightly seasoned.

Chaco, 3-14-13, Ginza, Chuo-ku, Tokyo. Tel: (03) 3542-1828. Open Monday–Friday 11.30am–2pm, 5–10.30pm; Saturday, Sunday and holidays 5–10.30pm.

Ginza Shabu Tei, M1 Bldg, 2nd Floor, 2-12-23 Ueno, Taito-ku. Tel: (03) 3832-1096. Open daily 4–10.45pm. Closed Sunday and holidays.

Ginza Suehiro (Tsukiji branch), 4-1-15 Tsukiji, Chuo-ku. Tel: (03) 3542-3951. Lunch and dinner 11am–9pm.

Difficult Choices

The truth is that the traveller need only walk down any street or back alley in any town or city and find more possibilities for eating than one can sample in a year. Plastic food in display cases or photographic menus make decisions both easier and more difficult – too many choices. Look, sniff, and enter.

Ginza Suehiro, 6-11-2 Ginza, Chuo-ku. Tel: (03) 3542-2411. The most famous Japanese steak house serving steak, shabu-shabu, and sukiyaki.

Imaasa, Imaasa Bldg, 2nd Floor, 1-1-21 Higashi Shimbashi, Minato-ku. Tel: (03) 3572-5286. Lunch 11.30am–2pm; dinner 5–9.30pm. Closed Sunday and holidays.

Naruse, JBP Bldg, B1, 6-8-17 Roppongi, Minato-ku. Tel: (03) 3403-7666. Open daily 5–10.30pm. All the shabu-shabu or sukiyaki you can eat.

Serina Roppongi, 3-12-2 Roppongi, Minato-ku. Tel: (03) 3403-6211. Open daily 5–10.30pm.

Shabusen, 2F & 2BF, Ginza Core Bldg, 5-8-20, Ginza, Chuo-ku, Tokyo. Tel: (03) 3572-3806. Open daily 11am–10pm.

Shabusen, Ginza Core Bldg, B2 and 2nd Floor, 5-8-20 Ginza, Chuo-ku. Tel: (03) 3572-3806. Open daily 11am–9.30pm. One of the inexpensive shabu-shabu restaurants in town.

Shinjuku, Sumitomo Bldg, 52nd Floor, 2-6-1 Nishi Shinjuku, Shinjuku-ku. Tel: (03) 3344-6761. Open daily 11.30am–9.30pm. A favorite with tourists.

Volks, 1BF., Sports Shinko Bldg, 2-8-12, Ginza, Chuo-ku, Tokyo. Tel: (03) 3561-3602. Weekdays 11.30am–11pm; Saturday and Sunday 10.30am–11pm.

Tempura

Mostly fish and vegetables dipped in batter and then deep-fried for a short time. It should be eaten hot. Tempura is dipped into a soy-based sauce mixed with ginger and radish.

Daikokuya, 1-38-10 Asakusa, Taito-ku. Tel: (03) 3844-1111. Open daily 11am–8pm. Closed Monday. Real shitamachi atmosphere and cheap.

Hageten, 3-4-6, Ginza, Chuo-ku, Tokyo. Tel: (03) 3561-1668. Open daily 11am–10pm.

Hashizen, 1-7-11 Shimbashi, Minato-ku. Tel: (03) 3571-2700. Open daily 11.30am–8.30pm.

Ten-Ichi, 6-6-5 Ginza, Chuo-ku. Tel: (03) 3571-1949. Open daily 11.30am–10pm. Closed Sunday and holidays. One of the most famous tempura restaurants in Tokyo. There are over ten branches throughout Tokyo.

Ten-mo, 4-1-3 Hashimoto, Nihombashi, Chuo-ku. Tel: (03) 3241-7035. Lunch midnight–2pm; dinner 5–8pm. Closed Sunday and holidays.

Tenkuni, 8-9-11 Ginza, Chuo-ku. Tel: (03) 3571-0686. Open 11.30am–9pm. Closed 1st and 3rd Wednesday.

Tenshige, Daisan Seiko Bldg, 2nd Floor, 3-6-10 Akasaka, Minato-ku. Tel: (03) 3583-3230. Lunch 11.40am–1.40pm; dinner 6–8.30pm. Closed Sunday and holidays.

Soba and Udon

Soba are buckwheat noodles, served in hot or cold soup, often with vegetables and/or meat. Udon are thick white noodles served in the same way as soba.

Sunaba, 4-1-13 Nihombashi, Muromachi, Chuo-ku. Tel: (03) 3241-4038. Open 11am–7.30pm.

Closed Sunday and holidays. From ¥500–¥2,000.

Matsuya, 1-12 Kanda, Sudacho, Chiyoda-ku. Tel: (03) 3251-1556. Open 11am–8pm. Closed Sunday and holidays. From ¥1,000.

Raman

Popular Chinese noodles served in a similar way to soba and udon.

Bannai Yurakucho, 2-4-4 Yurakucho, Chiyoda-ku. Tel: (03) 3215-4669. Open 11am–noon. Closed Sunday. From ¥490.

Hope-Ken, 2-33-9 Sendagaya, Shibuya-ku. Tel: (03) 3405-4249. Open 24 hours daily. From ¥500.

Keika, Nakagawa Bldg, 1st Floor, 3-7-2 Shinjuku, Shinjuku-ku. Tel: (03) 3354-4591. Open daily 11am–10.45pm. From ¥520–¥780.

Chinese

Aoba, 1-1-15 Okubo, Shinjuku-ku. Tel: (03) 3205-3184. Open daily 11.30am–11pm.

Chao, Arisugawa West, B1, 5-14-15 Minami Azabu, Minato-ku. Tel: (03) 3444-2255. Open daily 11am–9.30pm.

Daini's Table, 6-3-14 Minami Aoyama, Minato-ku. Tel: (03) 3499-2408. Open daily 5–11pm.

Peking Hanten, 4-4-5 Shimbashi, Minato-ku. Tel: (03) 3431-7651. Lunch 11.30am–2pm; dinner 5–9pm. Closed Sunday.

Sasan, Court Daikanyama, B1, 1-33-18 Ebisu-nishi, Shibuya-ku. Tel: (03) 3770-0777. Open 5pm–midnight. Closed Sunday.

Xing Fu, Harajuku Torim, B1, 6-28-6 Jingumae, Shibuya-ku. Tel: (03) 3498-4412. Lunch 11.30am–2pm; dinner 5.30–10pm. Closed Sunday and holidays. Kanpo ryori (Chinese herbal cooking).

Vegetarian

JAPANESE

Karo, 6F, Tokyo Grand Hotel, 2-5-3 Shiba-koen, Minato-ku. Tel: (03) 3454-0311. Shibakoen Station on Toei Mita Line. Open 11.30am–2pm, 5–9.30pm.

Daigo, 2-4-2 Atago, Minato-ku. Tel: (03) 3431-0811. Onarimon Station on the Toei Mita Line. Open daily noon–3pm, 5–9pm except Thursday. Expensive. Advanced reservation is required.

INDIAN

Maharao, B1F, Hibiya Mitsui Bldg, 1-1-2 Yurakucho, Chiyoda-ku. Tel: (03) 3580-6423. Hibiya Station on Hibiya LIne. Open daily 11am–10pm.

GM Nair's, 4-10-7 Ginza, Chuo-ku. Tel: (03) 3541-8246. Higashi-Ginza Station on the Hibiya Line (Exit A2). Open 11.30am–9.30pm; Sunday and National holidays 11.30am–8pm. Closed on Thursday.

Ashoka, 2F, Pearl Bldg, 7-9-18 Ginza, Chuo-ku. Tel: (03) 3572-2377. Ginza Station on Ginza Line (Exit A3). Open Monday–Saturday 11.30am–9.30pm; Sunday noon–7.30pm.

The following have Japanese vegetable dishes but are cooked with soup stock using dried bonito.

Healthy-kan, 2F, Asahi Rokubancho Mansion, 4 Rokubancho, Chiyoda-ku. Tel: (03) 3263-4023. Ichigaya Station on Chuo Line & Yurakucho Line. Open 10am–9.30pm. Closed on Sunday and national holidays.

Tenmi, 1-10-6 Jinnan, Shibuya-ku. Tel: (03) 3496-7100. JR and subway stations. Open Monday–Friday 11am–2pm, 5–9.30pm; Saturday 11.30am–7pm; Sunday 11.30am–6pm. Inexpensive.

Shizen-kan, 3-6 Maruyamacho, Shibuya-ku. Tel: (03) 3476-0591. JR and Shibuya Station (Hachiko Exit). Open 11.30am–7pm. Closed on Sunday and national holidays.

SALAD BAR

Cafe Bon Cing, 2-2-11 Ginza, Chuo-ku. Tel: (03) 3564-6721. Ginza Station on Maruouchi Line. Open 8am–11pm.

Sizzler, 2F, Mitsui Bldg, Annex, 2-1-1 Nishi-Shinjuku, Shinjuku-ku. Tel: (03) 3342-5814. JR and Shinjuku Station (West Exit). Open 11am–11pm.

Culture

Museums and Art Galleries

In Japan, there are more than 1,400 museums and art galleries and their numbers are increasing year by year.

Listed are art galleries, folk history museums, treasure houses and folk art museums. Major science museums and those of a unique nature are also included.

These institutions are arranged geographically from north to south and are classified roughly by district and city according to their location.

SAPPORO (HOKKAIDO)

Historical Museum of Hokkaido, 53-2 Konoppuro, Atsubetsucho, Atsubetsu-ku, Sapporo 061-004. Tel: (011) 898-0456. 40 minutes by bus from Sapporo Station, 5 minutes by bus from Shinrinkoen Station or 10 minutes by taxi from Shin-Sapporo Station. Palaeontological and biological specimens, archeological remains, implements and utensils used by the Ainu and immigrants, progress of colonisation and industries of Hokkaido. Open 9.30am–4.30pm, closed Mondays and national holidays.

The Natural History Museum of Agriculture, Hokkaido University, 8-chome, Nishi, Kita-Sanjo, Chuo-ku, Sapporo 060 (in the botanical garden). Tel: (011) 251-8010. 10 minutes walk from Sapporo Station. Specimens of fauna and flora peculiar to Hokkaido, implements and utensils of the old Ainus and Gilyaks are on display. Open 29 April –3 November 9am–4pm, closed Mondays and 4 November–28 April.

NORTHEASTERN HONSHU

Munakata Shiko Memorial Museum of Art, 2-1-2, Matsubara, Aomori, Aomori Pref. 030. Tel: (0177) 77-4567. 15 minutes by bus from Aomori Station. Prints and paintings by Munakata Shiko (1903–75), Aomori's best-known artist. Open April–September 9.30am–4.30pm; October–March 9.30am–4pm, closed Mondays, national holidays and end of every month.

Chusonji Treasury, Chusonji, Hiraizumicho, Nishiiwaigun, Iwate Pref. 029-41. Tel: (0191) 46-2211. 5 minutes by bus from Hiraizumi Station to Chusonji bus stop, then a 20-minute walk. A fine collection of the art of the late Heian period, some 800 years ago. The collection includes Buddhist images, paintings and other cultural and historical relics of that period. Open April–October 8am–5pm; November–March 8.30am–4.30pm.

Homma Museum of Art, 7-7, Onaricho, Sakata, Yamagata Pref. 998. Tel: (0234) 24-4311. 5-minute walk from Sakata Station. Japanese paintings, calligraphy, prints, swords and various articles associated with the local culture and the folk arts. Many were the property of the Homma family, wealthy merchants in Sakata. Open April–October 9am–5pm; November–March 9am–4.30pm, closed Mondays of December–March.

Chido Museum, 10-18, Kachu-Shinmachi, Tsuruoka, Yamagata Pref. 997. Tel: (0235) 22-1199. 10 minutes by bus from Tsuruoka Station. Art objects, archaeological relics and folk items related to the rural customs of the area, and some of the possessions of the Sakai family, a feudal lord of the region. They are housed in a group of buildings among which are the former police station, government office and an old farm house. Open 9am–5pm, closed 28 December–1 January.

Sendai City Museum, Sannomaruato, Kawauchi, Sendai, Miyagi Pref. 980. Tel: (022) 225-

2557. 10 minutes by bus from Sendai Station. *Samurai* armours, swords, old costumes and other art objects, many of which were possessed by the Date family, the well-known feudal lord of Sendai. Also on display are Japanese paintings, ukiyo-e, and pottery. Open 9am–4.45pm, closed Mondays and the day following national holidays.

Kurita Museum, 1542, Komabacho, Ashikaga, Tochigi Pref. 329-42. Tel: (0284) 91-1026. 10-minute walk from Tomita Station. A large collection of Imari and Nabeshima porcelains. There is a branch of this museum in Tokyo. (See Tokyo section.) Open 9.30am–5pm, closed 29-31 December.

Mashiko Reference Collection Museum, 3388, Mashiko, Mashiko-machi, Haga-gun, Tochigi Pref. 321-42. Tel: (0285) 72-5300. One hour by bus from Utsunomiya Station. Works of late Shoji Hamada and his collection. (Eastern and Western ceramics, fabrics, furniture, paintings etc.) Open 9.30am–4.30pm, closed Mondays, 28 December–4 January and all February.

TOKYO

Bridgestone Museum of Art, 1-10-1, Kyobashi, Chou-ku, Tokyo 104. Tel: (03) 3563-0241. 5-minute walk from Tokyo Station (Yaesuguchi side). Western paintings, prints, sculpture, pottery and metal items, and paintings by contemporary Japanese artists. Open 10am–5.30pm, closed Mondays.

Communications Museum, 2-3-1, Otemachi, Chiyoda-ku, Tokyo 100. Tel: (03) 3244-6821. 1-minute walk from Otemachi subway station. A large collection of postage stamps and various exhibits and information on communications and assorted technology. Open 9am–4.30pm; Fridays 9am–6.30pm, closed Mondays.

Furniture Museum, JIC Building, 3-10, Harumi, Chuo-ku, Tokyo 104. Tel: (03) 3533-0098. 15 minutes by bus from Ginza. Old Japanese furniture. Open 10am–4.30pm, closed Wednesdays.

The Gotoh Museum, 3-9-25, Kaminoge, Setagaya-ku, Tokyo 158. Tel: (03) 3703-0661. 4-minute walk from Kaminoge Station on the Tokyu Oimachi Line. Fine arts and crafts of ancient Japan, China and other Oriental nations. Open 9.30am–4.30pm, closed Mondays and the day following a national holiday.

Hatakeyama Collection, 2-20-12, Shiroganedai, Minato-ku, Tokyo 108. Tel: (03) 3447-5787. 6-minute

Tokyo Galleries

There are art galleries all over the Ginza area and other parts of Tokyo, but below are four well-known ones that almost always hold interesting shows.

Kaneko Art Gallery, Mitsunari Bldg, 3-7-13 Kyobashi, Chuo-ku. Tel: (03) 3564-0455. 11am–6.30pm. Closed Sundays and public holidays.

Maruzen Gallery, 2-3-10 Nihombashi, Chuo-ku. Tel: (03) 3272-7211. 10am–6.30pm. Closed Sundays.

Nichido Gallery, 7-4-12 Ginza, Chuo-ku. Tel: (03) 3571-2553. 10am–7.30pm daily.

Parco Gallery, Parco Part 1, Udagawacho, Shibuya-ku. Tel: (03) 3477-5781. 10am–8.30pm daily.

walk from Takanawadai subway station. Fine arts and crafts of ancient Japan, Korea and China. Many objects are relating to the tea ceremony. A tea ceremony room on the upper floor. Open April–September 10am–5pm; October–March 10am–4.30pm, closed Mondays.

Idemitsu Museum of Arts, 9th floor of Kokusai Building, 3-1-1, Marunouchi, Chiyoda-ku, Tokyo 100. Tel: (03) 3213-9402. 3-minute walk from Yurakucho Station. Zenga by Zen priest Sengai, Japanese ceramics, crafts & paintings, hand-painted Ukiyo-e and Chinese ceramics, crafts & bronzes. Open 10am–5pm, closed Mondays.

The Japan Folk Crafts Museum, 4-3-33, Komaba, Meguro-ku, Tokyo

153. Tel: (03) 3467-4527. 5-minute walk from Komaba-Todaimae Station on the Keio-Inokashira Line. Folk art of various parts of Japan and Korea, and other countries of the world, mostly assembled by Yanagi Soetsu. Open 10am–5pm, closed Mondays.

Japanese Sword Museum, 4-25-10, Yoyogi, Shibuya-ku, Tokyo 151. Tel: (03) 3379-1386. 10-minute walk from Sangubashi Station on the Odakyu Line. Works of noted swordsmiths, ancient and modern. Open 9am–4pm, closed Mondays.

Kite Museum, 5th floor of Taimeiken Building, 1-12-10, Nihombashi, Chuo-ku, Tokyo 103. Tel: (03) 3271-2465. 2-minute walk from Nihombashi subway station. Kites collected from throughout Japan and other countries. Open 11am–5pm, closed Sundays and national holidays.

Museum of Maritime Science, 3-1, Higashi-Yashio, Shinagawa-ku, Tokyo 135 (in the reclaimed land area). Tel: (03) 3528-1111. 20 minutes by bus from Shinagawa Station. Various nautical exhibits housed in a ferro-concrete replica of a 60,000-ton liner in the seaside park. Open 10am–5pm daily.

Matsuoka Museum of Art, 8th floor of Matsuoka Tamuracho Building, 5-22-10, Shimbashi, Minato-ku, Tokyo 105. Tel: (03) 3437-2787. 3-minute walk from Onarimon subway station. Oriental ceramics and Japanese paintings, and Egyptian, Greek, Roman and Indian sculptures. Open 10am–5pm, closed Mondays.

Meiji-Jingu Treasure Museum, 1-1, Kamizonocho, Yoyogi, Shibuya-ku, Tokyo 151. Tel: (03) 3379-5511. 13-minute walk from JR Yoyogi Station or 5 minutes walk from Sangubashi Station on the Odakyu Line. Objects used by the Emperor Meiji (1852–1912). Open March–October 9am–4.30pm; November–February 9am–4pm, closed 3rd Friday.

Meiji Memorial Picture Gallery, Meiji Jingu Gaien, Meiji-jingu Gaien, 9, Kasumigaoka, Shinjuku-ku, Tokyo 160. Tel: (03) 3401-5179. 3-minute walk from Shinanomachi Station. Pictures showing the main events in

the reign of the Emperor Meiji. Open 9am–4.30pm daily.
National Museum of Modern Art, Tokyo, 3, Kitanomaru-koen, Chiyoda-ku, Tokyo 102 (in Kitanomaru Park). Tel: (03) 3214-2561. 5-minute walk from Takebashi subway station. Japanese paintings, sculptures, prints, and calligraphy. Open 10am–5pm, closed Mondays.
Crafts Gallery, National Museum of Modern Art, Tokyo, 1, Kitanomaru-koen, Chiyoda-ku, Tokyo 102 (in Kitanomaru Park). Tel: (03) 3211-7781. 7-minute walk from Takebashi subway station. Contemporary Japanese handicrafts. Open 10am–5pm, closed Mondays.
National Science Museum, 7-20, Ueno-koen, Taito-ku, Tokyo 110 (in Ueno Park). Tel: (03) 3822-0111. 5-minute walk from Ueno Station. Exhibits in the field of natural history and physical sciences and technology. Open 9am–4.30pm, closed Mondays.
National Museum of Western Art, 7-7, Ueno-koen, Taito-ku, Tokyo 110 (in Ueno Park). Tel: (03) 3828-5131. 3-minute walk from Ueno Station. Works of famous Western painters and sculptors, mostly French artists from the 19th century to the recent past. Open 9.30am–5pm, closed Mondays.
Nezu Institute of Fine Arts, 6-5-1, Minami-Aoyama, Minato-ku, Tokyo 107. Tel: (03) 3400-2536. 10-minute walk from Omotesando subway station. Japanese paintings, calligraphy, sculpture, ceramics, lacquer and Chinese bronzes, Korean ceramics; a Japanese garden in which there are several tea houses. Open 9.30am–4.30pm, closed Mondays.
NHK Broadcast Museum, 2-1-1, Atago, Minato-ku, Tokyo 105. Tel: (03) 5400-6900. 6-minute walk from Kamiyacho subway station. Materials showing the history of the development of radio and TV broadcasting in Japan. Open 9.30am–4.30pm, closed Mondays (when Monday falls on a holiday, it is open) 26 December–4 January.
Sumo Museum, 1-3-28, Yokoami,

Sumida-ku, Tokyo 130. Tel: (03) 3622-0366. 1-minute walk from Ryogoku Station. Records and documents concerning the history of sumo (Japanese wrestling) since the 18th century. Open 9.30am–4.30pm, closed Saturdays, Sundays and national holidays.
Ukiyo-e, Ota Memorial Museum of Art, 1-10-10, Jingumae, Shibuya-ku, Tokyo 150. Tel: (03) 3403-0880. 3-minute walk from Meiji-Jingumae

Largest Museum

The **Tokyo National Museum**, in Ueno Park and a 10-minute walk from Ueno Station, is the largest museum in Japan. It offers excellent displays of Japan's fine arts and archaeology, including many that are designated as National Treasures or Important Cultural Properties (both designations are highly revered in Japan). Also offered are collections of Chinese, Korean and Indian art and archaeology. Open 9am–4.30pm, closed Mondays. Tel: (03) 3822-1111.

subway station and Harajuku Station. A large collection of ukiyo-e woodblock prints collected by Mr Seizo Ota. Open 10.30am–5.30pm, closed Mondays and 25th–end of each month.
The Okura Shukokan, 2-10-3, Toranomon, Minato-ku, Tokyo 105. Tel: (03) 3583-0781. 8-minute walk from Kamiyacho subway station or 10 minutes walk from Toranomon subway station. Fine arts and crafts of ancient Japan and other Asian countries. Adjacent to Okura Hotel. Open 10am–4pm, closed Mondays.
Paper Museum, 1-1-8, Horifune, Kita-ku, Tokyo 114. Tel: (03) 3911-3545. 1-minute walk from JR Oji Station. Various kinds of Japanese paper. Products and utensils for the making of hand-made paper. Open 9.30am–4.30pm, closed Mondays and national holidays.
Pentax Gallery, Kasumicho Corporation, 3-21-20, Nishi-Azabu, Minato-ku, Tokyo 106. Tel: (03) 3401-2186. 8-minute walk from

Roppongi subway station. Cameras. Open 10am–5pm, closed Sundays and national holidays.
Hiraki Ukiyo-e Museum, 6th floor, Yokohama Sogo Department Store, 2-18-1, Takashima, Nishi-ku, Yokohama, Kanagawa Pref. 220. Tel: (045) 465-2233. Adjacent to Yokohama Station. Hikaki collection of ukiyo-e prints. Open 10am–7pm, closed Tuesdays.
Science Museum, 2-1, Kitanomaru-koen, Chiyoda-ku, Tokyo 102 (in Kitanomaru Park). Tel: (03) 3212-8471. 5-minute walk from Takebashi subway station. Machinery of the latest type. Open 9.30am–4.50pm.
Suntory Museum of Art, 11th floor of Suntory Building, 1-2-3, Moto-Akasaka, Minato-ku, Tokyo 107. Tel: (03) 3470-1073. 3-minute walk from Akasakamitsuke subway station. Japanese lacquer, ceramics, glass, costumes, masks and other fine arts. A tea ceremony room is in the museum. Open 10am–5pm; Fridays 10am–7pm, closed Mondays.
Tobacco and Salt Museum, 1-16-8, Jinnan, Shibuya-ku, Tokyo 150. Tel: (03) 3476-2041. 8-minute walk from Shibuya Station or 10 minutes walk from Harajuku Station. Items and documents relating to smoking and salt. Special exhibits: – "Ukiyo-e prints depicting smoking custom" and others – on the 4th floor. Open 10am–6pm, closed Mondays, 1st Tuesday of June and 29 December–3 January.
Tokyo Central Museum, 5th floor of Ginza Boeki Building, 2-7-18, Ginza, Chuo-ku, Tokyo 104. Tel: (03) 3564-4600. 3-minute walk from Ginza subway station. Contemporary paintings, sculptures, prints, calligraphy and handicrafts. Open 10am–6pm, closed Mondays.
Hara Museum of Contemporary Art, 4-7-25, Kita-Shinagawa, Shinagawa-ku, Tokyo 140. Tel: (03) 3445-0651. 15-minute walk from Shinagawa Station. Collection of paintings and sculptures, after 1950 up to now, by leading artists of America, Europe and Japan. Open 11am–5pm; Wednesdays 11am–8pm, closed Mondays.

Tokyo Metropolitan Art Museum, 8-36, Ueno-koen, Taito-ku, Tokyo 110 (in Ueno Park). Tel: (03) 3823-6921. 7-minute walk from Ueno Station. Works of contemporary Japanese artists. Open 9am–5pm, closed 3rd Monday. (Gallery for Museum is closed on every Monday.)

Transportation Museum, 1-25, Kanda Sudacho, Chiyoda-ku, Tokyo 101. Tel: (03) 3251-8481. 4-minute walk from Awajicho subway station or 5 minutes walk from Akihabara Station. Various items showing the progress of railways and other means of transportation in Japan. Open 9.30am–5pm, closed Mondays. (Open daily in August, 26 March–6 April.)

Tsubouchi Memorial Theatre Museum, Waseda University, Waseda University, 1-6-1, Nishi-Waseda, Shinjuku-ku, Tokyo 169. Tel: (03) 3203-4141, ext. 5214. 6-minute walk from Waseda subway station. Items and documents connected with the Oriental and Occidental theatres. Open 9am–5pm, Sundays 10am–5pm, closed national holidays.

Yamatane Museum of Art, 8th and 9th floors of Yamatane Building, 7-12, Nihombashi-Kabutocho, Chou-ku, Tokyo 103. Tel: (03) 3669-7643. 1-minute walk from Kayabacho subway station. Japanese paintings of the Meiji period to the present. Tea ceremony rooms adjoin the museum. Open 10am–5pm, closed Mondays.

TOKYO ENVIRONS

Japan Open-air Folkhouse Museum, 7-1-1, Masugata, Tama-ku, Kawasaki, Kanagawa Pref. 214. Tel: (044) 922-2181. 15-minute walk from Mukogaoka-yuen Station on the Odakyu Line. Outdoor museum featuring old and rare Japanese farmhouses. Open 9.30am–4pm, closed Mondays.

Toshiba Science Institute, 1, Komukai-Toshibacho, Saiwai-ku, Kawasaki, Kanagawa Pref. 210. Tel: (044) 511-2300. 10 minutes by bus from Kawasaki Station to Komukai-koban bus stop and then 3-minute walk to the institute. The newest technologies, concepts and visitor-operated displays on electricity along with electronic products. Open 9am–5pm, closed Saturdays, Sundays and national holidays.

Silk Museum, 2nd floor of Silk Centre Building, 1, Yamashitacho, Naka-ku, Yokohama, Kanagawa Pref. 231. Tel: (045) 641-0841. 10-minute walk from Kannai Station or 15 minutes walk from Sakuragicho Station. Silk goods of various kinds and educational materials relating to silk. Open 9am–4.30pm, closed Mondays. (When Monday falls on a holiday, it is closed on Tuesday.)

Kanagawa Prefectural Kanazawa-Bunko Museum, 142, Kanazawacho, Kanazawa-ku, Yokohama, Kanagawa Pref. 236. Tel: (045) 701-9069. 10-minute walk from Kanazawa-Bunko Station on the Keihin-Kyuko Line. Sculpture, paintings, calligraphy, historical documents and a large library of the Chinese and Japanese classics. This Kanazawa Bunko was founded about 1260 by the Hojo family. Open 9am–4.30pm, closed Mondays, last two days of every 2 months and the day following national holidays.

Kamakura Museum, 2-1-1, Yukinoshita, Kamakura, Kanagawa Pref. 248 (in the precincts of the Tsurugaoka Hachiman-gu). Tel: (0467) 22-0753. 15-minute walk from Kamakura Station. Paintings, sculpture and other art objects of the 12th–16th centuries. Well worth a visit if interested in such things. Open 9am–4pm, closed Mondays.

Traditional Tea Ceremony (in English)

Imperial Hotel (Toko-an), 1-1-1 Uchisaiwai-cho, Chiyoda-ku, Tokyo. (4F the Main Wing). Tel: (03) 3504-1111. Near Hibiya Station on Hibiya, Chiyoda, or Toei Mita Line. Open 10am–4pm. Closed on Sunday and holidays. Fee, 20-minute participation periods. Advanced reservation is required.

Hotel Okura (Chosho-an), 2-10-4 Toranomon, Minato-ku, Tokyo. (7F of the Main Bldg.). Tel: (03) 3582-0111. Near Toranomon Station on Ginza Line or Kamiyacho Station on Hibiya Line. Open daily 11am–5pm. Fee, 20–30-minute participation periods. Advanced reservation is required.

Hotel New Otani, 4-1 Kioi-cho, Chiyoda-ku, Tokyo. (7F of Tower Bldg.). Tel: (03) 3265-1111, ext. 2443. Near Akasaka-mitsuke Station on Ginza or Marunouchi Line. Open Thursday, Friday and Saturday 11am–noon, 1–4pm. Fee, 15–20-minute participation periods. No reservation is needed if guests total less than 5 or 6.

Chado Kaikan, 3-39-17 Takadanobaba, Shinjuku-ku, Tokyo. Tel: (03) 3361-2446. 15-minute walk from Takadanobaba Station or take a bus for Otakibashi-Shako to Takadanobaba 4-chome stop. Open Monday–Thursday 10.30am–2.30pm. Closed on holidays. Fee, 1-hour participation periods. Advanced reservation is required.

Kenkyusha Nihongo Centre, 1-2 Kagurazaka, Shinjuku-ku, Tokyo. Tel: (03) 5261-8940. 5-minute walk from the west exit of Iidabashi Station on JR Sobu Line, or the B-3 exit of Iidabashi Station on Yurakucho or Tozai Line. Open Monday 6–8pm; Friday 2–4pm or 6–8pm. Fee, 2-hour participation periods. Advanced reservation is required.

Happoen (Muan), 1-1-6 Shiroganedai, Minato-ku, Tokyo. Tel: (03) 3443-3111. 15-minute walk from Meguro Station on JR Yamanote Line. Open daily, when tour groups participate in the tea ceremony 10am–6pm. Only up to 1 or 2 persons can join the tea ceremony with them. Tea is served to the guests seated on chairs and not on tatami. Fee, 30-minute participation periods. Private tea ceremony is available (¥20,000 per person).

**Museum of Modern Art,
Kanagawa,** Annex; 2-1-53,
Yukinoshita, Kamakura, Kanagawa
Pref. 248 (in the precincts of the
Tsurugaoka Hachiman-gu). Tel:
(0467) 22-5000, 7718. 10-minute
walk from Kamakura Station.
Japanese and foreign art: paintings,
sculpture, prints, from the 19th
century to the present. Open
10am–5pm, closed Mondays and
the day following national holidays.

HAKONE
Hakone Open-Air Museum,
Ninotaira, Hakonemachi, Ashigara-
shimo-gun, Kanagawa Pref. 250-04.
Tel: (0460) 2-1161. 2-minute walk
from Chokoku-no-mori Station on
the Hakone-Tozan Railway. A
collection of late 19th and 20th
century sculpture by Western and
Japanese artists. Open
March–October 9am–5pm,
November–February 9am–4pm.
Hakone Art Museum, 1300, Gora,
Hakonemachi, Ashigara-shimo-gun,
Kanagawa Pref. 250-04. Tel: (0460)
2-2623. 1-minute walk from Koen-
kami cable car stop. Cable car
leaves from Gora Station on the
Hakone-Tozan Railway. A collection
of pottery and porcelain from
Japan. bamboo and moss garden in
the museum grounds. Open
April–November 9.30am–4.30pm,
December–March 9am–4pm, closed
Thursdays.

ATAMI
MOA Museum of Art (MOA), 26-2,
Momoyama-cho, Atami, Shizuoka
Pref. 413. Tel: (0557) 84-2511. 20-
minute walk or 5 minutes by taxi
from Atami Station. A collection of
Japanese and Chinese art objects
which belong to the Church of World
Messianity. Open 9.30am–5pm,
closed Thursdays. (Open when
Thursday falls on a holiday.)

CENTRAL HONSHU
**Utsukushigahara Open-Air
Museum,** Utsukushigahara-daijo,
Takeshi-mura, Chiisagata-gun,
Nagano Pref. 386-05. Tel: (0268)
86-2331. 1.5 hours by bus from
Matsumoto Station or 1 hour 40
minutes by bus from Ueda Station.

Collection of contemporary
sculptures. Open 9am–5pm, closed
mid-November–24 April.
Tokugawa Art Museum, 1017,
Tokugawacho, Higashi-ku, Nagoya
461. Tel: (052) 935-6262. 20
minutes by bus from Nagoya
Station. Japanese paintings,
screens, swords and noh costumes
belonging to the feudal lords, and
Chinese paintings and ceramics.
Open 10am–5pm, closed Mondays.
Museum Meiji-mura, 1, Uchiyama,
Inuyama, Aichi Pref. 484. Tel:
(0568) 67-0314, 3263-5566 (Tokyo
Office). 20 minutes by bus from
Inuyama Station on the Meitetsu
Line. 60 buildings of the Meiji and
Taisho periods (1868–1926) in a
large landscaped park. Open
March–October 10am–5pm,
November–February 9.30am–4pm.
Hida Folklore Village, 1-590,
Kamiokamotocho, Yakayama, Gifu
Pref. 506. Tel: (0577) 33-4714. 10
minutes by bus from Takayama
Station. The Village is composed of
several Japanese old farmhouses in
"gassho-zukuri" style moved from
the villages in the Hida district.
Many folklore articles are preserved
in each house. Open 8.30am–5pm.
Edo Village, A-36, Kitabukuromachi,
Kanazawa, Ishikawa Pref. 920. Tel:
(0762) 35-1336. 50 minutes by
bus from Kanazawa Station.
Restored Edo period (1603–1867)
buildings: thatched farmhouses,
merchants' houses, gates, etc, in a
large open space. Open 8am–5pm.
**Ishikawa Prefectural Museum of
Art,** 2-1, Dewamachi, Kanazawa,
Ishikawa Pref. 920 (beside
Kenrokuen Park). Tel: (0762) 31-
7580. 20 minutes by bus from
Kanazawa Station. Old Japanese
paintings, lacquer, textiles and
Kutani ware. Oil paintings,
sculptures, Japanese-style paintings
and art by modern and
contemporary artists who are
connected with Ishikawa prefecture.
Open 9.30am–5pm, closed 29
December–3 January.
Seisonkaku, 1-2 Kenrokumachi,
Kanazawa, Ishikawa Pref. 920 (in
Kenrokuen Park, near the
Ishikawa Prefectural Museum of
Art). Tel: (0762) 21-0580. 15

minutes by bus from Kanazawa
Station. A collection of objects
belonging to the Maeda family, the
feudal lord of the region, displayed
in a large Japanese-style house
erected in 1863. Open
8.30am–4.30pm, closed
Wednesdays and 29 December–2
January.

KYOTO
Chishaku-in Temple Storehouse,
Higashiyama-Shichijo, Higashiyama-
ku, Kyoto 605 (in the grounds of
the Chishaku-in). Tel: (075) 541-
5361. Near Higashiyama-Shichijo
bus stop. Japanese paintings on
walls and screens of the
Momoyama period (1573 1615).
The Japanese garden is one of the
best gardens in Kyoto. Open
9am–4pm.
Costume Museum, 5th floor of
Izutsu Building, Shin-Hanayacho-
Horikawa-kado, Shimogyo-ku, Kyoto
600. Tel: (075) 361-8388. 10-
minute walk from Kyoto Station
(near Nishi Hongan-ji). Japanese
costumes, from ancient to modern
times, displayed on life-sized dolls.
Open 9am–5pm, closed Sundays
and national holidays.
Domoto Art Museum, 26,
Kamiyanagicho, Hirano, Kita-ku,
Kyoto 603. Tel: (075) 463-1348.
Near Ritsumeikan Daigaku-mae bus
stop. Japanese paintings, prints,
ceramics by the famous artist,
Domoto Insho (1891–1975). Open
9.30am–5pm, closed Mondays.
Taiga, Ike Art Museum, 57,
Matsuomangokucho, Nishikyo-ku,
Kyoto 615. Tel: (075) 381-2832. In
front of Kokedera bus stop
operated by the Kyoto Bus. Sumi-e
(black and white paintings) and
calligraphy by Ike Taiga
(1723–1776). Open 10am–5pm,
closed Wednesdays.
Kawai Kanjiro's House, Kaneicho,
Gojozaka, Higashiyama-ku, Kyoto
605. Tel: (075) 561-3585. 2-minute
walk from Umamachi bus stop.
Works of the famous potter, Kawai
Kanjiro (1890–1966), the folkcraft
objects used in his traditionally-
styled Japanese house. His
workroom and 2 kilns are
preserved. Open 10am–5pm,

closed Mondays, 24 December–7 January and 10–20 August.

Koryu-ji Reihoden Treasury, 36, Uzumasa Hachigaokacho, Ukyo-ku, Kyoto 616 (in the grounds of the Koryu-ji). Tel: (075) 861-1461. Near Uzumasa Station on the Keifuku Line. Japanese sculpture, calligraphy, documents, and costumes, owned by the temple. The wooden image of Miroku Bosatsu is especially famous nationwide. Open March–November 9am–5pm; December–February 9am–4.30pm.

Kyoto Municipal Museum of Art, 124, Enshojicho, Okazaki, Sakyo-ku, Kyoto 606 (in Okazaki Park). Tel: (075) 771-4107. In front of Kyoto Kaikan Bijutsukan-mae bus stop. Works of modern Japanese artists. Japanese paintings of the Kyoto School are predominant. Open 9am–5pm, closed Mondays. (Open when Monday falls on a holiday.)

Kyoto Yuzen Dyeing Hall, 6, Mamedacho, Nishikyogoku, Ukyo-ku, Kyoto 615. Tel: (075) 311-0025. 5-minute walk from Nishikyogoku Station on the Hankyu Line. Demonstration of the process of Yuzen dyeing and display and sale of Yuzen products. Open 9am–5pm, closed Mondays.

Kyoto National Museum, 527, Chayamachi, Higashiyama-ku, Kyoto 605 (near the Sanjusangendo Hall). Tel: (075) 541-1151. 13 minutes by bus from Kyoto Station. Fine arts and archaeology of Japan, mainly from the museum collection. Many of exhibits include the art treasures principally from the shrines and temples in and around Kyoto. Open 9am–4.30pm, closed Mondays.

National Museum of Modern Art, Enshojicho, Okazaki, Sako-ku, Kyoto 606 (in Okazaki Park). Tel: (075) 761-4111. In front of Kyoto Kaikan Bijutsukan-mae bus stop. Contemporary arts of Japan and other countries. Open 9.30am–5pm, closed Mondays.

The Raku Museum, Aburanokoji, Nakadachiuri Agaru, Kamigyo-ku, Kyoto 602. Tel: (075) 414-0304. 5-minute walk from Horikawa Nakadachiuri bus stop. Open 10am–4.30pm, closed Mondays.

Sen'oku Hakkokan (Sumitomo Collection), 24, Shimo-Miyanomaecho, Shishigadani, Sakyo-ku, Kyoto 606. Tel: (075) 771-6411. Near Higashi Tennocho bus stop. Open March–June and September–November 10am–4pm, closed Mondays and national holidays. (Open when Monday falls on a holiday.)

To-ji Treasure House, 1, Kujocho, Minami-ku, Kyoto 601 (in the grounds of the To-ji). Tel: (075) 691-3325. 15-minute walk from the southwest exit of Kyoto Station (Hachijoguchi exit). Buddhist statues, paintings, sutras and other objects owned by the temple. Open 9am–4.30pm.

NARA AND VICINITY

Horyu-ji Daihozo-den Treasure Museum, 1-1, Horyuji-sannai, Ikarugacho, Ikoma-gun, Nara Pref. 636-01 (in the grounds of the Horyu-ji). Tel: (0745) 75-2555. 20-minute walk from Horyuji Station. Buddhist statues, shrines and other works of Buddhist art belonging to the Horyu-ji. Open 11 March–19 November 8am–4.30pm, 20 November–10 March 8am–4pm.

Kofuku-ji National Treasure House, 48, Noboriojicho, Nara 630 (in the grounds of the Kofuku-ji). Tel: (0742) 22-5370. 7-minute walk from Kintetsu Nara Station. Buddhist statues of national treasure merit and sculpture of the Nara Period (710–784) and the Kamakura Period (1192–1333). Open 9am–5pm.

Nara National Museum, 50, Noboriojicho, Nara 630. Tel: (0742) 22-7771. 15-minute walk from Kintetsu Nara Station. The best Buddhist art in Japan, belonging to temples in the Nara area. Open 9am–4.30pm, closed Mondays.

Nara Prefectural Museum of Art, 10-6, Noboriojicho, Nara 630. Tel: (0742) 23-3968. 10-minute walk from Kintetsu Nara Station. Contemporary arts of Japan and other countries. Old Japanese paintings, textiles, and contemporary arts of Japan and other countries. Open 9am–4.30pm, closed Mondays.

Neiraku Museum, 74, Suimoncho, Nara 630. Tel: (0742) 22-2173. 15-minute walk from Kintetsu Nara Station. Ancient Chinese bronze, old Korean celadon, and some quantity of famous Japanese art objects. The Isuien Japanese landscape garden is opposite the museum. Open 10am–4.30pm, closed Tuesdays. (Open when Tuesday falls on a holiday, but closed on the following day.)

Shoso-in Treasure Repository, 129, Zoshicho, Nara 630. Tel: (0742) 26-2811. Located in the northwestern part of the Daibutsu-den. 15-minute walk from Kintetsu Nara Station. Precious art works of the late Nara period (710–784). Many of these objects formerly belonged to the Emperor Shomu. Some of the items are shown to the public annually at the Nara National Museum for a short period between late October and early November.

Toshodai-ji Treasure House, Toshodai-ji, Gojocho, Nara 630 (in the grounds of the Toshodaiji Temple). Tel: (0742) 33-7900. 10-minute walk from Nishinokyo Station on the Kintetsu Kashihara Line. Buddhist statues, paintings and art objects of national treasure merit of the Nara period (600–784). The statue of Ganjin, normally housed in a separate building, is shown only at the time of the temple festival, from 5–7 June usually. Open 21 March–19 May and 15 September–3 November 9am–4pm.

Museum Yamato Bunkakan, 1-11-6, Gakuen-Minami, Nara 631. Tel: (0742) 45-0544. 7-minute walk from Gakuen-mae Station on the Kintetsu Nara Line. Art objects – paintings, sculpture, ceramics, lacquer, prints, textiles – of Japan, China, Korea and other Asian countries. Open 10am–5pm, closed Mondays.

OSAKA AND VICINITY

Fujita Museum of Art, 10-32, Amijimacho, Miyakojima-ku, Osaka 534. Tel: (06) 351-0582. 7-minute walk from Katamachi Station. Japanese and Chinese fine arts and crafts. Many objects are related to

the tea ceremony. Open mid-March–mid-June and mid-September–early December 10am–4pm, closed Mondays.
Museum of Old Japanese Farm Houses, 1-2, Hattori-Ryokuchi, Toyonaka, Osaka Pref. 560. Tel: (06) 862-3137. 13-minute walk from Ryokuchi-koen Station on the Kita-Osaka Kyuko Line. Old Japanese farmhouses are reassembled and put on display in a village setting. Open April–October 9.30am–5pm, November–March 9.30am–4pm, closed Mondays.
National Museum of Art, Osaka, 10-4, Senri-Banpaku-Koen, Suita, Osaka Pref. 565 (in Expo Park). Tel: (06) 876-2481. Get off at JR Ibaraki Station, Hankyu Railways Ibarakishi Station, then take the bus to Nihon Teien-mae bus stop and then a 10-minute walk. Contemporary paintings and other works of art relating to the interchange of fine arts between the East and the West. Open 10am–5pm, closed Wednesdays. (Open when Wednesday falls on a holiday, but closed on the following day.)
National Museum of Ethnology, 10-1, Senri-Banpaku-Koen, Suita, Osaka Pref. 565 (in Expo Park). Tel: (06) 876-2151. 15-minute walk from Nihon Teien-mae bus stop. Display of artifacts from Japan and other countries and booths for individual viewing of films relating to the exhibits. Open 10am–5pm, closed Wednesdays.
Osaka Japan Folk Crafts Museum, 10-5, Senri-Banpaku-Koen, Suita, Osaka Pref. 565 (in Expo Park). Tel: (06) 877-1971. 10-minute walk from Nihon Teien-mae bus stop. Japanese folk craft objects which have been chosen with great care. Open 9.30am–5pm (last admittance at 4pm), closed Wednesdays. (Open when Wednesday falls on a holiday, but closed on the following day.)
Osaka City Museum, 1-1, Osakajo, Chou-ku, Osaka 540 (in the grounds of the Osaka Castle). Tel: (06) 941-7177. 15-minute walk from Morinomiya Station. Materials and records connected with the history, economy, and culture of Osaka.

Open 9.15am–4.45pm, closed every 2nd and 4th Monday of the month. (Open when the 4th Monday falls on a holiday, but closed on the following day.)
Osaka Municipal Museum of Art, 1-82, Chausuyamacho, Tennoji-ku, Osaka 543 (in Tennoji Park). Tel: (06) 771-4874. 8-minute walk from Tennoji Station (Subway or JR). Japanese, Chinese, and Korean art objects, both ancient and modern. Open 9.30am–5pm, closed Mondays.
Osaka Museum of Natural History, 1-23, Nagai-koen, Higashi-Sumiyoshi-ku, Osaka 546 (in Nagai Park). Tel: (06) 697-6221. 10-minute walk from Nagai subway station. Material for study of natural science. Open 9.30am–4.30pm, closed Mondays.
Modern Transportation Museum, 3-11-10, Namiyoke, Minato-ku, Osaka

552. Tel: (06) 581-5771. Near JR Bentencho Station. Various items relating to air, land, and sea transportation and more specifically the modernising of the Japanese National Railways. Open 9.30am–5pm, closed Mondays. (Open daily during spring holiday and summer holiday seasons.)

KOBE AND VICINITY
Hakutsuru Art Museum, 6-1-1, Sumiyoshi-Yamate, Higashi-Nada-ku, Kobe 658. Tel: (078) 851-6001. 15-minute walk from Mikage Station on the Hankyu Line. Chinese bronzes, ceramics, lacquer ware, and ancient Japanese art objects. Open mid-March–end May and mid-September–end November 10am–4.30pm, closed Mondays and day following national holidays.
Hyogo-ken Togei-kan, 5th floor of Zentan Kaikan Building, 4-5-1,

Visiting Imperial Villas in Kyoto

Any visit to an Imperial residence in Tokyo or Kyoto is an honour and a privilege. Only the grounds of Tokyo's **Imperial Palace** are opened to the public on January 2 and December 23, Emperor Akihito's birthday, a national holiday (*Tenno Tanjobi*). The Imperial Palace and villas in Kyoto are open by appointment only, on the same day of visit for foreigners (it's more difficult and time-consuming for Japanese to arrange visits, ironically) through the Imperial Household Agency.

To see the **Kyoto Imperial Palace, Shugaku-in Imperial Villa**, or **Katsura Imperial Villa** in Kyoto, apply for permission at the Imperial Household Agency office on the Palace grounds in Kyoto. Admission to the Palace and villas is free. For palace tours, you must apply – with passport – 30 minutes before tour times: 10am and 2pm weekdays and Saturday morning. (The palace is closed on Sundays and national holidays.) While the palace is open on Saturday mornings, the agency office is closed, so you need to

apply on weekdays. Only overseas visitors can apply and visit on the same day. Japanese must apply months in advance or wait for the week in April and October when the palace is open to the general public – a good time to avoid visiting. Palace tours begin at Seisho gate in the middle of the western wall and take about an hour. Most, but not all, tours are conducted in English, but an English-language pamphlet is provided. You must also apply to the same office for visits to either of the imperial villas; this can normally be done a few days before your intended visit. Some restrictions do apply on children, so check with the Imperial Household Agency office before your visit. Hotels can be helpful in pre-planning any visit.

It might seem like a lot of work, but then, how many imperial residences have you ever visited?
Imperial Household Agency, Kyoto Palace – Kyoto Gosho, 3 Kyoto Gyoen, Kamigyo-Ku, Kyoto 602. Tel: (075) 211-1215. Office hours 9am to 4.30pm weekdays.

Shimo-Yamatedori, Chou-ku, Kobe 650. Tel: (078) 321-0769. 3-minute walk from JR Motomachi Station. A large collection of Japanese ceramics. Among the pieces, Tamba ware are predominant. Open 10am–5pm, closed Mondays.

Hyogo Prefectural Museum of Modern Art, Kobe, 3-8-30, Harada-dori, Nada-ku, Kobe 657. Tel: (078) 801-1591. 5-minute walk from Hankyu Ojikoen Station on the Hankyu Kobe Line. Contemporary arts of Japan and other countries. Open 10am–5pm, closed Mondays.

Kobe City Museum, 24 Kyomachi, Chou-ku, Kobe 650. Tel: (078) 391-0035. 10-minute walk from JR Sannomiya Station. A newly-opened museum of archaeology and history of Kobe. It also houses a fine collection of Japanese paintings and art objects of the 16th to 17th centuries produced under the influence of Portugal and Spain (Namban Art), Kohmoh Art (the 17th to 19th centuries, influenced by Holland) and old maps. Open 10am–5pm, closed Mondays and the day following national holidays.

Tekisui Art Museum, 13-3, Yama-Ashiyacho, Ashiya, Hyogo Pref. 659. Tel: (0797) 22-2228. 8-minute walk from Ashiyagawa Station on the Hankyu Line. Japanese art objects, collection of toys and games, Kyoto wares. Open 10am–5pm, closed Mondays, mid-July–mid-September and mid-December–mid-January.

CHUGOKU

Bizen Pottery Traditional and Contemporary Art Museum, 1659-6, Imbe, Bizen, Okayama Pref. 705. Tel: (0869) 64-1400. 2-minute walk from Imbe Station. A large collection of Bizen ware by contemporary potters. Open 9.30am–5pm, closed Mondays.

Japanese Rural Toy Museum, 1-4-16, Chou, Kurashiki, Okayama Pref. 710. Tel: (0864) 22-8058. 10-minute walk from Kurashiki Station. Old Japanese folk toys collected from all parts of the country. Open 8am–5pm, closed 1 January.

The Kei Fujiwara Art Museum, Honami, Bizen, Okayama Pref. 705. Tel: (0869) 67-0638. 10-minute taxi from JR Bizen-Katakami Station. Bizen Pottery made by Kei Fujiwara and old Bizen pottery. Open 10am–4.30pm, closed Mondays.

Kurashiki Archaeological Museum, 1-3-13, Chuo, Kurashiki, Okayama Pref. 710. Tel: (0864) 22-1542. 14-minute walk from Kurashiki Station. Archaeological relics unearthed in the Inland Sea districts. Open December–February 9am–4.30pm, March–November 9am–5pm, closed Mondays.

Kurashiki Museum of Folkcraft, 1-4-11, Chuo, Kurashiki, Okayama Pref. 710. Tel: (0864) 22-1637. 15-minute walk from Kurashiki Station. Folkcraft objects of Japan and other countries. Open December–February 9am–4.15pm, March–November 9am–5pm, closed Mondays (when Monday falls on a holiday, it is open), 29 December–1 January.

Ohara Museum of Art, 1-1-15, Chuo, Kurashiki, Okayama Pref. 710. Tel: (0864) 22-0005. 13-minute walk from Kurashiki Station. The art museum exhibits Western paintings and sculpture of the 17th to the 20th centuries while the craft museum displays contemporary Japanese ceramics, textiles, wood-block prints, etc. Open 9am–5pm, closed Mondays.

Hiroshima Museum of Art, 3-2, Motomachi, Naka-ku, Hiroshima 730 (in Chuo Park). Tel: (082) 223-2530. 15 minutes by bus or streetcar from Hiroshima Station. Works of Impressionists' and other European artists since the 19th century and also modern Japanese artists' works. Open 9am–5pm, closed Mondays.

Hiroshima Peace Memorial Museum, 1-3, Nakajimacho, Naka-ku, Hiroshima 730. Tel: (082) 241-4004. 20 minutes by bus from Hiroshima Station. Records on the 1945 atomic bomb explosion. Open 1 May–30 November 9am–6pm, 1 December–30 April 9am–5pm, closed 29 December–2 January.

Seto Inland Sea Folk History Museum, 1412-2, Tarumicho, Takamatsu, Kagawa Pref. 761. Tel: (0878) 81-4707. 35 minutes by bus from Takamatsu Station to Ogoshi, then a 25-minute walk. Wooden fishing boats and all kinds of fishing gear, farm tools and archaeological items that have been excavated in and around the Inland Sea. The museum is located atop one of the hills in the Goshikidai region with a magnificent view over the Inland Sea. Open 9am–5pm.

KYUSHU AND OKINAWA

Fukuoka Art Museum, 1-6, Ohori-koen, Chuo-ku, Fukuoka 810 (in Ohori Park). Tel: (092) 714-6051. 30 minutes by bus from Hakata Station. Objects once owned by the Kuroda family, the local feudal lord, the Matsunaga collection, which is noted for tea ceremony utensils, and oil paintings from both the West and Japan. Open 9.30am–5.30pm, closed Mondays.

Nagasaki Municipal Museum, Heiwa Kaikan, 7-8 Hirano-machi, Nagasaki 852. Tel: (0958) 45-8188. 5-minute walk from Hamaguchi-machi bus and streetcar stops. Art objects and materials associated with Christianity and trade which were brought in by Holland and China, allowed to trade at Nagasaki, the only open port during the isolation. Open 9am–5pm, closed Mondays.

Okinawa Prefectural Museum, 1-1, Onakacho, Shuri, Naha, Okinawa Pref. 903. Tel: (0988) 84-2243. 2-minute walk from Shurijo Koen Iriguchi bus stop. Art objects of the Okinawa islands including paintings, sculpture, pottery vessels, clothing and lacquer ware. Not terribly exceptional. Open 9am–5pm, closed Mondays and holidays.

Ceramic Art & Crafts

Japan is a country of earthenware, a ceramic-loving nation and a storehouse of ceramic art and crafts. The origin of Japanese ceramic art is generally regarded to date back to the beginning of the 13th century, when Chinese ceramic techniques were introduced. There are a large number of kilns in Japan, especially in the south and each with a long and interesting history.

SHIBUKUSA-YAKI, KOITO-YAKI AND YAMADA-YAKI

Takayama City, Gifu Pref. (0577)
Hokokusha Pottery Works.
Shibukusa-yaki. Located in Kami-nino machi, Takayama City. Tel: 34-0504. Open all year round.
Koito-yaki Kamamoto. Located in Kami-Okamotocho, Takayama City. Tel: 32-1981. Open 9am–5pm. Closed Sunday.
Kobayashi Tosha Pottery Works.
Yamada-yaki. Located in Yamadacho, Takayama City. Tel: 32-4077. Open 8am–5pm. Closed Sunday.

MINO-YAKI (OR TAJIMI-YAKI)

Tajimi and Toki, Gifu Pref. (0572)
Mino-yaki Centre. Tel: 27-7111. Located in Higashi-machi, Tajimi City. Display of Mino ware by contemporary potters. Open 8.30am–5pm. Closed Sunday.
Gifu Prefectural Ceramic Museum. Tel: 23-1191. Open 9.30am–4.30pm. Old Mino ware and the tools and instruments used for making Seto ware in olden times.

KIYOMIZU-YAKI (OR KYO-YAKI)

Kyoto City, Kyoto Pref. (075)
Kyoto Tojiki Kaikan (Pottery Centre). Tel: 541-1102. Located in Gojozaka Higashi-iru, Higashiyama-ku. Display and sale of Kyo-yaki ware. Open 9.30am–5pm.
Kawai Kanjiro's House. 569 Kaneimachi, Gojozaka, Higashiyama-ku. Tel: 561-3585. Works of the famous potter, Kanjiro Kawai (1890–1966) and folkcraft objects used in his daily life are in his traditional Japanese house. Open 10am–5pm. Closed Monday.
Kyoto National Museum. Tel: 541-1151. Located in Higashi-oji, Higashiyama-ku (near the Sanjusangendo Hall). Open 9am–4.30pm. Closed Monday.
The Raku Museum. Tel: 414-0304. Located in Aburanokoji, Nakadachiuri-agaru, Kamigyo-ku. Open 10am–4.30pm. Closed Monday.

Ceramic Qualities

The characteristics of Japanese ceramics are:

- an expression that is gentle and suave;
- they are noted for their irregularity and freedom, simplicity and homeliness;
- they are free from artificiality and monotony.

The decorations on Japanese wares are quiet and not piquant. Gentleness of expression, which is the chief feature of Japanese ceramics, has been influenced by Japanese taste, fostered by the unique climatic conditions, and geographical features of the country. Korean influences are considerable in the south and west of Japan, especially in northern Kyushu.

BIZEN-YAKI

Imbe, Bizen, Okayama Pref. (0869)
Bizen Ceramics Hall, 1659-6 Imbe, Bizen City. Tel: 64-1400. Bizen ware by well-known contemporary potters. Open 9.30am–4.30pm. Closed Monday.
Kei Fujiwara Art Museum. Tel: 67-0638. Located in Honami, Bizen City. Bizen pottery made by Kai Fujiwara and old Bizen pottery. Open 10am–4.30pm. Closed Monday.

HAGI-YAKI

Hagi City, Yamaguchi Pref. (0869)
Kumaya Art Museum, 47 Imauonotanacho, Hagi City. Tel 2-7547. Old Hagi ware and various art objects owned by the Kumaya family. Open 9am–5pm (December–February), 8.30–5.30pm (March–November).

TOBE-YAKI

Ehime Pref. Shikoku Island (0899)
Tobe Ceramic Hall. Tel: 62-3900. Display and sale of Tobe-yaki ware created by 30 kilns.
Ehime Prefectural Products Association. Tel: 41-7584. Located in Ichibancho, Matsuyama City.

Display and sale of Tobe-yaki ware, Iyo-Kasuri fabric, lacquer ware and other products of the prefecture. Open 8.30am–5pm. Closed Saturday afternoon, Sunday and national holidays.
Umeno Seitojo Workshop. Tel: 62-2311. You can try your hand in the workshop and observe Tobe-yaki ware on display. Open 8am–5pm. Closed Monday and second Sunday.

KOISHIWARA-YAKI AND TAKATORI-YAKI

Koishiwara, Fukuoka Pref.
40 kilns are in the village. Almost all of them can be observed.
Koishiwara Potteries Hall. Tel: 74-2138. Display of Koshiwara ware. Open 9am–5pm. Closed Monday.
Takatori Seizan Kiln. Tel: 74-2045. Located in Kamatoko, Oaza-Tsuzumi. Open 8am–5pm. Open all year.
Takatori Hassen Kiln. Tel: 74-2211. Located in Sarayama, Koishiwara-mura. Open 8am–5pm.

ONTA-YAKI (ONDA-YAKI)

Hita City, Oita Pref. Kyushu. (0973)
Onda Potteries Hall. Display of Onda-yaki ware. Open 9am–5pm. Closed on 15th every month.
Sakamoto Haruzo Kiln. tel: 29-2405.
Sakamoto Shigeki Kiln. tel: 29-2404.

KARATSU-YAKI

Karatsu, Saga Pref. Kyushu. (0955)
Karatsu Castle Donjon, 8-1 Higashi-Jonai, Karatsu City. Tel: 72-5697. Old Karatsu ware and local archaeological material are on display. Open 9am–5pm.
Nakazato Taroemon Kiln. Tel: 72-8171. Only the exhibition hall can be observed. Located in Choda, Karatsu City. Open 8.30am–5.30pm.
Ochanomizu Kiln. Tel: 72-6513. Located in Kami-Koda, Karatsu City. Visitors can make hand-molded earthenware. Open 9.30am–5.30pm. Closed Monday.

IMARI-YAKI

Imari, Saga Pref., Kyushu. (0955)
Imari Arita Ceramics Hall. Tel: 22-6333. Display of Imari and Arita wares. Open 9am–5pm. Closed Monday.
Imari Ceramics Hall. Tel: 23-7293. Located where the Imari Arita Ceramics Hall is. Display and sale of Imari ware. Open 9am–5pm.

ARITA-YAKI

Arita, Saga Pref., Kyushu. (0955)
Arita Ceramics Museum. Tel: 42-3372. Display of local ceramics and documents and a large number of shards excavated at the kiln sites in the region. Open 9am–4.30pm. Closed Monday and National holidays.

Rise of Ceramics

The development of the ceramic arts was stimulated in the 16th century because of the popularity of the tea ceremony, and soon new kilns were opened in various parts of the country. The one in Arita, constructed in 1598 by a Korean potter who came from Korea that same year, deserves special mention.

Arita Folk History Museum. Tel: 43-2678. Located in Arita-machi, Nishi-Matsuura-gun. Display of old Imari, other ceramics and their documents of the region. Open 9am–4.30pm. Closed Monday.
Imaemon Kiln. Tel: 43-2267. Visitors can only observe Imaemon Gallery, across from the Imaemon Kiln, which displays Nabeshima and Imari wares. Open 8am–5pm.
Kakiemon Kiln. Tel: 43-2267. Only the exhibition hall can be observed. Open 9am–5pm.

HASAMI-YAKI

Nagasaki Pref., Kyushu. (0956)
Hasami Ceramics Hall. Tel: 85-2214. Located in Ishigo, Hasami-machi, **Higashi-Sonoki-gun**. Display and sale of Hasami ware. Open 9am–4.30pm. Closed Tuesday and national holidays.

KODA-YAKI & SHODAI-YAKI

Yatsushiro and Kumamoto (0965)
Mr Saisuke Agano's Kiln. Tel: 38-0416. Located in Hinagu Higashimachi, Yatsushiro City. Open 8am–6pm.
Mr Masae Sakai's Kiln. Tel: 33-2859. Kamikata-cho, Yatsushiro City. Open 9am–5pm. Closed Sunday.
Shodai-yaki: There are seven kilns. (0968)
Shirohei Kiln. Tel: 62-0538. Located in Oshima, Arao City. Open 9am–5pm.
Sueyasu Kiln. Tel: 68-0058. Located in Fumoto-Kami, Arao City. Open 9am–5pm.
Kumamoto Prefectural Traditional Crafts Hall. Tel: 324-4930. Located in Chibajo-mcahi, Kumamoto City. Display of Koda and Shodai wares, bamboo wares and cutleries. Open 9am–5pm. Closed Monday.

TSUBOYA-YAKI

Naha City, Okinawa Pref. (0988)
Kobashigawa Seitojo Workshop. 1-28027, Tsuboya, Naha City. Tel: 53-4617.
Aragaki Seitojo Workshop, 1-21-23 Tsuboyacho, Naha City. Tel: 63-1107.
Tsuboya Pottery Cooperative Union. Tel: 66-3284. To visit the workshops listed above, please contact the union first. Information on kilns can be obtained here.
Tsuboya Pottery Hall, 1-21-14 Tsuboya, Naha City. Tel: 66-3284. Display and sale of Tsuboya ware. Open 9am–6pm.
Okinawa Prefectural Museum. Tsuboya ware, Bingata dyed goods, paintings, etc are exhibited. Open 9am–4.30pm. Closed Monday and national holidays.

Theatres and Concerts

Bunkamura, 2-24-1 Dogenzaka, Shibuya-ku 150. Tel: Info: (03) 3477 3244, tickets: (03) 3477 9999.
Hibiya Kokaido (public hall), 1-3 Hibiya-koen, Chiyoda-ku. Tel: (03) 3591-6388.
Kabuki-za (kabuki), 4-12-15 Ginza, Chuo-ku. Tel: (03) 3541-3131.
Kinokuniya Hall (Japanese drama), 3-17-7 Shinjuku, Shinjuku-ku. Tel: (03) 3354-0141.
Kokuritsu Gekijo (contemporary Japanese drama), 4-1 Hayatocho, Chiyoda-ku. Tel: (03) 3265-7411.
Kosei Nenkin Hall, 5-3-1 Shinjuku, Shinjuku-ku. Tel: (03) 3356-1111.
Meijiza (historical Japanese drama), 2-31-1 Hamacho, Nihombashi, Chuo-ku. Tel: (03) 3660-3939.
National Theatre Nogakudo (noh), 4-18-1 Sendagaya, Shibuya-ku. Tel: (03) 3423-1331.
NHK Hall (classical), 2-1 Jinan, Shibuya-ku. Tel: (03) 3465-1111.
Nihon Budokan, 2-3 Kitanomaru Koen, Chiyoda-ku. Tel: (03) 3216-0781.
Nissei Gekijo, 1-1-1 Yurakucho, Chiyoda-ku. Tel: (03) 3503-3111.
Shibuya Kokaido, 1-1 Udagawacho, Shibuya-ku. Tel: (03) 3463-5001.
Suehirotei (rakugo), 3-6-12 Shinjuku, Shinjuku-ku. Tel: (03) 3351-2974.
Sunshine Gekijo (Japanese versions of Broadway hits), Sunshine City Bunka Kaikan, 3-1-4 Higashi-Ikebukuro, Toshima-ku. Tel: (03) 3987-5281.
Suntory Hall (classical), 1-13-1 Akasaka, Minato-ku. Tel: (03) 3505-1001.
Teikoku Gekijo (Imperial Theatre), 3-1-1 Marunouchi, Chiyoda-ku. Tel: (03) 3213-7221.
The Tokyo Globe (Shakespeare/opera), 3-1-2 Hyakunincho, Shinjuku-ku. Tel: (03) 3360-1151.
Tokyo Bunka Kaikan (classical/opera), 5-45 Ueno Park, Taito-ku. Tel: (03) 3828-2111.
Tokyo Dome (Big Egg), 1-3 Koraku, Bunkyo-ku. Tel: (03) 3811-2111.
Tokyo Takarazuka Gekijo (female revue), 1-1-3 Yurakucho, Chiyoda-ku. Tel: (03) 3591-1711.

Festivals

General

Festivals, or matsuri seem to be happening at any given time somewhere in Tokyo, and indeed have been an important part of Japanese life for hundreds of years. Many of the festivals have their roots in the long history of Japan's agricultural society. In today's ever modernising Japan, they are one of the few occasions when the Japanese can dress up and live a nostalgic past. Below is a short list of the main national holidays and the most important festivals. For information on upcoming events going on during any particular week or month, please consult tic or any of the tourist publications.

See the chapter on Kyoto (page 272) for festivals unique to Kyoto.

JANUARY

The first **sumo** tournament of the year, **Hatsu-basho**, is held for fifteen days at Tokyo's **Kokugikan** in mid January.

FEBRUARY

On the 3rd is **Setsubun**, the traditional bean throwing ceremony that is meant to purify the home of evil. Roasted beans are scattered from the inside of the house to the outside while people shout, "*Oni wa soto*" (Devils, go out!), and from the outside of the home to the inside while "*Fuku wa uchi*" (good luck, come in) is shouted. The same ceremony is also held at temples and shrines.

MARCH

On the 3rd is **Hina Matsuri** (Girl's Day), a festival for little girls. Small *Hina* dolls, representing imperial court figures, are displayed at home and in several public places.

APRIL

From early to mid April is **O-hanami** (cherry-blossom viewing), one of the important spring rites. People love to turn out and picnic, drink *sake* and sing songs under the pink blossoms.

On the 8th is **Hana Matsuri** (Birthday of Buddha), when commemorative services are held at various temples such as **Gokoku-ji**, **Senso-ji**, **Zojo-ji** and **Hommon-ji**.

MAY

In mid May, the **Natsu-basho** (summer **sumo** tournament) is held for fifteen days at the **Kokugikan**.

On the 3rd Saturday and Sunday, the **Sanja Matsuri** is held. This is one of the big Edo festivals honouring the three fishermen who found the image of Kannon in the river. The **Asakusa-Jinja (Senso-ji)** is a great place to go at this time to see the dancing, music and many portable shrines.

JUNE

On the second Sunday is **Torigoe Jinja Taisai**, a night-time festival, when the biggest and heaviest portable shrine in Tokyo is carried through the streets by lantern light. It all happens at the **Torigoe Shrine**.

From the 10th to the 16th is **Sanno Sai**, another big Edo festival featuring a *gyoretsu* (people parading in traditional costumes) on Saturday at the **Hie Shrine**.

JULY

From the 6th to the 8th is the **Asagao Ichi** (Morning Glory Fair), when over one hundred merchants set up stalls selling the morning flower at **Iriya Kishibojin**.

On the 7th is the **Tanabata Matsuri**, a festival celebrating the only day of the year when, according to the legend, the Weaver Princess (Vega) and her lover the Cowherder (Altair) can cross the Milky Way to meet. People write their wishes on coloured paper, hang them on bamboo branches, and then float them down a river the next day.

On the 9th and 10th is the **Hozuki Ichi** (Ground Cherry Fair) at **Senso-ji** from early morning to midnight. A visit to this temple on the 10th is meant to be equal to 46,000 visits at other times.

On the last Saturday of July, the **Sumida-gawa Hanabi Taikai** (Sumida River Fireworks) is held. This is the biggest fireworks display in Tokyo, and the best places to watch the display is between the **Kototoi** and **Shirahige bridges**, or at the **Komagata Bridge**.

AUGUST

Between the 13th and the 16th is the **Obon** festival, when people return to their hometowns to clean up the graves and offer prayers to the souls of departed ancestors. The traditional **Bon Odori** folk dances are held all over around this time.

OCTOBER

From mid to late October is chrysanthemum viewing time. There are flower displays dotted around the cities.

NOVEMBER

The 15th is **Shichi-Go-San** (Seven-Five-Three), a ceremony for 5-year-old boys and 3- and 7-year-old girls. The children usually dress up in *kimono* or Sunday best and are taken to visit a shrine.

DECEMBER

The 14th is **Gishi Sai**, a memorial service for the famous 47 Ronin who, on this day in 1702, avenged the death of their master and later committed ritual suicide. They are buried at the **Sengaku-ji** where the service is held.

On the 31st at the stroke of midnight, every temple bell throughout the country begins to toll. The bells toll 108 times representing the 108 evil human passions. This is called **Joya no Kane**, and the general public is allowed to strike the bells at various temples.

Shopping

Shopping Areas

Japan is a very expensive place to shop, but there are still bargains to be had if you look them up. The quality of Japanese products is well known, and there are some items which can only be bought in Japan. Certain areas promote only certain kinds of merchandise, which means that some domestic travel is involved for the serious shopper.

Following is a guide to the main shopping attractions in the cities and other areas throughout Japan.

IN AND AROUND TOKYO

Akihabara: The electronic jungle of the world featuring hundreds of discount stores.
Aoyama: High-class fashion boutiques.
Asakusa: Traditional Japanese toys, souvenirs, workmen's clothes, etc.
Ginza: The most expensive shopping centre. Several major department stores are located here, such as Hankyu, Matsuya, Matsuzakaya, Mitsukoshi, Printemps, Seibu and Wako, and exclusive boutiques. Also some traditional Japanese goods stores.
Harajuku: Another fashion area, though mostly geared to the young, which makes shopping relatively cheap. Several antique shops, and Kiddyland for the kids.
Hibiya: Mostly antique shops, jewelry shops, and art galleries.
Kanda and **Jimbocho:** Many second-hand bookstores.
Nihombashi: A good place to pick up traditional craft work. Two of Japan's oldest department stores, Mitsukoshi and Takashi-maya.
Roppongi: Several antique shops in the area, the Axis design building which features interior design as its main theme, and Seibu's Wave building which specialises in audio-visual equipment.
Shibuya: A good place to start with, Shibuya has a little bit of everything. Tokyu Hands is a must to visit; probably the most complete do-it-yourself department store in the world. Also here are the Seibu, Tokyu and Marui departments stores, the Parco "fashion buildings" besides the hundreds of small boutiques geared to young shoppers.
Shinjuku: Several big camera and electronic discount stores such as Yodobashi and Sakuraya. Also, Isetan and Marui department stores.
Ueno: Ameyoko is good for cheap food, cosmetics, clothing and toys. One of the few open markets in Tokyo. The shops in the back streets sell traditional Japanese goods.

Antiques

In most of the shops listed here, the staff speak English and are helpful. Watch out for badly restored pieces that have been given a quick coat of glossy lacquer and sold like new at steep prices.
Antique Gallery Kikori, Hanae Mori Building, B1, 3-6-1 Kita Aoyama, Minato-ku. Tel: (03) 3407-9363. Small but interesting selection of *tansu* and other items.
Antique Gallery Meguro, Stork Building, 2nd Fl, 2-24-18 Kamiosaki, Shinagawa-ku. Tel: (03) 3493-1971. Antique market of sorts covering 740 sq. metres (885 sq. yards) that houses several small antique shops.
Edo Antiques, 2-21-12 Akasaka, Minato-ku. Tel: (03) 3584-5280. Large selection of *tansu* and *hibachi*.
Harumi Antiques, 9-6-14 Akasaka, Minato-ku. Tel: (03) 3403-1043. Mostly *tansu* that have been restored, but some unrestored pieces can be purchased.
Japan Old Folkcraft and Antique Centre (Tokyo Komingu Kotto-kan), 3-9-5 Minami Ikebukuro, Toshima-ku. Tel: (03) 3980-8228. 35 dealers covering 600 sq. metres (718 sq. yards) and displaying various antique items.
Oriental Bazaar, 5-9-13 Jingæmae, Shibuya-ku. Tel: (03) 3400-3933. Apart from antiques, it is also a nice place to browse and pick up traditional Japanese toys, paper (*washi*), kimono, etc.

Ceramics

Besides workshops, department stores are the best places for Japanese ceramics offered at reasonable prices. On back streets, small shops also sell ceramics but prices are higher.
Iseryu Shoten, 3-8-2 Ningyocho, Nihombashi, Chuo-ku. Tel: (03) 3661-4820. Closed Sundays and holidays.
Saga Toen, 2-13-13 Nishi Azabu, Minato-ku. Tel: (03) 3400-3682.
Tachikichi & Co. Ltd, 6-13 Ginza, Chuo-ku. Tel: (03) 3571-2924.

Department Stores

Daimaru, 1-9-1 Marunouchi, Chiyoda-ku. Tel: (03) 3212-8011. Closed Thursdays.
Isetan, 3-14-1 Shinjuku, Shinjuku-ku. Tel: (03) 3352-1111. Closed Wednesdays.
Marui, 3-30-16 Shinjuku, Shinjuku-ku. Tel: (03) 3354-0101. 10.30am–7.30pm.
Matsuya, 1-4-1 Hanakawado, Taito-ku. Tel: (03) 3842-1111. Closed Thursdays.
Matsuzakaya, 3-29-5 Ueno, Taito-ku. Tel: (03) 3832-1111.
Mitsukoshi, 1-7-4 Muromachi, Nihom-bashi, Chuo-ku. Tel: (03) 3241-3311. Closed Mondays.
Printemps, 3-2-1 Ginza, Chuo-ku. Tel: (03) 3567-0077. 10am–7pm. Closed Wednesdays.
Seibu (Main Store), 1-28-1 Minami Ikebukuro, Toshima-ku. Tel: (03) 3981-0111. Closed Thursdays.
Sogo, 1-11-1 Yurakucho, Chiyoda-ku. Tel: (03) 3284-6711. Closed Tuesdays.
Takashimaya, 2-4-1 Nihombashi, Chuo-ku. Tel: (03) 3211-4111. Closed Wednesdays.
Tokyu, 2-24-1 Dogenzaka, Shibuya-ku. Tel: (03) 3477-3111. Closed Thursdays.

Japanese Paper (Washi)
Haibara, 2-7-6 Nihombashi, Chuo-ku. Tel: (03) 3272-3801. Closed Sundays and holidays.
Isetasu, 2-18-9 Yanaka, Taito-ku. Tel: (03) 3823-1453.
Kurodaya, 1-2-11 Asakusa, Taito-ku. Tel: (03) 3845-3830. Closed Mondays.
Kyækyodo, 5-7-4 Ginza, Chuo-ku. Tel: (03) 3571-4429.
Ozu Shoten, 2-6-3 Nihombashi Honcho, Chuo-ku. Tel: (03) 3663-8788. Closed on Sundays
Washikobo, 1-8-10 Nishi Azabu, Minato-ku. Tel: (03) 3405-1841. Closed Sundays and public holidays.

Kimonos (antique)
These shops specialise in antique *kimono*, *obi*, traditional blue and white textiles, *furoshiki*, *hanten*, etc. Prices from ¥1,000 up.
   Flea markets (see list under *Flea Markets*) also sell them, and you can usually pick up very beautiful old *kimono* and *obi* in good condition.
Ayahata, 2-21-2 Akasaka, Minato-ku. Tel: (03) 3582-9969. Closed Sundays and public holidays.
Hayashi Kimono, International Arcade, 1-7 Uchisaiwaicho, Chiyoda-ku. Tel: (03) 3581-9826.
Ikeda, 5-22-11 Shiroganedai, Minato-ku. Tel: (03) 3445-1269. Closed Sundays.
Konjaku Nishimura, Hanae Mori Building, B1, 3-6-1 Kita Aoyama, Minato-ku. Tel: (03) 3498-1759. Closed Thursdays.

Lacquerware (Shikki)
Bushi, Axis Building, B1 5-17-1 Roppongi, Minato-ku. Tel: (03) 3587-0317. Closed Mondays.
Heiando, 3-10-11 Nihombashi, Chuo-ku. Tel: (03) 3272-2871. Closed Sundays and public holidays.
Inachu Japan, 1-5-2 Akasaka, Minato-ku. Tel: (03) 3582-4451.
Kuroeya, Kuroeya Kokubu Building, 2nd Floor, 1-2-6 Nihombashi, Chuo-ku. Tel: (03) 3271-3356. Closed Saturdays, Sundays and public holidays.

Musical Instruments
Bachi Ei Gakkiten (*Shamisen*), 2-10-11 Ningyocho, Nihombashi, Chuo-ku. Tel: (03) 3666-7263. Closed Sundays and holidays.
Kikuya Shamisen Ten (*Shamisen*), 3-45-11 Yushima, Bunkyo-ku. Tel: (03) 3831-4733. Closed Sundays and holidays.
Tsurukawa Gakki Honten (*Koto*), 1-12-11 Kyobashi, Chuo-ku. Tel: (03) 3561-1872. Closed Sundays and holidays.
Ishida Biwa Ten (*Biwa*), 3-8-4 Toranomon, Minato-ku. Tel: (03) 3431-6548. Closed Sundays and holidays.
Miyamoto Unosuke Shoten (*drums*), 6-1-15 Asakusa, Taito-ku. Tel: (03) 3874-4131. Closed Sundays and public holidays.

Paper Lanterns
Hanato, 2-25-6 Asakusa, Taito-ku. Tel: (03) 3841-6411. 10am–9pm. Closed 2nd and 4th Tuesdays.
Kashiwaya, 2-3-13 Shintomi, Chuo-ku. Tel: (03) 3551-1362. Closed Sundays.

Umbrellas (Kasa)
Hasegawa Hakimonoten, 2-4-4 Ueno, Taito-ku. Tel: (03) 3831-3933. Closed Sundays.
Iidaya, 1-31-1 Asakusa, Taito-ku. Tel: (03) 3841-3644.

Woodblock Print (Ukiyo-e)
Asakusa Okuramae Shobo, 3-10-12 Kuramae, Taito-ku. Tel: (03) 3866-5894. Closed on Sundays, but will stay open for appointments. Specialist on books and prints on *Edo* and *sumo*.
Hara Shobo, 2-3 Jimbocho, Kanda, Chiyoda-ku. Tel: (03) 3261-7444. All types of prints old and new, from the highest quality to a "bargain drawer." English is spoken here.
Matsushita Associates, Inc., 6-3-12 Minami Aoyama, Shibuya-ku. Tel: (03) 3407-4966. Closed Sundays.
Oya Shobo, 1-1 Kanda, Jimbocho, Chiyoda-ku. Tel: (03) 3291-0062. Closed Sundays.
Sakai Kokodo Gallery, 1-2-14 Yurakucho, Chiyoda-ku. Tel: (03) 3591-4678.

Bookstores
There are bookstores all over Tokyo, and it is quite acceptable to browse through the books and magazines in the shop without having to buy them, so don't feel guilty. In spite of the large number of bookstores, there are relatively few that specialise in English books. Below is a list of the major stores in Tokyo that stock foreign books and books on Japan. They are usually helpful when phoning about information on books in stock. Besides these places, you can also get foreign newspapers and magazines in most hotels.
Aoyama Book Centre. Tel: (03) 3479-0479. Open daily 10–5.30am; Sunday and holidays 10am–10pm. 1 minute from Roppongi Stn (Hibiya Line).
Kinokuniya, 3-17-7 Shinjuku, Shinjuku-ku. Tel: (03) 3354-0131. Open 10am–7pm. Closed 3rd Wednesday of each month. Foreign books on the 6th floor. One of the most popular.
Libro (Ikebukuro Branch), 1-28-1 Minami Ikebukuro, Toshima-ku (Seibu Dept. SMA BIF, B2F). Tel: (03) 5992-8800. Open daily 10am–8pm, except Tuesday.
Maruzen, 2-3-10 Nihombashi, Chuo-ku. Tel: (03) 3272-7211. Open 10am–6pm. Closed Sunday. Foreign books on the 3rd floor. Very popular, as is...
Jena (pronounced "yena"), 5-6-1 Ginza, Chuo-ku. Tel: (03) 3571-2980. Weekdays 10.30am–7.50pm; Sunday 12.30–6.45pm. Closed holidays. Foreign books on the 3rd floor.
Kitazawa Shoten, 2-5-3 Kanda Jimbocho, Chiyoda-ku. Tel: (03) 3263-0011. Open 10am–6pm. Closed Sunday. Second-hand books on the 2nd floor, and English literature on the 1st floor.
Biblos, F1 Bldg, 4th Floor, 1-26-5 Takadanobaba, Shinjuku-ku. Tel: (03) 3200-4531. Open daily 10.30am–7.30pm; Sunday and holidays 11am–6.30pm. Closed 3rd Sunday of each month.

OUTSIDE TOKYO

Within Tohoku
• **Matsushima**
**Shiogama Suisan Nakaoroshi
Ichiban**; morning market.
Owariya, in front of Suigen-ji; wind
bells.
• **Aomori**
Murata Kogei-sha, Shinmachi Dori;
local crafts.
• **Morioka**
Kyabatake, near Minami Ohashi on
the Kitagami River, daily from 5am;
morning market.
Zaimoku-cho, every Saturday, April
to November, 3–9pm; night market
offering colorful array of items for
sale.
Iwachu, Nanbu Tekki; local iron
crafts.
• **Iizaka Spa**
Kodai Gangu, Nihonmatsu; local
crafts.

ON HOKKAIDO

• **Hakodate**
Chiaki-kan, in Horai-cho; handmade
Japanese confections.
• **Noboribetsu**
Kagetsu Do, Hyotan Ame; Japanese
candy, gifts and souvenirs.
• **Akan National Park**
Rakan, on Route 240; local crafts.
Akan Kohan Visitor Centre; local
crafts.

WITHIN KANSAI

• **Ise**
Akafuku Honten, near Ise Naiguu;
Japanese confections, souvenirs.
• **Nara**
Ikeda Gankohdo; Nara fans.
Somekawa Hakurokuen; Nara
dolls.
• **Kyoto**
Kawaramachi, main north-south
street: **Matsuya**, Kawaramachi Dori,
Kyoto dolls.
Kiyamachi (parallels the Takase
River, north-south): **Murakami Ju-
honten**, at the end of 4-jo Dori,
Japanese pickles; **Tachibana
Syokai**, antiques.
Teramachi (downtown arcade):
Ippodo, tea and accessories;
Kyukyodo, Japanese stationery;
Miyawaki Baisen-an, fans.
Shijyo, main east-west street:

Erizen, kimono and accessories;
Ichihara Heibei Shoten, chopsticks;
Morita Wash, paper crafts.
**Arashiyama: Ishikawa Taki no
Mise**, bamboo crafts.
• **Kobe**
Hon Takasagoya, Motomachi Dori
3-2-11; colorful gift items,
souvenirs and Japanese
confections.

IN SOUTHERN HONSHU

• **Himeji**
Azumadou, Kawahara Shoutengai;
Japanese confections.
• **Hagi**
Ochadokoro, near Kikuya Yokocho;
Japanese tea and confections.

ON SHIKOKU

• **Tokushima**
Fujiya; Japanese confections.
Aigura, Nishishinmachi Arcade;
local crafts.
• **Kochi**
Kitaura, Konyacho; dyed goods.
Tosa Mingei Ten; folk handicrafts.

ON KYUSHU

• **Nagasaki**
Art Hata, in Kajiya-cho; original
Nagasaki dolls.
• **Beppu Spa**
Kishima; bamboo crafts.
• **Kagoshima**
Satsuma Glass Kogei, near
Shuseikan; local glass crafts.

ON OKINAWA

• **Naha**
Hirugi, Keizairen Mingei Centre 2F,
Kokusai Dori; Ryukyuan dishes,
dances; crafts for sale; in other
words, a place to shop and eat.
Morita Sango no Mise, Kokusai
Dori; Okinawan coral jewelry.
• **Okinawa City**
Chuo Park Avenue, more than 100
shops and restaurants.

Sport

Spectator Sports

SUMO TOURNAMENTS

Six tournaments annually, each
lasting for 15 days, are held in
January, May and September in
Tokyo, in March in Osaka, in July in
Nagoya, and in November in
Fukuoka. During the tournament,
matches are televised daily from
4–6pm. Matches by junior wrestlers
begin at about 10am; by senior
wrestlers at 3pm on the first and
the last days, and at 3.30pm on
other days. Don't expect to sit close
to the ring, or *dohyo*. These seats
are both expensive and are usually
booked by large corporations or
simply the very wealthy.

Tokyo
January, May and September:
Kokugikan Sumo Hall, 1-3-28
Yokoami, Sumida-ku, Tokyo. Tel:
(03) 3623-5111. Near JR Ryogoku
Station.

Osaka
March: Osaka Furitsu Taiikukaikan
(Osaka Prefectural Gymnasium), 3-
4-36 Namba Naka, Naniwa-ku,
Osaka. Tel: (06) 631-0121. Near
Namba subway station.

Nagoya
July: Aichi Ken Taiikukan (Aichi
Prefectural Gymnasium), 1-1
Ninomaru, Naka-ku, Nagoya. Tel:
(052) 971-2516. 15 minute by car
from Nagoya Station. Tickets are
sold from 9am. Competition starts
from 9.20am.

Fukuoka
November: Fukuoka Kokusai Centre
Sogo Hall, 2-2 Chikuko-Honcho,
Hakata-ku, Fukuoka. Tel: (092) 272-
1111.

Language

General

The visitor will have few language problems within the confines of airports and the major Western-style hotels, but outside these the going can get tough for those who are unescorted. Quite apart from being unable to communicate verbally, the hapless visitor will also have the disconcerting experience of being almost totally illiterate.

The written language is made up of three different sets of characters: two simple home-grown syllabaries, *hiragana* and *katakana*, consisting of 46 characters each; and the much more formidable Chinese ideograms, *kanji*. Knowledge of just under two thousand of these is necessary to read a daily newspaper.

While the expenditure of the enormous effort required to memorise this number of kanji (it takes the Japanese most of their school career to do so) is clearly unjustifiable for those with only a passing interest in the language, a few hours spent learning the two syllabaries (on the plane trip to Japan, for example) would not be time completely wasted for those who can afford it.

Hiragana can be useful for identifying which station your train has stopped at; the platforms are plastered with hiragana versions of the station name so that children who have not yet learned kanji can see where they are. Station names are usually (but not always) posted in roman script (*romanji*) as well, but not always as obviously. Katakana is useful in that it is used to transliterate foreign words. Western-style restaurants often simply list the foreign names for the dishes on their menus in katakana.

Pronunciation: With its small number of simple and unvarying vowel sounds, the pronunciation of Japanese should be easy for those who speak Western languages, which are rich in vowel sounds. Japanese has nothing like the dreaded tonal system of Chinese to frustrate the student.

Vowels have but one sound, much like Spanish. Don't be sloppy with their pronunciations.

a – between fat and the u in but
e – like the e in egg
i – like the i in ink *
o – like the o in orange
u – like the u in butcher *

* When they occur in the middle of words, i and u are often almost silent. For example, *Takeshita* is really pronounced *Takesh'ta* while *sukiyaki* sounds more like *s'kiyaki*.

In spite of the seemingly simple pronunciation of Japanese, a lot of foreigners manage to mangle the language into a form which is almost impossible for the native speaker to understand. It is mainly intonation that is responsible for this. It would be fallacious to claim that the Japanese language has no rise and fall in pitch – just listen to a group of schoolgirls conversing on the train to confirm this – but it is certainly "flatter" in character than Western languages.

It is important to avoid stressing syllables within words; whereas an English speaker would naturally stress either the second or third syllable of *Hiroshima*, for example, in Japanese the four syllables should be stressed equally. Another problem lies in long (actually double) vowel sounds. These are often indicated by a line above the vowel, or simply by a double vowel, e.g. *Iidabashi*. To pronounce these long vowels properly, it is simply necessary to give the vowel sound double length.

GREETINGS

Good morning/*Ohayo gozaimasu*
Hello (afternoon)/*Konnichi-wa*
Good evening/*Komban-wa*
Good night/*Oyasumi nasai*

Goodbye/*Sayonara* (*Shitsure shimasu* for formal occasions)
How do you do?/*Hajime mashite?*
How are you?/*Ogenki desu ka?*
My name is.../*...to moshimasu*
I'm American/*Amerika-jin desu*
I'm British/*Igirisu-jin desu*
I'm Australian/*Osturaraia-jin desu*
I'm Canadian/*Kanada-jin desu*

ASKING FOR DIRECTIONS

Excuse me, where is the **toilet**?/ *Sumimasen. **Toire** wa doko desu ka?*
Excuse me, is there a **post office** near here?/*Sumimasen. Kono chikaku ni, **yubin-kyoku** wa arimasu ka?*
bakery/*pan-ya*
greengrocer's/*yao-ya*
stationery store/*bumbogu-ya*
pharmacy/*kusuri-ya*
barber shop/*toko-ya*
bookshop/*hon-ya*
supermarket/*supa-maketto*
department store/*depato*
restaurant/*restoran*
hotel/*hoteru*
station/*eki*
taxi stand/*takushii noriba*
bank/*ginko*
hospital/*byoin*
police station/*koban*

OUT SHOPPING

This one/*Kore*
That one (near the other person)/ *Sore*
That one (near neither of you)/*Are*
Do you have...?/*...(wa) arimasu ka?*
Could you show me that one please?/*Sore o misete kudasai?*
How much is it?/*Ikura desu ka?*
Do you accept (credit) cards?/ *(Kurjitto) kado tsukaemasu ka?*
I'll take this./*Kore o kudasai.*

BOARDING THE TRAIN

Ticket (office)/*kippu (uriba)*
reserved seat/*shitei seki*
unreserved seat/*jiyuseki*
first-class car/*guriin (green) sha*
Which platform does the train for Nagoya leave from?/*Nagoya yuki wa namban sen desu ka?*
Thank you (very much)/*(Domo) arigato gozaimasu* (informally, *domo* is enough)

Don't mention it./*Doitashimashite*
Thanks for the meal./*Gochisosama deshita.*
Here you are./*Dozo*
After you./*Dozo*
Sure, go ahead./*Dozo* (in answer to "May I...?")

DAYS/TIME

(On) Sunday/*Nichi-yobi (ni)*
(Next) Monday/*(Raishu no) Getsu-yobi*
(Last) Tuesday/*(Senshu no) Ka-yobi*
(Every) Wednesday/*(Maishu) Sui-yobi*
(This) Thursday/*(Konshu no) Moku-yobi*
Friday/*Kin-yobi*
Saturday/*Do-yobi*
Yesterday/*kino*
Today/*kyo*
This morning/*kesa*
This evening/*konya*
Tomorrow/*ashita*
What time is it?/*Nan-ji desu ka?*

NUMBERS

Counting is very complicated in Japanese! Counting up to ten on their fingers, the Japanese will go: *ichi, ni, san, shi (yon), go, roku, shichi* (or *nana*), *hachi, ku* (or *kyu*), *ju.* If they are counting bottles, they will go: *ip-pon, ni-hon, sam-bon, yon-hon, go-hon...* Pieces of paper and oranges are counted differently, as are goats and coins. (Depending on what is being counted, the suffix will change.) You will be fairly safe with the numbers below that don't need suffixes:

one/*hitotsu*
two/*futatsu*
three/*mittsu*
four/*yottsu*
five/*itsutsu*
six/*muttsu*
seven/*nanatsu*
eight/*yattsu*
nine/*kokonotsu*
ten/*to*

If you want five of something, simply point at it and say, *Itsutsu kudasai.* Or, when in doubt, just count with your fingers, or write the number down. Both will work just fine in Japan.

Further Reading

History and Culture

Barr, Pat. *The Coming of the Barbarians: A Story of Western Settlement in Japan 1853–1870.* Penguin 1988.
Borton, Hugh. *Japan's Modern Century.* Ronald Press. 1955.
Dunn, Charles J. *Everyday Life in Traditional Japan.* Charles E. Tuttle Company, Ltd. 1987.
Frederic, Louis. (Translated from the French by Eileen M. Lowe) *Daily Life in Japan at the Time of the Samurai.* Tuttle 1972.
Fukutake, Tadashi. *The Japanese Social Structure: Its Evolution in the Modern Century* Univ. of Tokyo Press 1989.
Kaempfer, Englebert. *The History of Japan.* (3 volumes). James MacLehose and Sons 1906.
Meech-Pekarik, Julia. *The World of the Meiji Print: Impressions.* Weatherhill 1986.
Neary, Ian. *Political Protest and Social Control in Prewar Japan: The Origins of Buraku Liberation.* Manchester University Press 1989.
Reischauer, Edwin & Fairbank, John *East Asia: The Great Tradition.* Houghton Mifflin 1960.
Sansom, Sir George B. *Japan, A Short Cultural History.* Appleton-Century-Crofts 1943.
Sansom, Sir George B. *The Western World and Japan.* Alfred A. Knopf, Inc. 1950.
Schiffer, Robert L. *The Exploding City.* St Martin's Press 1989.
Seidensticker, Edward. *Low City, High City: Tokyo From Edo to the Earthquake.* Tuttle 1983.
Tanizaki, Jun'ichiro. *In Praise of Shadows.* (Translated by Thomas J. Harper and Edward Seidensticker. Tuttle 1984.
Tsunoda, de Bary and Keene. *Sources of the Japanese Tradition.* (2 volumes).

Yazaki, Takeo. *Social Change and the City in Japan: From earliest times through the Industrial Revolution.* Japan Publications, Inc. 1968.

General

Condon, Camy & Nagasawa, Kimiko. *Kites, Crackers and Craftsmen.* Shufunotomo 1974.
Elkin, Judith. *Japanese Family.* A. & C. Black 1986.
Gunji, Masakutsu. *The Kabuki Guide.* Kodansha 1987.
Kenny, Don. *A Guide To Kyogen.* Hinoki Shoten 1968.
O'Neill, P.G. *A Guide To No.* Hinoki Shoten 1953.
Popham, Peter. *Tokyo: The City at the End of the World.* Kodansha International Ltd. 1985.
Waley, Paul. *Tokyo: City of Stories.* Weatherhill, New York 1991.
Walters, Gary D.A. *Day Walks Near Tokyo.* Kodansha 1988.
Japan Travel Bureau. *Japan In Your Pocket* (series).
Tokyo: A Bilingual Atlas. Kodansha, Tokyo 1990.
Japan: A Bilingual Atlas. Kodansha, Tokyo 1990.

Internet Sites

Japan Window: comprehensive and categorised links for every occasion on site set up by NTT. **www.jwindow.net/**
Stanford University: scholarly links for the more high-brow surfer. **fuji.stanford.edu/jguide/**
Tokyo Q: events, the arts, and nightlife in Tokyo. Fun. **www.so-net.or.jp/tokyoq/**
Japan Nat'l Tourist Organisation: excellent links and travel info. www.jnto.go.jp/
Ministry of Foreign Affairs: a site of questionable function but with comprehensive, useful links. **jin.jcic.or.jp/**
The Japan Times: a good online site for Japan's English-language newspaper of record. Has nearly everything covered. **www.japantimes.co.jp/**

ART & PHOTO CREDITS

Maps Polyglott Kartographie
Berndtson & Berndtson Publications
Cartographic Editor Zoë Goodwin
Production Caroline Low
Design Consultant Graham Mitchener
Picture Research Hilary Genin

Index

The World of Insight Guides

400 books in three complementary series cover every major destination in every continent.

Insight Guides

Alaska
Alsace
Amazon Wildlife
American Southwest
Amsterdam
Argentina
Atlanta
Athens
Australia
Austria
Bahamas
Bali
Baltic States
Bangkok
Barbados
Barcelona
Bay of Naples
Beijing
Belgium
Belize
Berlin
Bermuda
Boston
Brazil
Brittany
Brussels
Budapest
Buenos Aires
Burgundy
Burma (Myanmar)
Cairo
Calcutta
California
Canada
Caribbean
Catalonia
Channel Islands
Chicago
Chile
China
Cologne
Continental Europe
Corsica
Costa Rica
Crete
Crossing America
Cuba
Cyprus
Czech & Slovak Republics
Delhi, Jaipur, Agra
Denmark
Dresden
Dublin
Düsseldorf
East African Wildlife
East Asia
Eastern Europe
Ecuador
Edinburgh
Egypt
Finland
Florence
Florida
France
Frankfurt
French Riviera
Gambia & Senegal
Germany
Glasgow
Gran Canaria
Great Barrier Reef
Great Britain
Greece
Greek Islands
Hamburg
Hawaii
Hong Kong
Hungary
Iceland
India
India's Western Himalaya
Indian Wildlife
Indonesia
Ireland
Israel
Istanbul
Italy
Jamaica
Japan
Java
Jerusalem
Jordan
Kathmandu
Kenya
Korea
Lisbon
Loire Valley
London
Los Angeles
Madeira
Madrid
Malaysia
Mallorca & Ibiza
Malta
Marine Life in the South China Sea
Melbourne
Mexico
Mexico City
Miami
Montreal
Morocco
Moscow
Munich
Namibia
Native America
Nepal
Netherlands
New England
New Orleans
New York City
New York State
New Zealand
Nile
Normandy
Northern California
Northern Spain
Norway
Oman & the UAE
Oxford
Old South
Pacific Northwest
Pakistan
Paris
Peru
Philadelphia
Philippines
Poland
Portugal
Prague
Provence
Puerto Rico
Rajasthan
Rhine
Rio de Janeiro
Rockies
Rome
Russia
St Petersburg
San Francisco
Sardinia
Scotland
Seattle
Sicily
Singapore
South Africa
South America
South Asia
South India
South Tyrol
Southeast Asia
Southeast Asia Wildlife
Southern California
Southern Spain
Spain
Sri Lanka
Sweden
Switzerland
Sydney
Taiwan
Tenerife
Texas
Thailand
Tokyo
Trinidad & Tobago
Tunisia
Turkey
Turkish Coast
Tuscany
Umbria
US National Parks East
US National Parks West
Vancouver
Venezuela
Venice
Vienna
Vietnam
Wales
Washington DC
Waterways of Europe
Wild West
Yemen

Insight Pocket Guides

Aegean Islands★
Algarve★
Alsace
Amsterdam★
Athens★
Atlanta★
Bahamas★
Baja Peninsula★
Bali★
Bali Bird Walks
Bangkok★
Barbados★
Barcelona★
Bavaria★
Beijing★
Berlin★
Bermuda★
Bhutan★
Boston★
British Columbia★
Brittany★
Brussels★
Budapest & Surroundings★
Canton★
Chiang Mai★
Chicago★
Corsica★
Costa Blanca★
Costa Brava★
Costa del Sol/Marbella★
Costa Rica★
Crete★
Denmark★
Fiji★
Florence★
Florida★
Florida Keys★
French Riviera★
Gran Canaria★
Hawaii★
Hong Kong★
Hungary
Ibiza★
Ireland★
Ireland's Southwest★
Israel★
Istanbul★
Jakarta★
Jamaica★
Kathmandu Bikes & Hikes★
Kenya★
Kuala Lumpur★
Lisbon★
Loire Valley★
London★
Macau★
Madrid★
Malacca★
Maldives★
Mallorca★
Malta★
Mexico City★
Miami★
Milan★
Montreal★
Morocco★
Moscow
Munich★
Nepal★
New Delhi
New Orleans★
New York City★
New Zealand★
Northern California★
Oslo/Bergen★
Paris★
Penang★
Phuket★
Prague★
Provence★
Puerto Rico★
Quebec★
Rhodes★
Rome★
Sabah★
St Petersburg★
San Francisco★
Sardinia
Scotland★
Seville★
Seychelles★
Sicily★
Sikkim
Singapore★
Southeast England
Southern California★
Southern Spain★
Sri Lanka★
Sydney★
Tenerife★
Thailand★
Tibet★
Toronto★
Tunisia★
Turkish Coast★
Tuscany★
Venice★
Vienna★
Vietnam★
Yogyakarta
Yucatan Peninsula★

★ = Insight Pocket Guides
with Pull out Maps

Insight Compact Guides

Algarve
Amsterdam
Bahamas
Bali
Bangkok
Barbados
Barcelona
Beijing
Belgium
Berlin
Brittany
Brussels
Budapest
Burgundy
Copenhagen
Costa Brava
Costa Rica
Crete
Cyprus
Czech Republic
Denmark
Dominican Republic
Dublin
Egypt
Finland
Florence
Gran Canaria
Greece
Holland
Hong Kong
Ireland
Israel
Italian Lakes
Italian Riviera
Jamaica
Jerusalem
Lisbon
Madeira
Mallorca
Malta
Milan
Moscow
Munich
Normandy
Norway
Paris
Poland
Portugal
Prague
Provence
Rhodes
Rome
St Petersburg
Salzburg
Singapore
Switzerland
Sydney
Tenerife
Thailand
Turkey
Turkish Coast
Tuscany

UK regional titles:
Bath & Surroundings
Cambridge & East Anglia
Cornwall
Cotswolds
Devon & Exmoor
Edinburgh
Lake District
London
New Forest
North York Moors
Northumbria
Oxford
Peak District
Scotland
Scottish Highlands
Shakespeare Country
Snowdonia
South Downs
York
Yorkshire Dales

USA regional titles:
Boston
Cape Cod
Chicago
Florida
Florida Keys
Hawaii: Maui
Hawaii: Oahu
Las Vegas
Los Angeles
Martha's Vineyard & Nantucket
New York
San Francisco
Washington D.C.
Venice
Vienna
West of Ireland